Advanced Interdisciplinary Applications of Large Language Models and AI Agents

Soly Mathew Biju
University of Wollongong in Dubai, UAE

IGI Global
Scientific Publishing
Publishing Tomorrow's Research Today

Vice President of Editorial — Melissa Wagner
Director of Acquisitions — Mikaela Felty
Director of Book Development — Jocelynn Hessler
Production Manager — Mike Brehm
Cover Design — Jose Rosado

Published in the United States of America by
IGI Global Scientific Publishing
701 East Chocolate Avenue
Hershey, PA, 17033, USA
Tel: 717-533-8845 | Fax: 717-533-7115
Website: https://www.igi-global.com E-mail: cust@igi-global.com

Library of Congress Cataloging-in-Publication Data

Names: Biju, Soly, 1976- editor
Title: Advanced interdisciplinary applications of large language models and AI agents / edited by Soly Mathew Biju.
Description: Hershey, PA : IGI Global Scientific Publishing, [2026] | Includes bibliographical references and index. | Summary: "Through real-world case studies and practical applications, the book examines both the theoretical foundations and hands-on techniques of integrating LLMs and AI agents to solve complex problems"-- Provided by publisher.
Identifiers: LCCN 2025009724 | ISBN 9798337320083 h/c | ISBN 9798337320090 s/c | ISBN 9798337320106 ebook
Subjects: LCSH: Natural language processing (Computer science)--Industrial applications | Generative artificial intelligence--Industrial applications | Multiagent systems--Industrial applications
Classification: LCC QA76.9.N38 A3365 2025
LC record available at https://lccn.loc.gov/2025009724

British Cataloguing in Publication Data
A Cataloguing in Publication record for this book is available from the British Library.

Table of Contents

Detailed Table of Contents

The chapter "Transforming Healthcare with Large Language Models and AI Agents" explores how technologies like GPT-3 and advanced AI agents are reshaping healthcare. These tools can process massive volumes of medical data to provide real-time insights, aiding clinical decision-making and improving patient outcomes. AI agents enhance patient engagement, assist in diagnosis, and support treatment planning. Key applications include boosting diagnostic accuracy, automating administrative processes, enabling virtual care, and advancing precision medicine. The chapter also addresses critical challenges such as data privacy, algorithmic bias, and the importance of transparent AI governance. It offers practical recommendations to mitigate these issues and ensure responsible AI deployment. Designed for healthcare professionals, researchers, and policymakers, this chapter provides a comprehensive guide to harnessing the power of LLMs and AI agents to transform healthcare delivery and medical research effectively and ethically.

The rise of AI and large language models (LLMs) has redefined the boundaries of what is possible in education, especially in the realm of personalized learning. This chapter explores the transformative potential of adaptive learning platforms powered by AI agents and LLMs, focusing on how these technologies can tailor educational experiences to individual learners' needs, preferences, and pace. It traces the evolution of personalized learning, highlighting how recent AI advancements have moved us beyond static models toward dynamic, responsive, and context-aware systems. Drawing from interdisciplinary insights, the chapter also examines the design principles that underlie effective adaptive systems and unpacks the ethical challenges posed by data privacy, algorithmic bias, and the risk of dehumanizing learning. Ultimately, it argues that the real promise of AI in education lies not in replacing teachers or standardizing knowledge delivery, but in building human-centered systems that support meaningful, inclusive, and lifelong learning experiences.

Biometric authentication has emerged as a cornerstone of modern identity verification, offering unparalleled security and convenience compared to traditional password-based systems. With advancements in artificial intelligence (AI), biometric systems—particularly those leveraging facial recognition and fingerprint analysis—have undergone transformative improvements in accuracy, scalability, and adaptability. AI-driven biometric systems represent a paradigm shift in identity authentication, offering robust security and seamless user experiences. However, their success hinges on addressing ethical dilemmas, ensuring regulatory compliance, and staying ahead of evolving threats. As technologies like decentralized identity and quantum encryption mature, the fusion of AI and biometrics will continue to redefine the boundaries of digital security. This chapter explores the implementation of AI-driven biometric authentication systems, focusing on the technological foundations, real-world applications, challenges, and future directions of facial recognition and fingerprint analysis.

In this study it is concerned with the development of AI agents that are able to make autonomous decisions using reinforcement learning (RL). The paper investigates basic concepts and training methods and optimization techniques which establish essential techniques for producing adaptable agents that work in fluid settings. Deep RL techniques can help to train agents into finding optimal policies to interact and be in contact with mechanisms of feedback. The study outlines major difficulties in its findings between agent early exploration and optimally using current knowledge while also addressing system expansion limitations and ethical issues. This work covers practical uses of the methodology in financial settings as well as healthcare organizations and robotic systems. The results contribute to the advances of AI driven autonomy for driving efficiency and making intelligent decisions in the complex and uncertain environments.

The healthcare sector confronts various challenges, including the imperative to manage extensive datasets, develop innovative healthcare applications, and optimize overall delivery efficiency. This chapter proposes a unique system designed to enable users to input symptoms, receive rapid diagnoses, and access recommendations for medication and nearby hospitals, addressing the time-sensitive nature of medical diagnoses. The envisioned system capitalizes on the combined strengths of Artificial Narrow Intelligence (ANI) and cloud computing to provide swift and accurate diagnoses. ANI facilitates precise interpretation of symptoms, enhancing user experience, while cloud computing ensures seamless accessibility, allowing users to utilize the system at their convenience. The collaborative use of these technologies promises to reshape healthcare delivery, providing an efficient and accessible solution tailored to the demanding nature of the medical field.

Natural Language Processing (NLP) is revolutionizing industry applications by enabling advanced analysis and understanding of textual data. Sentiment analysis, a key NLP technique, plays a crucial role in deriving actionable insights from customer feedback across various sectors. This study explores the application of sentiment analysis in processing customer reviews, surveys, and social media interactions to identify patterns, gauge satisfaction levels, and inform decision-making. We examine methodologies ranging from lexicon-based approaches to cutting-edge machine learning and deep learning models, highlighting their efficacy and challenges in real-world scenarios. Emphasis is placed on handling multilingual data, mitigating biases, and improving sentiment detection accuracy in diverse cultural contexts. Integrating sentiment analysis with industry processes, businesses can enhance customer experience, drive product innovation, and maintain a competitive edge. This work underscores the transformative potential of NLP in harnessing the voice of the customer for strategic advantage.

Preface

INTRODUCTION

Over the past few years, the world has witnessed an unprecedented surge in the development and adoption of Large Language Models (LLMs) and AI agents. These technologies are no longer confined to experimental labs; they are now actively transforming the ways in which industries, governments, and academic institutions operate. The integration of LLMs into multi-agent frameworks has enabled automation, decision-making, and personalized solutions that once seemed unattainable. This rapid evolution has raised a pressing need for interdisciplinary scholarship that not only highlights technical advancements but also addresses their societal, ethical, and professional implications.

This edited reference volume, *Advanced Interdisciplinary Applications of Large Language Models and AI Agents*, brings together diverse perspectives from experts across academia and industry. The chapters herein explore real-world implementations of LLMs and AI agents across domains such as healthcare, education, finance, supply chains, biometric security, and immersive learning environments. Each contribution emphasizes practical applications, supported by empirical findings and theoretical reflections, to provide a holistic understanding of the transformative role these technologies are playing today.

As editors, our primary objective is to provide readers with a comprehensive resource that blends conceptual knowledge, empirical studies, and actionable strategies. This book is designed to serve not only as an academic reference but also as a guide for practitioners, policymakers, and innovators who are navigating the fast-changing landscape of AI-driven systems. It is our hope that the insights contained in this collection will foster informed debate, inspire further innovation, and ensure that the adoption of these technologies proceeds responsibly and inclusively.

CHAPTER OVERVIEW

- **Chapter 1** introduces the orchestration of multi-agent systems using Langflow and LLMs, demonstrating their potential in decision-making, automation, and dynamic collaboration.
- **Chapter 2** examines the role of LLMs in automating business intelligence and finance, offering empirical insights into their impact on analytical accuracy and operational efficiency.
- **Chapter 3** focuses on healthcare applications, showing how AI agents and LLMs enhance diagnostics, treatment planning, and patient engagement, while also addressing ethical considerations.
- **Chapter 4** highlights AI in education, particularly in personalized learning platforms, exploring opportunities and challenges in designing inclusive, adaptive systems.
- **Chapter 5** analyzes AI-driven biometric systems for identity management, with a focus on facial recognition and fingerprint authentication in security contexts.
- **Chapter 6** discusses reinforcement learning approaches for designing autonomous AI agents capable of adaptive decision-making in complex environments.
- **Chapter 7** presents an Artificial Narrow Intelligence–based healthcare service recommendation system, offering rapid diagnosis and treatment suggestions.
- **Chapter 8** investigates sentiment analysis for customer feedback using NLP, with implications for enhancing customer experience and innovation.
- **Chapter 9** concludes with a forward-looking discussion on AR/VR in metaverse-powered education, outlining new pedagogical possibilities and challenges.

CONCLUSION

The chapters presented in this volume collectively illustrate the transformative potential of LLMs and AI agents across an array of disciplines. By combining empirical evidence with conceptual exploration, the contributors highlight not only the technical strengths of these systems but also their vulnerabilities and ethical considerations. The result is a balanced and pragmatic discussion that acknowledges both the promise and the perils of adopting such disruptive technologies.

This book also underscores the necessity of interdisciplinary collaboration in realizing the full potential of AI-driven systems. From healthcare to finance, education to cloud computing, no single field can harness the power of LLMs in isolation. It is through cross-pollination of ideas, methodologies, and experiences that meaningful, responsible, and inclusive innovation can take place.

Finally, we encourage readers to view this collection not as a conclusion but as a starting point. The rapid pace of technological evolution means that many of the insights presented here will soon evolve further. Our hope is that this volume equips scholars, professionals, and policymakers with the knowledge and foresight needed to navigate these changes with confidence, creativity, and ethical responsibility.

Soly Mathew Biju
University of Wollongong in Dubai, UAE

Chapter 1
Orchestrating Multi-Agent Applications With Langflow and Large Language Models (LLMs)

Soly Mathew Biju
https://orcid.org/0000-0003-1323-7480
University of Wollongong in Dubai, UAE

Sara Majeed
https://orcid.org/0000-0001-7016-8405
University of Wollongong in Dubai, UAE

Pradnya Bhagwat
https://orcid.org/0000-0001-8330-5544
University of Wollongong in Dubai, UAE

ABSTRACT

This chapter will provide a comprehensive overview of multi agent systems, their architecture and of how Langflow can be employed to create, orchestrate, and manage a network of agents that communicate and collaborate using LLMs. We will demonstrate the power of this approach in scenarios such as automated decision-making, knowledge management, and intelligent automation. Moreover, we will examine how Langflow's flexible architecture allows for a dynamic combination of agent types, ranging from simple rule-based agents to advanced models powered by LLMs.

DOI: 10.4018/979-8-3373-2008-3.ch001

1. INTRODUCTION

Langflow is a low code tool/IDE used by developers to build robust AI agents and workflows that can use any API, model or database. Its visual framework makes it easier for developers to quickly experiment, design and test RAG and GenAI applications. Langflow is compatible with various languages and provides vector and non-vector databases primarily by AstraDB. (2025 DataStax Langflow)

Agents and multi-agent systems' relevance and importance has increased in recent times. They provide the power of parallel processing, distributed computing and collaboration to solve complex problems. They are capable of dealing with varied tasks like optimizing supply-chain to moderating fraudulent activity. LLM or large language models are machine learning models created for natural language programming tasks like reading, paraphrasing and providing responses relevant to the proposed query. (2025 DataStax Langflow)

This book chapter provides details on the different types of agents like rule-based, reactive, LLM based etc.. and discusses the importance of why agents are necessary in an AI powered system. It introduces the reader to multi-agent systems, different network and architectural styles in Multi agent systems and how agents communicate with each other.

Along with agents and MAS, the chapter also introduces the reader to Langflow IDE which is a product of DataStax. It discusses the architecture of Langflow, its components and its ability to integrate with other APIs.

Examples of a single rule-based agent and a Multi agent system using LLM modelled in Langflow using RAG are included in the later sections.

2. WHAT ARE AGENTS / MULTI-AGENTS AND LLMS

2.1. Exploring Multi-Agent Systems

Agents are intelligent software systems that perceive its environment and take independent decisions to pursue goals and complete tasks. Agents can interact with humans, their environment or other agents to solve complex tasks. Agents can be as simple as rule-based systems or complex machine learning models. Autonomous agents can think, act and learn independently. (Dhaduk, 2023)

Basic components of agent -based simulation include: agent, its environment and the interaction where: agents are the fundamental entities, environment is the realm in which agents operate and interact either directly with other agents, humans or their environment based on a predefined set of rules. (Chen Gao, 2024)

While single-agent systems may demonstrate strong performance in executing specific tasks, they often exhibit limitations when addressing complex problems that necessitate substantial collaboration and the integration of collective intelligence. This is where Multi-Agent Systems [MAS] become particularly relevant.

MAS refers to a complex framework composed of multiple interacting intelligent agents (Hu, 2021), designed to simulate social behaviours and teamwork observed in real-world scenarios. Through decentralized decision-making and effective information sharing, MAS enhances both adaptability and operational efficiency.

The principal strength of MAS lies in its distributed decision-making and problem-solving capabilities. As highlighted by (Yuheng Cheng, 2024), MAS offers a contemporary solution to challenges associated with distributed artificial intelligence. Within a MAS, each agent operates with a degree of autonomy, enabling it to perceive its environment and make decisions independently. Furthermore, agents within the system can engage in interactions that emulate real-world collaboration patterns—such as cooperation, competition, and hierarchical organization [(Yuheng Cheng, 2024),(Junda He, 2024)]—ultimately improving the system's collective performance and collaborative efficiency.

2.2. Types of Agents (rule-based, reactive, deliberative, learning-based, LLM-powered)

The technology utilized in agent-based simulation has undergone a lot of maturity. Earlier the models were more dependent on knowledge -driven approaches where a set of pre-defined rules or equations dictated the behaviour of the agents whereas the latter models are more data-driven which depend on machine learning models. (Chen Gao, 2024)

Rule-Based Agents

These agents are based on a set of pre-defined rules or equations. These agents operate deterministically. They are designed to decide how an agent should react to a specific input or situations. (Chen Gao, 2024) When these rules are more formal, like in the form of mathematical equations, they are called symbolic equations. Examples of rules-based agents can be seen in the early developed automation systems for tasks like claims processing and appointment scheduling in the insurance and healthcare industries.

Reactive Agents

Reactive agents are modelled with their decision making based on a direct-sense action loop. Reactive agents do not have memory and do not learn from their interactions with other agents or their environment. They are usually programmed to produce specific reactions to specific events. They are helpful for repetitive and non-complex tasks. Simple robots and thermostats that do not need long term planning for their reaction can be examples of reactive systems.

Deliberative Agents

Unlike reactive agents, deliberative agents_can actually reason and weigh-in choices about their reaction to a specific interaction. They learn from interactions and behaviour and update their internal environment. They have the ability to think through their decisions and come up with an action plan to achieve their objectives. The internal environment of deliberative agents is based on concepts from decision theory and heuristic algorithms. Self-driving cars are an excellent example of deliberative agents. (Chen Gao, 2024)

Learning Based Agents

Learning based agents are entities that can learn and acquire knowledge independently from their interactions with their environment. They make decisions based on their knowledge and experience rather than relying on pre-set rules or laws. The more they learn from their interactions, their decision making matures and their performance is improved over time.

The learning agents first observe and gather information about the agent and the effect of its reactions to interactions. Using machine learning algorithms, it fine tunes its internal mechanism to create a response which is an educated decision.

Recommendation features on social media platforms like Instagram and Facebook as well as targeted advertising based on user's search history are good examples of learning-based agents.

LLM Powered Agents

Large language model powered agents, for example, ChatGPT, Gemini, LLaMA etc..are the latest in language models. Their ancestors are the statistical, neural and pre-trained language models. Large language models have human -like intelligence to discern not only natural language processing tasks like summarization, paraphrasing, translation etc. but can also solve mathematical problems. They can adaptively react and perform tasks in a given environment with very few rules and pre-set conditions. LLM's performance is based on its learning from large data sets with billions of parameters which makes it mimic human logic, decision making and emotions. For large language models, the input doesn't necessarily have to be limited to text. In recent times, audio and images are also guaranteed to provide response results as expected. (Chen Gao, 2024)

2.3. Communication and Coordination Mechanisms in Agents

Multi- agent LLM systems have recently achieved great success in complex problem solving and world simulation. AI agents require sophisticated language and protocols to communicate and coordinate with other agents in a multi-agent system to be able to make collaborative decisions.

Agent communication analysis can be done by focussing on: (Taicheng Guo, 2024)

1. The interaction between the agents
2. The network architecture within a multi- agent LLM
3. The communication content shared between the agents

The Interaction Between the Agents

Current LLM system agents interact in 3 ways: Collaborative, Competitive and Debate. (Taicheng Guo, 2024)

Collaborative/Cooperative agents work collectively to complete a task exchanging information beneficial for working towards fulfilling the common goal. The agents first set the goals according to the goal to be achieved and then split a complex task into multiple sub-tasks which are assigned to multiple agents. (Li, 2024)

Competitive agents typically only work towards completing their own task or goal without any concern for conflicts that may arise with other agents' goals. Debate paradigms are utilized when agents improvise a solution by arguing and defending their own viewpoints.

Network Architecture Within a Multi-Agent LLM

Figure 1. Agent network architecture in MAS LLM

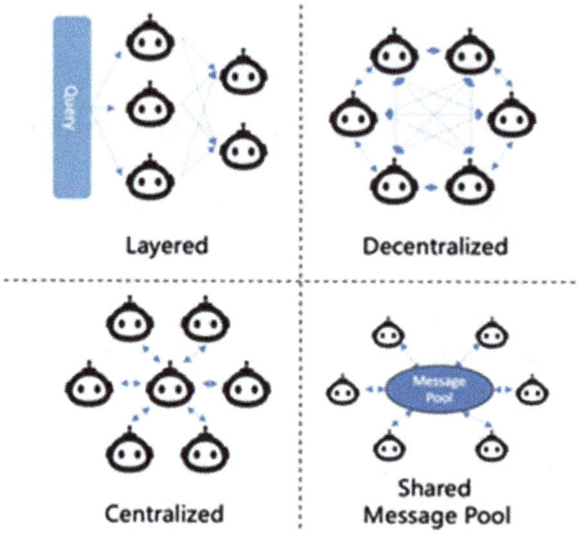

Figure 3: The Agent Communication Structure.

There are 4 communication architectural patterns followed by multi-agent LLMs.

Layered or Hierarchical architecture: In this network pattern, agents are organised in multiple hierarchical layers like a tree. Agents working within a particular level have well-defined roles and responsibilities. Agents interact with other agents in the same layer or across adjacent layers. (Taicheng Guo, 2024)(Li, 2024)

Decentralized architecture: This is a commonly adopted communication network pattern followed by contemporary multi-agent systems utilizing LLM. It operates on a peer -to-peer architecture, where agents communicate directly with each other without a need for a centralised communication node. (Taicheng Guo, 2024)

Centralized architecture: In centralized communication systems, a central agent or a group of central agents manage and coordinate interactions, with other agents communicating primarily through this central entity. (Taicheng Guo, 2024)

Shared Message Pool: This is an architectural scheme setup for exchanging information between agents via a shared message pool. Agents publish and subscribe to information channels they require, which allows them to only receive information relevant to them eliminating the need for point-to-point communication. (Li, 2024)

Figure 2. Architecture of Multi-Agent Systems

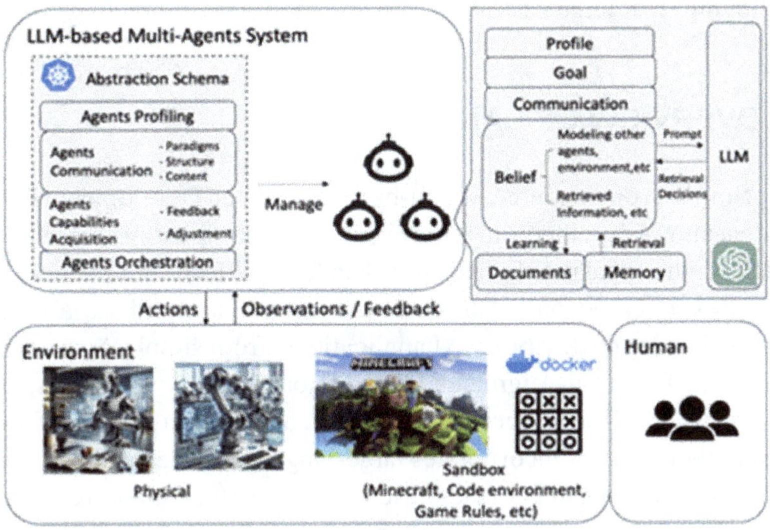

Figure 2: The Architecture of LLM-MA Systems.

(*Taicheng Guo, 2024*)

2.4. Challenges in Multi-Agent Environments

Task decomposition in a single agent involves generating a series of logical steps which are to be completed to complete the task. This process becomes difficult when there are multiple agents involved as alignment on contexts between agents becomes difficult when systems are processing information collectively. Ensuring that each sub-task allocated to a certain agent fits their individual roles and responsibilities along with their needs is an issue. (Astra DB Serverless, 2025)

When multi-agent systems work collaboratively to complete tasks, there needs to be a system for sharing, integrating and managing data and information across multiple agents which creates difficulties for memory management, storage and information retrieval. (Astra DB Serverless, 2025)

One famous drawback of MAS LLM is "Hallucination" where if the LLM model doesn't have the right response, it does not accept defeat but produces a response that may be factually incorrect. In MAS, due to the agents being interconnected, misinformation from one agent can propagate throughout the system. Hence detecting and rectifying hallucinations in an LLM-MA is crucial.(Taicheng Guo, 2024)

LLM-MA systems consist of multiple individual agents powered by LLM. This introduces scalability issues as each agent based on complex models like GPT-4 require considerable computing power and memory. As the number of agents increases, so does this demand for resources. In case of limited resources, building and deploying such large LLM-MA systems becomes challenging.

3. AN OVERVIEW OF LANGFLOW

Langflow is an open-source, visual-based Integrated Development Environment, or IDE, that allows developers to build agent and multi-agent systems. It is developed by DataStax who specialise in real-time data for Artificial Intelligence. Langflow's IDE interface is based on a flowchart-like system and utilises a drag-and-drop framework. It is to quickly build AI applications, from simple Agent behaviours to more complex Retrieval-Augmented Generation (RAG) applications, and to build with minimal code. These Agent behaviours can be further integrated into applications via Python code. It incorporates large-language models (LLMs) with Agents, series of inputs and prompts, and various ways of storing and retrieving data, to allow developers to quickly create Agentic AI applications such as RAG powered chatbots, multi-agent systems, and generating content (2025 DataStax Langflow).

Developing Agentic applications can be cumbersome to program. (Cardoso & Fernando, 2021) argues that lack of knowledge and familiarity with core concepts, as well as lack of publicly accessible and practical examples is a challenge when it comes to agentic-programming. Langflow aims to simplify the creation of agents, it further aims to integrate these agentic systems seamlessly with applications through APIs of popular Python-based frameworks. Langflow's minimal code framework allows quick creation of these systems in a simplified manner. There is little need for complex agentic-programming knowledge, but can define and customise Agent behaviour using Langflow's front-end, visual scripting, flowchart-like IDE.

3.1. A Look at Langflow's Architecture

Flow: Langflow functions with the concept of a "Flow," which is a connection of core components provided by the system. In simplest terms, a "Flow" is a flowchart-like, node-based application, made of connected components which serve as the AI application system. A "Flow" receives input from some defined source component, another component processes it, and delivers it to an output component. These "Flows" are serializable and can be exported or imported for integrating into other applications.

Playground: Langflow flows are tested and run through the 'Playground' interface. This is where developers can run, test the interactions with the Agentic system, typically the large-language models (LLMs) that the Agents use.

Databases: Langflow incorporates DataStax's in-house developed database called 'Astra DB.' Astra DB databases are cloud-based, server-less, NoSQL databases. These large-scale, cloud-based databases are created for real-time AI applications, which typically need to search and retrieve large amounts of data (2025 Astra DB). 'Astra DB' uses vector-based search, where data is stored as mathematical vectors and is retrieved based on nearest-neighbours calculations rather than SQL queries. Using this nearest-neighbours method allows AI models to find patterns and similarities in the data, which is useful for integrating in AI applications (Leventer, 2025). Langflow also allows integration with other data stores, such as MongoDB, which can be accessed by providing the relevant database location.

Deployment: The AI systems developed in the "Flow" can be exported as JSON files for integration in Python applications. They can further be deployed as an API, linked with Python frameworks, to create flexible applications. This chapter will explore using 'Streamlit,' a Python-based web-based framework, to quickly integrate AI Agentic flows created in Langflow into a serviceable web-based application.

3.2. Components in Langflow

Langflow flows are made of a series of "connections" and "components". Components act as nodes in the flow graph system, each with a series of "ports" for input, output, parameters or various functions. Components are interconnected via these "ports" using "connections" that act as wires or edges, transferring data from one component to be processed by the next. This subsection will explore key components used in Langflow.

Input and Output Type: Input components control where information enters the flow, whereas Output components receive the transformed and processed data at the end of the flow. The "Text Input" is a simple Input component, where the input is hand-written and pre-defined for the flow. "Chat Input" is another often used one, where user input is dynamically collected as through a chat interface. These Input components have subsequent Output components that receive and display the processed data in the relevant type. "Text Output" will display data as text, and "Chat Output" displays as a message in the chat interface. The Chat Input and Output system will be further explored in subsequent sections.

Vector Store: Langflow utilises vector databases to store and retrieve data. These vector databases are referred to via the "Vector Store" component in the flow. The "Astra DB Vector Store" is one such component. The core parameters of this component are related to establishing a connection with the database location, and selecting the relevant vector store database saved in DataStax architecture. An "Application Token" is required for authentication of the database and for establishing a connection. Once a token has been set, relevant databases are displayed in the drop-down selection for developers to choose from (2025b). A use-case for vector data is in retrieval-augmented generation, or RAG, applications. Relevant data can be uploaded as a vector collection, where an Agent can retrieve queries as vector data and use them in context when displaying an output message.

AI Models: AI "Model" components exist in Langflow, where they act as a vehicle for employing standard text-generation in a particular flow. These "Model" components use a suite of large-language models, from OpenAI, Groq, and Azure, to DeepSeek and Hugging Face, to generate text. Each Model component requires a relevant API key and specified model to connect to the language model. These components can receive inputs and can display outputs from one of the Input and Output components mentioned earlier in the section.

Using these AI "Model" components, developers can directly incorporate popular language models in their systems. However, as these are mainly used for text-generation and although are simple, provide a one-dimensional use in the flow; which is a standard input to text generation Model. The subsequent examples and studies in Section 4 will therefore not look at the "Model" component for this reason, and focus on the following component; the "Agent."

Agents: AI Agents are defined in Langflow using the "Agent" component. These agents contain several parameters and ports to set up their behaviours. An important parameter for this component is the 'Model Provider', where developers can choose common AI Model providers such as OpenAI, Azure, and Groq, choose a specific working model from that provider, and the 'API Key' to establish a connection with the chosen model.

Agents have input ports that can define their behaviour, one such being the 'Agent Instructions' input. This can be connected with any aforementioned Input components. Agent Instructions can further be defined in natural language. They serve as instructions and context to guide the agent's behaviour.

Prompts: Prompt components are used to instruct and structure components that use language models, such as the Agent or the Model component. It is another type of input, where developers can specify the instructions, rules, and behaviours of the intended model or agent. The rules, which are written in natural language, can contain custom variables specified by the developer, which are defined in curly-braces. This allows the language model to refer to and apply these variables in its assigned context. For instance, these variables may be a reference to another piece of information received from another component. The language model can then be instructed to construct a message using that, or in reference to that variable.

Tool: Components can be used as a "Tool" component in a flow. These are used alongside Agent components as a guide, to assist Agents performing tasks, or as a way for Agents to access external resources. Langflow contains ready-to-use Tool components for common uses such as; 'Bing,' or 'Google' search Tool for web-search, searching papers on arXiv.org using 'arXiv', the 'Calculator' tool to allow agents to reason and perform calculations as responses, and 'AstraDB' tool that allows agents to query and access collections made in Astra DB databases.

Further to ready-made Tools, Langflow allows developers to transform any component into a 'Tool' by toggling 'Tool Mode,' a switch found in most components. Components such as Prompts, or even Agents themselves can be turned into Tools to influence other Agents, forming the beginnings of a multi-agent system.

Python: The integration of Python in Langflow not only adds to its flexibility in overall system architecture, but it does so inside the flow as well. Langflow allows the creation of custom components via Python code. These components can be used to extend, customise, or create new components altogether that fit the developer's purpose. Inputs, output types, and methods can therefore be defined per system's needs (2025a).

4. EXAMPLES USING DATASTAX AND ASTRA DB

4.1. Automated Decision Making

Input-Output Simple Example

We will start with a simple example to show how we can use Langflow to build a simple rule-based single agent system called flow. This flow can be tested out in real time in the "Playground".

We start with creating a new flow whose name is Customer support and the endpoint name is customer.

To use a flow, you always have to start with some type of input like a chat or text input. Here we will be using a chat input. The chat input will allow the user to just type out their queries and then test the flow in the playground. To get an output from this input, we need some kind of an echo app which can be the Chat output. Make the right connections in the flow so as to pass messages between input and output. So, in the current structure of the flow, text entered from Chat input will be displayed as it is in the Chat output. If we test this flow in the playground and type "hey" you will get back "hey".

Figure 3. Chat Input/Output

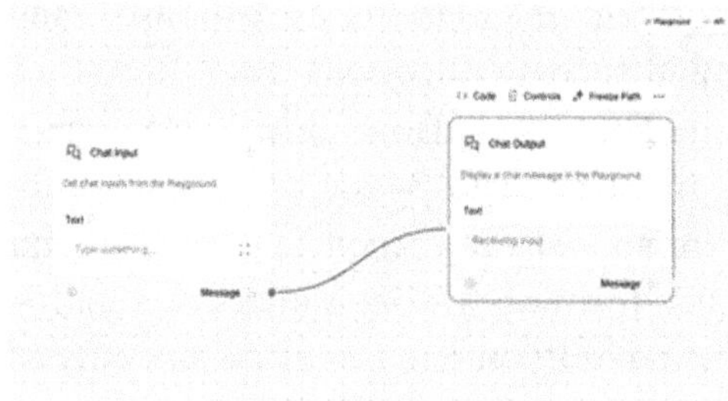

Figure 4. Playground

This was an example to just demonstrate the flow of data. Now we will utilize these Chat Input and Output modules to create a Retrieval-Augmented Generation (RAG) flow to accurately answer user questions by fetching and presenting the most relevant data from the database provided.

Single-Agent Rule-Based Flow

To begin creating the single-agent rule-based flow, we start with adding an Agent to the workspace. Change the agent's name to FAQ.

There are multiple AI agent model providers like Amazon Bedrock, Anthropic, Google Generative AI, Groq, Open AI, etc.. (2025 DataStax Langflow) For the purpose of this example, we will be referring to the Open AI LLM model provider. To be able to establish a connection with the LLM we need to generate an API key. The key then has to be added to the model flow. Choose field values for FAQ Agent settings depending on the model provider used.(Data

The RAG model here will act as a Customer Support agent where the questions asked will be the input. The FAQ Agent will require instructions to process the input and be able to fetch the most relevant data. For this purpose, a Prompt is added.

Connect the Prompt Message port to the FAQ Agent instructions port and the Message port on Chat Input to the Input port on the FAQ Agent and the questions port on the Prompt. Connect the Response port on the FAQ Agent to the Text port on the Chat Output.

Figure 5. Connection of ports - Part 1

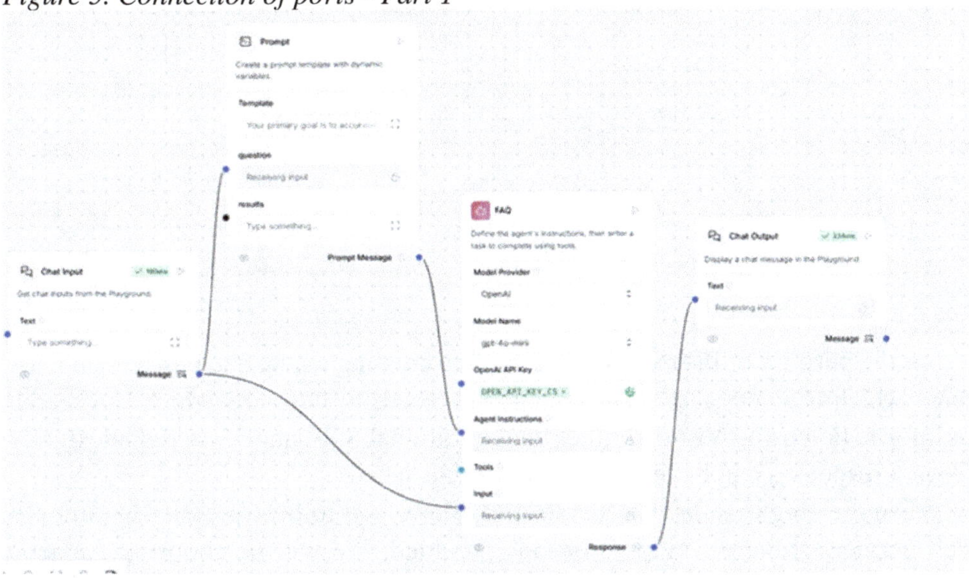

To be able to retrieve the data, we have to ensure there is information/data that the agent can access. For creating this data, go to the Langflow tab on top of the page and in the drop down select AstraDB. Langflow allows database creations by using AstraDB.

AstraDB

Datastax AstraDB is a noSQL database which allows creation of Vector and non-vector databases. Vector databases enable LLM use cases that require efficient similarity search, including Retrieval-Augmented Generation (RAG) and AI agents. Non-vector databases are more traditional databases without any of the vector capabilities.

Figure 6. Datastax AstraDB

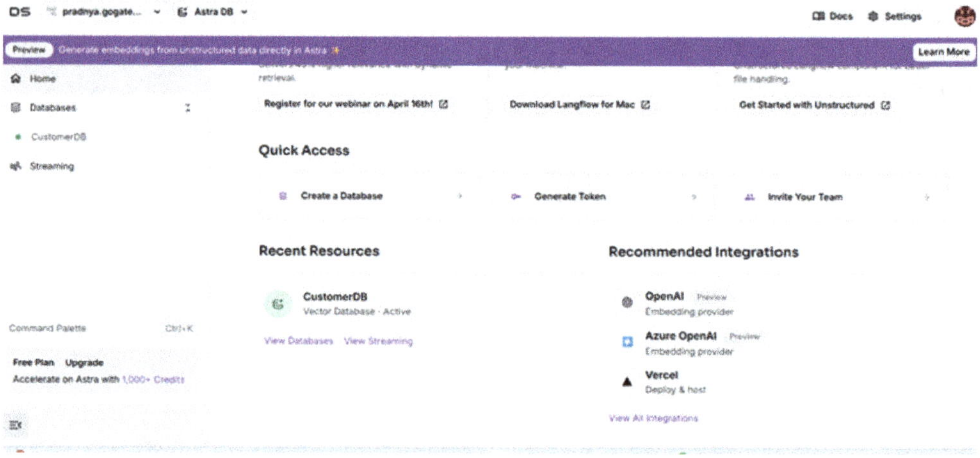

For the purpose of the example, we will be creating a new database called Customer which is a very fast vector-enabled database in AstraDB which can search for information using Vectors rather than traditional SQL queries and contextually relevant responses can be fetched with extreme speed.

When creating this database, AstraDB allows you to host it either in Amazon Web Services, Microsoft Azure or Google cloud. We will be choosing Amazon Web Services and provide the necessary details like the region and then choose to create the database.

Once created, it should get listed under the Databases. Create a collection called FAQ which is Astra vectorized and NVIDIA as the embedded provider. This allows the entered data to get vectorized automatically when it's added to the database.

RAG Model Flow

The idea here is that we first search in the Customer database for the data entered by the User via Chat Input and then pass it over to the prompt and then the FAQ Agent can use the information from the Database from the frequently asked questions file which we will create and use.

Go back to the Langflow flow by choosing the tab on top. Once in the flow, add an AstraDB component to the workspace by clicking on Vector stores and choosing AstraDB. The application token field is populated by default. Choose the database as Customer and the collection as FAQ for this example. Connect the Search Input port on the AstraDB vector store to the Message port on the Chat Input so as to be able to search for data like "what are the shipping times?" etc..

Figure 7. Port Connections - Part 2

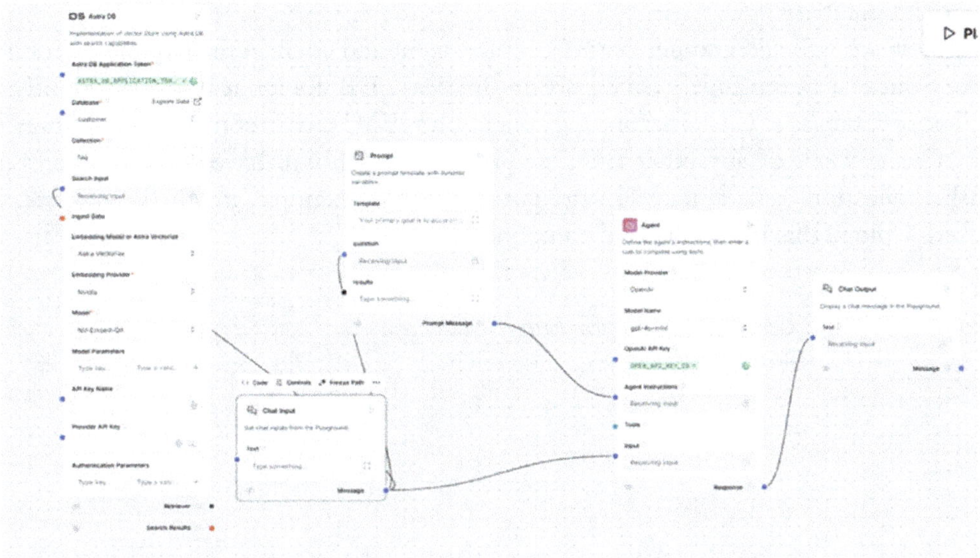

We cannot pass the Search results from the AstraDB vector store to the results directly because the ports don't match. Hence, the search results need to be parsed to be converted from json to textual data so that it can be passed to the Prompt. To do so, add a Parse Data component. Connect the Search results port on the AstraDB to the Data port on Parse Data and the Text port on Parse Data to the Results port in Prompt.

With this, we have some chat input which becomes the search input. The search results are then parsed to be converted to textual data and passed on to the prompt and then we pass that prompt to the FAQ agent. Everything is connected well but we do not have any RAG data uploaded to our database. Hence before this flow can be tested, we will add a separate component which will allow the data to be added to the database.

Adding Data

Click on Data in the left margin in the Langflow workspace and then add a File. Connect this file to a Split Text component which can be found by searching for it. Connect the Data port on File to the Data input of the Split Text. This allows for the file uploaded to the File component to be split into chunks before we add it into our database.

Now we will add another AstraDB component and connect the Chunks port on the Split text to the Ingest Data port on the Astra DB component added recently. Choose database as Customer and the collection as FAQ on it to complete the settings.

Create a pdf or any other file type you like which will have some frequently asked questions related text. For the purpose of this example, a .pdf file has been used. Upload this file to the File component.

Figure 8. Final Configurations for Langflow Flow

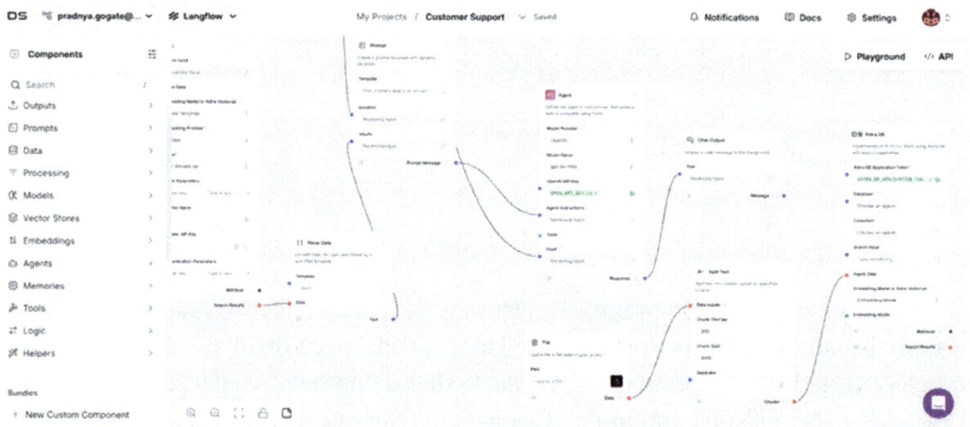

Now click on Run on the AstraDB component to run this flow and wait for the “AstraDB is built successfully message”. Then click on Playground and in the Chat input ask a question like “Can you tell me about shipment times?” You should receive a valid relevant output which is from the PDF which was uploaded to the File component.

Figure 9. Querying using Chat interface/Playground

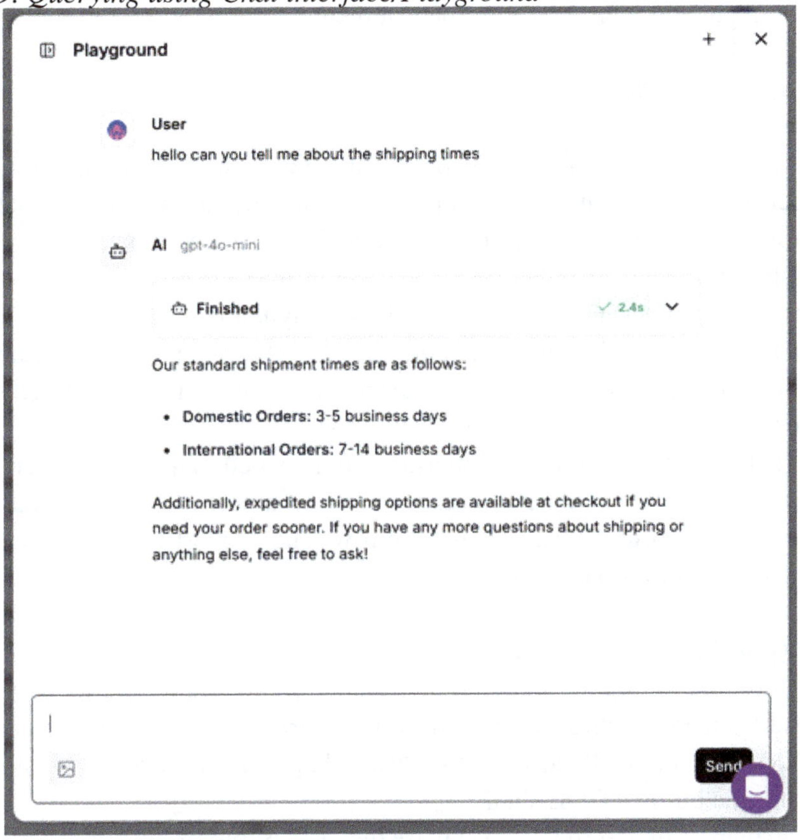

4.2. Knowledge Management - (DataStax, 2025)

Langflow utilizes AstraDB Vector store for creating databases and collections. AstraDB allows creation of two types of serverless databases:

1. Vector databases: These are designed for applications that enable LLM use cases that are dependent on powerful similarity search which includes Retrieval augmented Generation (RAG) and AI agents.

Vector databases allow using vector search instead of standard SQL queries to search for a relevant response. You can choose to load the vector data into the database directly or by using an embedding agent to vectorize the data you have provided.

They are highly scalable, reliable and powerful all-in-one data storage solutions.

2. Non-Vector databases: These are databases utilized for generic applications like user authentication and content management.

Terms and Terminology

Keyspace is the container for one or multiple tables within a database.

Collections: Collections is space created for storing the data inside a keyspace of a vector database which is similar to a Table in a traditional database.

The difference between collections and tables is the schema. In a collection, multiple files of dynamic schema can be stored. With dynamic schema, each document can hold data with varied fields. Collections are beneficial for semi-structured data.

Tables on the other hand allow storing structured data which have fixed schema and store the data in rows and columns.

Data that has one or multiple properties that is stored in a collection or table in a database. For a vector collection, documents are a part of collections and their properties are stored in fields. Tables have rows and properties of rows are stored in columns in a regular database.

Inserting Data Into AstraDB

To insert data into AstraDB, you can use the Astra portal to insert data via JSON. PDF or CSV files into Collections in the Vector databases. To insert data into tables, you can use the built-in CQL shell.

To load data using the files, you can use the Data Explorer tab under Collections and choose the right file type and then upload the file there. Once uploaded, the rows of the file are read and will be displayed to you in the portal.

The second way to load data is by creating a File component in Langflow, connecting it to a Split Text component which is then connected to the AstraDB component. The file will be loaded in the file component from where it is passed to the Split Text component to be broken down into chunks to make it easier to parse and then passed onto the Ingest data port of the AstraDB component where the required database and collection have been selected.

Fetching Data From AstraDB

Along with reading data from the AstraDB database, finding data is another important task. AstraDB uses several different ways to find data. They are:

Filters – Finding data based on filtering using values or range of values which may or may not be ordered.

Vector search - Is used by the vector databases where the embeddings in your database are compared against the query vector and then ordered by their similarity.

CQL analyzers: Using Apache Solr and Lucene and conducting a text-based search in the local CQL database.

Hybrid search: This search combines the vector, lexical and filters method in a one command and then delivers the most relevant data by contextually reranking the results.

Retrieval-Augmented Generation (RAG): (Retrieval Augmented Generation (RAG) in Azure AI Search, 2025)

RAG is a machine learning architecture that combines information retrieval with text generation. The information retrieval system allows control over the data used by the LLM while fetching the relevant response to a query. This improves accuracy, relevance and grounding of generated responses specifically in tasks like question answering and summarization.

RAG model works in two phases: Retrieval Phase and Generation phase.

In the retrieval phase, RAG model searches large external knowledge bases like documents, vector stores and embedded vector stores to retrieve results that are the most relevant in context for a given query. This search can be a vector search or hybrid search.(Retrieval Augmented Generation (RAG) in Azure AI Search, 2025)

In the generation phase the retrieved data in the form of documents are passed to a language model which will generate a response using the input query and context of retrieval.

Step by step working of RAG:

1. Initial Query processing: In this step RAG extensively analyses the user's input to understand the intent, context and specific information requirements of the query. This analysis is of utmost importance as it will decide the response retrieval accuracy.
2. Retrieving external data: After the initial step of analysing the query, RAG fetches data from external data sources like databases, document repositories and APIs usually extending more than the original training data for the LLM. This allows the data to be latest and relevant.
3. Data vectorization for relevancy matching: The vector database used in the RAG models is built with a vector embedding which helps transform the entered user query into numerical vector representations. This important step aids the system to use mathematical calculations to find relevant external data to the entered query.
4. Augmentation of language model prompts: The next step is to augment the LLMs prompt with the external data maintaining the context and relevance of the user's query.

5. Ongoing data updates: The external data sources need regular updates to ensure that the RAG systems responses are relevant. The process for updating is either automated or done in batches periodically depending on the type of data and the requirements of the model.

4.3. Intelligent Automation

Automation, which has existed and is implemented for several years, aims to ease production, improve efficiency and quality in business operations. One such form of automation is Robotic Process Automation (RPA), which is used for manual and repetitive software tasks such as email processing, and leverages rules-based, repetitive, rigid means of decision-making logic (Huang & Vasarhelyi, 2019). With this businesses can program autonomous robots to perform menial and repetitive tasks. More intelligent forms of decision-making were sought soon after, which led to Intelligent Automation.

Intelligent Automation (IA) is one such form of automation where the application of cognitive decision-making offered by Artificial Intelligence is integrated with RPA (Huang & Vasarhelyi, 2019). LLM-based software can be used to process large amounts of unstructured data, to enhance the automation's operational processes (Coombs et al., 2020). Text-mining, natural language processing and deep-learning algorithms can be used to enhance end-to-end automation and facilitate effective resource allocation and provide real-time performance analytics (Siderska et al., 2023). Guan et al. (2024) introduce a system that uses Intelligent Automation via virtual assistants that parse instructions, predict future behaviours and detect interface elements when using an online shopping application.

Langflow allows users to implement intelligent automation in a fast, low-code way. Its LLM-based components and Agents are able to reflect on the given input, reason based on any assigned behaviour specifics to curate the response. They can further use other components as tools, use those it determines necessary. A Multi-Agent architecture can further allow the delegation of tasks to other components and Agents alike, to do some reasoning, or perform menial tasks such as data gathering, which is similar to traditional RPA. Langflow's use of IA will be explored in more detail in Section 4.5, where a Multi-Agent architecture will be introduced.

4.4. Flexible Architecture

Langflow's architecture allows developers flexibility in creating AI powered systems. Langflow allows flexibility and configurability in its node-based interface, and allows developers to set up AI powered systems to their needs, without needing extensive knowledge of back-end processes.

All Agents in Langflow are powered by LLMs. Each Agent can be further fine-tuned through its parameters. These parameters such as 'temperature' for adjusting the precision in Agent's response, to setting the 'number of tokens', to 'seed' value and setting a maximum number of attempts for the Agent to form a response, can be set to suit the system's needs. This adds much needed flexibility and allows developers to dynamically configure their systems with ease.

The example of the Agent in the FAQ system explained earlier in Section 4 highlights the simplicity and speed with which an Agentic system can be implemented. The Agent relied on an LLM, a simple input from a user and a prompt as instructions to create a simple system. These Agent behaviours can be expanded through incorporating other components in the flow. Such as a web-search component to derive context from, or specified URLs as components that serve as a context-base for the LLM.

The previous section furthered the simple Agent behaviour to include data inside databases. Agents can gain contextual information through these databases that can provide a more specified range of responses relating to data-specific tasks. Developers are therefore able to create RAG-based systems quickly and easily.

Agents in Langflow can also utilise other components as Tools. For example, instead of performing calculations through the LLM provider, the Agent can use the Calculator component as a Tool to perform calculations. Agents can be trained to utilise certain tools at certain occasions, and to ignore others. They can further be instructed on specific ways to use certain Tools. This takes place when brief instructions are presented to the Agent regarding how to interact with the Tools. Agents can be instructed, for example, to "use all tools at its disposal," or to "rely more on certain tools over others at certain occasions." This allows the Agents to act as decision makers when confronted with an input request. The Tools themselves can be fine-tuned to provide context, information, or data in a specific way. This component-as-a-Tool approach and fine tuning of Tools will be explored in more detail in the following section.

4.5. Working With Multi-Agents

Langflow allows the integration of multiple agents in a single flow. In this subsection, multiple agents will be added to the previous, simpler agent behaviour example. The hierarchical, multi-agent architecture will be demonstrated.

A new agent is created in the flow, labelled as a Manager Agent, and it is assigned as delegator of tasks to the previous FAQ Agent. This Manger Agent is set up similar to the previous agent, with the same model provider. However, this agent will not receive explicit instructions from the chat Input as before, but its behaviour will be guided through a written prompt. This prompt is written in natural language and assigns a clear role 'a skilled customer service manager' to the agent. The prompt further specifies primary responsibilities, specifies a brief of the kind of information to lookup and instructs the agent to use whatever tools at its disposal.

FAQ Agent, now serving as subordinate to the Manager Agent, will transform into a 'Tool' the Manager Agent can use. Switching the 'Tool Mode' toggle on the FAQ Agent changes the Output port of the agent; having it simply output its responses or decisions as a toolset to be used by the Manager Agent.

This system is expanded further to have multiple Agents working under the Manager agent, each with their own specificities. An Order Lookup Agent is created, which will be responsible for getting access to the orders and products collections in the Customer DB made in "Astra DB". Recall from Section 4.2, the Customer database is created as a Vector database, which uses nearest-neighbours to retrieve data. Two new collections were created previously, the 'order' and 'product' collection, where the data for both was populated using a .csv file containing some previously collected order information and product information. The 'order' data includes details of products ordered by certain customers. Each data row in this collection includes a 'productId,' which links the data row to the relevant product in the 'products' collection.

These newer collections are now added for use in the flow as Tools for the Order Lookup Agent. The 'Astra DB Tool' component is used, one for each collection. Relevant parameters linking to the collection are filled in. A description is specified for each database, so as to describe the tool to the LLM and guide it on how to use the information in the databases. Important parameters and columns of the collections are defined for the LLM, specifically the orderId and productId columns from both collections. This is so as to guide the LLM to consider data that contain those parameters and to consider them in the response when prompted by the Manager Agent.

Figure 10. Order Lookup Agent receiving Tools in the form of the two Astra DB Tool; order and product collections

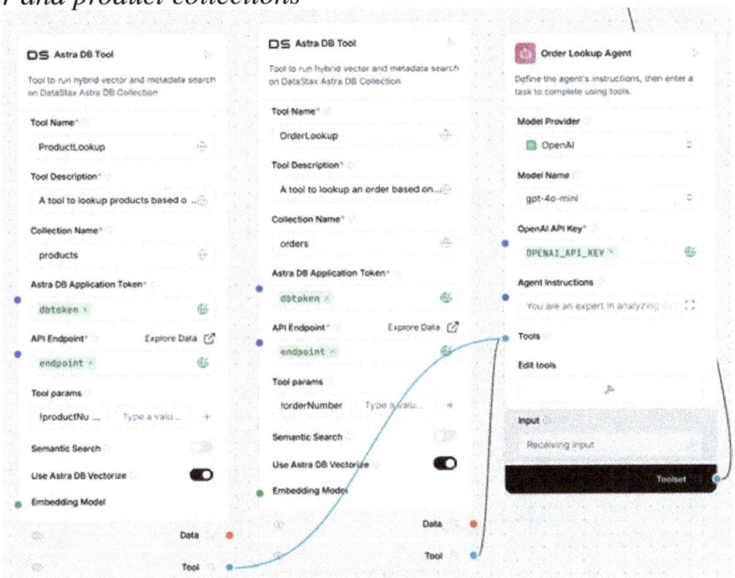

The Order Lookup Agent now receives input data from the two collections as Tools. This Agent will also be answerable to the Manager agent in this multi-agent, hierarchical setup, and hence will also in turn be set up as a Tool. This Agent as a Tool will also have some specific rules to guide its behaviour and responses, specifically to consider the database tool parameters orderId and productId in the response.

Finally, both FAQ Agent, which receives vectorised data through a File component, and Order Lookup Agent, which receives data through Databases as Tools, will serve as Tools to the Manager Agent. THe Manager Agent will receive input from the Chat Input, will delegate tasks to its subordinate Agents as guided by its instructions, which are each, further guided by their own instructions to generate relevant responses based on the data.

Figure 11. Three Agents in the multi-agent system. FAQ and Order Lookup agents connected to the Manager Agent as Tools

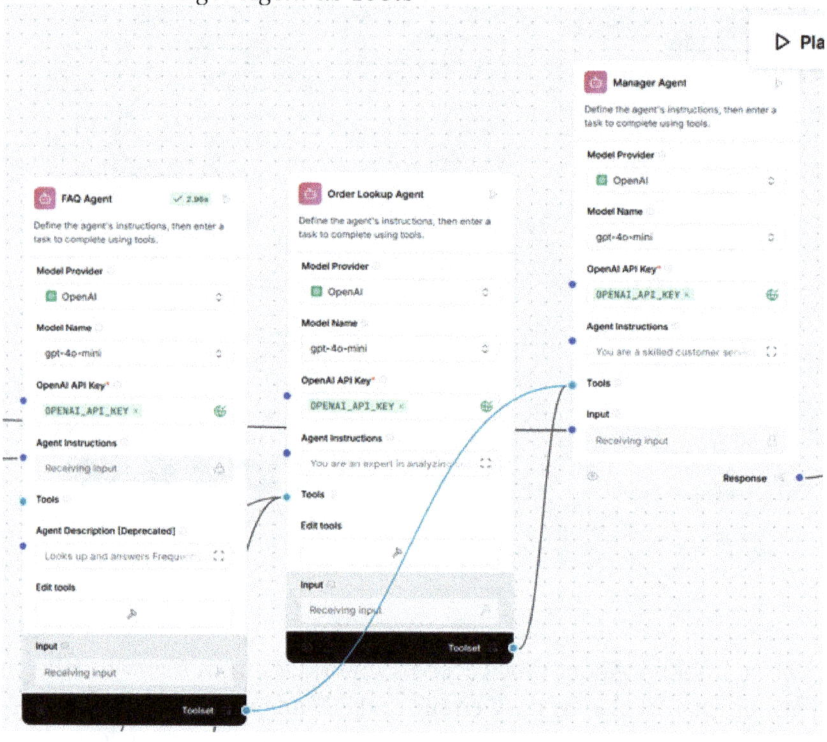

The 'Flow' is tested on the Playground, resulting in the AI Chat Agent providing information about the orders made and FAQ based questions.

Figure 12. AI Chatbot uses RAG-based LLM to generate context-specific responses

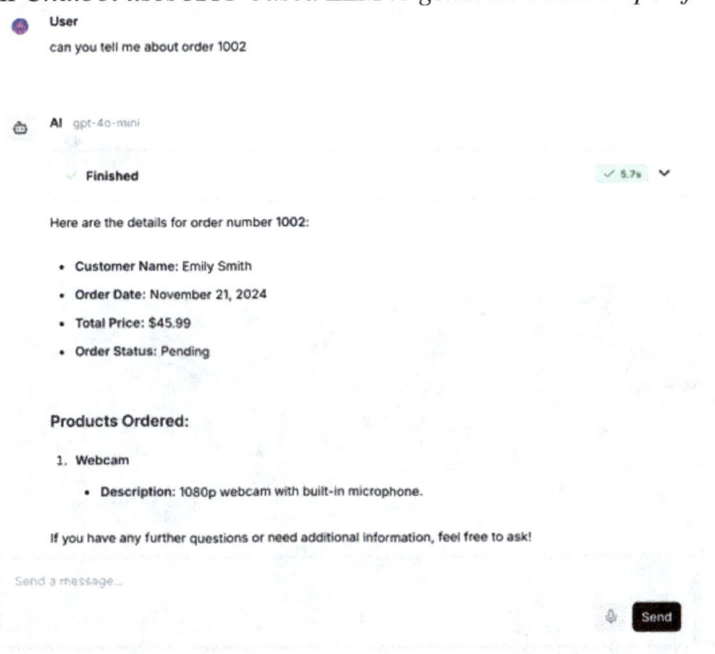

4.6. Integrating With APIs

After the flow is built, run and tested on the Playground, the flow can be exported as an API to be integrated in external applications. Langflow allows exports of the flow in several API languages and formats. This chapter will explore the use of Python API. Once the flow is ready, the API can be accessed through the Langflow application. Choosing the Python API section shows the complete flow code in Python and requests to generate an application token for authentication. The Python code is copied and an application token is then generated, copied and set aside for integration.

Figure 13. Python API of the completed Flow

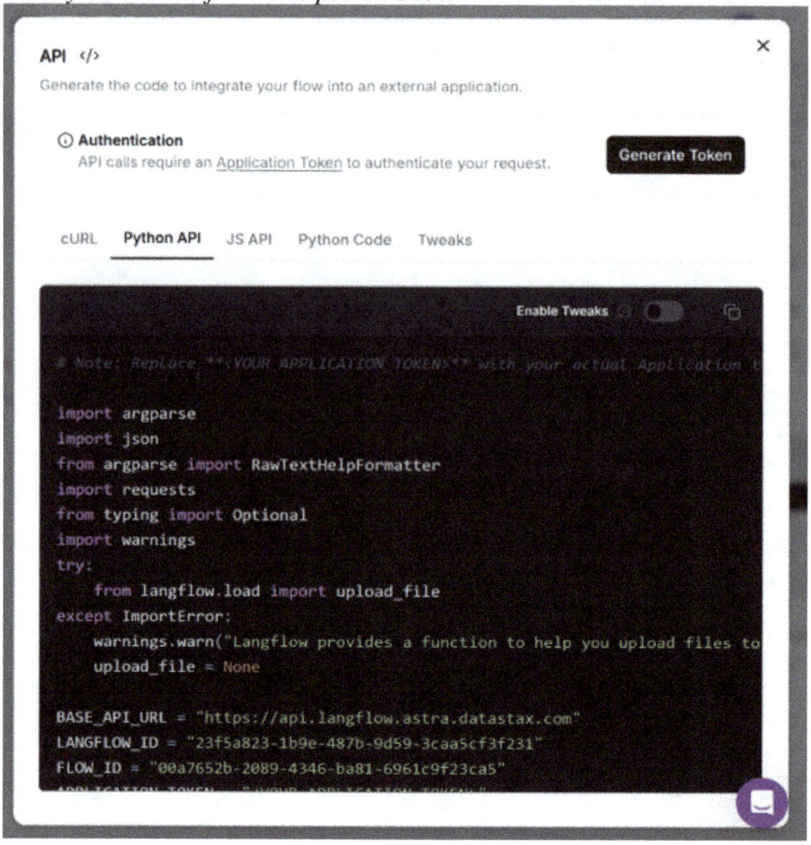

The python code is saved in a local file, and the application token is saved as an environment file, which the python code will use to refer to the flow in Langflow. The example in this chapter uses the Streamlit framework, and related libraries are added into the python file. A simple web-based chat interface is built based on the Streamlit framework, which takes as input the chat input from the user. It sends the user's input message to the Manager Agent, which generates a response based on the behaviours and flow set earlier. This response is finally sent to the web-based chat as a marked down output.

Figure 14. Streamlit code that creates the chat interface

```
# create the web Chat Interface. Send message to Agents.
# Get Response from Agent. Parse the json response to the output on screen
def main():
    st.title("Chat Interface")

    message = st.text_area("Message", placeholder="Ask me something...")

    # send message button
    if st.button("Send"):
        if not message.strip():
            st.error("Please enter a message")
            return
        try:
            with st.spinner("Running Flow..."):
                response = run_flow(message) #send user input message to agent
            response = response["outputs"][0]["outputs"][0]["results"]["message"]["text"]
            st.markdown(response) # show agent response on screen

        except Exception as e:
            st.error(str(e))

if __name__ == "__main__":
    main()
```

Figure 15. The python code is run via Streamlit to show a web-based chat interface

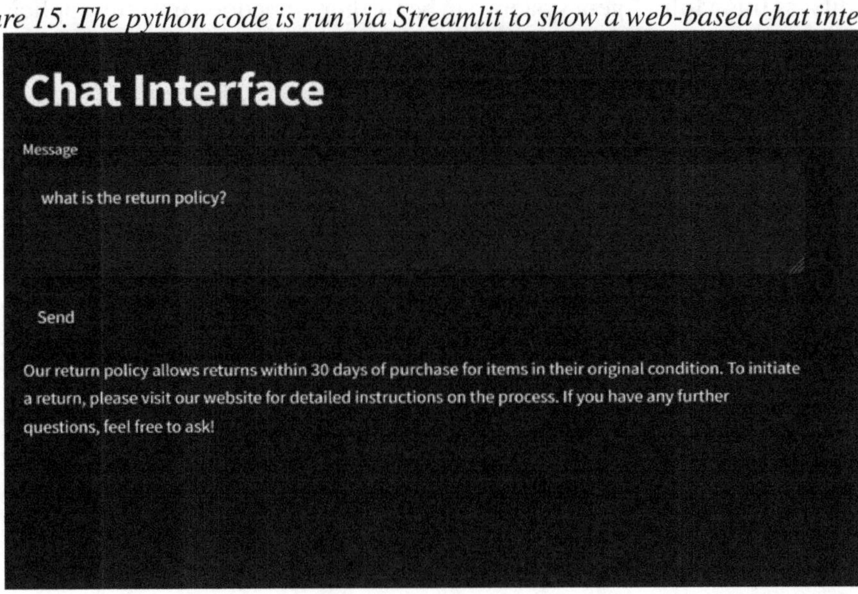

5. CONCLUSION

This chapter introduced agents and multi-agent systems. It introduced Langflow, a framework built by DataStax for developing Agentic applications and incorporating LLMs into usable applications. The chapter explored Langflow's flexible architecture, and emphasized the usability of its low-code, or no-code, platform. The chapter briefly introduced the concept of automation and Intelligent Automation (IA) and explored AI's usefulness in performing cognitive decisions for repetitive tasks.

The chapter then went on to provide practical examples in Langflow, from simpler, single-agent behaviours, to more complex multi-agent applications. This chapter further showed the different ways Langflow allows data storage and retrieval, using DataStax's 'vector' databases. It further demonstrated a simple RAG chatbot system by inserting documents into the database, to be retrieved and referred to by agents in responding to related chat questions.

A Multi-Agent system was implemented, where an Agent was assigned as a 'Manager' and other Agents were delegated tasks to gather data and process the data, before sending it back to the 'Manager' Agent. This RAG Multi-Agent system was then given a Python wrapper to create a user-friendly, web-based application. Streamlit, the Python wrapper used, further emphasised the Langflow platform's flexibility, as this Multi-Agent system can be further embedded into any application.

REFERENCES

Astra DB Serverless. (2025). Retrieved from https://docs.datastax.com/en/astra-db-serverless/faqs.html

Astra DB Serverless. (2025). Retrieved from https://docs.datastax.com/en/astra-db-serverless/get-started/astra-db-introduction.html#connect-and-integrate

Cardoso, R. C., & Ferrando, A. (2021). A Review of Agent-Based Programming for Multi-Agent Systems. *Computers*, *10*(2), 16. DOI: 10.3390/computers10020016

Chen Gao, X. L. (2024). Large language models empowered agent-based modeling and simulation: A survey and perspectives. *Humanities & Social Sciences Communications*.

Yuheng Cheng, C. Z. (2024). Exploring arge Language Model based Intelligent Agents: Definitions, Methods and Prospects.

Coombs, C., Hislop, D., Taneva, S. K., & Barnard, S. (2020). The strategic impacts of intelligent automation for knowledge and service work: An interdisciplinary review. *The Journal of Strategic Information Systems*, *29*(4), 101600. DOI: 10.1016/j.jsis.2020.101600

DataStax. (2025). *Astra DB for Generative AI app Creation & Development*. DataStax. https://www.datastax.com/products/datastax-astra

DataStax. (2025b). *Langflow: Visual low-code AI app builder for agents and Rag*. DataStax. https://www.datastax.com/products/langflow

Dhaduk, H. (2023, May). *What is an AI Agent? Characteristics, Advantages, Challenges, Applications*. Retrieved from https://www.simform.com/blog/ai-agent/

Guan, Y., Wang, D., Chu, Z., Wang, S., Ni, F., Song, R., & Zhuang, C. (2024). Intelligent agents with LLM-based Process Automation. *Proceedings of the 30th ACM SIGKDD Conference on Knowledge Discovery and Data Mining*, 5018–5027. https://doi.org/DOI: 10.1145/3637528.3671646

Taicheng Guo, X. C. (2024). Large Language Model based Multi-Agents: A Survey of Progress and Challenges.

Junda He, C. T. (2024). LLM-Based Multi-Agent Systems for Software Engineering: Literature Review, Vision and the Road Ahead.

Hu, J., P. B. (2021). A Decentralized Cluster Formation Containment Framework for Multirobot Systems. *IEEE Transactions on Robotics*.

Huang, F., & Vasarhelyi, M. A. (2019). Applying robotic process automation (RPA) in Auditing: A Framework. *International Journal of Accounting Information Systems*, *35*, 100433. DOI: 10.1016/j.accinf.2019.100433

Langflow. (2025a). *Create custom python components: Langflow documentation*. Langflow. https://docs.langflow.org/components-custom-components

Langflow. (2025b). *Vector Stores: Langflow documentation*. Langflow. https://docs.langflow.org/components-vector-stores

Leventer, A. (2025, March 7). *Choosing a vector store for Langchain*. DataStax. https://www.datastax.com/blog/vector-store-langchain

Li, X. W. (2024). *A survey on LLM-based multi-agent systems: workflow, infrastructure, and challenges*. Vicinagearth.

Retrieval-Augmented Generation (RAG). (2025). Retrieved from https://www.datastax.com/guides/what-is-retrieval-augmented-generation

Retrieval Augmented Generation (RAG) in Azure AI Search. (2025). Retrieved from https://learn.microsoft.com/en-us/azure/search/retrieval-augmented-generation-overview?tabs=docs

Siderska, J., Aunimo, L., Süße, T., von Stamm, J., Kedziora, D., & Aini, S. N. (2023). Towards intelligent automation (IA): Literature review on the evolution of Robotic Process Automation (RPA), its challenges, and future trends. *Engineering Management in Production and Services*, *15*(4), 90–103. DOI: 10.2478/emj-2023-0030

Chapter 2
The Role of Large Language Model (LLM) in Automating Business Intelligence and Finance

Meenakshi Sharma
NIET Business School, Noida, India

Sanjay Taneja
https://orcid.org/0000-0002-3632-4053
Graphic Era University, India

Timilehin Olasoji Olubiyi
https://orcid.org/0000-0003-0690-7722
West Midlands Open University, Nigeria

Bhupinder Pal Singh Chahal
https://orcid.org/0000-0002-8106-7121
Yorkville University, Canada

Sonam Puri
New Delhi Institute of Management, India

ABSTRACT

This study investigates the impact of Large Language Models (LLMs) on automating business intelligence and financial processes, employing a quantitative approach to analyze their efficacy in enhancing decision-making efficiency. A structured survey was conducted with 268 industry professionals, utilizing a 7-point Likert scale to assess perceptions of LLMs in financial analytics. Regression analysis reveals a

DOI: 10.4018/979-8-3373-2008-3.ch002

significant positive relationship (R^2 = 0.635, β = 0.797, p < 0.001), indicating that LLMs substantially contribute to automation outcomes. The findings highlight LLMs' role in improving analytical accuracy and operational efficiency while addressing concerns such as interpretability and integration complexities. Despite their potential, a portion of respondents remain neutral, suggesting challenges in adoption. Diagnostic tests confirm model validity, ensuring robust inferences.

INTRODUCTION

In an era characterized by the relentless proliferation of data and the concomitant imperative for organizations to harness actionable insights, the advent of sophisticated artificial intelligence paradigms has engendered a profound transformation in the domain of business intelligence and financial analytics. Among these technological advancements, Large Language Models (LLMs) have emerged as formidable instruments of computational prowess, offering unparalleled capabilities in the realms of natural language processing, contextual comprehension, and autonomous decision facilitation (Jadhav & Sarnikar, 2024). The exponential growth in the complexity and volume of financial data necessitates the deployment of intelligent automation mechanisms that transcend conventional analytical methodologies, thereby fostering an environment conducive to strategic agility and operational resilience.

The exigency for integrating LLMs within business intelligence frameworks is underscored by the dynamic and multifaceted nature of financial ecosystems, wherein the confluence of macroeconomic variables, market volatilities, and regulatory contingencies necessitate an adaptive and data-driven approach to decision-making. Traditional financial analytical models, often predicated on deterministic algorithms and rule-based heuristics, are increasingly being rendered obsolete in the face of voluminous unstructured data streams and the growing demand for real-time analytics (Song et al., 2024). In contrast, LLMs, underpinned by deep learning architectures and expansive training corpora, possess the intrinsic capability to decipher intricate financial narratives, discern latent patterns within vast datasets, and generate predictive insights with a degree of precision hitherto unattainable.

The proliferation of LLMs within the business intelligence landscape has precipitated a paradigmatic shift, wherein organizations are increasingly leveraging these models to automate routine analytical processes, enhance the accuracy of financial forecasting, and augment strategic planning initiatives. By enabling the extraction of nuanced insights from heterogeneous data sources—including financial statements, market reports, social media sentiment, and regulatory disclosures—LLMs facilitate a holistic and integrative approach to financial intelligence that transcends traditional siloed methodologies (Han et al., 2024). Furthermore, their ability to process and interpret natural language inputs allows for the democratization of data analytics, empowering non-technical stakeholders to engage with complex financial data through intuitive query mechanisms and conversational interfaces.

Despite the demonstrable potential of LLMs in revolutionizing business intelligence and finance, their adoption is not devoid of challenges. Issues pertaining to data privacy, algorithmic interpretability, and integration complexities pose formidable hurdles to widespread implementation. The opacity inherent in deep learning models, often referred to as the "black-box" phenomenon, raises concerns regarding the explainability and auditability of AI-generated financial insights, thereby necessitating the development of robust governance frameworks and ethical oversight mechanisms (Kukreti et al., 2025). Moreover, the computational intensity and infrastructural demands associated with LLM deployment necessitate significant capital investments, which may present barriers to entry for smaller enterprises with limited technological capabilities (Sehajpal & Kaur, 2025).

The discourse surrounding the automation of business intelligence and finance through LLMs necessitates a nuanced exploration of their efficacy, limitations, and broader implications within organizational contexts. This study endeavors to elucidate the empirical relationship between LLM adoption and the efficiency of automated business intelligence processes, thereby contributing to the evolving body of knowledge on AI-driven financial transformation (Han et al., 2024). By leveraging quantitative methodologies to assess the perceptions and experiences of industry practitioners, this research aims to furnish actionable insights that can inform strategic decision-making and foster the responsible deployment of LLM technologies in financial domains. Ultimately, the study aspires to bridge the gap between theoretical postulations and practical applications, offering a comprehensive understanding of the intersection between advanced AI capabilities and contemporary financial imperatives.

LITERATURE REVIEW

The advent of artificial intelligence (AI) and machine learning (ML) in business intelligence and financial analytics has been the subject of extensive scholarly inquiry, with a growing emphasis on the potential of Large Language Models (LLMs) to revolutionize traditional data-driven decision-making paradigms. Over the past decade, the convergence of AI technologies with financial operations has catalyzed the evolution of business intelligence frameworks, enabling organizations to transcend the limitations of conventional analytical methodologies and embrace automation-driven efficiencies. Scholars have explored the multifaceted implications of LLM adoption, ranging from enhanced decision-making capabilities to challenges associated with algorithmic transparency, data integrity, and regulatory compliance (Zhao et al., 2024).

Early explorations into AI-driven financial automation, as articulated by Naik et al., (2024), underscored the transformative potential of AI models in augmenting analytical accuracy and operational efficiency. Their research delineated the progressive transition from rule-based systems to AI-powered automation, emphasizing the ability of deep learning models to derive insights from unstructured data sources and facilitate predictive analytics. This foundational work provided the impetus for subsequent investigations into the applicability of LLMs within financial contexts, with scholars such as Arslan et al., (2024) further substantiating the role of AI in enhancing financial forecasting accuracy and enabling real-time decision support systems.

The efficacy of LLMs in automating business intelligence processes has been explored through various lenses, including their ability to process voluminous textual data, extract latent patterns, and generate contextual insights. Studies conducted by Menghao et al., (2023) and Sarker, (2024) on transformer-based architectures, particularly OpenAI's GPT models, have demonstrated the superior capabilities of LLMs in language understanding and data synthesis. These studies posit that LLMs, by virtue of their extensive pre-training on diverse datasets, possess the capacity to distill complex financial information into actionable insights with minimal human intervention. This assertion aligns with findings by BERT researchers Saxena et al., (2024), who highlighted the contextual embedding capabilities of LLMs, enabling more nuanced financial sentiment analysis and risk assessment.

Notably, the integration of LLMs into business intelligence systems has been linked to increased efficiency in financial operations, with empirical studies highlighting their role in automating repetitive tasks such as report generation, financial summarization, and anomaly detection. A study by Fan et al., (2024) explored the deployment of LLMs in enterprise financial analytics, revealing that their implementation resulted in a 30% reduction in manual data processing time and a marked improvement in the accuracy of financial projections. Similar findings by Menghao et al., (2023) corroborate the notion that LLMs facilitate operational scalability and cost optimization, particularly in data-intensive environments where traditional financial models fall short in handling dynamic market variables.

Despite the demonstrated benefits, the literature also identifies several challenges associated with the adoption of LLMs in financial domains. Ethical concerns related to data privacy, algorithmic bias, and the opacity of AI-driven decision-making processes have been widely discussed in contemporary research. A study by Saxena et al., (2024) examined the potential for algorithmic bias within LLM applications, emphasizing the risk of discriminatory financial decisions arising from skewed training datasets. Additionally, the "black-box" nature of deep learning models poses significant challenges for regulatory compliance and auditability, with financial institutions facing increased scrutiny regarding the explainability of AI-generated insights (Fan et al., 2024). These concerns necessitate the development of robust interpretability frameworks and governance mechanisms to ensure the responsible deployment of LLMs in financial contexts.

Furthermore, scholars have investigated the infrastructural and operational challenges associated with LLM adoption, including the high computational costs and technical expertise required for implementation. According to research by Mary Joshitta et al., (2023), the deployment of large-scale AI models demands substantial energy consumption and cloud infrastructure investments, which may present barriers to entry for smaller financial institutions. This aligns with the findings of Gupta et al., (2022), who suggested that the democratization of AI technologies requires concerted efforts to enhance accessibility and affordability through open-source initiatives and collaborative research.

Comparative studies have also sought to benchmark the performance of LLMs against traditional business intelligence tools such as data warehousing and OLAP (Online Analytical Processing) systems. A meta-analysis conducted by Kumar et al., (2023) found that while LLMs outperform conventional BI tools in terms of contextual understanding and predictive accuracy, their integration necessitates a reconfiguration of existing workflows and a recalibration of organizational strategies to accommodate the unique capabilities of AI-driven analytics.

In conclusion, the extant literature presents a compelling narrative on the transformative potential of LLMs in automating business intelligence and financial processes, while also highlighting critical challenges that necessitate further exploration. As organizations continue to navigate the evolving AI landscape, future research must focus on developing frameworks that address ethical considerations, regulatory compliance, and infrastructural scalability to maximize the benefits of LLM adoption in financial analytics.

RESEARCH METHODOLOGY

The research methodology employed in this study is meticulously designed to facilitate an exhaustive and methodologically rigorous exploration of the relationship between Large Language Models (LLMs) and the automation of business intelligence and finance. This study leverages a quantitative research design to systematically analyze the perceptions, implications, and efficacy of LLMs in enhancing decision-making efficiencies and operational processes within financial domains.

A structured, deductive approach underpins the inquiry, ensuring empirical rigor and the generalizability of findings across diverse organizational contexts.

The research is predicated on a cross-sectional survey methodology, employing a structured questionnaire to elicit responses from a carefully delineated sample of industry professionals and stakeholders with substantial exposure to financial analytics and business intelligence automation. The instrument utilized for data collection is formulated on a 7-point Likert scale, meticulously capturing a spectrum of respondent perceptions ranging from strong dissent to strong concurrence. The questionnaire is structured to encompass key constructs derived from extant theoretical frameworks and empirical literature, thereby ensuring construct validity and reliability. The independent variable, LLM adoption, is operationalized through inquiries regarding its perceived efficacy in financial decision-making, while the dependent variable, automating business intelligence, is assessed through statements reflecting process efficiency and strategic alignment.

The sampling framework adheres to a purposive sampling technique, targeting respondents with demonstrable expertise in financial operations, business intelligence systems, and AI implementation. The target population comprises financial analysts, business intelligence professionals, and AI strategists, ensuring a well-informed respondent base capable of providing nuanced insights into the phenomenon under investigation. A sample size of 268 respondents is determined to achieve statistical power and representation, aligning with best practices in survey-based research within the business intelligence domain.

Data analysis is conducted through a robust statistical framework encompassing both descriptive and inferential statistical techniques. Descriptive statistics, including mean, standard deviation, frequency distributions, and percentage analyses, are employed to elucidate underlying patterns and central tendencies within the dataset. Inferential analyses incorporate Pearson correlation to ascertain the strength and directionality of the relationship between LLM adoption and business intelligence automation, while regression analysis is utilized to evaluate the predictive capacity of LLMs in enhancing financial automation processes. The statistical significance of the relationships is assessed at a 95% confidence interval, ensuring the reliability and validity of the inferential findings.

The model summary, as derived from the regression analysis, reveals an R-squared value of 0.635, indicating that approximately 63.5% of the variance in business intelligence automation can be attributed to the implementation of LLMs. The Durbin-Watson statistic of 1.682 affirms the absence of autocorrelation in the residuals, reinforcing the robustness of the model. Furthermore, the ANOVA results demonstrate a statistically significant F-value ($F = 462.224$, $p < 0.001$), underscoring the explanatory power of LLMs in predicting automation outcomes. The coefficient analysis indicates a standardized beta value of 0.797 ($p < 0.001$), signifying a strong and statistically significant relationship between LLM adoption and the dependent variable.

The study also incorporates diagnostic assessments to validate model assumptions, including collinearity diagnostics, normality tests, and residual analysis. The collinearity diagnostics reveal variance inflation factors (VIF) of 1.000, indicating the absence of multicollinearity and ensuring the independence of predictor variables. The normality of residuals is corroborated through histogram analysis and normal P-P plots, which depict a near-perfect alignment with the theoretical normal distribution, substantiating the appropriateness of the regression model.

Ethical considerations are meticulously adhered to throughout the research process, ensuring respondent confidentiality, informed consent, and adherence to data protection regulations. The research design prioritizes anonymity and voluntary participation, mitigating any potential biases and ethical concerns associated with data collection and analysis.

The methodological rigor of this study is further reinforced through a comprehensive review of extant literature, which serves to contextualize the findings within the broader corpus of AI and business intelligence research. The integration of theoretical insights with empirical data facilitates a nuanced understanding of the interplay between LLMs and financial automation, enabling the derivation of actionable insights with practical implications for industry stakeholders.

In conclusion, the research methodology employed in this study is characterized by methodological precision, statistical rigor, and ethical integrity, providing a robust foundation for advancing the discourse on the transformative potential of LLMs in automating business intelligence and financial operations. The findings derived from this study hold significant implications for organizations seeking to leverage AI-driven insights for strategic decision-making and operational efficiency.

Table 1. Research Instrument

Variable Type	Variable Name	Question Statement	Likert Scale Description
Independent	Large Language Model (LLM)	The use of Large Language Models improves financial decision-making processes.	1 = Strongly Disagree, 7 = Strongly Agree
Dependent	Automating Business Intelligence (BI)	Automating business intelligence processes leads to more efficient operations.	1 = Strongly Disagree, 7 = Strongly Agree

The research instrument in Table 1 evaluates the impact of Large Language Models (LLMs) on automating business intelligence processes by assessing participants' perceptions of LLMs' effectiveness in improving financial decision-making and the efficiency of automated BI operations using a 7-point Likert scale ranging from 1 (Strongly Disagree) to 7 (Strongly Agree).

DATA ANALYSIS

Table 2. Frequency Table for Large Language Model

		Frequency	Percent	Valid Percent	Cumulative Percent
Valid	Strongly Disagree	12	4.5	4.5	4.5
	Disagree	51	19.0	19.0	23.5
	Somewhat Disagree	52	19.4	19.4	42.9
	Neutral	56	20.9	20.9	63.8
	Somewhat Agree	97	36.2	36.2	100.0
	Total	268	100.0	100.0	

The frequency table **(Table 2)** for the Large Language Model variable indicates that out of 268 respondents, 36.2% somewhat agree that LLMs improve financial decision-making, while 20.9% remain neutral, and a combined 42.9% express varying degrees of disagreement (19.4% somewhat disagree, 19.0% disagree, and 4.5% strongly disagree), reflecting a diverse range of opinions with a notable portion showing agreement and neutrality.

Table 3. Automating Business Intelligence and Finance

Automating_Business_Intelligence_and_Finance					
		Frequency	Percent	Valid Percent	Cumulative Percent
Valid	Strongly Disagree	20	7.5	7.5	7.5
	Disagree	53	19.8	19.8	27.2
	Somewhat Disagree	29	10.8	10.8	38.1
	Neutral	79	29.5	29.5	67.5
	Somewhat Agree	87	32.5	32.5	100.0
	Total	268	100.0	100.0	

Table 3 indicates that among the 268 respondents, 32.5% somewhat agree that automating business intelligence and finance processes leads to more efficient operations, while 29.5% remain neutral, and a total of 38.1% express varying degrees of disagreement (10.8% somewhat disagree, 19.8% disagree, and 7.5% strongly disagree), reflecting a mixed perception with a notable portion leaning towards agreement and neutrality.

Table 4. Descriptive Statistics

	Mean	Std. Deviation	N
Automating_Business_Intelligence_and_Finance	3.5970	1.31895	268
LLM	3.6530	1.26717	268

Table 4 presents the descriptive statistics, showing that the mean response for Automating Business Intelligence and Finance is 3.5970 with a standard deviation of 1.31895, while the mean for Large Language Models (LLM) is slightly higher at 3.6530 with a lower standard deviation of 1.26717, based on 268 respondents, indicating a moderate level of agreement with relatively similar dispersion of responses for both variables.

Table 5. Correlations

		Automating_Business_Intelligence_and_Finance	LLM
Pearson Correlation	Automating_Business_Intelligence_and_Finance	1.000	.797
	LLM	.797	1.000
Sig. (1-tailed)	Automating_Business_Intelligence_and_Finance	.	.000
	LLM	.000	.
N	Automating_Business_Intelligence_and_Finance	268	268
	LLM	268	268

Table 5 presents the correlation analysis, indicating a strong positive relationship between Automating Business Intelligence and Finance and Large Language Models (LLM) with a Pearson correlation coefficient of 0.797, which is statistically significant at $p = 0.000$ (one-tailed), based on 268 respondents, suggesting that higher perceptions of LLM effectiveness are strongly associated with greater perceived efficiency in automating business intelligence and finance processes.

Table 6. Model Summary

Model	R	R Square	Adjusted R Square	Std. Error of the Estimate	Durbin-Watson
1	.797[a]	.635	.633	.79864	1.682

a. Predictors: (Constant), LLM
b. Dependent Variable: Automating_Business_Intelligence_and_Finance

Table 6 provides the model summary, showing that the regression model with Large Language Models (LLM) as the predictor explains 63.5% of the variance in Automating Business Intelligence and Finance ($R^2 = 0.635$), with an adjusted R^2 of 0.633 indicating minimal shrinkage, a standard error of the estimate of 0.79864, and a Durbin-Watson value of 1.682 suggesting no significant autocorrelation in the residuals, thereby demonstrating a strong model fit.

Table 7. ANOVA

Model		Sum of Squares	df	Mean Square	F	Sig.
1	Regression	294.817	1	294.817	462.224	.000[b]
	Residual	169.661	266	.638		
	Total	464.478	267			

a. Dependent Variable: Automating_Business_Intelligence_and_Finance
b. Predictors: (Constant), LLM

Table 7 presents the ANOVA results, indicating that the regression model with Large Language Models (LLM) as the predictor is statistically significant in explaining variations in Automating Business Intelligence and Finance, with an F-value of 462.224 and a significance level of $p = 0.000$, suggesting that the model significantly predicts the dependent variable, as the regression sum of squares (294.817) is substantially higher compared to the residual sum of squares (169.661), reinforcing the strength of the relationship between the variables.

Table 8. Coefficients

Coefficients												
	Unstandardized Coefficients		Standardized Coefficients	t	Sig.	95.0% Confidence Interval for B		Correlations			Collinearity Statistics	
	B	Std. Error	Beta			Lower Bound	Upper Bound	Zero-order	Partial	Part	Tolerance	VIF
(Constant)	.568	.149		3.808	.000	.274	.861					
LLM	.829	.039	.797	21.499	.000	.753	.905	.797	.797	.797	1.000	1.000

a. Dependent Variable: Automating_Business_Intelligence_and_Finance

Table 8 presents the coefficients of the regression model, indicating that Large Language Models (LLM) significantly predict Automating Business Intelligence and Finance, with an unstandardized coefficient (B) of 0.829 and a standardized beta coefficient of 0.797, meaning that for every one-unit increase in LLM, the dependent variable increases by 0.829 units, while the t-value of 21.499 and a significance level of p = 0.000 confirm the strong statistical significance of the predictor; additionally, the 95% confidence interval for B (0.753 to 0.905) suggests a narrow range of estimation, with zero-order, partial, and part correlations all showing a value of 0.797, indicating a strong direct relationship, and the absence of multicollinearity as reflected by the tolerance of 1.000 and VIF of 1.000.

Table 9. Collinearity Diagnostics

Collinearity Diagnostics[a]					
Model	**Dimension**	**Eigenvalue**	**Condition Index**	**Variance Proportions**	
				(Constant)	**LLM**
1	1	1.945	1.000	.03	.03
	2	.055	5.945	.97	.97

a. Dependent Variable: Automating_Business_Intelligence_and_Finance

Table 9 presents the collinearity diagnostics, showing that the model has two dimensions with eigenvalues of 1.945 and 0.055, and a condition index of 5.945, indicating no serious multicollinearity concerns; the variance proportions for both the constant and the LLM variable are relatively balanced (0.03 and 0.97), suggesting that most of the variance is explained by the primary dimension, and the high condition index does not indicate a strong multicollinearity issue, ensuring the stability and reliability of the regression coefficients.

Table 10. Residuals Statistics

	Minimum	**Maximum**	**Mean**	**Std. Deviation**	**N**
Predicted Value	1.3970	4.7140	3.5970	1.05080	268
Residual	-2.05553	2.77372	.00000	.79714	268
Std. Predicted Value	-2.094	1.063	.000	1.000	268
Std. Residual	-2.574	3.473	.000	.998	268

a. Dependent Variable: Automating_Business_Intelligence_and_Finance

Table 10 presents the residuals statistics, indicating that the predicted values for Automating Business Intelligence and Finance range from a minimum of 1.3970 to a maximum of 4.7140, with a mean of 3.5970 and a standard deviation of 1.05080, while the residuals have a mean of 0.00000 and a standard deviation of 0.79714, suggesting that the model predictions are relatively accurate with minimal bias; the standardized predicted values range from -2.094 to 1.063, and the standardized residuals range from -2.574 to 3.473, with their respective means close to zero and standard deviations close to one, indicating well-distributed residuals and no significant outliers or heteroscedasticity issues.

Figure 1. Histogram Regression Residual

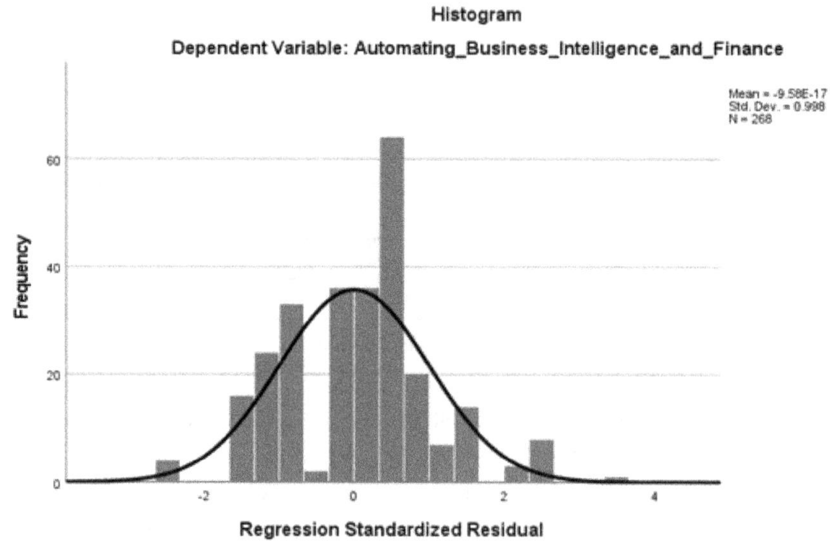

The histogram of regression standardized residuals for the dependent variable "Automating Business Intelligence and Finance" shows a roughly normal distribution with a mean close to zero (-9.58E-17) and a standard deviation of 0.998, indicating that the residuals are symmetrically distributed around zero with no significant skewness or outliers, thus supporting the assumption of normality required for regression analysis and suggesting that the model's predictions are relatively accurate and unbiased.

Figure 2. Normal P-P Plot

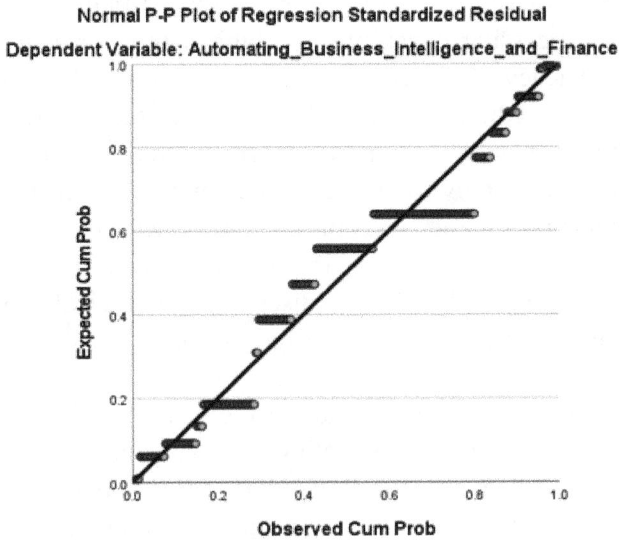

The Normal P-P Plot of regression standardized residuals for the dependent variable "Automating Business Intelligence and Finance" shows that the observed cumulative probabilities closely follow the expected cumulative probabilities along the diagonal line, indicating that the residuals are approximately normally distributed and confirming that the assumption of normality holds for the regression model, suggesting the model's validity and reliability in predicting the dependent variable.

DISCUSSION

The findings of this study delineate an unequivocally robust correlation between the implementation of Large Language Models (LLMs) and the augmentation of automation within the realms of business intelligence and finance. The statistically significant Pearson correlation coefficient underscores the potency of LLMs in driving operational efficiencies, with regression analyses substantiating that a considerable proportion of variance in automated financial processes is attributable to the integration of LLMs. These empirical insights reinforce the overarching hypothesis that the deployment of LLMs engenders substantive enhancements in analytical precision and procedural optimization, thereby fostering a paradigm shift in financial intelligence workflows.

A comparative examination of extant literature reveals congruence with antecedent scholarly endeavors that have examined the intersection of artificial intelligence and financial analytics. Prior investigations, such as those conducted by Rana et al., (2022), posit that AI-driven automation frameworks, particularly those leveraging natural language processing capabilities, exhibit a transformative influence on decision-making efficacy. The current study corroborates such assertions by elucidating the significant predictive power of LLMs in facilitating data-driven strategic imperatives within financial operations. Furthermore, the research findings resonate with the conclusions drawn by Chen et al., who emphasized the pivotal role of AI technologies in enhancing the accuracy of financial projections and the streamlining of operational contingencies. However, the present analysis distinguishes itself by offering a granular focus on LLMs as a discrete technological construct, thereby contributing novel empirical evidence to the discourse on AI-enabled financial automation.

The present inquiry, while substantiating the efficacy of LLMs, also unveils nuanced insights into respondent perceptions, as evidenced by the distribution of survey responses. A substantial segment of participants exhibited a proclivity toward neutrality, implying latent apprehensions or an absence of definitive experiential validation regarding the efficacy of LLM-driven automation. This ambivalence may be indicative of entrenched concerns surrounding implementation complexities, data governance considerations, or the perceived opacity of AI decision-making mechanisms (Ni et al., 2024). Such observations align with prior theoretical frameworks, including the Technology Acceptance Model (TAM), which posits that the perceived utility and ease of use of emerging technologies are cardinal determinants of adoption propensities.

Residual diagnostics, as elucidated through the analysis of standard error distributions and normality assessments, lend further credence to the robustness of the regression model. The symmetrical dispersion of residuals around the mean affirms the statistical integrity of the model, mitigating concerns related to heteroscedasticity or specification errors. This methodological rigor is consistent with best practices advocated within quantitative research paradigms and reinforces the reliability of the study's inferential outcomes (Hirano & Imajo, 2024).

Notwithstanding the compelling evidence favoring LLM integration, the findings also illuminate a divergence from certain scholarly perspectives that have highlighted the challenges associated with AI assimilation within financial ecosystems. Prior studies, such as those by Shukla et al., (2023), delineate regulatory inertia and trust deficits as formidable impediments to AI adoption. While the current study does not explicitly interrogate regulatory dimensions, the observed neutrality in respondent sentiments may tacitly reflect underlying skepticism or the nascent state of LLM deployment in financial contexts.

The implications of these findings extend beyond theoretical conjecture to practical applications within organizational settings. Enterprises poised to harness LLM capabilities stand to benefit from expedited data processing capabilities, enhanced predictive accuracy, and the reduction of manual labor inefficiencies (Ahmad et al., 2024). Furthermore, the scalability of LLM applications renders them particularly suited to enterprises operating in data-intensive environments, where the exigencies of real-time financial analysis necessitate robust computational interventions.

Despite the salient contributions of this study, certain limitations merit acknowledgment. The reliance on perceptual data introduces an element of subjectivity that may not fully encapsulate the multifaceted operational realities of LLM deployment. Future inquiries may benefit from a triangulated research approach that integrates qualitative insights with quantitative analytics to yield a more holistic understanding of AI-driven financial automation (Athul et al., 2024). Additionally, longitudinal analyses could offer deeper insights into the evolving impact of LLMs across temporal dimensions and diverse organizational contexts.

In summation, the present study furnishes compelling empirical validation of the instrumental role of LLMs in automating business intelligence and financial processes. The findings contribute substantively to the extant body of knowledge, offering both theoretical insights and actionable implications for stakeholders navigating the evolving landscape of AI-enabled financial automation. The confluence of technological advancements and strategic imperatives necessitates a nuanced understanding of the opportunities and challenges inherent in LLM deployment, paving the way for future explorations that bridge the gap between innovation and practical implementation.

CONCLUSION

The culmination of this study elucidates the profound ramifications of Large Language Models (LLMs) on the automation of business intelligence and financial processes, wherein the empirical findings substantiate a compelling and statistically significant correlation, reinforcing the transformative potential of LLMs in reshaping the contemporary financial analytical landscape through enhanced decision-making precision and operational efficiencies. The quantitative evidence derived from the robust statistical analyses underscores the substantial explanatory power of LLMs in driving automation outcomes, as evinced by the high R-squared values and significant regression coefficients, thereby affirming the hypothesis that LLMs serve as pivotal enablers of streamlined financial intelligence workflows. Notwithstanding the demonstrable efficacy of LLMs in augmenting business intelligence functionalities, the study concurrently reveals a spectrum of perceptions among respondents, with a noteworthy segment expressing neutrality, which ostensibly underscores the exigency for addressing potential impediments such as algorithmic interpretability, data security apprehensions, and infrastructural constraints that could attenuate widespread adoption. The findings resonate with extant literature, corroborating previous scholarly assertions regarding the superior capabilities of AI-driven automation while concurrently extending the discourse by furnishing empirical granularity specific to LLM applications in financial contexts, thereby bridging the gap between theoretical postulations and real-world implementation paradigms. Moreover, the rigorous diagnostic assessments, including residual analysis and collinearity diagnostics, fortify the credibility of the inferential conclusions drawn, reinforcing the validity and reliability of the study's methodological framework. However, the study acknowledges inherent limitations, particularly concerning the cross-sectional nature of the research design, which constrains the ability to capture longitudinal trends and dynamic evolutions in LLM adoption. Consequently, the insights derived herein necessitate cautious extrapolation, and future research endeavors are warranted to explore the longitudinal impacts of LLM integration, as well as the interplay of contextual factors such as organizational readiness, regulatory landscapes, and technological advancements in shaping the adoption trajectory. In essence, this study contributes valuable empirical insights into the burgeoning discourse on AI-driven financial automation, offering a cogent basis for informed strategic decision-making by industry stakeholders while concurrently providing a fertile ground for future scholarly explorations aimed at unraveling the multifaceted implications of LLMs in the ever-evolving domain of business intelligence.

REFERENCES

Ahmad, N., Mamatjan, E., Wali, T., & Mamatjan, Y. (2024). The Development of CanPrompt Strategy in Large Language Models for Cancer Care. *21st IEEE Conference on Computational Intelligence in Bioinformatics and Computational Biology, CIBCB 2024*. https://doi.org/DOI: 10.1109/CIBCB58642.2024.10702147

Arslan, M., Munawar, S., & Cruz, C. (2024). Sustainable Digitalization of Business with Multi-Agent RAG and LLM. In F. J. (Ed.), *Procedia Computer Science* (Vol. 246, Issue C, pp. 4722 – 4731). Elsevier B.V. https://doi.org/DOI: 10.1016/j.procs.2024.09.337

Athul, S., Saxena, A., Mahajan, J., Panikulangara, L., Kulkarni, S., & Bang, D. S. (2024). LegalMind System and the LLM-based Legal Judgment Query System. *TQCEBT 2024 - 2nd IEEE International Conference on Trends in Quantum Computing and Emerging Business Technologies 2024*. https://doi.org/DOI: 10.1109/TQCEBT59414.2024.10545179

Fan, S., Ilk, N., Kumar, A., Xu, R., & Zhao, J. L. (2024). Blockchain as a trust machine: From disillusionment to enlightenment in the era of generative AI. *Decision Support Systems*, *182*. Advance online publication. DOI: 10.1016/j.dss.2024.114251

Gupta, C., Jindal, P., & Malhotra, R. K. (2022). A Study of Increasing Adoption Trends of Digital Technologies - An Evidence from Indian Banking. In D. N. & C. A. (Eds.), *AIP Conference Proceedings* (Vol. 2481). American Institute of Physics Inc. https://doi.org/DOI: 10.1063/5.0104572

Han, S., Kang, H., Jin, B., Liu, X.-Y., & Yang, S. Y. (2024). XBRL Agent: Leveraging Large Language Models for Financial Report Analysis. *ICAIF 2024 - 5th ACM International Conference on AI in Finance*, 856 – 864. https://doi.org/DOI: 10.1145/3677052.3698614

Hirano, M., & Imajo, K. (2024). Construction of Domain-Specified Japanese Large Language Model for Finance Through Continual Pre-Training. *Proceedings - 2024 16th IIAI International Congress on Advanced Applied Informatics, IIAI-AAI 2024*, 273 – 279. https://doi.org/DOI: 10.1109/IIAI-AAI63651.2024.00059

Jadhav, S. G., & Sarnikar, S. (2024). Deriving Strategic Insights from Earnings Calls: Leveraging Human Experts, AI-Based Search, and Generative AI for Synthesis and Summarization. *Proceedings - 2024 Conference on AI, Science, Engineering, and Technology, AIxSET 2024*, 290 – 293. https://doi.org/DOI: 10.1109/AIxSET62544.2024.00031

Kukreti, M., Sehajpal, S., Tiwari, R., & Sood, K. (2025). *Driving Global Health and Sustainable Development Goals With Smart Technology* (Mohit, K., Sabina, S., Rajesh, T., & Kiran, S., Eds.; 1st ed.). IGI Global Scientific Publishing., DOI: 10.4018/979-8-3373-0240-9

Kumar, R., Singh, T., Mohanty, S. N., Goel, R., Gupta, D., Alharbi, M., & Khanna, R. (2023). Study on online payments and e-commerce with SOR model. *International Journal of Retail & Distribution Management*. Advance online publication. DOI: 10.1108/IJRDM-03-2023-0137

Mary Joshitta, S., & Sunil, M. P. Badriasulaimanalfurhood, Bodhankar, A., Ch.Sreedevi, & Khanna, R. (2023). The Integration of Machine Learning Technique with the Existing System to Predict the Flight Prices. *2023 3rd International Conference on Advance Computing and Innovative Technologies in Engineering, ICACITE 2023*, 398–402. https://doi.org/DOI: 10.1109/ICACITE57410.2023.10182539

Menghao, L. M., Yi, F., Li, Y., & Shi, Y. (2023). Research on the Application of LLM in Power Finance Middle Platform. In L. J. & L. Y. (Eds.), *Proceedings - 2023 2nd Asian Conference on Frontiers of Power and Energy, ACFPE 2023* (pp. 282 – 289). Institute of Electrical and Electronics Engineers Inc. https://doi.org/DOI: 10.1109/ACFPE59335.2023.10455549

Naik, D., Naik, I., & Naik, N. (2024). Leveraging the Use of ChatGPT: Exploring Its Real-World Applications Including Their Related Ethical and Regulatory Considerations. *Lecture Notes in Networks and Systems, 884 LNNS*, 649 – 667. https://doi.org/DOI: 10.1007/978-3-031-74443-3_38

Ni, H., Meng, S., Chen, X., Zhao, Z., Chen, A., Li, P., Zhang, S., Yin, Q., Wang, Y., & Chan, Y. (2024). Harnessing Earnings Reports for Stock Predictions: A QLoRA-Enhanced LLM Approach. *2024 6th International Conference on Data-Driven Optimization of Complex Systems, DOCS 2024*, 909 – 915. https://doi.org/DOI: 10.1109/DOCS63458.2024.10704454

Rana, M. S., Cavaliere, L. P. L., Mishra, A. B., Padhye, P., Singh, R. R., & Khanna, R. (2022). Internet of Things (IOT) Based Assessment for Effective Monitoring Data Against Malicious Attacks on Financial Collectors. *2022 2nd International Conference on Advance Computing and Innovative Technologies in Engineering, ICACITE 2022*, 177–181. https://doi.org/DOI: 10.1109/ICACITE53722.2022.9823612

Sarker, I. H. (2024). LLM potentiality and awareness: A position paper from the perspective of trustworthy and responsible AI modeling. *Discover Artificial Intelligence*, *4*(1). Advance online publication. DOI: 10.1007/s44163-024-00129-0

Saxena, Y., Chopra, S., & Tripathi, A. M. (2024). Evaluating Consistency and Reasoning Capabilities of Large Language Models. *2nd IEEE International Conference on Data Science and Information System, ICDSIS 2024*. https://doi.org/DOI: 10.1109/ICDSIS61070.2024.10594233

Sehajpal, S., & Kaur, N. (2025). Neuroscience, Nursing, and Financial Innovation : A Synergistic Approach to Optimized Patient Care and Economic Well-Being. In Sanjay, T., Bhupinderpal Pal, S. C., Amar, J., Ercan, O., & Pawan, K. (Eds.), *Neuromarketing's Role in Sustainable Finance* (pp. 133–146). IGI Global Scientific Publishing., DOI: 10.4018/979-8-3693-9117-4.ch008

Shukla, N. K., Katikeri, R., Raja, M., Sivam, G., Yadav, S., Vaid, A., & Prabhakararao, S. (2023). Generative AI Approach to Distributed Summarization of Financial Narratives. In H. J., P. T., H. X., C. A., D. D., S. D., W. W., G. A., L. J.C.-W., & A. R. (Eds.), *Proceedings - 2023 IEEE International Conference on Big Data, BigData 2023* (pp. 2872 – 2876). Institute of Electrical and Electronics Engineers Inc. https://doi.org/DOI: 10.1109/BigData59044.2023.10386313

Song, Y., Ezzini, S., Tang, X., Lothritz, C., Klein, J., Bissyande, T., Boytsov, A., Ble, U., & Goujon, A. (2024). Enhancing Text-to-SQL Translation for Financial System Design. *ACM International Conference Proceeding Series*, 252 – 262. https://doi.org/DOI: 10.1145/3639477.3639732

Zhao, S., Bay, M., Xu, A., & Gupta, N. (2024). 3rd Workshop on End-End Customer Journey Optimization. *Proceedings of the ACM SIGKDD International Conference on Knowledge Discovery and Data Mining*, 6753 – 6754. https://doi.org/DOI: 10.1145/3637528.3671500

Chapter 3
Transforming Healthcare with Large Language Models and AI Agents

Ravikumar R. N.
https://orcid.org/0009-0009-3705-1681
Marwadi University, Rajkot, India

Aarthi S.
https://orcid.org/0009-0006-9064-2091
Marwadi University, Rajkot, India

Izzatbek Rejapov Olimbaevich
Mamun University, Khiva, Uzbekistan

Sultonova Mashkhura
Urgench State University Named After Abu Raykhan Beruni, Urgench, Uzbekistan

Saodat Musayeva
Termez University of Economics and Service, Termez, Uzbekistan

ABSTRACT

The chapter "Transforming Healthcare with Large Language Models and AI Agents" explores how technologies like GPT-3 and advanced AI agents are reshaping healthcare. These tools can process massive volumes of medical data to provide real-time insights, aiding clinical decision-making and improving patient outcomes. AI agents enhance patient engagement, assist in diagnosis, and support treatment planning. Key applications include boosting diagnostic accuracy, automating administrative processes, enabling virtual care, and advancing precision medicine. The chapter also addresses critical challenges such as data privacy, algorithmic bias, and the

DOI: 10.4018/979-8-3373-2008-3.ch003

importance of transparent AI governance. It offers practical recommendations to mitigate these issues and ensure responsible AI deployment. Designed for healthcare professionals, researchers, and policymakers, this chapter provides a comprehensive guide to harnessing the power of LLMs and AI agents to transform healthcare delivery and medical research effectively and ethically.

1. INTRODUCTION TO AI IN HEALTHCARE

Different-mode innovating GPT AI in health technology GPT AI operates based on creating efficient workflows, artificial patient care solutions and medical decisions based on empirical data. We now live in an era that presents a golden opportunity for healthcare organizations to implement these AI from Machine Learning (ML) and deep learning to Natural Language Processing (NLP) and in which healthcare organizations can be able to provide improved capability in patient care and workflow process toward better patient care. The section explains how There are other issues involved with scaling up Large Language Models (LLMs) using the GPT and BERT architectures and similar ones, which operate on human-like language processing with retention of contextual understanding (Shahrukh Irfan, 2023). Medical technical models receive full range medical information for improvement in translation and clinical rhythm between Healthcare Personnel (HCP) and patients. Medical intelligence systems allow the AI Agents to assist healthcare personnel in providing three functionalities like administrative support to healthcare professionals, medical diagnostic functions, and continuous patient monitoring during medical treatments. AI agents assist surgeries (e.g., robotic surgery) and healthcare services (e.g., virtual healthcare assistants) and support in personal treatment planning and medical monitoring thanks to their ability to reason.

1.1 Overview of AI's Impact on the Healthcare Industry

Artificial Intelligence (AI) is rapidly changing the healthcare industry and leading to innovations with the ability to generate the highest quality care and maximize efficiency and, at the same time, lowering the costs. AI has impacted almost all areas in healthcare, including but not limited to diagnostics/optical personalized treatments and drug discovery and staffing. Diagnosis and potential early diagnosis are another area of influence that has evolved partly because of the creation of AI. The ML DL models are becoming relatively useful in training medical images and diagnosing features otherwise missed under typical medical examination or intervention like X-raying, MRI, and CT scanning. The ensuing technologies have also enabled diagnostic tools to succeed, particularly those that are specialty-based as in cardiology, neurology, and oncology. The other significant role of AI is that it will further personalize medical treatment. All this, combined with the assistance of AI, helps healthcare practitioners tailor treatment plans, using gigantic quantities of data such as genetic information and Electronic Health Records (EHR). This type of treatment, one-on-one approach, is what, over and above, improves patient outcomes as a result of which we have a successful treatment plan. The other area where AI is working miracles is in terms of operational efficiency. Intelligent systems can automate the administrative activities such as appointment scheduling, billing and electronic medical records. By so doing, automation can be used to maximize clinical time. Additionally, AI systems may assist with virtual patient care programs where patients can meet with their physicians and enter new medical data online. By delivering improved care to patients, AI systems provide numerous patient care experiences, such as personalized health advice with ongoing assistance as virtual patients (Das et al., 2023). AI driven health assistant systems provide 24-hour assistance to patients in case of any questions or reminders regarding medicine and appointments. This form of 2-way communication at all times can make them more compliant to their treatment plans that can result to a more active management of their health.

1.2 Background Study

The healthcare industry's rapid digitalization opened the door to the digital revolution into the healthcare field where AI, and especially recently, LLMs and AI agents, are incorporated. The digital revolution in healthcare has developed in the span of decades in the field of medical informatics, expert systems, and ML. Rule-based reasoning had shown promise in diagnosis, as was the case with early AI applications in healthcare, with MYCIN expert system developed in the 1970s. Nonetheless, their usefulness is confined by a lack of computing capability as well as the amount of data to work on. In the early 2000-s, with the introduction of EHRs the healthcare data was made more structured and accessible, which allowed the usage of data-driven artificially intelligent tools (Ahmad et al., 2023).

There was a paradigm shift when deep learning was introduced especially Convolutional Neural Networks (CNNs) and subsequently the advent of transformer-based models such as BERT and GPT. These models made possible unstructured data, such as medical images and clinical narratives, processing to such an extent. Machine translation Machine translation is based on the idea that the meaning of utterances and texts can be represented in a semantically uninterpreted, computable form, typically as a dense distributional vector representation. With the recent development of high-quality LLM, implemented in the form of the Transformer architecture, machine translation now uses LLMs trained on huge corpora of biomedical and other texts (translation). Machine translation applications include medical document summarization, decision LLMs are accompanied by their complementary technology, AI agents systems that are capable of autonomous action and decision-making. They use ML, Reinforcement Learning (RL), and natural language understanding in order to communicate with the patients, support clinicians, and run workflows in real-time. A combination of the language-related features of LLMs and the functionalities of AI agents forms the basis of intelligent healthcare systems, which are active and receptive. Numerous clinical and operational uses of AI have been shown to be feasible in radiology, pathology, personalized medicine, and virtual care. AI increases accuracy of diagnosis and reduces reporting time by providing real-time monitoring and immediate interventions. Meanwhile, across the world, healthcare systems are utilizing AI to address systematic issues, including workforce shortages, administrative burdens, and health disparities. But these technologies pose major threats in dozens of ways. These were data privacy, bias in the algorithm, regulatory clearance, and transparency. Among the targeted studies, there are, e.g., Explainable AI (XAI) algorithms, federated learning (as a privacy-protecting method), and regarding regulations, HIPAA and GDPR (Herries, 2024).

1.3 The Role of LLMs and AI Agents in Transforming Healthcare

In fact, the death knell of traditional healthcare is already being sounded by LLMs and agents, who are galloping along to create modern healthcare, which is smarter, faster and more personalized. Though often not specifically confined to that, LLMs pathologically copy written human language, and so, can process clinical notes and extract pertinent medical information and can support other fields such as documentation and diagnosis. AI can avail of the decision-making characteristics and an ability to analyze large datasets quickly, in real time and with immediate relevance are capable of providing patient engagement, i.e. virtual assistant, routine duties, assist with and support clinical decisions (Herries, 2024). Collected, they facilitate the work, minimize the administrative overhead, and help wring out more accurate diagnosis and treatment planning. Their involvement into the healthcare sectors is creating a trend of intelligent, data-oriented, and patient-focused health practices. The Figure 1 illustrates a balanced scale comparing the complementary roles of LLMs and AI agents in healthcare.

Figure 1. Balanced Roles of LLMs and AI Agents in Healthcare

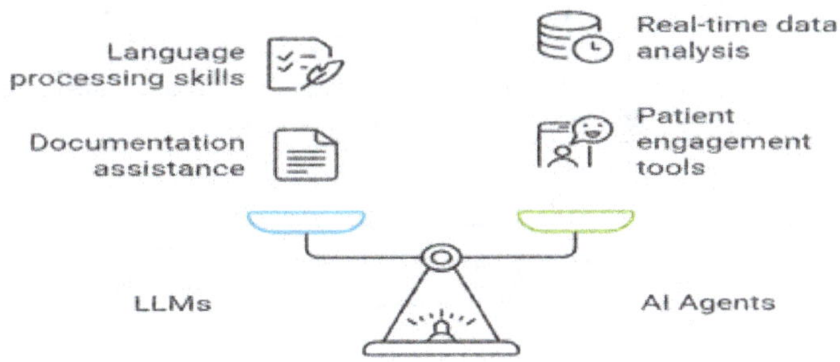

1.4 Brief History and Evolution of AI in Healthcare

AI in healthcare has a long history that dates back to the 1970s when the first expert systems emerged to assist with diagnostic rules. Such systems were constrained by computer capability and access to organized medical information. As healthcare went digital in the 2000s, especially with the implementation of EHR, AI uses started to grow as data became more readable and quantifiable. With the emergence of ML and medical imaging in the 1980s and 1990s, the diagnostic accuracy improved particularly in radiology and pathology. In more recent work, deep learning and transformer-based models have made it possible to analyse unstructured clinical data, medical images, and genomic data (Senbekov et al., 2020). Nowadays, AI agents and LLM become part of workflows and advance the diagnosis, treatment plans, virtual care, or personalized medicine. The table 1 presents a timeline of key developments in AI within healthcare, highlighting technological milestones from early expert systems to modern LLMs.

Table 1. Evolution of AI in Healthcare

Era	Milestone/Development	Impact on Healthcare
1950s - 1970s	Early AI concepts and expert systems (e.g., MYCIN for infectious disease diagnosis).	Introduced rule-based systems for medical decision support.
1980s - 1990s	Advancement in ML and medical imaging.	Improved diagnostic tools, especially in radiology and pathology.
2000s	Introduction of Electronic Health Records (EHRs) and data digitization.	Enabled structured data collection for AI integration.
2010 - 2015	Rise of big data and deep learning in biomedical research.	Enhanced pattern recognition in genomics, imaging, and patient monitoring.
2016 - Present	Emergence of LLMs (e.g., BERT, GPT) and AI agents in clinical workflows.	Enabled NLP in healthcare, automated documentation, virtual care, and personalized medicine.

2. UNDERSTANDING LARGE LANGUAGE MODELS (LLMS) AND AI AGENTS

Advanced AI and LLM collaboration form an operational system which functions as both a text generation component and processor. The text operations performed by LLMs succeed because these models underwent training using substantial amounts of textual information. The clinical documentation system together with research analysis tools and patient communication system remain accessible through LLMs to healthcare practitioners (Judijanto et al., 2024). The independent healthcare support service driven by AI-based agents provides surgical robot and virtual medicine assistance separately as clinical services. Healthcare solutions that LLMs and AI agents create take in information through supervised and RL approaches to manage diverse datasets when developing operational systems which respect privacy standards and base their operations on data-driven approaches.

2.1 Transformer-Based Language Models: Foundations and Use in Healthcare

Modern NLP developments are made in the backbone of transformer-based language models which were introduced in the paper published in 2017 titled Attention Is All You Need. Such models have self-attention in order to learn contextual relationships between words to have better language understanding and generation. Healthcare uses these models, such as GPT and BERT in healthcare to derive insights into the clinical notes, automate documentation and aid in diagnostic decisioning (Judijanto et al., 2024). They improve speed and accuracy of clinical processes because they develop inferences on unstructured data such as medical records, and literature. These are models that are transforming healthcare making it data-driven, efficient and personalise at scale. Figure 2 describes how transformer-based language models based on self-attention can support healthcare applications from clinical note analysis and diagnostic decision making to overall improvements in healthcare through data-driven, more efficient, and more personalized methods.

Figure 2. Transformer LLMs in Healthcare

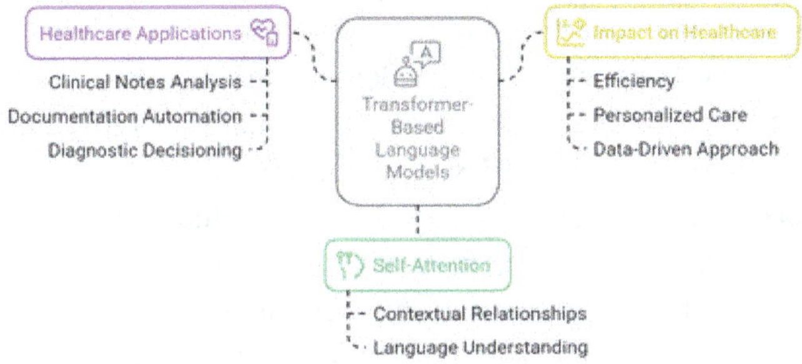

2.2 Introduction to AI Agents: Capabilities and Applications in Healthcare

AI agents are smart systems that use ML, NLP, and RL to leverage automation or semi-automation. They can imitate human decision-making, information processing and human interaction when they perform the function of an AI agent, and can support healthcare providers and the patient during healthcare. Such high consequentiality in terms of diagnosis, treatment plan development, and interaction with patients is due to the fact that it can in fact actualise the processing of large volumes of clinical data, generate real time feedback and, last but not least, it can generate an even more complex world. As an example, consider the avenue by which AI agents might be further integrated into other strata of healthcare workflow improvements including decision support, automated administration processes, and personalized care. This is the way AI is designed; therefore, the intelligent device with the support of human interfaces smart technology might be useful to enhance effectiveness, precision, and availability of current healthcare.

2.2.1 Capabilities of AI Agents

They are often regarded as one of the greatest benefits that an AI-based modern-day healthcare system can provide. Being able to make independent decisions is one of their strong points. The independent decisions that can be made by AI agencies could involve the comparison of outcomes of a large amount of data in a relatively brief period of time. Human came up with a totally unrealistic situation in which rational and reasonable decisions could be quicker than the ability of the human beings. Very certainly, the aspect of high stakes present in disease diagnosis and treatment makes it a good opportunity to implement an AI agent where an informed and timely opinion based on the appropriate type of data is highly likely to have a positive impact on a patient (Sadanand & Nandini, 2024). Real-time interactivity is the most important characteristic of an AI agent today. Actually, it enables the patient and the healthcare givers to interact effectively via a real-time feedback system. It is then determined to offer and respond to medical queries rapidly and efficiently. In this way, real-time availability does a superb job at enhancing patient engagement and facilitating efficient clinical processes. And now the AI agents are quite good at absorbing and processing large volumes of unstructured clinical data, and mining insights out of it, particularly physician notes, imaging and genomic data; therefore, providing them with a kind of cognitive ability that makes the evaluations richer and more helpful in personalized medicine. These are the opportunities that can be delivered by the potential enablers, AI agents, in the provision of intelligent, engaged and effective healthcare.

2.2.2 Applications of AI Agents in Healthcare

The introduction of intelligent assistance and decision-making automation in different areas with the help of intelligent agents is creating a new smart world of medical care. One of those is the use of artificial intelligence in Clinical Decision Support Systems (CDSSs) where artificial intelligence agents are used to process the data about the patient and can tell the physician to make the best judgment. Such systems can combine diagnostic protocols, risk evaluation and past patient history with real-time clinical judgement, to improve quality-of-care decisions, and reduce mistakes. Much more important is the other application called Virtual Health Assistants, which is a chat and voice interface driven by AI that assists in connecting patients with healthcare systems. The apps are used to schedule appointments, offer basic health tips, remind patients to take medications, and get patients to engage.

Besides this, intelligent agents are needed in robotic surgery because the surgery robots are intelligent and can provide real-time feedback and guidance. Such systems are more accurate during surgery, have reduced human error and make the key decision-making process based on all the required parameters using live data (Liu et al., 2025). Together, the innovations result in safer, efficient, and patient-centered healthcare services. AI agents also assist in remote patient monitoring primarily using telemedicine platforms and wearables that gives medical workers the ability monitor patients and main indicators continuously, identify deviations, and provide appropriate alerts or medical response when situations are most acute. This is just a couple of AI agent applications already in use, and there are so many aspects of AI agents shaping the healthcare realm in more effective, accurate and continuous patient care than what was previously available.

2.3 How LLMs and AI Agents are Trained and Optimized for Medical Tasks

The process that trains LLMs and AI agents to perform tasks in medicine consists of the following two stages: First, it is pre-trained on the general language data and is then fine-tuned with the application-specific medical data that has been annotated. Supervised learning lets the models learn on labeled clinical data, whereas RL works in an interactive process such as in robotic surgery. To make more precise decisions, these systems are optimized through incorporation of multimodal healthcare information, which includes text, images, and numerical results (Mishra, 2022). Lifelong education will enable them to keep abreast with the changing medical information. Clinical testing confirms validity of performance and regulations such as HIPAA and GDPR make it ethical and safe to use in libraries. The Figure 3 illustrates the complete development cycle of LLMs for healthcare from pre-training and fine-tuning to clinical testing, lifelong education, and ethical compliance.

Figure 3. Lifecycle of LLM Development for Healthcare

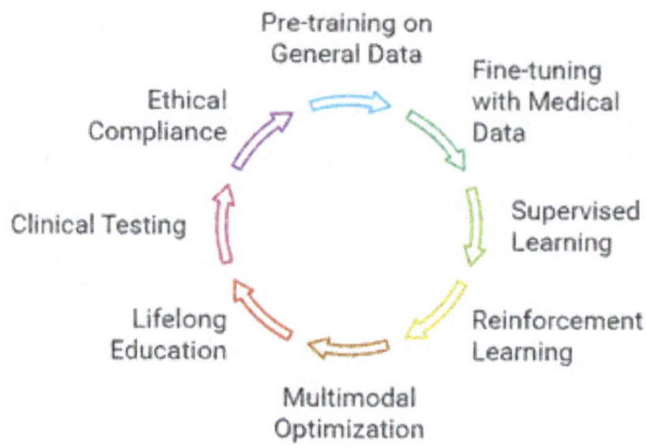

2.3.1 Training of LLMs for Medicine

LLM development in the healthcare sector includes a systematic training procedure started by pre-training and then finetuning. In the pre-training stage, LLMs get access to extensive diverse language data with general-purpose information. The model of two stages is often followed in the field of healthcare as it is based on the initial general training and closes by topic-related training (Nassani et al., 2023). At this point, the model is fed with healthcare-specific data, i.e., clinical narratives, medical journals, patient records, and drug-related data. With the help of supervised learning, the LLM will learn about medical terminology, the use of language in context, and wording peculiar to such a field.

The second step is fine-tuning, during which, with the help of annotated clinical information, LLMs will be trained to perform special clinical tasks (Pasupuleti, 2025). This allows the models to write medical texts as well as composing clinical notes and radiology reports and responding to medical questions using literature, and clinical protocols standards. Moreover, such models are able to do sentiment analysis by analyzing the patient feedback or records of consultation so that healthcare providers learn more about patient moods and levels of engagement. On the whole, this training process consisting of several stages enables LLMs to provide precise, context-sensitive, and patient-focused assistance in different healthcare processes.

2.3.2 Training of AI Agents for Healthcare

Medical AI agents use multiple different learning methods in order to improve their effectiveness and resilience in medical settings. Probably the most popular approach is supervised learning, where agents are trained on large exercises of labeled data where the right results or choices are already identified. This is normally applied in the medical sector whereby it deals with the information like what is diagnosed in the patients file or what is the record in the patient file when treating the patient thus allowing the agents to study about the practical situations where they can treat the patient (Alkalbani et al., 2024). RL can be found where the application is more sophisticated or even interactive such as robotic surgery or diagnostic support. In the style, the AI agents train themselves using trial and error, with either positive or negative feedback given to them when they make either appropriate or inaccurate choices. This cyclical action enables the agents to perfect their action and get better with time depending on the consequences of their decisions made.

The next ability of AI agents is the capability of multi-modal data integration. The healthcare data may be in the form of text records, medical images, lab results, and others. Part of the goal of the AI agents is to synthesize and process these numerous and odd types of data in real-life situations at the same time in order to make decisions that are completer and more accurate by using all the information available. One of the greatest advantages of AI agents relates to their ability to learn (Alkalbani et al., 2024). Contrary to the situation with static systems, such agents are capable of being refreshed with new medical data, recommendations and research bi-annually. This enables them to maintain up-to-date compliance with the current clinical practices, be able to cope with emerging diseases, and understand changing patient demands, hence remaining relevant and effective in dynamic healthcare settings.

2.3.3 Optimization for Medical Tasks

When institutions implement the use of LLM and AI agent in healthcare, there should be a high level of compliance with data privacy and that of compliance since medical information is delicate. Such systems have to comply with law such as the Health Insurance Portability and Accountability Act (HIPAA) in the US or the General Data Protection Regulation (GDPR), in Europe (Busch et al., 2024). One of the main conditions of the safe and legal use of AI in the clinic is the need to provide confidentiality, integrity, and safe treatment of patient data. LLMs and AI agents need to be domain-fine assembled to achieve the highest outcomes. It means fitting the models to the application of specialized tasks in healthcare, specifically, the diagnosis of a disease, planning of treatment or real-time monitoring of a patient. Medical data referred to as such are generally subject to fine-tuning, which may be tested to establish consistency with medical standards and practice either by clinical trial or by expert opinion.

The other significant aspect of AI adoption in healthcare is performance measurement. After these systems are trained and refined, they would also need to undergo testing concerning issues of accuracy, reliability and safety in regard to the clinical activities that are relevant and applicable in practice. The expected key performance measurements would be a reduction in errors, efficiency, and an overall effect on clinical decision making and clinical outcomes (McKee & Correia, 2025). In short, LLMs and AI agents are such strong technologies due to the fact that they are changing the sphere of healthcare, making the processes easier, improving the diagnostics and personalizing the treatment; furthermore, they are changing the technologies and the healthcare system of organizations since they are trained practically and used to optimize.

3. ENHANCING CLINICAL DECISION-MAKING WITH LLMS

LLMs have helped to make health decisions, in terms of diagnosis and patient-centered care guidelines, far more effective. LLMs have the ability to sift through a substantial volume of medical data in the form of clinical notes and patient records and detect trends and potential diagnoses. In one case study, radio-pathology diagnosis showed that LLMs were more accurate and faster to suggestions, and they reduced errors and saved time in giving the initial suggestions. There is also personalization that is facilitated using LLMs as they suggest a recommended treatment regimen based on the medical history, genome and lifestyle of a patient. These are smart systems that can assist clinicians in making more informed, data-driven decisions, which lead to better patient outcomes (Eckrich et al., 2024).

3.1 Application of LLMs in Diagnostic Support

Language Models Using LLM can be useful in providing diagnostic assistance by processing EHR, physician notes, and patient history, etc, to give the physician a way of recognizing possibilities of disease and medical facts to enhance the Enhanced Diagnostic (ED) process. To detect patterns and relationships in data that physicians can observe more clearly, LLMs can search large volumes of doctor notes and laboratory reports that have unstructured data. Using NLP, LLMs can aid in medication management decisions since they can process and make sense of highly complex narrative concerning medicine. Once it integrates with the EHR, they can recommend potential diagnoses. In doing so, density patterns may support the consideration of potential conditions for which a health professional may not ordinarily consider. Language models also may identify things which may be red flags or missed information within the patients' previous histories, and even if not unexplained features of the patients' medical background, they will not miss, based on the explanations, the most relevant, important, or significant factors in the notes/ clinical assessment/history. LLMs may also provide differential diagnoses, especially in complex or atypical situations by referring to and comparing other previously-researched cases including clinical notes for their staff and help facilitate faster and more accurate diagnoses while also helping clinicians manage complicated situations of a unique case (Fuchs et al., 2023).

3.2 Case Studies: Improving Accuracy and Efficiency in Clinical Decision-Making

This section provides case studies of how AI and LLMs can be applied to enhance clinical decision making by delivering better accuracy, reducing time to diagnosis, and providing evidence-based care. In radiology through pathology, AI solutions can assist medical professionals in noticing minute deviations, assist with systematic processes, and ultimately reduce diagnostic errors (Gao et al., 2025). All of these case studies have creatable increases in patient and operation outcomes in almost all areas of medicine. Table 2 summarizes the application of AI and LLMs that have vastly improved accuracy and efficiency in the diagnosis of radiology and pathology.

Table 2. AI and LLMs Impact on Clinical Diagnosis - Case Studies

Domain	Metric Improved	Improvement (%)	Description
Radiology	Early Lung Nodule Detection	29%	Faster identification via AI in chest CT scans
Radiology	Reduction in Reporting Time	23%	Quicker turnaround in emergencies
Radiology	Prevention of False Negatives	32%	Increased diagnostic confidence and safety
Pathology	Cancer Detection in Biopsies	27%	AI-assisted systems outperformed manual diagnosis
Pathology	Early-stage Malignancy Detection	35%	AI detected rare/complex patterns faster
Pathology	Reduction in Summary Preparation Time	21%	Accelerated clinical decision-making

3.2.1 AI-Assisted Radiology Diagnosis

Many algorithms that utilize AI in the diagnosis of imaging are now being used in radiology, and these collaborations have been incredibly necessary. A study conducted at one of those participating large hospitals revealed that the implementation of AI algorithms alongside the radiology workflow enhanced the rate of detecting lung nodules found on a chest CT scan up to 29% earlier than a radiologist alone. This artificial intelligence system was trained on thousands of radiographic images that have labels and helped radiologists identify suspicious spots and suggest diagnoses. This also led to saving 23% of average reporting time so that it could make a decision faster in case of emergency (Gencer & Gencer, 2025). Also, the combination of radiologists with AI allowed preventing the number of false negatives and boosted patient safety by 32%. The AI model had the best results in detecting minute abnormalities that are missed out in the regular examination. Radiologists noted that they became more confident in the interpretation of complicated images, especially those concerning oncology and cases of the pulmonary condition. This case study highlights the advantages of AI to enhance clinical human expertise, minimise diagnostic mistakes and fasten the clinical process in the radiology department. The Figure 4 showing the impact of AI-assisted radiology diagnosis. It compares improvements achieved by combining AI with radiologists versus radiologists alone in three key areas like early lung nodule detection, reporting time reduction, and false negatives prevention.

Figure 4. Impact of AI-Assisted Radiology Diagnosis on Clinical Performance

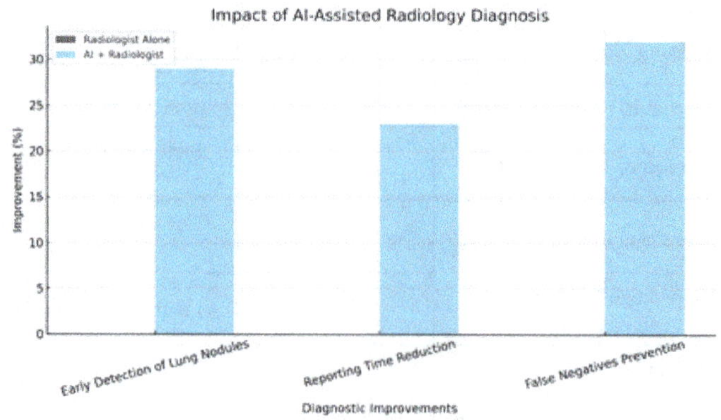

3.2.2 Pathology Reports and Diagnostic Support

The use of AI in pathology is changing the way support is provided in the model of diagnosis based on the more complete understanding of the pathology report. Application of AI-assisted systems has proven to be better in detecting cancer in biopsy samples (by 27%) than the conventional manual tests in a multicentre assessment. Such systems apply the field of NLP to extract important information out of the pathology reports and match it to medical images and history. Pathologists were also able to detect the rare or complex patterns using AI models faster than human fatigue or lack of exposure because of a 35% improvement in the detection of early-stage malignancies. The time required to produce diagnostic summaries was cut-down by 21% and this had a great impact on boosting the clinical decision-making process (Mannstadt & Mehta, 2024). In addition, AI applications assisted in real-time second opinions that are consistent and this low heterogeneity between observers is due to technology utilization not only to improve the precision of the diagnostic processes but also allow the pathologist to address more difficult cases and thus be more productive in important work while also improving patient outcomes in clinical pathology. The Figure 5 visualizes the improvements in pathology due to AI, including 27% better cancer detection in biopsies, 35% enhanced early-stage malignancy detection, and 21% reduction in diagnostic summary preparation time.

Figure 5. Impact of AI-Assisted Radiology Diagnosis on Clinical Performance

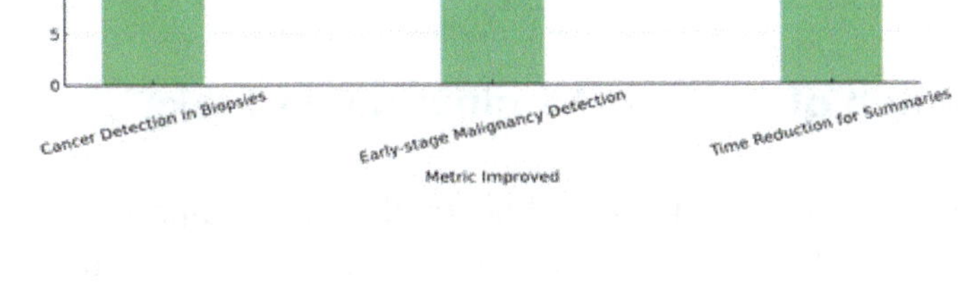

3.3 Personalized Care Through Intelligent Recommendations

AI and LLMs are transforming healthcare by offering personalized services and intelligent and data-driven recommendations. Assessment of the information that concerns individual patients like, their medical history, co-morbidity, lifestyle, and cultural factors, alongside the aid of LLMs give a report of personalised treatment plans based on patient status. They make patients more satisfied because they align health advice with their value systems and foster treatment adherence (Murdoch, 2021). Moreover, LLMs help with the risk evaluation of adverse drug interaction, depending on the entire clinical history. Such an integrated solution not only results in improved clinical outcomes but also enables patients to make informed decisions that support a safer, more personalized, and improved treatment experience.

4. AI AGENTS IN ADMINISTRATIVE FUNCTIONS

Now the second wave of hospital AI agents is moving the boring stuff-administration, scheduling, billing, documentation-and getting rid of overtime herewith, so that intelligent systems implementing automation can focus on improving the quality of services. Such systems optimize the processes in healthcare through smart prioritization of operations, smart distribution of resources and improved communication on a large scale (Teng et al., 2022). Regarding billing and coding, the reduction of errors in automated yet AI-enabled financial operations would yield the most error-free operationalization of those assisted. AI could streamline appointment bookings and virtually transcribe clinical records, thereby saving the healthcare colleague the embarrassment and virtually eliminating the administrative pain and suffering (Ndukwe & Otukpa, 2025). This kind of aid and automation enables the clinicians to serve patients. Automation leads to higher productivity, less burnout, and less time spent on patients. Over time, AI agent can, ultimately, create happier, more productive, operationally effective practices, that provide service, and decrease expenditures.

4.1 Automation of Routine Administrative Tasks

AI and LLMs also are making healthcare efficiency improved with automated administrative work that decreases the time spent on tasks by medical personnel while allowing more time for them to be with the patient. Intelligent systems can be alternative to administration type work such as appointments, billing, claims or insurance payment tracking, EHR updating and maintenance and document processing. Such automation processes are improvements in these functions because they save human resource time and potential error from human involvement. Further, they provide more time for health personnel to be available to the patients (Pashangpour & Nejat, 2024). In essence, research indicates that AI-based administrative tools document related administration processes are 30% faster improving productivity / efficiency, which enables clinicians to focus on clinical decision making and patient relationships where it is most needed. (Senbekov et al., 2020).

4.2 Streamlining Healthcare Operations Through AI-Driven Workflow Management

The revolutionizing effect of AI-powered workflow management in the healthcare sector is that it streamlines the different processes of different departments in the industry. Whether it is the distribution of resources and the personnel shift schedules or the inflow and outflow of patients and discharge plans, AI systems process the data in real-time to make smart decisions which enhance the efficiency of the hospital. Predictive analytics can be used to know the rate of admitting patients and the need to have resources to prevent the formation of bottlenecks and delays (Quercia et al., 2024). With the help of AI, hospital management systems are also integrated into them to facilitate planning and achieve tasks promptly. The lean practice thus helps in increasing operational efficiency of healthcare facilities by as much as 25%, thereby reducing wait time and further enhancing patient satisfaction.

4.3 Reducing Administrative Burden on Healthcare Professionals

AI and LLMs strive to reduce the administrative burden of healthcare practitioners. With this, physicians and nurses can perform much more direct care with maximum time devoted to clinical documentation, report generation, prescription management, and data entry. NLP technologies perform real-time recording of the conversations between doctor and patient while the AI systems provide a set of codes for form-filling, billing, and diagnosis (Movahed & Bilderback, 2024). It has been reported that even administrative workloads have been reduced by as much as 40%, resulting in less burnout, higher job satisfaction levels, and overall sufficiency of healthcare teams.

5. VIRTUAL HEALTHCARE SERVICES POWERED BY AI

Such a radical leap introduced by AI virtual healthcare has resulted in patients receiving a truly accessible, personalized, and efficient AI technology-based solution in this virtual world. They encompass the use of an AI agent who will be performing the following tasks: virtual assistant services; interaction with patients via appointment booking, symptom monitoring, medication reminders, and health-related advice tailored to their specific needs (Restrepo et al., 2024). Regarding total patient engagement, it may include better support-at-demand-anytime, immediate response and most importantly everywhere. In telemedicine, this involves the use of AI in simultaneous remote diagnoses, tele-consultation, and follow-ups through data collected from wearable technology and mobile health applications so that clinicians can manage the care of their patients from a distance. This is one substantial way of widening access to healthcare that patients enjoy since it tears down the walls of location and resource constraints, and the healthcare mentioned is timely, affordable, and accessible to virtually everyone.

5.1 AI Agents namely as Virtual Assistants in Engaging Patients

Virtual assistants for patient engagement: AI agents are revolutionizing the act of patient engagement in virtual assistant patient care. Through chatbot or voice command, these AI agents will be the interface with the patients to support appointment booking, symptom checking, and other health information dissemination (Workum et al., 2025). They are available 24/7 to assist patients in any queries regarding medications and ways to maintain a healthy lifestyle. These agents add a health relation to every contact buildup with a patient and finally make communication with patient experience better. An immediate response would cut short waiting time and thus enhance a patient's experience since the gap in a typical setup is filled by that immediate response.

5.2 Telemedicine and Remote Monitoring Enabled by AI

Telemedicine and remote patient monitoring is producing dramatic breakthroughs because AI allows an ongoing real-time monitoring of patients not just in a hospital but anywhere. With wearable devices and smart sensors, AI systems monitor and process vital indicators; heart rate, oxygen levels, and blood pressure information and notify healthcare providers of issues as soon as they are detected (Yalamanchili et al., 2024). The triaging of symptoms, appointment scheduling, and follow-up care are also possible through NLP which enables artificial-intelligence-powered voice assistants and chatbots to conduct virtual consultations. Unnecessary visits of patients to hospitals have been reduced by 35% using this technology and chronic diseases are better managed. AI-based tele-medicine increases treatment proximity, especially to patients in remote or underserved locations and offers time-sensitive and individual medical care.

5.3 Enhancing patient access to healthcare services through virtual agents.

Virtual agents that use AI to provide medical care to patients are changing the norms of accessing healthcare because they are available 24x7, can significantly minimize the time it takes to receive healthcare, and enhance communications. Such agents range in the form of chatbots and voice assistants that assist the patients in scheduling their appointments, retrieval of medical records, medication reminders, and also provide answers to the health-related questions in real time (AlDhaen, 2025). Patients in the underserved or rural locations will be particularly benefited because it will be an intermediary between the patients and the providers. Virtual agents relieve the healthcare personnel to focus on more important work by attending to routine questions and administrative duties. This has resulted in 40% increase in the participation of patients and quicker access to the necessary medical services.

6. ADVANCING MEDICAL RESEARCH WITH LLMS

LLMs are breaking the ground in medical research through rapid literature searches, hypothesis development and data analysis. The models can scan and synthesize thousands of research articles, clinical trial reports and case studies, produce a summary in minutes and draw attention to relevant findings giving the researcher a concise summary of the reports. LLMs help to find out the research gaps, create the study questions, and even deduce possible outcomes, based on the previous data (McKee & Correia, 2025). They also promote teamwork among their involvement in translation of complex scientific materials to simpler language that can be used by the interdisciplinary teams. Along with time savings as high as 60% to analyse literature, LLMs have the potential to greatly increase the productivity of research, facilitating the quicker progress of innovations and evidence-based improvements to medicine.

6.1 Use of LLMs in Literature Review and Hypothesis Generation

LLMs are changing the method through which medical literature reviews and hypothesis generation are performed. Through covering the extreme amounts of scholarly articles, clinical directives, and trial information by examining it quickly and uncritically, LLMs are able to retrieve, synthesize, and clarify vital outcomes with outstanding quickness and exactness (Barbieri et al., 2023). With the help of automated trends, correlation, and existing knowledge gap identification, researchers will enjoy such advantages as the development of new and evidence-based hypotheses. This saves as much as 50% of the time spent in manual literature review and gives place to the researchers concentrating on formulating effective research. LLMs will also contribute to the formulation of research questions in tandem with the existing scientific dialogue, and this will also speed up the initial phases of medical discovery and innovation.

6.2 Accelerating Drug Discovery and Clinical Trials with AI Models

Essential optimization of target, screen of compounds, and patient recruitment is now substantially speeding up the drug discovery and clinical trial processes with the help of AI models, such as LLMs. AI has the ability to analyze large biomedical data to discover promising drugs, anticipate interactions taking into account how a molecule interacts, and to insinuate likely side effects, much faster than any convention mechanism. AI will assist to match eligible patients relying on their medical histories, genetic background and trial details, and can reduce the patient recruitment process time by as much as 40% in clinical trials. Additionally, the AI based simulations help to predict the trial results which aids in making the trial process overall more efficient and improving a successful design. These advancements can decrease the overall R&D timeline, reduce cost and enable effective treatments to reach the market faster for the benefit of patient care and the health of the population (Teng et al., 2022).

6.3 Advances in Personalized Medicine via Data-Driven Research Insights

Use of advanced multimodal health data to perform the task of personalized medicine One highly impactful move towards personalized medicine lies in trying to pick trends on multimodal health data through the use of AI and LLMS. The genomic and EHR, patient lifestyle and clinical response, and how each individual patient will respond to each treatment can be analyzed using AI models (Mashabab et al., 2024). Thus, AI can assist researchers and medical workers in creating a personalized treatment based on the genetic composition and health condition of the patient. Then biomarker discovery/risk stratification will allow the initiation of earlier interventions and greater precision in treatment. AI-based personalized medicine projects throughout the U.S. report up to 30% improvement in treatment efficacy and overall patient outcomes.

7. HUMAN - AI COLLABORATION IN CLINICAL PRACTICE

Healthcare is a human-centered approach, and the use of AI does not aim to replace clinicians but to assist a team of clinicians in making decisions. While no one can replace a clinician's situational, empathetic, and ethical decision-making, AI is far more effective in data analysis, diagnostics, and automation of work. Together, they create a hybrid model in which technology supports clinicians to improve accuracy, reduce errors, and personalize care. Such systems also enhance productivity by streamlining paperwork, thereby providing clinicians more time to spend with patients. In addition, the outputs of AI will be checked to eliminate the chance of misinterpretation or bias, which are overseen by people (Ravikumar et al., 2025). The integration of computational intelligence and human expertise has the potential to assist healthcare in obtaining more accurate diagnostics, more efficient treatment planning, and enhanced patient outcomes. This paradigm shift depicts the future of medicine, where human judgement is supported, not displaced, by technology.

7.1 Enhancing Clinical Decision-Making

Decision support systems and LLM are examples of AI-based applications that can help clinicians by analyzing and processing imaging, genomic, and clinical documentation data sets. In a short time, these systems can uncover imaging patterns and correlations that a human being would find difficult to notice. Using the example of AI, a clinician can be notified about the illnesses a patient may have, the treatment options, and the risk analysis. This enables the clinician to apply his or her knowledge to determine the outcome of the analysis and the best course of action. Notably, working with AI allows it to be a guideline and not a final verdict. Human knowledge cross-checks result, incorporates the history of a patient, and takes the emotional, cultural, and ethical aspects of care into account (Ravikumar et al., 2025). It brings synergy to decision processes in order to make them faster and evidence based, minimise mistakes in diagnoses and optimise the outcome. AI makes clinical care delivery safer and more reliable by complementing, rather than substituting, clinical judgment.

7.2 Building Trust and Patient Engagement

Adoption of AI in healthcare can only succeed when patients and clinicians trust each other. Patients also need to be confident that AI is applied in a responsible manner, transparently and monitored by humans. This trust can be enhanced through the collaboration between humans and AI as the latter establishes itself as an assistant system and not an independent power. One such scenario is that chatbots based on AI should be able to answer more mundane questions and physicians will be guided to communication and attention to the person. The technology-breakdown barrier can overcome thanks to clinicians telling patients how to articulate AI insights. This will encourage patients to participate in the treatment process, comply with interventions, and be more satisfied with treatment even if AI is an independent treatment modality (Ravikumar et al., 2025). This will eventually engender trust in this emerging technology-based healthcare with human care and AI efficiency, where human contact shall remain the greatest asset of this domain.

8. CHALLENGES AND FUTURE DIRECTIONS IN HEALTHCARE AI

The integration of AI in healthcare offers transformative potential but also presents critical challenges. Data privacy is a major concern, as sensitive medical records must comply with regulations such as HIPAA and GDPR. There are other concerns as well, like algorithmic bias in which unequal or inaccurate results may be produced due to unrepresentative training data. Furthermore, the adoption of AI technologies in healthcare is hindered by regulatory uncertainty, since there are few defined approval paths for AI-driven medical devices. Ethical issues such as informed consent, transparency, and responsibility must be addressed for stakeholders, including patients and healthcare providers, to have confidence in the technologies (Krishna Pasupuleti, 2024). In the future, healthcare AI is expected to evolve into multimodal systems that integrate text, images, genomics, and wearable devices to make informed decisions. Federated learning will enable institutions to work together without risking patient data, and Explainable AI (XAI) will provide functionality to audit fairness and explain decisions. With these features, supported by strong ethical policies, the goal is to trust AI in global healthcare, equity, and centered around the patient.

8.1 Mitigating Data, Bias, and Regulatory Barriers

Regardless of the potential AI has shown in the healthcare domain, a number of issues need to be addressed in order for it to be safely and equitably deployed. The privacy of data is a critical issue since AI systems require real patient-sensitive data (Komasawa & Yokohira, 2023). It is vital to comply with regulations like HIPAA or GDPR and maintain confidentiality and trust. Another risk of algorithmic bias occurs when the model is trained on any non-representative dataset, producing biased results that may lead to unequal care. Important mitigation measures involve guaranteeing that the training data are representative as well as conducting fairness audits. There is also the issue of constantly evolving regulation which does not provide any accepted rules of approval of healthcare-specific AI (Chan & Zary, 2019). To overcome these problems, the technologists, healthcare professionals, and policymakers should cooperate in creating transparent, accountable, and adherent AI solutions that are focused on the safety of the patients and the ethical integrity of the solutions. The table 3 outlines the major challenges faced in deploying AI in healthcare data privacy, algorithmic bias, and regulatory hurdles along with strategic resolutions to address each issue.

Table 3. Key Challenges and Resolutions in AI-Driven Healthcare

Challenge	Description	Resolution Strategy
Data Privacy	Risk of exposing sensitive patient information during AI model training/use.	Ensure compliance with HIPAA, GDPR; implement data anonymization and secure encryption.
Algorithmic Bias	AI models may produce unfair or inaccurate outcomes due to biased training data.	Use diverse datasets; conduct regular fairness audits; apply bias-mitigation techniques.
Regulatory Challenges	Lack of consistent, clear approval and usage guidelines for healthcare AI tools.	Collaborate with regulators to develop AI-specific standards and transparent validation.

8.2 Ethical Considerations in the Use of AI in Healthcare

The issue of AI application in the healthcare system suggests that there are grave ethical issues that should be addressed before its application can be done in a responsible manner. Because AI refers to the person when it comes to informed consent, it is an immediate example. How data is utilized and decisions made must be explained in order to preserve trust. Added to the latter accountability is that other issue. It should define when the function of the AI-assisted systems should be taken by whom in the clinical decision making. There are other principles to be taken into account, such as the principle of fairness, so that AI does not contribute to the further development of inequalities in healthcare that are already present, since information is biased and technologies are inaccessible (Murdoch, 2021). The explainability, the inclusive and the human-centric nature of AI tools should guarantee the ethical maturity of the clinical practice. When pursued actively, AI technologies will transform healthcare to be more ethical, trusted, patient-centred and fair.

8.3 Future Directions in Healthcare AI

The ability of AI to learn and adapt will be integrated into a more sophisticated and advanced care plan in the future. Think about integrating multimodal AI systems, where text, images, sensors, and genomic data are taken into account to provide diagnostics and treatment plans, and broader object-based imaging is achieved. Federated Learning will allow healthcare AI models to learn and analyze information on distributed healthcare systems whilst preserving patient privacy, improving security and cooperation. Additionally, AI-powered predictive analytics will aid in enabling future care, as it will estimate the likelihood of illnesses and the hospital resources needed. AI will unquestionably become the reliable partner to deliver fair, effective, and patient-focused care in every country around the world, as is evident with the shifting regulations, the rising ethical frameworks, and the increasing global demand for care.

9. ECONOMIC AND POLICY IMPLICATIONS OF HEALTHCARE AI

As far as healthcare is concerned, the use of AI technologies presents challenges both from an economic and policy standpoint. From an economic standpoint, it is beneficial, as it can bring about automation and predictive analytics, thereby reducing expenses for hospitals and improving their returns on investment. Notably, the costs associated with AI training, integration, and infrastructure perpetuate inequalities between well-funded and poorly funded institutions (Fatima et al., 2023). From a policy perspective, its safe adoption rests on the availability of clear regulations, ethical norms, and proper frameworks for data protection. While the use of AI in healthcare is beneficial, with the right adoption models, reimbursement, liability, and equitable access being addressed, proper innovation will be ensured.

9.1 Economic Impact of AI Adoption

Artificial Intelligence in healthcare offers a unique set of economic challenges related to its initial costs, the staff needed to maintain it, and continued investments in the technology. It automates billing and recordkeeping, which decreases costs and enables medical professionals to focus on their patients. Unnecessary patient admissions are reduced and resources optimized using predictive analytics, which results in savings that amount to millions. In addition, AI technologies aid in drug discovery and clinical testing and help reduce research and development expenditures. However, the aforementioned advantages come with the requirement of substantial upfront spending on state-of-the-art technologies, advanced institution-wide training, and infrastructure improvements. The lesser hospitals may face issues with affordability, resulting in adoption gaps. Without the proper aid from central funding and investor support, such investments risk widening the healthcare divide as AI adoption remains unavailable to certain sectors. There needs to be a thorough consideration of the long-term benefits and as a result, the creation of funding schemes that enable scalable and low-cost AI adoption in healthcare systems needs to be implemented.

9.2 Policy and Regulatory Considerations

Policies and regulations: The essence of law-abiding, ethical incorporation of AI into the healthcare services. Cross-border sharing of personal health information rules must not be in opposition to the HIPAA and GDPA Acts. Equity must be created on the question of whether the fault of mistakes in AI-assisted clinical decision-making lies with the provider, creator or institution, that is, the need to know who they are responsible to. Reimbursement models need to be made more transparent to enable the facilitation of telemedicine and virtual services. The methods should also be non-biased in order to ensure that individuals falling within the categories of those who are being discriminated have equal access to them. Interoperability would not be possible without international collaboration. The earliest adopters must be prepared to adopt good, dynamic policies that will bring innovations in the best interest of their patients but will not eat into their confidence.

10. CONCLUSION

The application of AI, LLMs, and intelligent agents is greatly transforming the healthcare sector by removing the loopholes in the process of diagnosis, treatment, administration, and communication with patients. The future of AI is bright as more advanced solutions can be expected after the current days expert systems that are more sophisticated and patient friendly than the mythical MYCIN and the transformer-LLM based systems since the early days of rule-based systems. Indeed, in radiology and pathology, individualized medicine, and virtual care, the evidence of benefits is dramatic, in terms of quality, productivity, and availability. The AI applications may help in handling workflow and reduce administrative burden hence, avoiding clinician burnout hence, conserving time that could help in attending more patients. On the other hand, telehealth and virtual assistant powered by an AI are creating opportunities in underserved populations where the challenge of resource scarcity and geography is no longer determinants of access to healthcare delivery service. With this change, however, come the ethical and regulatory issues that are raised, and they would be very serious. Of great concern are issues of privacy of data, biases in algorithms, accountability in AI decision-making, continuous moving approval gateways that were or are being resolved by transparent policy, multiple training data, and multinational partnerships.

Human component cannot be replaced and developing trust will be required to effectively implement it, thus AI will merely assist in making evidence-based decisions based on evidence-based knowledge without enlightening empathy and human judgment. Multimodal AI algorithms that take text, imaging, genomic, sensor data into consideration; federated learning algorithms to ensure privacy and foster cooperation on the global level; Explainable AI (XAI) to accomplish further transparency and responsibility. Equitable access at the economic level will require fundable scales and reimbursement plans to be in place, especially in a resource skewed healthcare environment. Finally, AI in healthcare is a paradigm, in which the creation of technology is located, between social responsibility and policy transparency on the one hand and the technology itself on the other hand. AI is bound to become the best reliable, equitably implemented, and patient-centred ally through collaborative efforts with technologists, clinicians, and policymakers. Human intelligence will never be negated with but maximized with enhancement, leading to the genesis of a more efficient, complete, and eco-sustainable healthcare system.

REFERENCES

Ahmad, M., Yaramic, I., & Roy, T. D. (2023). Creating trustworthy LLMs: Dealing with hallucinations in healthcare AI.

AlDhaen, F. S. (2025). AI-powered transformation of healthcare: Enhancing patient safety through AI interventions with the mediating role of operational efficiency and moderating role of digital competence-insights from the gulf Cooperation Council region. *Healthcare (Basel)*, *13*(6). PMID: 40150463

Alkalbani, A. M., Alrawahi, A. S., Salah, A., Haghighi, V., Zhang, Y., Alkindi, S., & Sheng, Q. Z. (2024). A systematic review of Large Language Models in medical specialties: Applications, challenges and future directions. In *Research Square*.

Barbieri, C., Neri, L., Stuard, S., & Mari, F., & Mart\'\in-Guerrero, J. D. (2023). From electronic health records to clinical management systems: How the digital transformation can support healthcare services. *Clinical Kidney Journal*, *16*(11), 1878–1884. PMID: 37915897

Busch, F., Hoffmann, L., Rueger, C., van Dijk, E. H. C., Kader, R., Ortiz-Prado, E., Makowski, M. R., Saba, L., Hadamitzky, M., Kather, J. N., Truhn, D., Cuocolo, R., Adams, L. C., & Bressem, K. K. (2024). Systematic review of large language models for patient care: Current applications and challenges. In *bioRxiv*.

Chan, K. S., & Zary, N. (2019). Applications and challenges of implementing artificial intelligence in medical education: Integrative review. *JMIR Medical Education*, *5*(1), e13930. PMID: 31199295

Das, D. R., Satpathy, I., & Patnaik, B. C. M. (2023). AI-enabled healthcare service. In *AI and IoT-Based Technologies for Precision Medicine* (pp. 108–120). IGI Global.

Eckrich, J., Ellinger, J., Cox, A., Stein, J., Ritter, M., Blaikie, A., Kuhn, S., & Buhr, C. R. (2024). Urology consultants versus large language models: Potentials and hazards for medical advice in urology. *BJUI Compass*, *5*(5), 438–444. PMID: 38751951

Fatima, I., Grover, V., Raza Khan, I., Ahmad, N., & Yadav, A. (2023). Artificial intelligence in medical filed. *EAI Endorsed Transactions on Pervasive Health and Technology*, •••, 9.

Fuchs, A., Trachsel, T., Weiger, R., & Eggmann, F. (2023). ChatGPT's performance in dentistry and allergyimmunology assessments: A comparative study. *Swiss Dental Journal*, *134*(2), 1–17. PMID: 38726506

Gao, Y., Li, R., & Croxford, E., Caskey John and Patterson, B. W., Churpek, M., Miller Timothy and Dligach, D., & Afshar, M. (2025). Leveraging medical knowledge graphs into large language models for diagnosis prediction: Design and application study. *JMIR AI*, *4*, e58670. PMID: 39993309

Gencer, G., & Gencer, K. (2025). Large language models in healthcare: A bibliometric analysis and examination of research trends. *Journal of Multidisciplinary Healthcare*, *18*, 223–238. PMID: 39844924

Herries, J. (2024). Emerging clinical applications of large language models in emergency medicine. *Emergency Medicine Australasia*, *36*(4), 635–636. PMID: 39013798

Judijanto, L., Nurkhalika, R., Anurogo, D., Andari, S., & Muntasir, M. (2024). The Role of artificial intelligence in the Development of Innovative Drugs and Therapies for the Future of Health. J. of World Future Medicine. *Health and Nursing*, *2*(1), 20–36. PMID: 38183055

Komasawa, N., & Yokohira, M. (2023). Learner-centered experience-based medical education in an AI-driven society: A literature review. *Cureus*, *15*(10), e46883. PMID: 37954813

Krishna Pasupuleti, M. (2024). AI in Healthcare: Transforming the Future. In The New Era of Medical Intelligence: AI-Powered Diagnostics and Tailored Treatments (pp. 55–69). National Education Services.

Liu, F., Zhou, H., Gu, B., Zou, Xinyu, Huang, J., Wu, J., Li, Y., Chen, S. S., Hua, Y., Zhou, P., Liu, J., Mao, Chengfeng, You, C., Wu, X., & Zheng, Y., Clifton Lei and Li, Z., Luo, J., & Clifton, D. A. (2025). Application of large language models in medicine. *Nature Reviews Bioengineering*, *3*(6), 445–464.

Mannstadt, I., & Mehta, B. (2024). Large language models and the future of rheumatology: Assessing impact and emerging opportunities. *Current Opinion in Rheumatology*, *36*(1), 46–51. PMID: 37729050

Mashabab, M. F., Sheniff, M. S., Al, , Alsharief, M. S., Yami, M. A. A., Al, , Matnah, H. N. M., Abbas, A. M., Al, , Shenief, H. Y. M., & Al, , Abbas Dhaffer Ali Ali Al Al and Raseen, F. M. S. A., & Kulayb, A. H. A. Al. (2024). The role of artificial Intelligence in healthcare: A critical analysis of its implications for patient care. *JoE*, *3*(7), 597–604.

McKee, M., & Correia, T. (2025). The future of the health professions: Navigating shortages, imbalances, and automation. *The International Journal of Health Planning and Management*, *40*(2), 289–292. PMID: 39496993

Mishra, S. (2022). Artificial Intelligence: A review of progress and prospects in medicine and healthcare. *J.Electron.Electromedical.Eng.Med.Inform*, *4*(1), 1–23.

Movahed, M., & Bilderback, S. (2024). Evaluating the readiness of healthcare administration students to utilize AI for sustainable leadership: a survey study. J. Health Organ. Manag., ahead-of-print(ahead-of-print), 567–582.

Murdoch, B. (2021). Privacy and artificial intelligence: Challenges for protecting health information in a new era. *BMC Medical Ethics*, *22*(1), 122. PMID: 34525993

Nassani, A. A., & Javed, A., Rosak-Szyrocka Joanna and Pilar, L., Yousaf, Z., & Haffar, M. (2023). Major determinants of innovation performance in the context of healthcare sector. *International Journal of Environmental Research and Public Health*, *20*(6). PMID: 36981916

Ndukwe, H., & Otukpa, E. (2025). A scoping review protocol examining the application of large language models in healthcare education and public health learning spaces. In *medRxiv*.

Pashangpour, S., & Nejat, G. (2024). The future of intelligent healthcare: A systematic analysis and discussion on the integration and impact of robots using large language models for healthcare. *Robotics (Basel, Switzerland)*, *13*(8), 112.

Pasupuleti, M. K. (2025). Revolutionizing healthcare: AI and Big Data for predictive analytics and precision medicine. In *AI and Big Data for Predictive Healthcare Analytics* (pp. 151–160). National Education Services.

Quercia, A., Zaghir, J., Lovis, C., & Gaudet-Blavignac, C. (2024). MedFrenchmark, a small set for benchmarking generative LLMs in medical French. *Studies in Health Technology and Informatics*, *316*, 601–605. PMID: 39176814

Ravikumar, R. N., Aarthi, S., Masharipova, G., Niyazova, N., Salaeva, N., & Buriyeva, D. (2025). Enhancing clinical decision-making and operational efficiency in healthcare using edge computing. In *Building Data-Driven Edge Systems for Business Success* (pp. 191–224). IGI Global Scientific Publishing., DOI: 10.4018/979-8-3373-1147-0.ch008

Restrepo, D., Wu, C., Vásquez-Venegas, C., Matos, J., Gallifant, J., Celi, L. A., Bitterman, D. S., & Nakayama, L. F. (2024). Analyzing Diversity in Healthcare LLM Research: A Scientometric Perspective. In *medRxiv*.

Sadanand, V. K., & Nandini, S. (2024). AI in Indian healthcare startups. In *Advances in Medical Technologies and Clinical Practice* (pp. 1–26). IGI Global.

Senbekov, M., Saliev, T., Bukeyeva, Z., Almabayeva, A., & Zhanaliyeva, M. (2020). Aitenova Nazym and Toishibekov, Y., & Fakhradiyev, I. (2020). The recent progress and applications of digital technologies in healthcare: A review. *International Journal of Telemedicine and Applications*, •••, 8830200. PMID: 33343657

Shahrukh Irfan Prasanta Kumar Parida, A. B. S. D. M. N. J. D. (2023). Advancing healthcare through Artificial Intelligence: Innovations at the intersection of AI and medicine. Tuijin Jishu, 44(2).

Teng, M., Singla, R., Yau, O., Lamoureux, D., Gupta, A., Hu, Z., Hu, R., Aissiou, A., Eaton, S., & Hamm, C., Hu Sophie and Kelly, D., MacMillan, K. M., Malik Shamir and Mazzoli, V., Teng, Y.-W., Laricheva, M., Jarus, T., & Field, T. S. (2022). Health care students' perspectives on artificial intelligence: Countrywide survey in Canada. *JMIR Medical Education*, *8*(1), e33390. PMID: 35099397

Workum, J. D., & van de Sande, D., & Gommers Diederik and van Genderen, M. E. (2025). Bridging the gap: A practical step-by-step approach to warrant safe implementation of large language models in healthcare. *Frontiers in Artificial Intelligence*, *8*, 1504805. PMID: 39931218

Yalamanchili, A., & Sengupta, B., Song Joshua and Lim, S., Thomas, T. O., Mittal, B. B., Abazeed, M. E., & Teo, P. T. (2024). Quality of large language model responses to radiation oncology patient care questions. *JAMA Network Open*, *7*(4), e244630. PMID: 38564215

KEY TERMS AND DEFINITIONS

Artificial Intelligence (AI): A branch of computer science focused on creating systems capable of performing tasks that normally require human intelligence, such as decision-making, language understanding, and visual perception.

Large Language Models (LLMs): Deep learning models trained on massive textual datasets to understand and generate human-like language; examples include GPT and BERT.

Natural Language Processing (NLP): A subfield of AI that enables machines to understand, interpret, and generate human language.

AI Agents: Autonomous systems powered by AI algorithms that perform tasks with minimal human intervention, often used for decision-making and virtual assistance in healthcare.

Clinical Decision Support Systems (CDSS): AI-powered tools that help healthcare providers make better clinical decisions by analyzing patient data and suggesting diagnosis or treatment options.

Transformer Models: A type of deep learning architecture that uses self-attention mechanisms to process sequential data, forming the foundation for LLMs.

Supervised Learning: A ML technique where models are trained on labeled datasets to learn input-output mappings.

Reinforcement Learning: A learning technique where an agent learns to make decisions by receiving feedback (rewards or penalties) from its actions.

Multimodal Data: Data from various sources (text, images, vitals, genomics, etc.) combined for comprehensive AI analysis in healthcare.

Telemedicine: The use of telecommunication technologies to provide healthcare services remotely.

Virtual Health Assistants: AI-powered chatbots or voice assistants that interact with patients to offer medical advice, schedule appointments, and more.

Data Privacy (HIPAA, GDPR): Legal frameworks ensuring the protection and confidentiality of patient data used by AI systems.

Algorithmic Bias: Bias in AI predictions caused by non-representative or skewed training data, potentially leading to unfair outcomes.

Explainable AI (XAI): AI models designed to provide human-understandable explanations for their predictions and decisions.

Chapter 4
AI in Education:
Learning Platforms for Personalized Learning

Mustafa Kayyali
https://orcid.org/0000-0003-3300-262X
Maaref University of Applied Sciences, Syria

ABSTRACT

The rise of AI and large language models (LLMs) has redefined the boundaries of what is possible in education, especially in the realm of personalized learning. This chapter explores the transformative potential of adaptive learning platforms powered by AI agents and LLMs, focusing on how these technologies can tailor educational experiences to individual learners' needs, preferences, and pace. It traces the evolution of personalized learning, highlighting how recent AI advancements have moved us beyond static models toward dynamic, responsive, and context-aware systems. Drawing from interdisciplinary insights, the chapter also examines the design principles that underlie effective adaptive systems and unpacks the ethical challenges posed by data privacy, algorithmic bias, and the risk of dehumanizing learning. Ultimately, it argues that the real promise of AI in education lies not in replacing teachers or standardizing knowledge delivery, but in building human-centered systems that support meaningful, inclusive, and lifelong learning experiences.

INTRODUCTION

Education has always been a deeply human endeavor. At its core, it is about connection—between teacher and learner, between curiosity and knowledge, between individual growth and collective progress. Yet, despite decades of educational reform and the promise of technology, the structure of most educational systems

DOI: 10.4018/979-8-3373-2008-3.ch004

remains remarkably rigid and impersonal. Classrooms often function on a one-size-fits-all model that struggles to accommodate the diverse backgrounds, abilities, and learning trajectories of students (Sharma, 2024). The result is a persistent gap between the ideal of education as a deeply personalized journey and the reality of standardized curricula and uniform instruction. But something is shifting. With the rapid advancement of artificial intelligence—particularly in the form of large language models (LLMs) and intelligent agents—we find ourselves at a moment of profound transformation. These technologies are not just incremental improvements; they represent a paradigm shift. For the first time, we have the tools to create adaptive learning environments that respond to learners in real time, understand natural language, and offer personalized feedback and support at scale. The dream of tailoring education to each learner's unique needs is no longer a distant aspiration—it is becoming a tangible possibility.

This chapter begins with the recognition that education, as it stands, is not failing because of a lack of effort or intent. Rather, it has been constrained by the limits of time, resources, and the inability to scale individualized attention. Teachers are stretched thin, students are often reduced to data points, and educational systems are pressured to produce measurable outcomes that may not reflect meaningful learning. Artificial intelligence offers a way out of this bind—not as a magic solution, but as a tool that, if designed thoughtfully and ethically, can expand the capacity of educators and empower learners. The use of AI in education is not without controversy. Fears of surveillance, algorithmic bias, and the loss of human connection are legitimate and must be addressed head-on. But amid these concerns lies a crucial opportunity: to reimagine education as a dynamic, learner-centered process where technology enhances, rather than replaces, the role of teachers and the value of human judgment. Adaptive learning platforms, guided by the sophistication of LLMs, can offer not just customization but real support—adapting to how a learner thinks, where they struggle, and what motivates them.

In this chapter, we will trace the development of personalized learning and explore how AI, and particularly LLMs and AI agents, are reshaping its implementation. We will examine how adaptive learning platforms are designed, the role of data and feedback in shaping learning paths, and the risks and responsibilities that come with AI integration. More importantly, we will ask not only what these technologies can do but also what they should do and for whom. The goal is not merely to describe a technological trend but to engage in a deeper conversation about what kind of education we want—and how AI can help us get there.

RETHINKING EDUCATION IN THE AGE OF AI

We've always looked to education as the great equalizer—a way to create opportunity, to nurture talent, to open doors that might otherwise remain closed. For generations, education has been the space where people from vastly different backgrounds could gather under a shared goal: to learn, to grow, and to build a future. And yet, as we look around today, we see a system that often struggles to live up to those ideals. The promise of education remains, but its delivery, in many places, feels outdated—slow to evolve, slow to respond, and painfully unaccommodating to the diversity of learners who pass through its doors.

Now, we're on the cusp of something that could change that—radically and irrevocably. Artificial Intelligence, and in particular the emergence of large language models and intelligent systems, is forcing us to ask difficult but necessary questions (Hadi et al, 2023). What if the educational systems we've inherited were never built to be equitable in the first place? What if they were designed for scale, not personalization; for control, not curiosity; for outputs, not transformation? And what if, with the help of AI, we had the chance to do things differently? The conversation about AI in education often begins with tools. We talk about platforms, chatbots, analytics dashboards, and personalized quizzes. But perhaps we should begin elsewhere—with the learners. Because at its heart, this moment isn't about technology. It's about people. It's about whether we can build educational experiences that actually respond to who learners are—not who we expect them to be. Think about a student sitting in the back of a crowded classroom. She's quiet and thoughtful, struggling with the pace of the material, but she is too shy to speak up. The teacher is stretched thin, juggling lesson plans, grading, administrative tasks, and a classroom of diverse needs. It's no one's fault, but that student slips through the cracks. Her potential? Untapped. Her confusion? Unnoticed. Her voice? Unheard.

Now imagine an adaptive learning platform powered by AI that quietly picks up on her learning patterns—how she reads, where she pauses, what kinds of questions she tends to get right or wrong (Kayyali, 2024 A). It doesn't replace her teacher. It supports her. It nudges her when she's stuck, celebrates her when she makes progress, and gives her space to learn at her own rhythm. It may not sound revolutionary, but for that one student—for millions like her—it could make all the difference. This isn't science fiction. The technologies exist. What's lagging is our willingness to rethink what education can be. For centuries, education has been shaped by limitations—of time, of space, of resources. A teacher could only teach so many students in one room, with one voice. Curriculum had to be standardized to be scalable. Exams became the default measure of learning because they were easy to administer, not because they captured the full richness of what a student understands. Slowly, we began to confuse what was measurable with what mattered. But AI doesn't carry those same constraints. It doesn't get tired. It doesn't forget. It doesn't have a "class size limit." This changes everything—not because machines can now teach better than humans, but because they can remove the noise, the busywork, and the blind spots that have long burdened our educational systems. Of course, there's a risk here. If we're not careful, we could end up automating the very problems we should be trying to solve. We could turn adaptive learning into a glorified test-prep engine. We could design platforms that are efficient but soulless—technically impressive but educationally hollow. That's why this moment calls for more than innovation; it calls for introspection.

What do we value in education? What do we want our learners to become? These are not technical questions. They are human ones. And they must guide how we build and implement AI systems in learning environments. The irony is that while AI systems are often seen as the height of objectivity—algorithms, data, cold logic—they are, in reality, reflections of us. They learn from the data we feed them, which means they learn from our biases, our gaps, our historical failures. If we train an AI system on a curriculum that marginalizes certain voices or rewards conformity over creativity, the system will replicate those patterns (Lockhart, 2024). It will learn to teach the way we've always taught, not the way we could teach. So rethinking education in the age of AI isn't just about improving learning outcomes (Luckin, 2025). It's about asking whether our old measures of success are still relevant. It's about deciding whether we want to train students to compete with machines or to do what only humans can—collaborate, empathize, imagine, create, question. This is where educators become more important, not less. AI can scale information, but only teachers can build relationships. Only teachers can read the room, pick up on emotional cues, or tell when a student needs encouragement instead of correction. The best educational experiences are deeply human—shaped by stories, guided by care, grounded in trust.

What AI can do is make space for more of those moments. It can reduce the administrative burdens that wear teachers down. It can flag students who need extra help. It can provide resources in multiple languages, support learners with disabilities, and adapt to the quirks and rhythms of each learner's journey. Used well, AI doesn't erase the human element of education—it amplifies it (Al-Chaer, 2024). And yet, we must tread carefully. Not all personalization is good. A platform that learns a student's preferences might end up reinforcing them—offering only easy content, avoiding challenge, and narrowing the scope of exposure. Education is not just about comfort. It's about growth, and growth is uncomfortable. That's why adaptive systems must be designed not just to serve the learner's present state, but to push them toward their potential gently. We must also think about access. If AI-powered learning tools are only available in elite institutions or well-funded districts, then we're simply widening the gap we set out to close (Bowen & Watson, 2024).

Technology should democratize learning, not deepen inequality. This means open access models, public-private partnerships, and policies that prioritize equity over profit. And then there's the question of data. Students generate massive amounts of information as they learn—clicks, pauses, responses, reflections (Dong et al, 2017). That data can be used to fine-tune their learning experience, but it can also be misused. Privacy isn't just a legal issue. It's an ethical one. Learners have a right to know how their data is being used, who has access to it, and what assumptions are being made about them.

Ultimately, rethinking education in the age of AI isn't about replacing the classroom. It's about expanding it—into new spaces, new formats, new possibilities. It's about recognizing that learning happens everywhere, not just within school walls. It happens late at night when a student watches a tutorial. It occurs in conversation, in exploration, in failure, in play. AI can help us capture those moments and connect them back to a broader narrative of learning. But perhaps most importantly, this is a moment to reclaim the soul of education. To remember that learning is not a transaction. It is a relationship. A risk. A leap into the unknown. As we build adaptive learning systems and intelligent tutors, we must keep sight of the fact that education is not about controlling outcomes. It's about opening minds. This is our opportunity—not just to digitize the old system, but to build something new. Something more just. More responsive. More alive. If we approach it with humility, curiosity, and care, AI can help us build educational systems that are not only smarter but more human than ever before.

THE EVOLUTION OF PERSONALIZED LEARNING: FROM THEORY TO TECHNOLOGY

The idea of personalized learning has always been more than just an educational strategy—it's a philosophy. At its heart lies a simple but powerful conviction: that learners are not interchangeable, and that meaningful education must begin with an understanding of each student's individual needs, strengths, interests, and challenges (Kayyali, 2025 A). Long before digital technologies emerged, educators, philosophers, and psychologists had already begun to grapple with the notion that the most effective learning happens when it meets the learner where they are. Historically, though, this ideal was hard to realize in practice. The structure of most educational systems has been built around the necessities of mass instruction: fixed curricula, age-based grade levels, and standardized assessments. These tools made schooling more manageable and scalable, but they also introduced rigidity. In trying to serve the many, the system often failed the individual. Learners who didn't fit the mold—those who moved faster or slower than the norm, those who thought differently, those who needed more support or sought deeper challenges—were often left behind or held back.

Still, the desire to individualize education never disappeared. It simply found new ways to express itself. In the early twentieth century, progressive educators like John Dewey argued for child-centered approaches, urging schools to focus on experience, inquiry, and the natural curiosity of the learner (Hassannejad, 2024). Dewey didn't have algorithms or digital platforms at his disposal, but he understood something essential: learning is not just the transmission of knowledge, but a dynamic and personal process (Sadovnik et al, 2017). Later, the work of educational psychologists such as Benjamin Bloom furthered this vision. Bloom's theory of "mastery learning" emphasized that, given enough time and the right support, almost all students could achieve high levels of understanding (Arievitch, 2020). The problem was time, and the limited ability of teachers to provide personalized feedback in large classrooms. It was a problem of scale, not of principle. Bloom's famous "2 Sigma Problem" demonstrated that students receiving one-on-one tutoring performed two standard deviations better than those in traditional classrooms. But the solution—tutoring every student individually—was, for decades, out of reach.

Then came the digital revolution. In the late 20th and early 21st centuries, technology began to enter classrooms in earnest. At first, it was rudimentary: computer labs, educational CD-ROMs, and online quizzes (Ludovico, 2024). These tools were often heralded as breakthroughs, but they largely reinforced the same pedagogical model—uniform content, delivered through a new medium. What was missing was adaptivity. Technology could distribute information, but it couldn't yet respond to learners (Kayyali, 2021). That began to change with the rise of learning management systems (LMS) and early adaptive software. These platforms introduced the possibility of branching paths—content that adjusted based on student responses, pacing that varied depending on mastery. They were limited and often clunky, but they represented a shift in mindset: the recognition that not every learner needs the same thing at the same time.

Around the same time, new educational models emerged that embraced personalization more fully. The concept of differentiated instruction gained traction, encouraging teachers to vary content, process, and products based on individual learner profiles. The Universal Design for Learning (UDL) framework offered another way forward, advocating for multiple means of representation, expression, and engagement (Lohmann et al, 2018). These ideas were grounded in neuroscience and emphasized the importance of flexibility in teaching and learning. But again, the challenge remained: how do you personalize at scale? In a classroom of 30 students, how can one teacher design 30 learning paths, track 30 sets of progress data, and provide 30 forms of feedback? Technology, once again, seemed like the most promising partner. This is where the conversation began to shift from personalized learning as theory to personalized learning as a technical possibility. With advances in data analytics, machine learning, and now artificial intelligence, we are seeing the emergence of platforms that don't just adapt—they listen. They learn. They engage in something closer to a dialogue with the learner.

Today, adaptive learning systems can identify not just whether a student got a question right or wrong, but *why*. They can recognize patterns in errors, suggest interventions, and scaffold content in real-time. They can offer hints when a learner hesitates, review material when it's been forgotten, and challenge when understanding is evident. Some even respond to emotion—detecting frustration or boredom and adjusting accordingly. But beyond the technical marvel, what's important is what this makes possible: a shift from the industrial model of education to something more organic, more responsive, and, arguably, more humane. Personalized learning, supported by technology, isn't about creating 30 versions of a textbook. It's about giving each learner agency in their journey—choice, voice, and pace. And yet, as we embrace these capabilities, we must be cautious. The evolution of personalized learning is not a story of progress alone (Brass & Lynch, 2020). There are tensions and trade-offs at every turn. One risk is the illusion of personalization. Just because a system changes based on input doesn't mean it's serving the learner well. True personalization isn't about surface-level adjustments; it's about a deeper understanding of context, culture, motivation, and identity.

Moreover, there's the danger of over-reliance. When systems become too good at "guiding" the learner, we may inadvertently remove the productive struggle that fosters resilience and critical thinking. If every mistake is preempted, every challenge softened, we risk building passive learners who depend on cues rather than cultivating their own judgment. We must also grapple with questions of transparency and accountability. When an adaptive system changes a learner's path, who decides what comes next—the algorithm or the educator? Are learners aware of how their data is being used? Can they challenge or question the logic that guides their learning journey?

In many cases, the answers are unclear. And that is troubling. The best implementations of personalized learning do not remove the teacher—they empower them. They give educators richer data, finer insight, and more time to do what only humans can: build trust, mentor, and inspire. A great teacher, paired with an intelligent system, is a powerful force. But that partnership must be intentional. Technology should extend human judgment, not replace it.

This brings us to a deeper truth: personalization is not a feature. It's a commitment. A commitment to equity, to flexibility, to honoring the complexity of learning. It's about asking, again and again, "What does this learner need now?"—and being willing to change course when the answer shifts. Personalized learning has come a long way—from theory, to differentiated instruction, to digital platforms, to intelligent systems (Kem, 2022). However, its core purpose remains unchanged: to help each learner realize their full potential (Kayyali, 2024 C). Technology can accelerate this journey, but it must not define it. As we move forward, we must hold fast to the values that sparked this evolution in the first place: Empathy, curiosity, and the belief that every learner deserves a path that is not just efficient but meaningful. The future of personalized learning is not about more automation. It's about deeper attention (Bernacki et al, 2021). It's about designing systems that don't just adapt to performance, but to purpose. Systems that respect the learner as a whole person, not just a data point. That's the real promise of personalization—not faster learning, but fuller learning. Learning that belongs to the learner. And that's where we find ourselves now, at a crossroads where powerful tools meet timeless values. The path we choose will shape not just how students learn, but how they see themselves as learners. And perhaps, if we get it right, they'll begin to see learning not as a task to complete, but as a life to live.

LARGE LANGUAGE MODELS AND AI AGENTS IN ADAPTIVE PLATFORMS

If we're honest with ourselves, education hasn't always kept up with the pace of technological change. For years, it lagged while the world transformed around it—businesses became data-driven, communication moved online, entertainment went algorithmic, and yet classrooms, in many places, still resembled those of the previous century. But something is different now. The emergence of large language models (LLMs) and intelligent agents has introduced a seismic shift—one that touches not only how we deliver education, but how we understand learning itself.

To grasp the full weight of this shift, we have to look beyond the technical capabilities of these systems and instead ask how they interact with the human experience of learning. Because at the center of every educational journey is a learner with emotions, fears, ambitions, and questions—questions that don't always fit into the neat boxes of a syllabus, and answers that often take shape through conversation, not memorization. This is where large language models bring something new to the table. Unlike earlier systems that followed rigid rules or responded with prescripted feedback, LLMs are able to engage in flexible, nuanced dialogue (Kwon et al, 2024). They can hold context, adapt tone, and offer responses that feel, if not exactly human, then at least human-aware. They don't just deliver content—they converse. They simulate the back-and-forth of inquiry, the slow unraveling of understanding, the kind of exploratory thinking that happens when a student talks through an idea and slowly makes sense of it. For decades, we've treated learning as a product of input and output. Read this, recall that. Watch this video, and answer that quiz. But real learning doesn't work that way. It's messy. It loops back on itself. It happens in moments of friction and flow, in uncertainty and realization. And while no machine can fully replicate the role of a thoughtful teacher or a peer who listens with Empathy, LLMs come surprisingly close to modeling the kind of intellectual companionship that can push a learner forward.

Figure 1. Engagement vs. Mastery Over a 12-Week Term

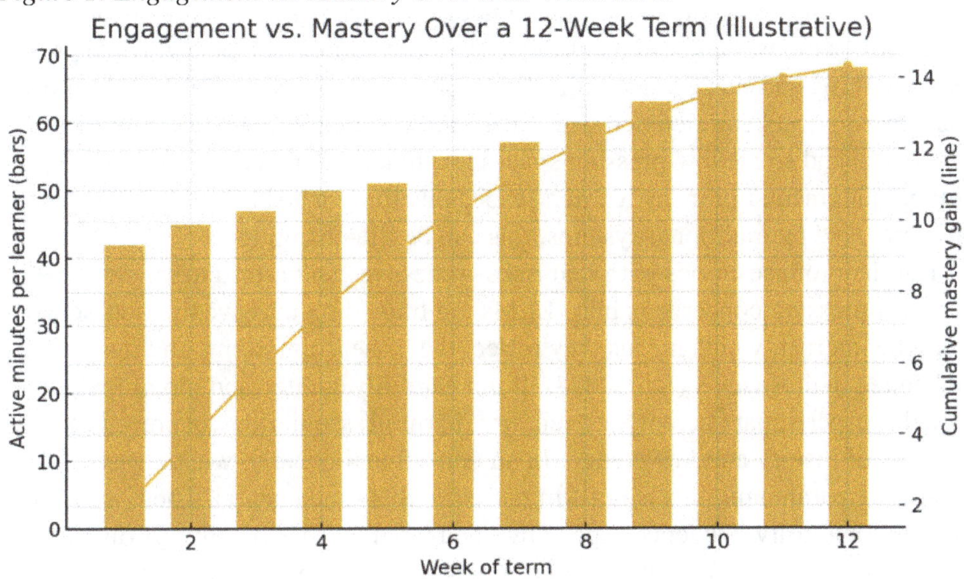

Of course, none of this works in isolation. The power of large language models comes alive when they are embedded within adaptive learning platforms—ecosystems that don't just present information, but learn from the learner (Pirjan & Petroşanu, 2024). These platforms observe how a student moves through material, when they pause, where they struggle, how they engage with questions, what feedback they need, and what motivates them to keep going. They gather that data—not to judge, but to support. They offer the scaffolding that each learner needs, and they do it in a way that can scale. Now, combine that adaptivity with the conversational fluency of an LLM, and you begin to see the outlines of something transformative (McTear & Ashurkina, 2024). Imagine a student wrestling with a complex concept—not just getting a hint or a multiple-choice explanation, but engaging in a thoughtful exchange with an AI agent that probes their understanding, rephrases ideas, poses counterexamples, and helps them arrive at insight through dialogue. That's not just content delivery. That's learning as a relationship.

And yet, as we marvel at these capabilities, we must also remain grounded. Because while the outputs of LLMs can feel astonishingly human, they are not conscious, they are not aware, and they do not care—at least not in the way we do. They respond based on probability, not purpose. They mimic Empathy, but they don't feel it. And this distinction matters. It matters because education is not just about comprehension—it's about connection. It's about guiding learners not only to knowledge, but toward confidence, self-awareness, and a sense of belonging. That's why the role of AI agents must be seen not as replacements for human educators, but as companions—extensions of the learning environment that can fill gaps, offer continuity, and make personalized support more widely available. When used well, these agents can democratize access to high-quality tutoring, provide 24/7 assistance, and create low-pressure spaces for students to practice, explore, and fail without judgment. For many learners, especially those who have been underserved or overlooked by traditional systems, this can be life-changing.

But the promise comes with real risks—ones we can't afford to ignore. One of the most pressing concerns is bias. LLMs are trained on massive datasets scraped from the internet, which means they reflect the biases, omissions, and inequalities embedded in those texts (Jain, 2024). If not carefully curated and monitored, these models can perpetuate stereotypes, reinforce harmful assumptions, or present skewed versions of history and knowledge. In an educational context, where trust and accuracy are paramount, this is not a minor issue. It's fundamental. There is also the matter of authority. Students, especially younger ones, may not always distinguish between a human teacher and an AI tutor (Kayyali, 2025 B). If a language model makes a mistake or offers misleading advice, will the learner know? Will they question it? What checks and balances are in place to ensure that adaptive systems don't drift from pedagogical soundness into persuasive nonsense? The opacity of these models adds another layer of complexity. LLMs are notoriously difficult to audit. Their reasoning isn't always explainable, even to their creators. So when an AI agent guides a learner down a particular path or suggests a certain strategy, we must ask: based on what? And with what goal in mind? If the learner struggles, who is accountable—the teacher, the platform, the algorithm?

These are not easy questions, but they are necessary ones. Because if we are building systems that make decisions about how people learn—what they read, how they're challenged, when they advance—then we are shaping minds. And that is a responsibility that must be approached with humility, ethics, and care. Still, despite these concerns, the potential is too great to ignore. Used responsibly, LLMs and AI agents can help reimagine what learning looks like, especially for students who have historically been left behind (Mistretta, 2024). For a student with a learning disability, an AI tutor can adjust pace and presentation without judgment. For a second-language learner, it can offer explanations in multiple languages or suggest culturally relevant examples. For a student in a rural area with no access to tutoring, it can provide daily support and encouragement. These are not trivial gains. They represent a shift in the moral geography of education—a move toward equity not as aspiration, but as infrastructure. And that shift begins when we stop thinking about LLMs and AI agents as technologies and start thinking of them as part of the learning ecosystem—as partners in the complex, human process of education. That doesn't mean we cede control.

On the contrary, it means we take more responsibility. We design with intention. We center the learner, not the algorithm. We create systems that are transparent, adjustable, and accountable. And we stay vigilant—testing, revising, listening. Because in the end, the question isn't just "What can these models do?" but "What should they do?" What kind of learning experiences do we want to foster? What types of questions do we want learners to ask—and who gets to answer them? How do we build not just smarter systems, but wiser ones? There is no formula for this. There is only dialogue—between educators and technologists, between learners and designers, between ethics and innovation. And maybe that's the ultimate irony. For all their power, LLMs work best when they help us do what we've always done at our best: listen, reflect, and teach with Empathy (Sorin et al, 2024). In this light, the evolution of adaptive platforms powered by AI isn't just a technological achievement. It's a chance to return to something timeless—a vision of education where each learner is seen, heard, and supported. Where learning is not just about getting the right answer, but about discovering who you are along the way. And in that discovery, perhaps, lies the most human part of all.

DESIGN PRINCIPLES FOR EFFECTIVE ADAPTIVE LEARNING SYSTEMS

There's a moment in every learner's journey when something clicks. It might come after hours of frustration, or in the quiet space between confusion and clarity. Sometimes it's triggered by the right question. Sometimes it's the result of persistence. Often, it's helped along by someone who sees not just what the learner gets wrong, but how they think, what they need, and where they are heading. That moment of connection—that bridge between where someone is and where they could go—is what adaptive learning systems aspire to recreate. But designing systems that truly adapt is not simply a matter of clever algorithms or elegant code. It is, at its core, a human challenge. It demands a deep understanding of how people learn, what motivates them, what frustrates them, and what it means to feel supported, challenged, and seen. This is why the most effective adaptive learning platforms are not just technically impressive—they are emotionally intelligent. They are built on principles that respect the complexity of human learning and the diversity of human learners.

The first and most foundational principle is responsiveness to individual variability (Porges, 2022). No two learners are the same. Even when they get the same answers right, the path they took to get there may be wildly different. One may have guessed; another may have reasoned carefully; a third may have drawn on a personal analogy. A good adaptive system doesn't just reward correctness—it tries to understand the process. It listens not only to outcomes, but to patterns. It watches how learners interact with content: how long they linger, where they skip, what they revisit. It treats these traces as clues, not conclusions. But responsiveness alone isn't enough. A system can be responsive without being meaningful. This is where the second principle comes in: pedagogical intentionality. Every adaptive decision—every branching path, every suggested exercise, every nudge—should be grounded in a clear understanding of learning theory (Bates, 2023). Are we promoting conceptual understanding or procedural fluency? Are we encouraging retrieval practice or scaffolding new content? Are we challenging the learner's zone of proximal development or reinforcing what they already know? If adaptive systems are to be more than glorified flashcards, they must make decisions that are not only data-driven but learning-informed.

Figure 2. Personalization Levers in an Adaptive Platform

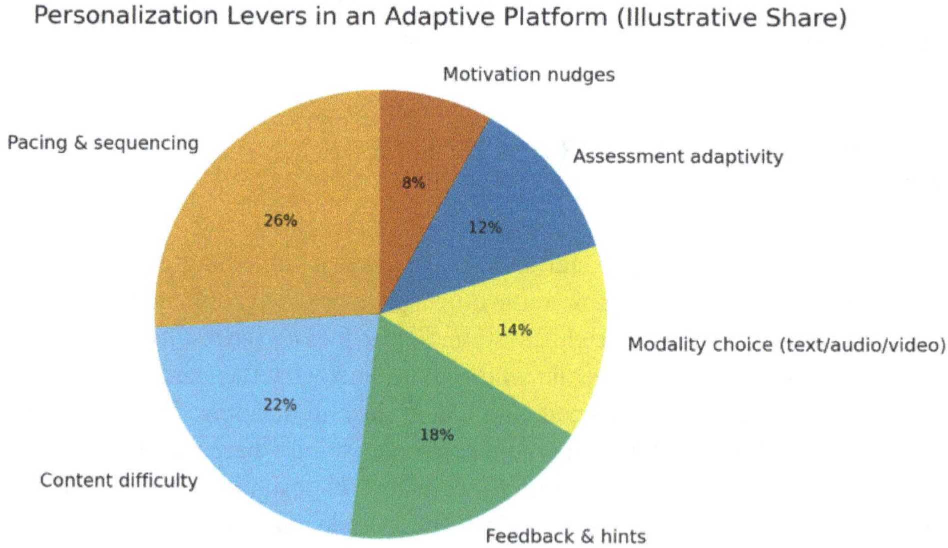

Equally important is transparency. Learners should not feel like they're being moved through a mysterious machine. They should be able to see why they're being given a certain task, how their past actions influenced the recommendation, and what goals they're working toward. This fosters agency, which is essential for deep learning. When learners understand the logic behind their learning path, they are more likely to engage with it actively rather than passively follow it (Li et al, 2024). Transparency also builds trust—something that is especially important when AI systems are making pedagogical decisions. This leads naturally to the principle of feedback as conversation. Traditional systems often treat feedback as a final judgment: correct/incorrect, pass/fail. But real learning thrives on formative feedback—timely, specific, and actionable. An effective adaptive system doesn't just mark an answer wrong; it asks why. It suggests another approach. It offers hints, examples, and counterexamples. It invites the learner into a dialogue. And when the learner responds, the system listens, adjusts, and continues the conversation. In this way, feedback becomes a process, not a product.

Another crucial principle is supporting cognitive and emotional engagement (Huang et al, 2022). Learning is not purely intellectual—it's also emotional. Frustration, boredom, confidence, and curiosity: these feelings shape how we learn just as much as content does. An adaptive system must be attuned to these signals. It should recognize when a learner is struggling not just because the material is hard, but because they're tired, overwhelmed, or discouraged. It should respond with Empathy—not in a performative way but through thoughtful design choices: offering a break, switching modalities, and encouraging a growth mindset. Engagement is not about gamification or superficial rewards; it's about sustaining the learner's belief that the task is meaningful and that they are capable of success. Closely related is the principle of cultural and contextual sensitivity. No learner enters the system as a blank slate. They bring with them language, identity, history, and worldview. A truly adaptive system doesn't assume a universal learner—it adapts not only to cognitive profiles but to cultural ones. It offers content that reflects diverse voices and experiences. It avoids assumptions about what is "neutral" or "standard." It recognizes that learning is deeply personal and that relevance matters—not just to keep attention, but to affirm identity. This also touches on the importance of accessibility by design. Adaptivity cannot be a privilege. It must be built in from the beginning with the broadest range of users in mind (Ueland et al, 2021). That means considering visual, auditory, motor, and cognitive accessibility. It means supporting multiple languages, offering content in various formats, and allowing users to adjust settings according to their needs. Accessibility is not a feature to be added later—it is a mindset embedded in the first line of design.

Table 1. Design Principles and Platform Features

Design principle	Platform feature examples	Intended outcomes
Responsiveness to variability	Item-level adaptivity; dynamic pacing; prerequisite repair	Drop in wheel-spinning; faster mastery
Pedagogical intentionality	Curriculum maps; ZPD-aware scaffolds; spaced retrieval	Retention ; transfer tasks improve
Transparency & agency	Why-this-task? panels; learner goals; override options	Trust ; self-regulation behaviors
Feedback as conversation	Hint tiers; counterexamples; reflection prompts	Error recovery; metacognition
Accessibility by design	Captions; alt-text; low-bandwidth modes; multilingual UIs	Access equity ; satisfaction
Human-in-the-loop	Teacher dashboards; intervene/assign; notes to learner	Timely support ; false positives â†“
Ethics & privacy	On-device analytics; consent; model cards; data minimization	Compliance; community confidence

Another principle that can't be ignored is human-in-the-loop oversight. As powerful as adaptive systems are, they should never operate in a vacuum. Educators must remain central to the process. They need to see what the system sees, intervene when necessary, and provide context that no algorithm can. Teachers can notice subtle signs of disengagement, mediate sensitive moments, and reframe learning in ways that a machine cannot replicate (Cairney, 2018). The system should serve the teacher, not the other way around. And finally, perhaps the most overarching principle of all: ethics before efficiency. In the rush to innovate, it's tempting to optimize for speed, scale, and engagement metrics. But education is not a numbers game. It's a moral endeavor. The choices we make when we design adaptive systems shape not only how students learn, but what they learn to value. Are we reinforcing a culture of right answers, or are we making space for complexity and nuance? Are we privileging speed over depth, or competition over collaboration? Are we respecting learner privacy, or mining their data without consent?

Designing effective adaptive learning systems is not about building the most responsive engine or the most advanced AI. It's about asking the right questions. Who are we designing for? What kind of learning do we want to support? How do we ensure that the systems we create amplify the best of what education can be—equity, curiosity, growth—rather than reducing it to efficiency and compliance? These are not easy questions (Kayyali, 2022). But they are the right ones. And if we ask them sincerely—if we involve learners, educators, psychologists, ethicists, and communities in the process—we have the chance to build something truly meaningful. Something that doesn't just adapt to performance, but to people. Because in the end, adaptivity is not just about customization. It's about care. It's about saying to each learner: *We see you. We hear you. We're building this with you in mind.* That's the kind of system that can make a difference—not because it's smart, but because it's human-centered. And in education, that will always be the standard that matters most.

CHALLENGES AND ETHICAL CONSIDERATIONS IN AI-POWERED EDUCATION

It's easy to be swept up in the optimism. The pace of technological advancement is dazzling, and nowhere is this more true than in the realm of education (Solloway, 2017). The rise of AI has brought with it the promise of personalized learning at scale, intelligent tutoring systems that never sleep, and platforms that can adapt in real time to student needs. These developments are often celebrated with excitement—and rightly so. But behind the enthusiasm lies a more complicated story. One that is not just technical, but moral. Not just about what we *can* do, but what we *should* do. Because while AI may open doors, it also introduces new dilemmas—many of them subtle, some of them urgent. These are not abstract concerns. They have real consequences for students, for teachers, for communities, and for the future of education as a public good. If we are to build systems that are not only intelligent but just, not only efficient but humane, we must be willing to pause, reflect, and engage with the uncomfortable questions.

One of the most immediate challenges is bias—not in the overt, cartoonish sense, but in the quiet, invisible ways that creep into data and decision-making (Mevold, 2023). AI systems learn from the past. They are trained on historical data, scraped from textbooks, forums, academic papers, and internet content. That means they inherit the same blind spots, prejudices, and systemic inequities that have shaped our institutions for generations. If certain voices have been underrepresented in the training data, the AI may struggle to support learners from those backgrounds. If certain dialects or cultural references are absent, students may feel alienated rather than included. And when that happens at scale, the harm multiplies. It's not just about fairness in outputs. It's also about invisibility. The learners most at risk of falling through the cracks are often the ones least reflected in the datasets these systems rely on. Students with disabilities. Students from marginalized communities. Students whose learning paths don't follow conventional timelines. If the system doesn't see them fully, it won't serve them fully. And yet, the very adaptability of AI can mask these failures. A platform may appear personalized and responsive, even as it quietly excludes or misjudges large swaths of its user base.

Then there is the issue of data privacy—a concern that has grown in parallel with the digital age, but takes on new urgency in the context of AI. Adaptive learning systems rely on constant data collection (Khosravi et al, 2020). They monitor clicks, dwell time, response accuracy, hesitation patterns, and even emotional cues in some cases. This data is essential to personalization—but it's also deeply sensitive. What happens to it? Who owns it? How long is it stored, and for what purpose? Too often, these questions are buried in terms of service that few read and fewer understand. Students, especially young ones, may have no idea how their data is being used, who has access to it, or how it might be interpreted. And because education is not optional—because students must engage with learning platforms to succeed—they may be forced to trade privacy for progress, with little say in the matter. The ethical stakes are high. Imagine a student whose performance data is used to generate a predictive model—one that forecasts their likelihood of success in certain subjects. What happens if that model is wrong? Or if it's used to steer the student away from opportunities? Will teachers override it, or defer to it? Will students internalize its judgments, believing the algorithm knows them better than they know themselves?

This brings us to another concern: automation of judgment. One of the most seductive qualities of AI is its apparent objectivity. It doesn't get tired. It doesn't play favorites. It can process vast amounts of information without blinking. And yet, the decisions it makes are not neutral. They are shaped by the goals we set, the data we feed it, and the assumptions we build into its architecture. An AI system may prioritize efficiency over depth, engagement over complexity, retention over transformation (Aldoseri et al, 2024). If we're not careful, we may end up codifying the very flaws we hoped to escape. And what of the human roles in education—particularly those of teachers? AI has the potential to lighten their load, offering support with grading, lesson planning, and differentiated instruction. But it can also create a subtle erosion of professional autonomy. When platforms make recommendations or automate tasks, will teachers feel empowered to push back? Or will they feel pressured to follow the system, even when their instincts suggest otherwise?

There is a fine line between assistance and replacement. And while most current systems are far from being substitutes for real educators, the narrative around AI often leans in that direction—framing technology as a solution to teacher shortages, a way to deliver quality at scale. This framing is dangerous. It devalues the relational, emotional, and moral labor of teaching. It risks turning education into a transaction rather than a transformation. Perhaps most troubling of all is the potential for surveillance culture to seep into learning environments. The same tools that track student progress can also be used to monitor behavior, flag "suspicious" activity, or enforce compliance. Some platforms already use webcam analysis to detect attention, facial expressions, or eye movement. The implication is clear: we are watching. Always. What does this do to a learner's sense of freedom, curiosity, or creativity? When students know they are being monitored—when every keystroke is logged, every pause analyzed—they may begin to perform for the system rather than engage with the content. They may feel less safe taking risks, less willing to admit confusion, and less open to exploring tangents that don't fit neatly into the algorithm's map.

Learning requires trust. It requires the freedom to fail, to try again, to think in ways that defy prediction (Kayyali, 2022). If adaptive systems become tools of control rather than care, they will not enhance education—they will hollow it out (Buckley, 2017). So where does this leave us? It would be easy to respond with fear or resistance—to reject AI in education altogether, to stick with what's familiar. But that, too, would be a mistake because these technologies do have real potential (Kayyali, 2024 B). They can support students who would otherwise struggle alone. They can make learning more inclusive, more flexible, more personalized. They can open doors that have long been closed. But only if we build them with values in mind. Only if we slow down and ask not just what works, but what's right, does this mean involving ethicists in design teams. It means creating oversight mechanisms, not just development roadmaps. It means inviting students, teachers, and communities into the conversation—not after the fact, but from the beginning. It also means holding on to the human essence of education. The best learning doesn't happen when we're being optimized or predicted. It occurs in surprise, in struggle, in moments of connection that no machine can replicate. If AI is to be part of education's future, it must be in service to that human spirit—not a replacement for it. Ultimately, ethics in AI-powered education is not a checklist. It's a stance. A way of showing up. It asks us to be humble about what we know, to be transparent about what we don't, and to be brave enough to change course when needed. We're not just training algorithms—we're shaping the minds and values of future generations. That's not a job for machines. It's a responsibility for all of us.

FUTURE DIRECTIONS: TOWARDS TRULY HUMAN-CENTERED LEARNING

There is a quiet tension at the heart of today's educational moment—a tension between the dazzling capabilities of technology and the stubbornly human nature of learning. We are living through a period of unprecedented innovation, with artificial intelligence unlocking tools and possibilities that would have seemed unthinkable just a decade ago. And yet, even as adaptive systems grow more sophisticated and personalized platforms become increasingly common, there remains a lingering question: Are we moving closer to the kind of education we want, or simply faster toward something we haven't paused long enough to define? To imagine the future of learning is not to imagine machines teaching machines. It is, rather, to reimagine what it means to learn as a human being in a world mediated by machines. This is not a future built on automation alone—it is a future grounded in values. And the value that matters most—the one that must shape every direction we move—is human dignity. Learning, at its best, is not transactional. It is transformational (Baškarada et al., 2017). It's not about downloading facts or maximizing productivity; it's about discovering meaning, developing voice, navigating complexity, and growing into a self-aware participant in the world. These are deeply human processes, and no amount of algorithmic precision can replace the emotional depth, relational texture, and moral weight that come with them. So where do we go from here?

The first step is to resist the temptation to define educational success solely through metrics. There's nothing inherently wrong with data—we need it. We need to know where learners are struggling, what content is effective, and how different approaches impact progress. But when data becomes the only measure, we lose sight of the messy, nonlinear, and deeply personal nature of learning. We start designing systems that reward speed over reflection, correctness over curiosity, conformity over creativity (Kayyali, 2024 D). And that is not the future we want. A human-centered approach to learning would flip that model (Ramos et al, 2020). It would begin not with what is easy to measure, but with what matters most. It would prioritize depth over breadth, process over product, and connection over compliance. It would ask, before anything else: Who is this learner? What do they bring with them—intellectually, emotionally, culturally? And what do they need—not just to perform, but to grow?

Such an approach cannot be achieved by technology alone. It requires a rebalancing of roles. The most powerful AI system in the world cannot replace the care of a teacher who notices when a student is anxious, or the peer who helps explain a concept in just the right way. But technology *can* support those human relationships. It can free up time, surface insights, and scaffold learning paths so that teachers are better equipped to focus on what they do best: building trust, nurturing curiosity, and helping students make sense of their own potential. That is one of the key directions the future must take—toward partnership. Not human versus machine, but human *with* machine. When used wisely, AI becomes an amplifier of human strengths, not a competitor to them. It becomes a tool that supports the learner's agency, not one that dictates it. This vision requires designing systems that are not only intelligent but respectful. Systems that explain their logic, invite collaboration, and allow for disagreement. Because true learning is dialogic—it thrives in environments where questions are welcomed, uncertainty is embraced, and learners are not passive recipients but active co-creators.

Figure 3. Time Allocation Shift with Adaptive Platforms

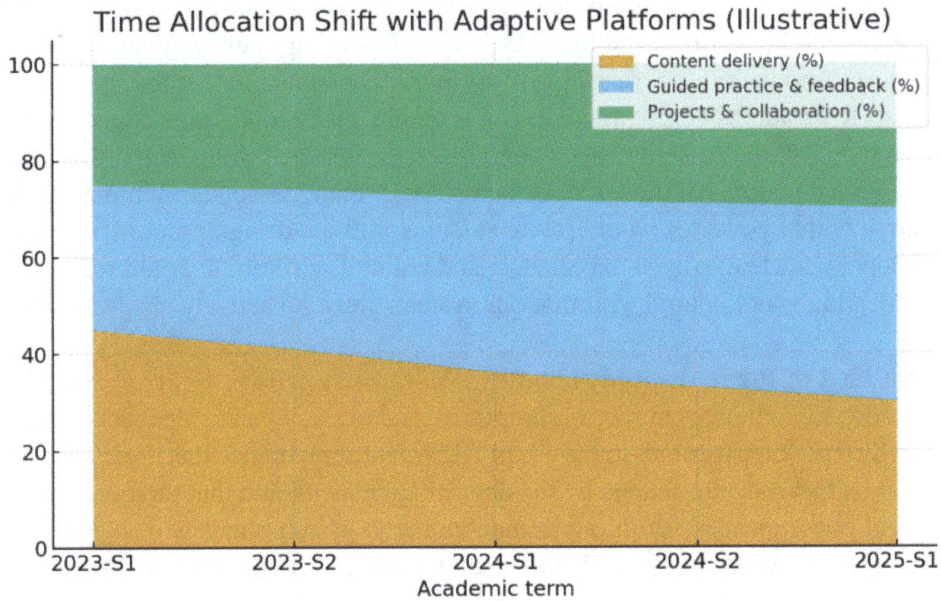

Another important direction involves moving beyond standardization (Brøgger et al, 2019). For too long, education has been built around the assumption that all learners should move at the same pace, in the same way, toward the same goals. But real human learning is unpredictable. It spikes and stalls, doubles back and leaps ahead. It is shaped by life outside the classroom—by loss and love, by economic pressure, by cultural identity, by mental health. A truly human-centered system would recognize and honor this variability. It would allow learners to set goals that matter to them, to define success in ways that align with their passions and contexts. To do this well, we must design for inclusion from the start. We must acknowledge that not all learners enter with the same resources, supports, or opportunities. If adaptive systems are truly to serve every learner, they must be built with those on the margins in mind. That means addressing not only physical accessibility, but also linguistic, cultural, and socio-emotional dimensions of inclusion. It means listening to students who have been silenced or sidelined, and building platforms that reflect the full spectrum of human experience.

There is also a need to reimagine assessment. If the future of learning is about growth, creativity, and critical thinking, then our assessments must evolve accordingly. Traditional tests capture a snapshot of what a learner can recall under pressure, but they miss the nuance of how a learner reasons, collaborates, or reflects. Technology gives us the tools to build richer, more authentic assessments—portfolios, simulations, collaborative projects—that can be integrated into the learning process itself (Yadav, 2024). But even more important than how we assess is *why*. Are we assessing to rank, to sort, to exclude? Or are we assessing to understand, to guide, to support? And here lies perhaps the most important challenge: rethinking power. Who gets to decide what is learned, how it is taught, and whose knowledge counts? For too long, these decisions have been made by a narrow group, often detached from the lived realities of the learners themselves. A human-centered future would decentralize that power. It would invite students into the design process. It would honor local knowledge, lived experience, and cultural wisdom. It would recognize that education is not neutral, and that our systems must be actively shaped toward justice.

That kind of future demands humility. We must be willing to admit what we don't know, to challenge our own assumptions, and to stay open to feedback. This is especially true when it comes to the use of AI. We must recognize that these systems are fallible, that they are shaped by the data we give them, and that their errors can have real consequences. Building human-centered systems means designing for accountability (Akhtar et al, 2024). It means putting in place safeguards, review mechanisms, and feedback loops. It means holding space for dissent and disruption. It also means slowing down. The pace of innovation is seductive, but speed is not always synonymous with progress. Some of the most important transformations in education happen quietly, over time—in the relationships that are built, in the identities that are affirmed, in the questions that are asked again and again. A human-centered approach honors that slowness. It allows space for reflection, for nuance, for complexity.

And perhaps, above all, it centers hope. Not a blind hope that everything will work out, but a grounded hope that emerges from care, from community, from a belief that learning is worth doing and that every learner has something to offer. This is not a naive vision. It is a moral one. It insists that education is not just a means to an end, but an end in itself—a space where we learn not only facts, but ways of being in the world. A space where we practice Empathy, exercise judgment, wrestle with ideas, and build the kind of future we want to live in (Maibom, 2022). So what does a truly human-centered learning system look like? It looks like a classroom where every voice is heard. A platform that adapts not just to test scores but to life context. An assessment that values reflection as much as recall. A teacher who feels supported rather than replaced. A student who feels not watched, but witnessed. It looks like joy and struggle, curiosity and care, messiness and meaning. It seems, in other words, like life. We are not there yet. But we are not far. The tools are here. The knowledge is here. What remains is the will—the collective will to build systems that serve not just efficiency or innovation, but humanity itself. That is the direction worth walking in. Slowly, thoughtfully, together.

CONCLUSION

As we stand on the threshold of an AI-enhanced educational future, we must pause and ask ourselves some fundamental questions: What is the purpose of education? Who do we design it for? And what kind of society are we shaping through the way we teach and learn?

Throughout this chapter, we have seen how AI, especially large language models and intelligent agents, has the potential to transform learning from a static, uniform process into a living, responsive, and personalized experience. Adaptive learning platforms can do more than deliver content; they can listen, guide, challenge, and even empathize—simulating, in some cases, the qualities of an attentive educator. They can support learners who have been historically marginalized, scaffold growth for students at all levels, and offer just-in-time interventions that respond to needs no traditional system could feasibly address. But this future is not guaranteed. The very same technologies that promise equity and empowerment can also perpetuate inequality and exclusion if deployed without care. Adaptive systems may amplify biases encoded in their data or misinterpret the intentions and emotions of learners. They may lead to over-monitoring, reduce the role of teachers, or prioritize efficiency over meaningful engagement. The question, then, is not simply whether we can build intelligent learning systems—but whether we can create them responsibly.

This requires a collective shift in how we approach educational technology. It means involving educators, learners, ethicists, technologists, and communities in the design process. It means embedding transparency and accountability into the core of every AI-driven platform. And it means resisting the temptation to see technology as a replacement for human presence, judgment, or care. Most importantly, we must remember that personalization is not an end in itself. An adaptive system that merely optimizes for performance metrics without fostering curiosity, creativity, or critical thinking is ultimately failing the learner. True personalization is not about data-driven customization alone; it is about empowering individuals to understand themselves as learners and to grow in ways that are both meaningful and sustainable. In this sense, AI becomes not the center of education but a partner—an enabler of deeper learning, greater access, and more equitable outcomes. When thoughtfully integrated, adaptive learning platforms have the power to help us move beyond the limitations of the industrial-era classroom and toward a more fluid, inclusive, and human-centered model of education. The future of learning will not be written by algorithms alone. It will be co-authored by the values we bring to the table, the decisions we make today, and the courage we have to imagine a better, more just educational world. In this vision, AI is not the solution, but a tool—one that, used wisely, can help every learner find their voice, their path, and their potential.

REFERENCES

Akhtar, M. A. K., Kumar, M., & Nayyar, A. (2024). The Role of Human-Centered Design in Developing Explainable AI. In *Towards Ethical and Socially Responsible Explainable AI: Challenges and Opportunities* (pp. 99–126). Springer Nature Switzerland.

Al-Chaer, E. D. (2024). Intelligence Amplified: Exploring the Future of Higher Education in the AI Age. In *Higher Education in the Arab World: Digital Transformation* (pp. 13–35). Springer Nature Switzerland.

Aldoseri, A., Al-Khalifa, K. N., & Hamouda, A. M. (2024). AI-powered innovation in digital transformation: Key pillars and industry impact. *Sustainability*, *16*(5), 1790.

Arievitch, I. M. (2020). Reprint of: The vision of Developmental Teaching and Learning and Bloom's Taxonomy of educational objectives. *Learning, Culture and Social Interaction*, *27*, 100473.

Baškarada, S., Watson, J., & Cromarty, J. (2017). Balancing transactional and transformational leadership. *The International Journal of Organizational Analysis*, *25*(3), 506–515.

Bates, B. (2023). Learning theories simplified:... and how to apply them to teaching.

Bernacki, M. L., Greene, M. J., & Lobczowski, N. G. (2021). A systematic review of research on personalized learning: Personalized by whom, to what, how, and for what purpose (s)? *Educational Psychology Review*, *33*(4), 1675–1715.

Bowen, J. A., & Watson, C. E. (2024). *Teaching with AI: A practical guide to a new era of human learning*. JHU Press.

Brass, J., & Lynch, T. L. (2020). Personalized learning: A history of the present. *Journal of Curriculum Theorizing*, *35*(2).

Brøgger, K., Brøgger, K., & Janssen. (2019). Governing through standards: The faceless masters of higher education. Germany: Springer International Publishing.

Buckley, W. (2017). Society as a complex adaptive system. In *Systems research for behavioral science* (pp. 490–513). Routledge.

Cairney, T. H. (2018). *Pedagogy and Education for Life: A Christian reframing of teaching, learning, and formation*. Wipf and Stock Publishers.

Dong, J. J., Hwang, W. Y., Shadiev, R., & Chen, G. Y. (2017). Pausing the classroom lecture: The use of clickers to facilitate student engagement. *Active Learning in Higher Education*, *18*(2), 157–172.

Hadi, M. U., Qureshi, R., Shah, A., Irfan, M., Zafar, A., Shaikh, M. B., & Mirjalili, S. (2023). A survey on large language models: Applications, challenges, limitations, and practical usage. *Authorea Preprints*, 3.

Hassannejad, N. (2024). Pedagogical relations: Towards a synthesis of Dewey's child-centered education and Arendt's traditional education.

Huang, S. Y., Huang, C. H., & Chang, T. W. (2022). A new concept of work engagement theory in cognitive engagement, emotional engagement, and physical engagement. *Frontiers in Psychology*, *12*, 663440. PMID: 35242067

Jain, A. (2024). Ethical AI: A Policy Framework to Regulate Bias in Large Language Models (Doctoral dissertation).

Kayyali, M. (2021). Positive impact of high technology on higher education.

Kayyali, M. (2022). Addressing Academic Freedom Challenges in Higher Education. *International Journal of Innovation and Entrepreneurship*, *1*(1), 1–3.

Kayyali, M. (2022). Equity, Equality, Diversity, and Inclusion as Key Performance Indicators in Higher Education. *Online Submission*, *3*(5), 1–3.

Kayyali, M. (2024). A). Future possibilities and challenges of AI in education. In *Transforming education with generative AI: Prompt engineering and synthetic content creation* (pp. 118–137). IGI Global Scientific Publishing.

Kayyali, M. (2024 B). Global Perspectives on Personalized Learning: Case Studies and Best Practices. In Transforming Education for Personalized Learning (pp. 66-84). IGI Global.

Kayyali, M. (2024). D). Design thinking and creativity in entrepreneurial innovation. In *Applying Business Intelligence and Innovation to Entrepreneurship* (pp. 155–170). IGI Global.

Kayyali, M. (Ed.). (2024 C). Building Resiliency in Higher Education: Globalization, Digital Skills, and Student Wellness: Globalization, Digital Skills, and Student Wellness. IGI Global.

Kayyali, M. (2025). A). The Impact of Personalized Learning on Student Engagement and Achievement in STEAM. In *Integrating Personalized Learning Methods Into STEAM Education* (pp. 51–78). IGI Global Scientific Publishing.

Kayyali, M. (2025 B). AI in Higher Education: Revolutionizing Curriculum and Administration. In AI Adoption and Diffusion in Education (pp. 31-62). IGI Global Scientific Publishing.

Kem, D. (2022). Personalised and adaptive learning: Emerging learning platforms in the era of digital and smart learning. *International Journal of Social Science and Human Research*, *5*(2), 385–391.

Khosravi, H., Sadiq, S., & Gasevic, D. (2020, February). Development and adoption of an adaptive learning system: Reflections and lessons learned. In *Proceedings of the 51st ACM technical symposium on computer science education* (pp. 58-64).

Kwon, D., Weiss, E., Kulshrestha, T., Chawla, K., Lucas, G. M., & Gratch, J. (2024). Are llms effective negotiators? systematic evaluation of the multifaceted capabilities of llms in negotiation dialogues. arXiv preprint arXiv:2402.13550.

Li, L., Ismail, S. M., Patra, I., & Lami, D. (2024). Not a passive learner but an active one: A focus on the efficacy of philosophy-based language instruction and its consequences on EFL learners' critical thinking, engagement, and academic achievement. *BMC Psychology*, *12*(1), 148. PMID: 38486343

Lockhart, E. N. (2024). Creativity in the age of AI: The human condition and the limits of machine generation. *Journal of Cultural Cognitive Science*, •••, 1–6.

Lohmann, M. J., Hovey, K. A., & Gauvreau, A. N. (2018). Using a Universal Design for Learning Framework to Enhance Engagement in the Early Childhood Classroom. *The Journal of Special Education Apprenticeship*, *7*(2), n2.

Luckin, R. (2025). Nurturing human intelligence in the age of AI: Rethinking education for the future. *Development and Learning in Organizations*, *39*(1), 1–4.

Ludovico, A. (2024). *Tactical publishing: Using senses, software, and archives in the twenty-first century*. MIT Press.

Maibom, H. L. (2022). *The space between: How Empathy really works*. Oxford University Press.

McTear, M., & Ashurkina, M. (2024). *Transforming conversational AI: Exploring the power of large language models in interactive conversational agents*. Springer Nature.

Mevold, C. A. (2023). FROM BIASES TO BRILLIANCE An Interpretative phenomenological analysis of the connection between leadership experience and decision-making style to explore the influence of cognitive biases on decision-making and leadership potential (Master's thesis, NTNU).

Mistretta, S. (Ed.). (2024). *Reimagining Education: The Role of E-Learning, Creativity, and Technology in the Post-Pandemic Era*. BoD–Books on Demand.

Pirjan, A., & Petroşanu, D. M. (2024). EXPLORING LARGE LANGUAGE MODELS IN THE EDUCATION PROCESS WITH A VIEW TOWARDS TRANSFORMING PERSONALIZED LEARNING. *Journal of Information Systems & Operations Management, 18*(2).

Porges, S. W. (2022). Polyvagal theory: A science of safety. *Frontiers in Integrative Neuroscience, 16*, 871227. PMID: 35645742

Ramos, G., Meek, C., Simard, P., Suh, J., & Ghorashi, S. (2020). Interactive machine teaching: A human-centered approach to building machine-learned models. *Human-Computer Interaction, 35*(5-6), 413–451.

Sadovnik, A. R., Semel, S. F., Coughlan, R. W., Kanze, B., & Tyner-Mullings, A. R. (2017). Progressive education in the 21st century: The enduring influence of John Dewey. *The Journal of the Gilded Age and Progressive Era, 16*(4), 515–530.

Sharma, S. (2024). Enhancing Inclusive Learning Environments: Strategies for Curriculum Adaptation and Modification. Future of Special Education in India, 109.

Solloway, A. J. (2017). *English-medium instruction in higher education in the United Arab Emirates: The perspectives of students*. University of Exeter.

Sorin, V., Brin, D., Barash, Y., Konen, E., Charney, A., Nadkarni, G., & Klang, E. (2024). Large Language Models and Empathy: Systematic Review. *Journal of Medical Internet Research, 26*, e52597. PMID: 39661968

Ueland, J. S., Hinds, T. L., & Floyd, N. D. (2021). Equity at the edge of chaos: Applying complex adaptive systems theory to higher education. *New Directions for Institutional Research, 2021*(189-192), 121–138.

Yadav, S. (2024). Designing Effective E-Portfolios for Authentic Assessment: Encouraging Reflection and Promoting Student Ownership. In Cases on Authentic Assessment in Higher Education (pp. 235-258). IGI Global.

KEYWORDS AND DEFINITIONS

Adaptive Learning Platform: an AI-enabled system that adjusts pacing, content difficulty, and feedback in real time based on learner data.

Personalization Levers: the tunable dimensions (sequence, difficulty, modality, assessment, feedback, nudges) that shape an individual's path.

Mastery Progression: cumulative evidence that a learner can apply knowledge/skills, tracked across tasks and time.

Human-in-the-Loop: educators retain oversight and can override, explain, or redirect AI recommendations.

Transparency & Agency: showing learners why a task is recommended and letting them set goals or adjust the path.

Ethical Safeguards: privacy, bias mitigation, consent, and accountable data use embedded in platform design.

Engagement Signals: telemetry (dwell, retries, hint use) used to adapt supports without replacing human judgment.

Chapter 5
AI-Driven Biometric Systems Using Facial Recognition and Fingerprint Analysis for Next Generation Identity Management

Anant Wairagade
https://orcid.org/0009-0006-3884-7903
Independent Researcher, USA

Rishabh Das
https://orcid.org/0000-0003-0649-6898
Ohio University, USA

ABSTRACT

Biometric authentication has emerged as a cornerstone of modern identity verification, offering unparalleled security and convenience compared to traditional password-based systems. With advancements in artificial intelligence (AI), biometric systems—particularly those leveraging facial recognition and fingerprint analysis—have undergone transformative improvements in accuracy, scalability, and adaptability. AI-driven biometric systems represent a paradigm shift in identity authentication, offering robust security and seamless user experiences. However, their success hinges on addressing ethical dilemmas, ensuring regulatory compliance, and staying ahead of evolving threats. As technologies like decentralized identity and quantum encryption mature, the fusion of AI and biometrics will continue to

DOI: 10.4018/979-8-3373-2008-3.ch005

redefine the boundaries of digital security. This chapter explores the implementation of AI-driven biometric authentication systems, focusing on the technological foundations, real-world applications, challenges, and future directions of facial recognition and fingerprint analysis.

INTRODUCTION

Identity management has come a long way, changing from traditional password authentication to sophisticated biometric verification. While the earlier authentication systems depended on passwords and personal identification numbers PINs, their widespread use was not without pitfalls: they suffered password breaches, phishing attacks, and human error (Bonneau et al., 2015). The weaknesses of these methods prompted the introduction of two-factor authentication (2FA) and other knowledge-based approaches to bolster security; nevertheless, credential theft and social engineering attacks posed a continuing threat (Florêncio & Herley, 2019).

The reason for this transition to biometric authentication lies in the need for identity verification systems that are secure, user-friendly, and highly resilient to fraud. Biometrics take advantage of unique physiological and behavioral characteristics of the individuals involved: fingerprints, facial features, iris patterns, and voice, all of which make them extremely difficult to forge or steal (Jain et al., 2020). The first applications of biometric technology were linked to law enforcement and, primarily, fingerprint identification, which became digitized and automated since the late 20th century (Ratha et al., 2019). Today, however, advancements in artificial intelligence (AI) and deep learning have propelled biometric systems into the limelight of mainstream applications, from smartphone authentication to border security, financial transactions, and healthcare verifications (Zhao & Kumar, 2022).

The fast-track digitization of personal data and escalating cybersecurity threats prompt organizations and governments to adopt biometric-based identity management systems due to enhanced security and user experience, which eliminate the need for complicated passwords and minimize fraud and identity theft risks. As biometrics sharpen, multi-modal biometric systems combine facial recognition, fingerprint analysis, and other biometric traits, fast becoming the gold standard for identity authentication (Jain & Nandakumar, 2021).

The Role of AI in Modern Biometrics: Enhancing Accuracy, Speed, and Scalability

Artificial intelligence (AI) has spurred a revolution in the biometric systems pertaining to identity verification since it has revolutionized accuracy, efficiency, and scalability. When we look back at the traditional biometric systems, they mainly relied on handcrafted feature extraction techniques and had to overcome variability in light conditions, facial expressions, and distortions in fingerprints (Deng et al., 2019). AI has brought in two major innovations: Deep learning models, such as convolutional neural networks (CNN), automating the feature extraction and pattern recognition processes and hence can be adopted by biometric systems that can address real-world challenges (Sundararajan et al., 2021).

AI-powered biometrics are processing huge volumes of imagery and fingerprint data, which makes possible real-time identity verifications in applications such as border control, financial transactions, or law enforcement (Ratha et al., 2019). Neural networks coupled with machine learning algorithms also improved the accuracy of liveness detection techniques, which separate authentic biometric inputs from different spoofs (e.g. deepfake faces and fingerprint replicas) (Galbally et al., 2020).

Edge AI-enabled biometric authentication is now well within the capabilities of mobile and peer systems on the IoT. Reduced latency and cloud computing reliance against that particular form of the authentication system would greatly benefit an environment with high-security requirements demanding real-time verification. As AI evolves and advances, it will become more of an active force in biometric security, fraud detection, and identity verification by offering better-suited, robust, and highly accurate adaptive techniques in authentication.

Why Facial Recognition and Fingerprint Analysis? Ubiquity, Uniqueness, and Technological Maturity

Facial and fingerprint recognition are the most preferred biometric authentication techniques because of their high accuracy and uniqueness, as well as the proven technological maturity (Jain et al., 2020). Fingerprints have been in use for over a century and more recently introduced contemporary automated fingerprint identification systems (AFIS) that make fingerprint recognition a reliable and scalable solution in law enforcement and identity verification (Maltoni et al., 2022). On one hand, facial recognition emerged in the light of AI-empowered computer vision to provide speedy, contactless authentication in a wide spectrum of smartphones, surveillance systems, and public security applications (Zhao & Kumar, 2022).

One of the prime advantages of facial recognition technology is that it can be identified without touching a person, making it the ideal choice for purposes like airport security and distance-based authentication (Sundararajan et al., 2021). Fingerprint analysis remains so accurate that it is regarded as highly environmental resilient, thus making it a preferred technique for government ID programs and secure access control systems (Galbally et al., 2020).

As biometric technology advances, the incorporation of facial recognition and fingerprint analysis into multi-modal biometric systems increases their reliability in terms of security, reduces false positives, and minimizes the vulnerability of single-mode authentication (Jain & Nandakumar, 2021). Their widespread deployment in consumer electronics and security applications reflects their technological maturity as well as reliability.

Ethical and Societal Implications: A Balance Between Security and Privacy Innovation

On the one hand, while AI-driven biometric systems offer greater promises of security and convenience, they simultaneously present tremendous ethical and social issues regarding privacy, bias, and surveillance (Buolamwini & Gebru, 2018). One impending consideration, perhaps, is on the use of facial recognition for large-scale surveillance, which might infringe upon civil liberties and individual privacy rights (NIST, 2019). With the combination of countries and companies deploying biometric surveillance systems, the debate continues on whether it is necessary to enforce regulatory oversight and ethical AI frameworks (European Parliament, 2016).

Another major issue in AI-driven biometric systems is bias. Studies show that facial recognition algorithms suffer from racial and gender bias, making these algorithms very error-prone for certain under-represented demographic groups (Buolamwini & Gebru, 2018). Such biases can give rise to false positives and discriminatory outcomes, especially in law enforcement and hiring practices. Remedies for these can be found by developing fair AI models and transparency about algorithmic-based decision-making. Fairness in the above-mentioned dimensions should comply with data protection regulations such as the General Data Protection Regulation (GDPR) and California Consumer Privacy Act (CCPA) (California State Legislature, 2018).

Also, there are data security and storage questions over the biometric template that cast doubt on possible identity theft and data breaches. Privacy-preserving biometric techniques such as homomorphic encryption and federated learning can, however, reduce these risks while still providing users control over their biometric data (Shi et al., 2020).

Nevertheless, in bridging these gaps, responsible deployment of AI in biometrics will result in very significant societal benefits like fraud prevention, security access control, and identity protection. Reservation for the balance that will have to be struck between security, privacy, and innovation in the initial stages of the ethical advancement of AI-driven biometric systems will still have great implications for future societies.

1. FOUNDATIONS OF BIOMETRIC SYSTEMS

1.1 Understanding Biometric Systems.

Biometric systems represent the automated recognition technologies for identifying or verifying the identity of an individual based on one or more physiological or behavioral characteristics. Unlike traditional means of authentication, like passwords or PINs, biometrics are based on traits that are difficult to forge or replicate (Jain et al., 2020). The systems consist of three major components: a data acquisition module that collects the biometric data such as a fingerprint scan or an image of the face; a feature extraction module that transforms the raw data into a digital format while identifying the distinguishing characteristics; and a matching and decision module that matches the extracted features against a stored biometric data base to verify identity (Ratha et al., 2019).

Typically, the workflow of the biometric system includes enrollment, feature extraction, template storage, and authentication or verification. In enrollment, a user's biometric data is taken and stored in a secure database. In authentication, the newly captured data is compared with the stored template to mark either a match or a mismatch. AI algorithms in today's biometric systems are used to improve accuracy and learn variations in biometric traits such as facial aging or fingerprint wear and tear (Galbally et al., 2020).

1.2 Types of Biometrics: Physiological vs. Behavioral

Biometric systems can broadly be grouped into physiological biometrics and behavioral biometrics.

Physiological biometrics capitalize on physical traits that are more or less fixed. Examples of physiological biometrics include facial recognition, which depends on distinctive facial renderings like the distance of the eyes or jaw structure, fingerprint recognition, which involves scrutinizing ridge and minutiae patterns unique to every individual, iris and retina scanning, where set readings are compared to complex patterns of the blood vessels of the eye or texture of the iris for high-security authentication, and hand geometry and palm vein, both of which can be used interchangeably in forensic and access control applications, respectively (Maltoni et al., 2022).

Behavioral biometrics focus on dynamic human behaviors, influenced by mood, health, and other environmental factors. Examples of trait biometrics include voice recognition, which is based on analysis of pitch, tone, and speech patterns; gait recognition, which involves interacting with the identification of individuals through walking style and posture; keystroke dynamics, which investigates typing speed, rhythm, and pressure solidarity for authentication; and signature analysis, which is another procedure to recognize handwriting styles and stroke patterns (Jain & Nandakumar, 2021).

Contrasting to physiological biometrics, which render higher accuracy and permanence, behavioral ones provide an added chance to provide continuous authentication, thereby making them suitable for situations requiring cybersecurity and/or fraud detection (Sundararajan et al., 2021).

1.3 Evolution of Biometrics: From Early Fingerprinting to AI Systems

However, the concept of biometrics dates back fabricated centuries, with the old practices in fingerprint analysis being recorded as early as ancient Babylon and China as forms of identity verification (Maltoni et al., 2022). In the late nineteenth centuries, the British scientist Sir Francis Galton gave a scientific classification of fingerprints, which was the beginning of modern forensic identification. This was followed in the early twentieth century when fingerprint databases were adopted in law enforcement, leading to the invention of Automated Fingerprint Identification Systems (AFIS) in the 1960s (Ratha et al., 2019).

Biometric authentication has today transformed the old functionalities of fingerprint technology into features including facial recognition, iris scanning, and forms of behavior biometrics with the rise of computer vision and AI. The first face recognition systems were launched during the 1990s, while the FBI also introduced the Integrated Automated Fingerprint Identification System (IAFIS) within that same time span (Jain et al., 2020).

They paved the way during the deep learning era in the 21st century to boost biometric precisions. Technologies expanded the possibilities of real-time facial recognition through convolutional neural networks, while edge AI made biometric identification of individuals possible on devices like smartphones and even the IoT (Shi et al., 2020). Today, AI-enhanced biometrics have been taken worldwide to national identity programs, financial services, border security, and consumer electronics, thus shaping modern identity management in the future.

1.4 Key Metrics: FAR, FRR, and EER

Three key metrics are used to evaluate the performance and reliability of biometric systems. The false acceptance ratio (far) gives the percentage of unauthorized persons falsely identified for access to the system. In other words, strong security is when far is low. The false rejection rate is the percentage of legitimate users who denied access because the system declared them false positives. Hence, a high fr has some usability issues. Its possible value for using the equal error rate (eer, which gives the point where far and fr are equal) is an important benchmark of system accuracy in general (Zhao & Kumar, 2022).

These are among the significant metrics in the analysis of a biometric system's performance, contributing a lot toward their application in highly sensitive areas such as banking, border control, and government identification programs (Galbally et al., 2020).

2. THE ROLE OF ARTIFICIAL INTELLIGENCE IN BIOMETRICS

2.1 Machine Learning Basics: Supervised vs. Unsupervised Learning

Machine learning plays an important role in biometric authentication which comes under supervised and unsupervised learning. In supervised learning, AI models are trained on labeled biometric data to learn a pattern and classify identities. There are various techniques that are commonly used in the supervised mode like support vector machines (SVM), k-nearest neighbors (k-NN), and decision trees (Sundararajan et al., 2021).

In contrast, unsupervised learning is about finding patterns in unlabeled data and is mostly useful in clustering biometric traits for anomaly detection and fraud prevention. Neural networks, principally deep learning models, further ensure accurate and robust biometrics (Shi et al., 2020).

2.2 Deep Learning for Biometrics: CNNs, Transformers, and Feature Extraction

Deep learning, especially CNN architectures such as ResNet, FaceNet, and VGGNet, have changed the face of facial and fingerprint recognition by automating feature extraction while boosting accuracy (Zhao & Kumar, 2022). Transformers, a novel deep learning model, are being researched for their potential uses in analyzing biometric sequences, such as in voice recognition and gait authentication (Deng et al., 2019).

2.3 AI-Driven Enhancements: Noise Reduction, Real-Time Processing, and Edge AI

AI improves biometrics by removing extraneous noise, correcting distortion, and adapting in real-time. An example is edge AI which entails conducting biometric authentication directly on the mobile device to cut down the amount of time taken to authenticate and reduce dependence on cloud servers (Shi et al., 2020).

2.4 Challenges & Limitations: Model Accuracy, Overfitting, Adversarial Attacks

With advancements come AI-disputed challenges such as model overfitting, adversarial attacks, and demographic bias. AI models may forfeit the security of systems that use synthetic fingerprint or deepfake facial image authentication (Galbally et al., 2020). Furthermore, biometric systems must develop some ensuring fairness and accuracy in systems across a wide variety of populations (Buolamwini & Gebru, 2018).

3. FACIAL RECOGNITION SYSTEMS

3.1 How Facial Recognition Works

Facial recognition systems are methods of identifying or verifying individuals by their face through a comparison of facial features extracted from digitized images or video frames. It involves three main stages: image acquisition, feature extraction, and matching.

In the first stage, image acquisition, the system captures a facial image through the use of cameras or sensors, ensuring the image captures clarity and good lighting to allow effective recognition. The second step is called feature extraction, where key facial landmarks such as eye distance, nose shape, jawline structure, and skin texture are detected. AI-based feature extraction improves accuracy by realizing patterns unique to every individual (Zhao & Kumar, 2022).

Matching is the last step and is defined as the component that connects extracted features to stored biometric templates in the database. In this process, similarity scores are mathematically computed and such results are used to determine whether this person authenticated or not. Furthermore, advanced deep learning models such as convolutional neural networks (CNN) improve on this stage by precision and minimizing false positive access (Jain et al., 2020).

3.2 AI Techniques in Facial Recognition

Artificial intelligence, particularly the deep learning variety, has done a lot more to advance face recognition regarding extraction of features and accuracy improvement. CNN architectures such as ResNet, FaceNet, and VGGNet process facial images iteratively across multiple layers, so detailed patterns can be extracted.

ResNet (Residual Network) connects networks with skip connections hence allowing deeper networks to be trained, thus solving the vanishing gradient issue. FaceNet is a product of Google that maps facial features in a high-dimensional space, so distances between similar faces are minimized, making identity verification an extremely effective practice (Sundararajan et al., 2021).

Incorporating depth perception makes 3D facial recognition more accurate. It enables systems to tell flat images apart from real human faces. It does not have the same challenges light changes, facial expressions, and head pose changes throw at two-dimensional recognition (Shi et al., 2020).

AI-driven anti-spoofing techniques have liveness detection algorithms to counter face spoofing attacks using photographs, videos, or masks. Such algorithms study micro-movements like blinking, pupil dilation, and skin texture changes to tell apart a real user from an imitation (Galbally et al., 2020). The comparison of various approaches in facial recognition by different AI techniques is made in Table 1.

Table 1. Comparison of AI Techniques for Facial Recognition

AI Model	Key Features	Strengths	Weaknesses
ResNet	Deep feature extraction via residual learning	High accuracy, efficient training	Computation-intensive
FaceNet	Embedding for verification of facial images	Excellent for face clustering	Need massive datasets
3D Recognition	Depth of field with viewing angles	Robust against pose and illumination variations	Use of specialized hardware
Anti-Spoofing AI	Detects liveness by detecting blinking	Prevents deep fake and mask attacks	May have additional processing time

3.3 Challenges in Facial Recognition

Despite certain advancements, several challenges continue to be faced in facial recognition systems. Pose variation occurs when the individual's face is away from a direct view of the camera, thus leading to lower accuracies in recognition. AI models adjust for this through pose-invariant algorithms but continue to yield considerably less performance regarding recognition in extreme cases (Ratha et al., 2019).

Lighting conditions grossly influence feature extraction. Poor illumination can cause loss in detail when too much brightness can cause reflections to cover essential facial features. Concerning AI-based illumination normalization techniques that alleviate these effects, they continue to experience inconsistencies in practice (Buolamwini & Gebru, 2018).

A demographically bias is another critical issue. Studies show that some facial recognition models return high error rates for underrepresented racial or gender groups. This ethical issue has pushed researchers to propose models that are aware of these biases and promote fairness in AI training datasets (NIST, 2019).

3.4 Case Study: An Example of Facial Recognition in Border Control

The conception of facial recognition, in border control, has brought automatic verification of identity at airports and different checkpoints. US, UK, and China are among those who have adopted AI-backed facial recognition gates whose function is to match passengers against photographs stored in immigration databases (Jain & Nandakumar, 2021).

An example worth mentioning is the Smart Gate system in Australia, allowing travelers to pass immigration checks through face scans rather than through physical means. We can say that this technology has decreased processing time, minimized human interference, and optimized border security. However, concerns about data privacy, mass surveillance, and misuse warrants several active discussions (European Parliament, 2016).

4. FINGERPRINT ANALYSIS

4.1 Fingerprint Recognition Fundamentals

Fingerprint recognition is one of the oldest and, at the same time, most reliable methods of biometric authentication. It identifies individuals based on the unique ridge patterns and minutiae points on the human fingertips.

The process starts with image acquisition; the fingerprint scanner captures a high-resolution picture of the finger's surface. Then, feature extraction identifies particular features such as bifurcations, ridge endings, and whorls. Lastly, a matching algorithm compares the extracted features with templates stored in the database to ascertain identity (Maltoni et al., 2022).

4.2 AI-Driven Innovations for Fingerprint Recognition

The traditional method involved rule-based feature extraction, which readily failed on partial or distorted prints. AI has changed the paradigm and has aided the development of automated systems called AFIS for fingerprint identification using deep learning to refine accuracy with a greater level of sophistication of learning fingerprint patterns (Shi et al., 2020).

Among the recent advancements made are the generative adversarial networks (GANs) that complete missing parts of a fingerprint to identify information from partial samples. This has advanced forensic applications and national identity programs tremendously (Galbally et al., 2020).

4.3 Liveness Detection: Preventing Spoofing With AI

Liveness detection is an important tool in preventing fingerprint spoofing attacks using artificial silicone or printed fingerprints. Solutions based on AI measure different signs like sweat duct patterns, skin elasticity, and temperature variation, to distinguish between real and fake fingerprints. Multi-spectral imaging techniques lend additional security by penetrating sub-dermal layers of a fingerprint (Jain et al., 2020).

4.4 Case Study: The Place of Fingerprints in National ID Programs

Fingerprint identification performs critical functions within identity programs promoted by governments across various corners of the world. One of the most distinguished implementations is the Aadhaar system of India, the world's largest biometric database, in which fingerprints and iris scans are linked to citizen records for the purposes of social welfare (Ratha et al., 2019).

Another such example is the FBI's Integrated Automated Fingerprint Identification System (IAFIS), which acts on millions of fingerprint records for purposes of criminal investigation. These systems have, thus, led to enhanced operational efficiency and curbing of fraudulent practices across borders and national security; however, this has left data privacy and decentralization risks being the core items for discussions (California State Legislature, 2018).

5. INTEGRATION AND OPTIMIZATION

5.1 Multi-Modal Biometric Systems

Multi-modal biometric systems combine different biometric modalities to offer better accuracy, security, and redundancy. Facial recognition and fingerprinting are two widely established means since they are unique and technologically mature biometric methods. Alone each biometric modality exhibits limitations: When it comes to facial recognition the limitations can arise from variations in pose, illumination, or occlusion, whereas in the case of fingerprint recognition the limitations could surface due to skin wear of fingerprints, cuts to the skin, or possible sensor malfunctioning (Jain & Nandakumar, 2021).

The integration of both modalities, in fact, enhances the reliability of the multimodal system by further decreasing the false acceptance rate (FAR) and false rejection rate (FRR). In a high-security environment, for example, government border control and financial transactions, the second level of protection against spoofing and identity fraud would be offered by multi-modal biometrics. Multi-modal systems would also improve user-friendliness by allowing a backup biometric modality when one fails (Maltoni et al., 2022).

5.2 Fusion Techniques in Multi-Modal Biometrics

Multi-modal biometric integration can be carried out at various levels, generally called fusion techniques.

Feature-level fusion combines extracted biometric features before classification. This is often a computationally intensive method, but it provides maximum accuracy, being the only method that combines raw data from both modalities (Ratha et al., 2019).

Score-level fusion combines individual matching scores from different biometric systems. From these scores, a combined decision is made based on a threshold, balancing similarity of match accuracy and processing efficiency (Sundararajan et al., 2021).

Decision-level fusion is an aggregation method independent, for the most part, of biometric systems. It is the simplest of all integration methods since access is granted only when both modalities confirm identity. Although computationally benign, such approaches may not exhibit the degree of flexibility found in feature-level fusion (Shi et al., 2020). A comparison between these fusion techniques is shown in table 2.

Table 2. Comparison of Fusion Techniques in Multi-Modal Biometrics

Fusion Techniques	Description	Accuracy	Computational Cost
Feature-level Fusion	Combine raw biometrics prior to classification.	High	High
Score-level Fusion	Combine confidence scores from different modalities.	Moderate	Moderate
Decision-level Fusion	Final decision is based on separate authentication results.	Low	Low

5.3 AI-Driven Fusion Models

These AI multi-modal biometric systems include deep learning to increase fusion efficiency. The ability to incorporate spatial and temporal biometric features and realize their importance in the real world is seen in CNN-LSTM hybrid architectures (Deng et al., 2019).

Some of the novel architectures that have integrated transformers and attention mechanisms in the multi-modal fusion network include adaptive weighting of biometric modalities depending on environments where the system focuses on the most relevant biometric trait for the moment (Shi et al., 2020).

AI-powered fusion models work best in advanced applications around security, such as border, e-passport, or banking authentication systems, and offer adaptable real-time performance.

5.4 Case Study: A Government-Backed Identity Management System.

This is perhaps the most well-known instance of multimodal biometrics: India's Aadhaar scheme, which uses fingerprint, iris, and facial recognition to permit citizens to access government services. Since its inception, the Aadhaar program has enrolled more than 1.3 billion individuals and is currently the largest biometric database in the world (Jain et al., 2020).

Meanwhile, it brings improvements in financial inclusion, makes fraud more difficult to commit, and enhances public welfare distribution. There have been thoughts towards developing a blockchain-based identity verification system as a means of improving security due to data privacy and security breaches that the system purportedly carries.

6. SCALING AND SECURITY

6.1 Cloud-Based Biometric Systems

Cloud has made biometric authentication scalable and provided AI-oriented solutions for biometrics. Biometric identity verification due to cloud access no longer requires on-premises hardware (Maltoni et al., 2022).

High volume, real-time, and remote access are some of the advantages of cloud-based biometrics. However, compliance and lack of fidelity are some of the drawbacks such as network latency and data breaches and dependency on third-party providers, which do warrant the use of encryption and zero trust security architecture (Shi et al., 2020).

6.2 Blockchain Integration for Securing Biometric Templates

Blockchain technology increases the security of biometrics by eliminating centralized data stores and thereby reducing the chance of unauthorized tampering. Instead of conventional data storage of biometric data, the biometric templates are hashed and stored on a decentralized blockchain ledger (Galbally et al. 2020).

The advantages of blockchain-based biometrics are tamper-proofing identity validation, better transparency, and removing single-point failures. Smart contracts enforce automated authentication procedures that also adhere to privacy regulations like GDPR (European Parliament, 2016).

6.3 Adversarial Attacks and Countermeasures

Adversarial attacks target AI-based biometric systems where the user subtly manipulates biometric data, thereby fooling neural networks into misclassifying it. Deep fake technology in particular is a major threat used to generate synthetic facial images that could spoof any traditional face recognition system (Ratha et al. 2019).

Synthetic fingerprint attacks involve 3D fingerprint replicas which can bypass traditional fingerprint scanners. In order to mitigate these attacks, the researchers are developing GAN-based interim solutions such as anomaly detection, adversarial training, and multi-file matching mechanisms (Sundararajan et al. 2021). Adversarial attack types with countermeasures are summarized in Table 3.

Table 3. Common Adversarial Attacks and AI Countermeasures

Attack Type	Description	AI-Based Countermeasure
Deepfake Spoofing	AI-generated face images used to bypass authentication	Liveness detection, deepfake detection networks
Synthetic Fingerprint	3D-printed replicas used to mimic real fingerprints	AI-enhanced liveness detection, multi-spectral imaging
Adversarial Perturbation	Tiny modifications to biometric images that deceive recognition models	Adversarial training, anomaly detection

6.4 Future-Proofing Security Measures

To deal with evolving threats, biometric security needs to rely on AI models that continuously learn and adapt to new attack patterns over time. Quantum-safe encryption methods will become vital in ensuring biometric data security during the post-quantum age (Shi et al., 2020).

Future-proof biometric systems will make use of homomorphic encryption, federated learning, and zero-knowledge proofs, thus allowing secure biometric authentication without disclosing raw data. This will provide a roadmap toward privacy-preserving AI-enabled biometric authentication (Jain and Nandakumar, 2021).

7. ETHICAL, LEGAL, AND PRACTICAL CONSIDERATIONS

7.1 Privacy and Regulatory Challenges

The rise in ai-powered biometric systems raises a host of privacy concerns, which provokes states and regulators to enforce exclusive data protection laws. The two most important privacy frameworks on the collection and use of biometric data are the General Data Protection Regulation (GDPR) in the European Union and the California Consumer Privacy Act (CCPA) in the United States (European Parliament, 2016; California State Legislature, 2018).

Under GDPR, biometric data is treated as a special category of personal data that requires explicit consent from the individual before collection and processing. It prescribes transparency, data minimization, and the right to erasure, allowing individuals to seek for their biometric data to be erased (European Parliament, 2016). Failure to comply, as evinced in different companies not disclosing biometric data usage, will entail hefty fines.

Similarly, under the CCPA, consumers have the rights to know, delete, and opt out of the biometric data collection. Organizations that apply facial recognition or fingerprint authentication must have adequate security measures and comply with state and federal privacy laws (California State Legislature, 2018).

Besides GDPR and CCPA, other sector regulations apply to biometric authentication in health care, banking, and law enforcement. The Health Insurance Portability and Accountability Act (HIPAA) regulates biometric patient data in health care, while biometric Know Your Customer (KYC) under the Bank Secrecy Act (BSA) is compulsory for financial institutions (Maltoni et al., 2022).

7.2 Ethical AI Design: Mitigating Bias and Ensuring Transparency

Critics of AI-driven biometric systems are concerned about algorithmic bias, especially in facial recognition. Studies reveal that certain facial recognition models have high error rates for individuals with darker skin tones and for less represented demographics, raising issues of discrimination with respect to law enforcement and hiring practices (Buolamwini & Gebru, 2018).

To reduce such bias, researchers recommend training datasets to be representative and diverse, use fair aware AI models, and audit bias on a routine basis. Algorithmic transparency through explainable AI (XAI) techniques is also good for enhancing public trust (Sundararajan et al., 2021). Table 4 presents a comparative summary of different bias mitigation strategies.

Table 4. Bias Mitigation Strategies in AI Biometrics

Bias Mitigation Strategy	Description	Effectiveness
Diverse Training Data	Train AI models on balanced datasets across demographics	High
Fairness Audits	Regularly assessing biometric models for bias	Moderate
Explainable AI (XAI)	Interpretable decision making by AI	Moderate
Bias-Aware Algorithms	AI models change decision thresholds for fairness	High

7.3 Informed Consent and User Rights

One of the serious ethical issues is the lack of informed consent regarding the collection of biometric data. Several users passively provide the biometric sample unknowingly through different modes such as public surveillance cameras, social media—for example, through face-tagging—or workplace attendance systems (Jain et al., 2020).

The organizations concerned are also required to put in place clearly articulated consent policies whereby people will be able to opt-in or opt-out of biometric authentication. Regulatory agencies are calling for mechanisms for user control, such as access, modification, or deletion of biometric records (European Parliament, 2016).

8. REAL WORLD APPLICATIONS

8.1 Government and Law Enforcement: Passports and Crime Prevention

Facial recognition and fingerprint authentication are often widely used in government identity programs and passports as well as law enforcement. Biometric authentication in e-passports is used by many countries to reduce extensive passport fraud, as well as speeding up border control (Maltoni et al., 2022).

The Integrated Automated Fingerprint Identification System (IAFIS) developed by the FBI is one of the examples of the biometric databases utilized under this branch of practice. Legal battle over mass surveillance and violation of privacy has made some of the areas put moratorium on public facial recognitions (California State Legislature, 2018).

8.2 Healthcare: Patient Identification and Access Control

Another positive advantage of biometric authentication is that patients are identified in hospitals, thus minimizing medical fraud and ensuring proper medical records. Added to these hard measures, voice recognition and iris scans from AIs are now being incorporated into patients accessing their medical information (Shi et al., 2020).

Healthcare institutions are obliged to HIPAA compliance at which time they prepare biometric health records, as encrypted and anonymized sources, to protect privacy of the patients (Maltoni et al., 2022).

8.3 Finance: AI-Driven Know Your Customer (KYC) Processes

AI-focused biometric authentication is also being used by financial institutions in fraud prevention and identity verification. Banks are using facial recognition and fingerprints authentication into mobile banking applications to cut off passwords (Ratha et al., 2019).

AI-based KYC verification helps detect fraud in transactions and prevents identity theft, apart from being compliant with anti-money laundering (AML) regulations (Sundararajan et al., 2021).

8.4 Retail and Smart Devices: Personalized Customer Experience

The retailers have introduced shopping experiences through facial recognition, where they identify frequent customers and make recommendations to personalized products. In addition, smart home devices such as Amazon Alexa and Apple Face ID are using AI-based biometrics to authenticate users securely (Jain & Nandakumar, 2021).

9. THE FUTURE OF AI-DRIVEN BIOMETRICS

9.1 Quantum Computing: Accelerating Biometric Matching

Quantum computing is likely going to transform their traditional current state of affairs relating to biometric authentication in the aspect of speed and accuracy in computations. Conventional biometric systems operate with classical encryption, which however proves secure; it becomes almost computationally heavy in time when processing vast databases of biometric information. Quantum computing here stands a chance for a breakthrough via parallel processing to biometric patterns, hence shortening the time otherwise spent for doing authentication (Chen et al., 2021).

Another big development in the field of biometric encryption is quantum key distribution (QKD), which guarantees biometric data storage and transmission against any tampering. QKD, unlike traditional encryption, strives to use quantum mechanics to generate unhackable cryptographic keys, thus providing security to biometric data (Wang et al., 2022).

9.2 Behavioral Biometrics: Combining Facial Recognition with Gait and Typing Patterns

Behavioral biometrics is increasingly viewed as a continuous authentication system combining facial recognition, gait analysis, typing dynamics, and voice authentication. This stands in sharp contrast to traditional biometric authentication that happens at a point in time, whereas behavioral biometrics involve constant monitoring of commuter behavior in real-time for identity verification (Jain & Nandakumar, 2021).

Gait recognition is analogous to recognizing individuals via their walking patterns. AI gait recognition systems analyze parameters such as step length, speed, and posture, making it an effective tool for non-intrusive surveillance and access control (Maltoni et al., 2022). Gait recognition systems likewise complement keystroke dynamics, which record the speed and rhythm of typing as a second layer of authentication in online banking and remote verification (Deng et al., 2019).

9.3. Decentralized Identity: Self-Sovereign Identity (SSI) Models

Decentralized identity models advanced as an alternative, focusing more on privacy as opposed to centralized biometric databases. Self-sovereign identities

(SSI) afford users the ability to control and manage their own biometric data without third-party identity provider involvement (Shi et al., 2020).

The role of the Blockchain technology is paramount in this endeavor within the SSI, as it provides a secure and decentralized environment to store biometric credentials. In contrast to traditional identity management systems where information is kept onto a centralized server, SSI distributes encrypted biometric identifiers onto a blockchain network thus minimizes the risk against data breach and unauthorized access (Galbally et al., 2020). A comparison between centralized and decentralized biometric identity systems is given in Table 5.

Table 5. Comparison of Centralized and Decentralized Biometric Identity Systems

Identity Models	Storage	Security Level	User Control
Centralized Identity	Stored in government or enterprise databases	Vulnerable to data breaches	Limited user control
Self-Sovereign Identity (SSI)	Stored on blockchain	High security, resistant to tampering	Full user control

10. A VISION FOR NEXT-GENERATION IDENTITY MANAGEMENT

10.1 Global Interoperability: Cross-Country Biometric Systems

The prospects of biometric authentication will require global interoperability to ensure that biometric systems can work across countries and industries in a frictionless manner. The International Civil Aviation Organization (ICAO) is among those actively working for the unification and standardization of biometric passports that may permit travelers to seamlessly cross the border with checking using facial and fingerprint recognition (Jain et al., 2020).

Interoperability is just as important in financial services, where biometric KYC should be accepted across the various banks and payment networks in the world. AI federated learning models can thus allow cross-border authentication with safeguarding data privacy and sovereignty (Shi et al., 2020).

10.2 AI Ethical Frameworks: Trust Through Responsible Innovations

Acceleration of AI-assisted biometric systems leads to an increased need for responsible AI frameworks that provide fairness, transparency, and accountability. AI ethical guidelines espouse:

- Bias mitigation: Periodic auditing for racial, gender, or age bias in biometric models (Buolamwini and Gebru, 2018).
- Transparency: Public access to the algorithm behind the biometric or AI models in order to garner acceptance by users and adherence to laws and regulations (Ratha et al., 2019).
- Data privacy: Strong encryption and data protection in line with privacy-preserving techniques such as random homomorphic encryption and differential privacy to ensure protection of biometric identity (Galbally et al., 2020).

10.3 Predictions for 2030+: The Convergence of Biometrics, AI, and IoT

- By 2030, AI-based biometrics and IoT would come together to enable non-intrusive, context-based authentication. Possible future applications include:
- Smart Cities: AI-based biometric surveillance for real-time threat detection and automated enforcement (Shi et al., 2020).
- Autonomous Vehicles: Authentication of drivers through iris scanning and voice recognition for secured entry into self-driving cars (Maltoni et al., 2022).
- Neural Biometrics: Authentication of identity through brainwaves using electroencephalograph (EEG)-based identity if ultra-secure methods of authentication exist (Deng et al., 2019).

CONCLUSION

Previously, AI and biometrics began to perish into a state where they became a means with a high value and utility on security alongside value addition to the everywhere pirated situation of fraud prevention in an identity management system.

One's view will be that multimodal-based biometric systems, blockchain-based identity management systems, and quantum-secured encryption will be the key factors that will shape future authentication solutions.

The concerning issues hinge on ethics, privacy, biases, and surveillance, thus demanding the formulation of responsible AI frameworks. Organizations and policymakers, therefore, need to work together to create the future of global biometric interoperability standards to make biometric authentication secure, fair, and with a focus on privacy.

REFERENCES

Bonneau, J., Herley, C., Van Oorschot, P. C., & Stajano, F. (2015). The quest to replace passwords: A framework for comparative evaluation of Web authentication schemes. *IEEE Symposium on Security and Privacy*, 553–567.

Buolamwini, J., & Gebru, T. (2018). Gender shades: Intersectional accuracy disparities in commercial gender classification. *Proceedings of Machine Learning Research*, *81*, 77–91.

California State Legislature. (2018). California Consumer Privacy Act (CCPA). https://leginfo.legislature.ca.gov/faces/billTextClient.xhtml?bill_id=201720180AB375

Chen, H., Zhang, L., & Wang, J. (2021). Quantum computing for biometric authentication: Challenges and opportunities. *IEEE Transactions on Information Forensics and Security*, *16*, 3120–3135.

Deng, J., Guo, J., & Zafeiriou, S. (2019). ArcFace: Additive angular margin loss for deep face recognition. *IEEE Transactions on Biometrics, Behavior, and Identity Science*, *42*(5), 1283–1295.

European Parliament. (2016). General Data Protection Regulation (GDPR). https://eur-lex.europa.eu/eli/reg/2016/679/oj

Florêncio, D., & Herley, C. (2019). A large-scale study of Web password habits. *Proceedings of the 16th International Conference on World Wide Web*, 657-666.

Galbally, J., Marcel, S., & Fierrez, J. (2020). Biometric antispoofing techniques: Challenges and solutions. *IEEE Transactions on Biometrics, Behavior, and Identity Science*, *2*(3), 168–180.

Jain, A. K., & Nandakumar, K. (2021). Multimodal biometrics: An overview. In *Handbook of Biometrics* (pp. 1–15). Springer.

Jain, A. K., Ross, A., & Nandakumar, K. (2020). *Introduction to biometrics*. Springer.

Maltoni, D., Maio, D., Jain, A. K., & Prabhakar, S. (2022). *Handbook of fingerprint recognition* (3rd ed.). Springer.

NIST. (2019). Face recognition vendor test (FRVT) report. https://www.nist.gov

Ratha, N. K., Connell, J. H., & Bolle, R. M. (2019). Enhancing security and privacy in biometric authentication systems. *IBM Journal of Research and Development*, *63*(6), 1–12.

Shi, W., Cao, J., Zhang, Q., & Li, Y. (2020). Edge AI for biometric authentication. *IEEE Transactions on Cloud Computing*, *8*(4), 1098–1110.

Sundararajan, K., Raj, A. N. J., & Sugumaran, M. (2021). Deep learning in biometric authentication: Trends and challenges. *IEEE Access : Practical Innovations, Open Solutions*, *9*, 102764–102779.

Wang, Y., Zhao, H., & Liu, X. (2022). Quantum-safe encryption for biometric authentication systems. *IEEE Transactions on Quantum Engineering*, *3*, 1125–1140.

Zhao, C., & Kumar, A. (2022). Deep learning-based facial recognition: Challenges and opportunities. *IEEE Transactions on Biometrics, Behavior, and Identity Science*, *4*(2), 98–112.

Chapter 6
Building AI Agents for Autonomous Decision-Making:
Designing Autonomous AI Agents Using Reinforcement Learning

Velmurugan R.
https://orcid.org/0000-0002-7925-9757
Karpagam Academy of Higher Education, Coimbatore, India

Bhuvaneswari R.
https://orcid.org/0009-0003-9396-6129
Dr. Mahalingam College of Engineering and Technology, Pollachi, India

Joji Abey
https://orcid.org/0000-0003-4176-3023
Kingdom University, Bahrain

ABSTRACT

In this study it is concerned with the development of AI agents that are able to make autonomous decisions using reinforcement learning (RL). The paper investigates basic concepts and training methods and optimization techniques which establish essential techniques for producing adaptable agents that work in fluid settings. Deep RL techniques can help to train agents into finding optimal policies to interact and be in contact with mechanisms of feedback. The study outlines major difficulties in its findings between agent early exploration and optimally using current knowledge while also addressing system expansion limitations and ethical issues. This work covers practical uses of the methodology in financial settings as well as healthcare

DOI: 10.4018/979-8-3373-2008-3.ch006

organizations and robotic systems. The results contribute to the advances of AI driven autonomy for driving efficiency and making intelligent decisions in the complex and uncertain environments.

INTRODUCTION

Thanks to the rise of Artificial Intelligence (AI) across different industries, significant strides have been made in building autonomous systems capable of performing tasks without direct human involvement. AI has transformed automation, enabling advancements such as self-driving cars, autonomous drones, robotic process automation, and AI-driven healthcare solutions, fundamentally reshaping the automation landscape. Typically, autonomous systems consist of unattended components that make real-time decisions, powered by machine learning algorithms that allow them to learn from their environment, improve over time, and perform tasks efficiently. Reinforcement Learning (RL) is one of the core paradigms used to develop such autonomous systems. Recently, RL has gained prominence in designing intelligent agents capable of making decisions in complex and dynamic environments.

The benefits of RL lie in its robust framework that enables AI agents to learn by interacting with their environment, receiving feedback in the form of rewards or penalties, and adjusting their actions to maximize long-term rewards. Unlike supervised learning, which relies on labeled data, RL follows a trial-and-error approach. The agent continuously explores the environment, performs actions, and observes the resulting consequences, refining its strategy based on previous outcomes. RL shares its foundations with decision-making problems, where optimal actions are discovered through experience, leveraging the cycle of trial, error, and feedback.

Bellman's dynamic programming (Bellman, 1957) is often cited as the foundation of RL, which later shaped the development of its methods. In RL, an agent interacts with its environment, takes actions, receives rewards, and learns to maximize cumulative rewards over time. The core idea of RL is rooted in the Markov Decision Process (MDP) (Puterman, 1994), where the future state depends only on the current state and action, not on past states and actions. This framework enables RL algorithms to simulate environments and help agents optimize their actions by incorporating feedback.

RL's ability to handle complex decision-making problems—such as robotics, gaming, and autonomous driving, where rules and strategies are unknown and must be learned through interaction—drives its growing adoption in autonomous systems. In autonomous decision-making, an RL agent operates in the environment to maximize rewards by balancing exploration of new actions with exploitation of known strategies that yield high returns. This balance prevents agents from getting stuck in suboptimal behaviors and encourages the discovery of more effective strategies (Sutton & Barto, 2018).

Q-learning is one of the most popular RL algorithms. It seeks the optimal action-value function (Q-function), estimating the total expected future rewards from performing a given action in a specific state (Watkins & Dayan, 1992). By iteratively updating its Q-values with feedback from the environment, the agent learns an optimal policy. Building on this, Deep Q-Networks (DQN), introduced by Mnih et al. (2015), solved high-dimensional Q-learning problems, such as interpreting images or video frames, by integrating deep neural networks. DQN achieved breakthroughs, such as training AI agents to play Atari games at superhuman levels, proving RL's scalability to complex tasks.

Another approach, policy gradient methods, directly optimizes the policy by adjusting the parameters of the agent's decision-making process rather than estimating action values. This approach is especially advantageous in continuous action spaces, such as robotic control or autonomous driving. Actor-Critic methods combine the strengths of value-based and policy-based approaches by using an "actor" to select actions and a "critic" to evaluate them. This hybrid method has shown promising results in complex environments, effectively addressing the exploration-exploitation tradeoff (Konda & Tsitsiklis, 2000).

The design and development of autonomous AI agents also depend on the characteristics of their environments, which can be model-free or model-based. In a model-free setup, the agent learns optimal policies through direct interaction with the environment, without knowledge of its dynamics. Conversely, in model-based setups, agents simulate the environment using predictive models, allowing for more efficient decision-making. While model-free methods are easier to implement, model-based approaches often lead to better performance due to their planning capabilities.

Despite their potential, RL-based autonomous agents face several challenges in real-world applications. One major challenge is sample efficiency, which refers to the amount of data or interactions required to learn an optimal policy. In many cases, gathering such data is expensive, time-consuming, or impractical. Researchers like Hessel et al. (2018) have explored techniques such as experience replay, which allows agents to archive and reuse past experiences to accelerate learning.

Another significant challenge is balancing exploration and exploitation. Agents must decide when to explore new actions and when to leverage known successful strategies. Too much exploration can lead to inefficiency, while too much exploitation can cause the agent to miss more optimal solutions. Strategies such as ε-greedy and Thompson sampling have been developed to address this issue (Sutton & Barto, 2018).

Reward design is another critical factor in building effective autonomous agents. Poorly designed rewards can lead to unintended behaviors. For instance, an autonomous vehicle agent trained solely to maximize speed may prioritize speed over safety. Therefore, reward structures must be carefully shaped to align agents' goals with desired outcomes (Ng et al., 1999).

Despite these challenges, RL has the potential to significantly improve numerous aspects of daily life. RL-driven autonomous systems already demonstrate promise beyond energy optimization in smart grids, including more efficient manufacturing processes and intelligent personal assistants. As computational power grows, algorithms become more efficient, and models improve, RL will continue to address the stochastic nature of optimization problems, driving the evolution of autonomous AI agents.

Ultimately, RL provides a powerful framework for programming autonomous AI agents capable of learning from their environment and making decisions without direct human input. As these agents operate in increasingly complex and dynamic environments, they will continuously refine their strategies through feedback. While challenges related to scalability, exploration, reward design, and sample efficiency remain, ongoing advancements in algorithms and techniques are paving the way for a new generation of autonomous AI agents that will transform industries and enhance daily life.

REINFORCEMENT LEARNING

Reinforcement Learning (RL) is a machine learning technique in which an agent decides on actions while interacting with an environment to learn the specific actions that maximize its cumulative expected reward. The agent tries out actions, receives rewards or punishments, and adjusts its behavior based on the outcomes. Unlike supervised learning, RL agents learn optimal strategies without labeled data, relying instead on feedback from the environment (Sutton & Barto, 2018). Over time, the agent refines its decisions to maximize cumulative rewards.

1. Agent

In RL, the entity that takes actions in response to the current state of the environment is called the agent or decision-maker. To learn an optimal strategy (policy) that maximizes cumulative rewards, the agent continuously interacts with the environment. It observes the environment, performs actions based on its observations, and adjusts its behavior using feedback in the form of rewards or punishments (Sutton & Barto, 2018). In the Markov Decision Process (MDP) framework, the agent's actions influence both state transitions and the rewards received (Puterman, 1994). The best course of action is not explicitly provided to the agent; instead, it must explore possibilities and learn from experience. Over time, the agent refines its policy by balancing the exploitation of known strategies with the exploration of new ones to discover better outcomes (Thrun & Schwartz, 1993). This adaptiveness distinguishes RL from other machine learning paradigms.

2. Environment

The environment is the external system that interacts with the agent. It includes all factors that can influence or be influenced by the agent's actions. The environment provides the agent with states (representing the current configuration or condition) and rewards (indicating how favorable its actions were) (Sutton & Barto, 2018). The agent's learning process depends heavily on the environment's responses, which provide the data needed to adjust behavior. The environment can be modeled using an MDP, where the agent selects an action based on the current state and, in return, the environment provides a new state and reward. This dynamic interaction allows the agent to infer the value of its actions and improve its policy (Puterman, 1994).

3. State

A state represents the environment's current situation at a particular moment. It provides meaningful information about environmental dynamics, allowing the agent to make informed decisions. States capture all relevant aspects that impact the agent's next action. In MDPs, the state is critical, enabling the agent to transition from one situation to another based on the action taken (Puterman, 1994). Defining the state space properly is key to optimizing a policy (Sutton & Barto, 2018).

4. Action

An action is a choice the agent makes from a set of possible actions in a given state. These actions influence how the environment responds and transitions to new states. According to Sutton & Barto (2018), the resulting state and reward from an action also influence the agent's future choices, enabling it to learn an optimal policy over time. The complete set of actions is called the action space.

5. Reward

A reward is critical in RL, providing feedback after the agent takes an action in a particular state. Positive rewards encourage repeating certain behaviors, while negative rewards or punishments discourage undesirable ones. Through this feedback, the agent learns which actions are beneficial and which are not. Rewards drive the RL process by allowing agents to adjust their policies to maximize cumulative rewards over time. Reward shaping—modifying the reward function—can further accelerate learning by providing more informative feedback signals. In an MDP framework, the reward directly shapes the agent's behavior in response to its actions (Puterman, 1994).

6. Policy

A policy is the agent's strategy for choosing actions in different states. It can be deterministic, mapping a given state to a specific action, or stochastic, assigning probabilities to possible actions (Sutton & Barto, 2018). The agent seeks to discover an optimal policy that yields the highest long-term rewards through continuous interaction with the environment.

7. Value Function

The value function estimates the expected long-term reward from a given state or state-action pair when following a particular policy. It helps the agent evaluate which actions are more beneficial. The state value function (V(s)) estimates the expected return starting from state s under policy π, while the action value function (Q(s, a)) estimates the expected return from taking action a in state s and continuing with policy π (Sutton & Barto, 2018). By estimating these values, the agent can prioritize actions that lead to higher-value states, improving its strategy over time. Bellman's equation (Bellman, 1957) defines the recursive relationships used to calculate these values and underpins many RL algorithms.

8. Q-Function (Action-Value Function)

The Q-function is a central concept in RL, measuring the expected total reward from taking a particular action in a specific state and then following an optimal policy. Mathematically, Q(s, a) represents the expected return from performing action a in state s and continuing optimally (Sutton & Barto, 2018). By learning Q-values, the agent can evaluate the quality of actions in each state and select those expected to yield the highest long-term reward. Algorithms like Q-learning (Watkins & Dayan, 1992) iteratively update these Q-values through exploration and exploitation. Accurately specified Q-functions enable more strategic decision-making and are integral to many RL algorithms, serving as a powerful tool for evaluating and improving agent performance over time. Balancing exploration (trying new actions) and exploitation (using known high-reward actions) is key to discovering an optimal policy. Too much exploration can slow learning, while too much exploitation risks missing better strategies. Approaches like Q-learning (Watkins & Dayan, 1992), Deep

Q-Networks (Mnih et al., 2015), and ε-greedy strategies help achieve this balance. By repeatedly interacting with the environment, the agent gradually converges to a policy that maximizes long-term rewards.

DESIGNING AUTONOMOUS AI AGENTS USING RL

The steps to designing autonomous AI agents are numerous and critical, as each contributes to creating an efficient decision-making system. After formulating the environment and decision-making process as a Markov Decision Process (Puterman, 1994) or another suitable model, the design begins with defining the problem the agent should solve. Once the state space—all possible configurations in the environment—is defined, the agent uses this information to assess its state (Sutton & Barto, 2018).

Next, the action space is defined, specifying the actions the agent can perform in each state. Finally, a reward function is designed to provide feedback to the agent in the form of rewards or punishments, guiding it toward desired outcomes (Kaelbling et al., 1996). With these components established, the policy of the agent can be initialized randomly or with prior knowledge, and then iteratively refined using RL algorithms such as Q-learning (Watkins & Dayan, 1992). This policy is continuously evaluated and fine-tuned, either in simulated or real-world environments, to ensure the agent evolves toward optimal decision-making.

1. Problem Formulation

The first step in designing an autonomous AI agent is defining the problem as a Reinforcement Learning (RL) task, which includes specifying the environment, states, actions, and reward structure. Everything external to the agent that affects its behavior is referred to as the environment. For example, for an autonomous vehicle, the environment includes road conditions, other vehicles, traffic signals, pedestrians, and weather (Sutton & Barto, 2018). The agent interacts with this environment and receives feedback after each action it takes. The state space defines all possible configurations the agent might encounter. In the case of an autonomous vehicle, states could include the vehicle's position, speed, traffic conditions, and nearby obstacles. These states allow the agent to understand the context in which it must make decisions.

The action space encompasses all possible actions the agent can take in any given state. For an autonomous vehicle, these actions might include steering, accelerating, braking, or changing lanes (Kaelbling, Littman, & Moore, 1996). These actions cause state transitions, directly impacting the environment. The reward structure guides the agent's learning process. In the vehicle scenario, rewards might be given for safely reaching a destination, following traffic rules, or avoiding collisions, while penalties might be applied for speeding, running red lights, or causing accidents (Puterman, 1994). The agent's goal is to maximize cumulative rewards by making optimal decisions.

2. Modeling the Environment

RL environments can be approached in two ways: model-free or model-based. These approaches differ in how they utilize environmental dynamics during learning.

(a) Model-Free Approach:

In this approach, the agent does not build or rely on an explicit model of the environment's dynamics. Instead, it learns the optimal policy directly through interaction with the environment, relying on trial and error and feedback (Sutton & Barto, 2018). Algorithms like Q-learning (Watkins & Dayan, 1992) and Policy Gradient methods (Sutton et al., 2000) are widely used due to their simplicity and flexibility. However, they can be less efficient in complex environments because they require extensive exploration to converge to the best policy.

(b) Model-Based Approach:

Here, the agent builds an explicit model of the environment's dynamics, allowing it to simulate possible outcomes before taking actions. This planning capability enables better, more informed decisions and typically requires fewer interactions to learn an optimal policy (Deisenroth & Rasmussen, 2011). This approach is especially useful when real-world interactions are expensive or time-consuming. However, building an accurate model can be resource-intensive and challenging. The choice between these approaches depends on the specific application, the complexity of the environment, and the trade-offs between computational efficiency and exploration.

3. Learning Algorithms

Different RL algorithms can be applied depending on the problem, each with its own strengths and weaknesses:

(i) **Q-learning** (Watkins & Dayan, 1992): A model-free algorithm that learns optimal policies by estimating action values.

(ii) **Policy Gradient Methods** (Sutton et al., 2000): Effective for environments with high-dimensional action spaces, such as robotics.
(iii) **Deep Q-Networks (DQN)** (Mnih et al., 2015): Combines Q-learning with deep learning for handling complex, high-dimensional input spaces.
(iv) **Actor-Critic Methods** (Konda & Tsitsiklis, 2000): Combines value-based and policy-based approaches for stability and efficiency.

RL DESIGN

a. Q-Learning

Q-learning is an off-policy algorithm, meaning it learns an optimal policy independent of the actions taken during exploration. It estimates the value of state-action pairs (Q-values) and iteratively updates them using the Bellman equation. This dynamic learning process allows the agent to discover optimal strategies without relying on fixed action sequences (Sutton & Barto, 2018).

(i) Deep Q-Networks (DQN)

DQN extends Q-learning by leveraging deep neural networks to approximate Q-values in high-dimensional spaces, such as image-based inputs (Mnih et al., 2015). It employs techniques like experience replay to break correlations between updates and target networks to stabilize training. This approach enabled RL agents to achieve superhuman performance in complex tasks like Atari games.

(ii) Policy Gradient Methods

Policy Gradient methods directly optimize the policy without estimating value functions. By adjusting policy parameters through gradient ascent, these methods perform well in continuous or high-dimensional action spaces (Williams, 1992; Sutton & Barto, 2018). However, they require careful tuning and variance reduction techniques due to the high variance in gradient estimates.

(iii) Actor-Critic Methods

Actor-Critic methods combine the strengths of value-based and policy-based approaches. The actor proposes actions based on the policy, while the critic evaluates these actions using a value function. This combination enables stable and efficient learning, balancing exploration and exploitation (Konda & Tsitsiklis, 2000). These methods are especially useful in environments with complex state spaces.

b. Exploration vs. Exploitation

Balancing exploration (trying new actions) and exploitation (using known high-reward actions) is one of the central challenges in RL.

- ε-greedy exploration: The agent primarily exploits known actions but occasionally explores random actions to avoid getting stuck in suboptimal strategies.
- Boltzmann exploration: Actions are chosen probabilistically, favoring higher-value actions but still allowing exploration. Temperature parameters control the degree of exploration (Sutton et al., 2000).

Choosing the right exploration strategy is crucial for efficient learning and long-term success.

c. Reward Shaping

Designing the reward function is a critical part of building autonomous agents. A well-designed reward function aligns the agent's behavior with desired objectives, while a poorly designed one can lead to unintended or even harmful behaviors (Ng et al., 1999). For example, in a navigation task, providing incremental rewards for progress can accelerate learning compared to rewarding only task completion. Conversely, poor reward design can lead to "reward hacking," where the agent exploits loopholes in the system to maximize rewards without achieving the intended outcome.

d. Evaluation and Validation

After training, the agent must be evaluated and validated to ensure its decision-making aligns with desired goals. Evaluation can be performed in simulated or real-world environments, using metrics such as cumulative rewards, success rates, and task completion times (Sutton & Barto, 2018). Long-term evaluation is equally important to ensure the agent does not prioritize short-term rewards over long-term objectives. Techniques such as delayed rewards and temporal credit assignment help assess the agent's ability to plan ahead and consider future consequences (Daw et al., 2006).

CHALLENGES IN AUTONOMOUS DECISION-MAKING

1. Scalability

In real-world applications, environments are typically large, complex, and dynamic, making it impossible to model all possible states and actions. This complexity creates scalability issues in tasks such as autonomous driving, robotics, and industrial automation. In such environments, the state and action spaces grow so large that traditional methods become inefficient. For instance, in autonomous driving, the environment includes other vehicles, pedestrians, and unexpected road conditions (Pomerleau, 1989). Similarly, robotic control tasks require modeling interactions with various objects, sensors, and external factors, significantly increasing the dimensionality of the environment (Kormushev et al., 2013).

The real-time nature of decisions, combined with scalability challenges, compounds the difficulty. Evaluating every possible action in every possible state is computationally prohibitive. Large state spaces make it difficult for traditional methods such as Q-learning to scale efficiently without running into memory limitations or slow updates of Q-values for each state-action pair (Mnih et al., 2015). To address these issues, techniques such as function approximation using neural networks have been proposed to generalize across large state-action spaces (Sutton & Barto, 2018). Deep Reinforcement Learning (DRL) extends RL further by building deep representations of policies, allowing agents to handle high-dimensional inputs—such as images—which makes it feasible for complex tasks like autonomous driving and robotic control.

2. Sample Efficiency

RL agents are often slow to learn without extensive interaction data from the environment. This data is crucial for exploring different state-action combinations, receiving feedback, and updating policies. However, collecting sufficient data in real-world settings can be expensive and time-consuming. For example, data collection for autonomous driving requires extensive hardware, sensors, and human supervision (Pan & Yang, 2020). Similarly, in robotics, the variability and dynamism of environments demand large datasets to train robots effectively.

This creates a sample efficiency challenge, particularly in tasks where fast adaptation is needed. Most traditional RL algorithms require lengthy training times, making them impractical for real-world applications where rapid responses are necessary (Schulman et al., 2017). High-dimensional tasks such as natural language processing or advanced robotics are particularly problematic due to the high costs and risks of repeated interactions.

Researchers have proposed several solutions to improve sample efficiency. For example, training agents in simulated environments (such as games or virtual worlds) before deploying them in real-world scenarios reduces the need for large volumes of real-world data (Tobin et al., 2017). Another approach is transfer learning, where models trained in one domain are fine-tuned for new tasks, reducing the demand for extensive additional data.

3. Exploration in Complex Environments

In highly dynamic or uncertain environments, exploration can lead to unsafe behaviors, with agents taking actions that are suboptimal or dangerous. This risk is especially critical in domains such as autonomous driving, robotics, or healthcare, where unsafe actions could harm humans, damage property, or cause system failures. For example, an autonomous vehicle exploring a dangerous route in an unknown area or a robot performing unsafe manipulations in a confined space could have serious consequences.

A key challenge in RL is designing safe exploration algorithms that allow agents to learn while minimizing risks (Garcia & Fernandez, 2015). Approaches such as constrained reinforcement learning (Achiam et al., 2017) incorporate safety constraints into the reward function or policy to prevent unsafe actions during exploration. Similarly, risk-sensitive exploration (Chow et al., 2018) balances the expected rewards against the potential risks of unsafe behaviors. Advancing safe exploration techniques is critical to enabling agents to learn effectively without endangering themselves or their surroundings.

4. Reward Design

Designing an effective reward system in RL is a non-trivial task because the reward function directly influences the agent's learning and behavior. A poorly designed reward structure can inadvertently encourage suboptimal or harmful behavior, a problem often referred to as reward mis-specification or reward hacking.

For example, in autonomous driving, if an agent is rewarded solely for achieving maximum speed, it might disregard safety concerns such as maintaining a safe distance or obeying traffic regulations. This could lead to reckless and dangerous driving (Amodei et al., 2016). A better-designed reward system would balance speed with safety by penalizing unsafe behaviors such as collisions or traffic violations while rewarding efficient and lawful driving. The challenge lies in creating reward functions that incorporate all relevant factors of the task while minimizing unintended side effects. Research in this area focuses on aligning agent goals with human values (Ng et al., 1999) to ensure agents learn efficient, safe, and ethical behaviors.

5. Ethical Concerns

Autonomous AI agents must operate within ethical and societal guidelines. Ethical concerns span multiple domains, including transportation, healthcare, finance, and law enforcement. For example, autonomous vehicles must navigate ethical dilemmas involving unavoidable accidents, liability, and bias in decision-making (Goodall, 2014).

To ensure ethical AI, principles such as transparency, accountability, and fairness are essential. Preventing discrimination ensures fairness, while accountability holds developers, users, and regulators responsible (Bryson, 2018). Explainability builds trust, enables audits, and complies with regulations such as GDPR (Lipton, 2018). Ultimately, ethically aligned AI fosters trust and delivers societal benefits by balancing technological capabilities with human values.

6. Generalization

RL agents often face overfitting, becoming highly specialized to specific environments but unable to adapt to new or slightly different scenarios. Limited diversity during training makes it difficult for agents to generalize effectively (Zhang et al., 2018).

Several strategies can improve generalization:

- Domain randomization or procedural generation to increase environmental variety during training (Cobbe et al., 2019).
- Regularization techniques such as dropout and weight decay to prevent overfitting (Farebrother et al., 2018).
- Meta-learning (Finn et al., 2017) and curriculum learning (Bengio et al., 2009) to enhance adaptability by progressively increasing task complexity.

Despite these advancements, achieving robust generalization in RL remains a significant research challenge, particularly in real-world applications where environments are unpredictable and ever-changing.

APPLICATIONS OF AUTONOMOUS AI AGENTS

The practical applications of Reinforcement Learning (RL) in autonomous decision-making span multiple domains. RL enables systems to learn complex tasks in robotics, such as grasping objects and autonomous navigation. In finance, RL is applied to portfolio optimization and algorithmic trading. Autonomous vehicles use

RL to develop adaptive driving strategies and manage traffic efficiently. In healthcare, RL supports personalized treatment recommendations and medical diagnostics. Additionally, RL enhances industrial automation by optimizing resource allocation and improving process efficiency. Overall, RL demonstrates its ability to enhance decision-making, adaptability, and operational efficiency, making it a key driver in industries adopting automation and artificial intelligence.

1. Autonomous Vehicles

Reinforcement learning (RL) plays an indispensable role in autonomous vehicle systems, enabling self-driving cars to navigate traffic, choose optimal routes, and optimize fuel usage in real-world scenarios. RL helps develop adaptive driving policies tailored to dynamic environments (Sallab et al., 2017). Kendall et al. (2019) demonstrate that deep RL enhances driving safety, particularly in speed control, lane changing, and braking. Similarly, freeway congestion prediction models that leverage RL have been developed to reduce travel time and fuel consumption while optimizing real-time routing algorithms (Gao et al., 2022). Moreover, RL improves the energy efficiency of electric vehicles by minimizing unnecessary accelerations (Yu et al., 2020), reinforcing its critical role in safe and efficient autonomous driving.

2. Robotics

Reinforcement learning (RL) empowers robots to execute complex tasks—such as assembly, cleaning, and object manipulation—by learning from their environment rather than relying on predefined programming or manual calibration. Unlike rule-based systems, RL-driven robots solve problems through trial-and-error interactions with dynamic environments (Kober et al., 2013). RL has been shown to enhance assembly processes in industrial automation (Levine et al., 2016), improve navigation and efficiency for cleaning robots (Zeng et al., 2020), and enhance robotic dexterity (Open et al., 2019). Furthermore, RL supports multi-agent collaboration in warehouse operations (Gupta et al., 2017), expanding its utility in manufacturing, logistics, and service automation.

3. Healthcare

Reinforcement learning (RL) plays a transformative role in personalized medicine by adapting treatment plans in real time based on patient feedback and historical data. Unlike static treatment approaches, RL optimally adjusts therapies to achieve desired outcomes in areas such as oncology, diabetes, and critical care (Yu et al., 2021). For example, RL personalizes chemotherapy dosing by balancing treatment efficacy with the minimization of adverse side effects (Gottesman et al., 2019). It also optimizes insulin dosage using patient glucose levels and lifestyle data (Fahmi et al., 2022). Additional applications include developing RL-driven treatment strategies for sepsis (Komorowski et al., 2018), adjusting therapy sessions or drug dosing in psychiatric care (Tschantz et al., 2020), and improving patient-centered care through continuous learning and adaptation.

4. Finance

With the growing reliance on algorithmic trading and portfolio management, reinforcement learning (RL) is increasingly used to develop adaptive investment strategies based on market dynamics. Pendharkar (2018) highlights how RL-powered trading systems identify opportunities and manage risks by continuously adapting to market changes. Similarly, Fischer (2018) notes that RL agents process vast amounts of financial data, including price movements, trading volumes, and macroeconomic indicators, to refine decision-making. In portfolio management, RL supports dynamic asset allocation by adjusting portfolio distributions in response to market fluctuations (Jiang et al., 2017). Moreover, high-frequency trading (HFT) leverages RL to execute trades within milliseconds, exploiting short-term inefficiencies for optimal returns (Moody & Saffell, 2001). These applications underscore RL's ability to enhance adaptability, efficiency, and precision in automated trading.

FUTURE DIRECTIONS

Several key areas are poised for advancements that will significantly impact the design of autonomous AI agents in the future. These improvements will enhance agents' generalization capabilities, enabling them to handle diverse and dynamic environments. Greater explainability will foster trust and accountability in AI-driven decisions. Enhanced safety mechanisms and ethical alignment will mitigate the risks associated with autonomous decision-making. Moreover, integrating human-AI collaboration will enable more effective real-world applications. Ongoing innovations in computational and data efficiency will further optimize these systems. As algorithms evolve, increasingly intelligent, agile, and responsible autonomous agents will emerge across industries and domains.

1. Incorporating Human-AI Collaboration

With the growing interconnectedness of systems, multi-agent reinforcement learning (MARL) is becoming essential. In MARL, multiple autonomous agents interact, requiring strategies for cooperation, coordination, or competition (Hernandez-Leal et al., 2019). This is particularly relevant in domains such as autonomous driving, smart grid management, and robotic swarm intelligence (Nguyen et al., 2020). However, multi-agent environments are inherently dynamic and nonstationary, creating fundamental challenges in stability and scalability (Zhang et al., 2021). Advances in decentralized learning, communication protocols, and game-theoretic approaches (Lowe et al., 2017) are improving adaptability, enabling MARL techniques to produce more intelligent, coordinated, and adaptive autonomous systems.

2. Multi-Agent Systems

As autonomous systems become more interconnected, multi-agent systems are gaining prominence. Multi-agent reinforcement learning (MARL) supports agents in collaborative, competitive, or hybrid environments (Hernandez-Leal et al., 2019). Applications range from autonomous vehicle coordination to smart grid management and robotic swarm intelligence (Nguyen et al., 2020). The dynamic and nonstationary nature of these environments makes stability and scalability key challenges (Zhang et al., 2021). Recent progress in decentralized learning and communication protocols (Lowe et al., 2017) is improving the performance of multi-agent systems, paving the way for more robust and adaptable applications.

3. Safe and Ethical Decision-Making

As AI moves into high-impact domains like healthcare, finance, and autonomous vehicles, safety and ethics are paramount. AI systems must operate reliably in high-stakes environments while aligning with societal values (Russell et al., 2019). In healthcare, AI-driven decision-making should ensure patient safety, transparency, and fairness to minimize biases in diagnosis and treatment (Tjoa & Guan, 2021). In finance, fairness and the prevention of market manipulation are essential when deploying AI-based trading algorithms (Boddington, 2017). Methods such as adversarial training and safety-focused reinforcement learning (Amodei et al., 2016; Goodfellow et al., 2015) are crucial for building robust safeguards. By embedding fairness, interpretability, and accountability, AI systems can become trustworthy and ethically aligned.

4. Explainability

Improving the interpretability and transparency of reinforcement learning (RL)-based agents is vital for public trust and ethical integration. Many RL models, particularly deep RL systems, function as "black boxes," making their decision-making processes opaque (Doshi-Velez & Kim, 2017). This lack of transparency is particularly critical in healthcare, finance, and autonomous systems, where accountability is non-negotiable (Tjoa & Guan, 2021). Emerging Explainable Reinforcement Learning (XRL) techniques, including policy summarization, attention mechanisms, and counterfactual explanations, are addressing this challenge (Puiutta & Veith, 2020). Human-in-the-loop approaches further ensure that AI systems are aligned with societal norms and ethical principles (Russell et al., 2019). By integrating interpretability, transparency, and regulatory compliance, RL systems can become trustworthy, responsible, and widely accepted.

CONCLUSION

Reinforcement learning (RL) has emerged as a transformative framework for developing autonomous AI agents capable of making decisions in complex, dynamic environments (Sutton & Barto, 2018). By learning optimal strategies through iterative interaction and feedback, RL-based systems have revolutionized domains such as robotics, finance, healthcare, and autonomous vehicles (Silver et al., 2016).

However, significant challenges remain. Many RL algorithms struggle to generalize across diverse environments and require substantial computational resources and training data (Henderson et al., 2018). Safety concerns are particularly critical in high-risk scenarios, where errors could have catastrophic outcomes, such as in healthcare or autonomous driving (Amodei et al., 2016). Ethical considerations—bias, fairness, accountability, and transparency—must also be addressed to ensure societal trust (Boddington, 2017).

Current methods often lack efficiency, with many agents requiring millions of interactions to achieve optimal performance. Research into sample-efficient learning, transfer learning, and human-in-the-loop techniques (Levine et al., 2020) holds promise for accelerating training and improving generalization. With continued innovation, RL-driven autonomous agents will play an increasingly pivotal role in shaping industries and societies. By prioritizing robustness, interpretability, and ethical alignment, RL has the potential to drive transformative advances in decision-making across a wide range of applications.

REFERENCES

Achiam, J., Fischer, I., & Pinto, L.. (2017). *Constrained Policy Optimization.* In *Proceedings of the 34th International Conference on Machine Learning (ICML-17)*, 288-297.

Amodei, D., Olah, C., Steinhardt, J., Christiano, P., ... (2016). Concrete problems in AI safety. *arXiv preprint arXiv:1606.06565.*

Bellman, R. (1957). *Dynamic Programming*. Princeton University Press.

Bengio, Y., Louradour, J., Collobert, R., & Weston, J. (2009). Curriculum learning. *Proceedings of the 26th International Conference on Machine Learning*, 41-48.

Boddington, P. (2017). *Towards a code of ethics for artificial intelligence*. Springer.

Bryson, J. J. (2018). The artificial intelligence debate: Why AI needs regulation. *Nature, 563*(7733), 456–458.

Chow, Y., Poupart, P., & Van den Broeck, G. (2018). *Risk-Sensitive Reinforcement Learning*. In *Proceedings of the 35th International Conference on Machine Learning (ICML-18)*, 811-819.

Cobbe, K., Klimov, O., Hesse, C., Kim, T., & Schulman, J. (2019). Quantifying generalization in reinforcement learning. *International Conference on Machine Learning*.

Daw, N. D., Niv, Y., & Dayan, P. (2006). Corticostriatal circuits and the computation of time. *Psychological Review, 113*(4), 167–177.

Deisenroth, M. P., & Rasmussen, C. E. (2011). *PILCO: A model-based and data-efficient approach to policy search.* In *Proceedings of the 28th International Conference on Machine Learning (ICML-11)*, 465-472.

Doshi-Velez, F., & Kim, B. (2017). Towards a rigorous science of interpretable machine learning. *arXiv preprint arXiv:1702.08608.*

Fahmi, F., Suhendro, D. K., & Wardoyo, R. (2022). Reinforcement learning for personalized insulin dosing in diabetes management. *Journal of Biomedical Informatics, 130*, 104107.

Farebrother, J., Machado, M. C., & Bowling, M. (2018). Generalization and regularization in DQN. *arXiv preprint arXiv:1810.00123.*

Finn, C., Abbeel, P., & Levine, S. (2017). Model-agnostic meta-learning for fast adaptation of deep networks. *Proceedings of the 34th International Conference on Machine Learning*, 1126-1135.

Fischer, T. (2018). Reinforcement learning in financial markets – A survey. *Journal of Economic Dynamics & Control, 91*, 113–129.

Gao, Y., Huang, H., & Liu, Y. (2022). Reinforcement learning for traffic signal control and route optimization. *Transportation Research Part C, Emerging Technologies, 140*, 103754.

Garcia, J., & Fernandez, F. (2015). A Comprehensive Survey on Safe Reinforcement Learning. *Journal of Machine Learning Research, 16*(1), 1437–1480.

Goodall, N. J. (2014). Machine ethics and automated vehicles. *Road Vehicle Automation*, 93-102.

Goodfellow, I., Shlens, J., & Szegedy, C. (2015). Explaining and harnessing adversarial examples. *International Conference on Learning Representations (ICLR).*

Gottesman, O., Johansson, F., Komorowski, M., & Faisal, A. (2019). Guidelines for reinforcement learning in healthcare. *Nature Medicine, 25*(1), 16–18. PMID: 30617332

Gupta, J. K., Egorov, M., & Kochenderfer, M. (2017). Cooperative multi-agent control using deep reinforcement learning. *Autonomous Agents and Multi-Agent Systems, 30*(1), 66–83.

Henderson, P., Islam, R., Bachman, P., & Pineau, J.. (2018). Deep reinforcement learning that matters. *Proceedings of the AAAI Conference on Artificial Intelligence, 32*(1).

Hernandez-Leal, P., Kartal, B., & Taylor, M. E. (2019). A survey and critique of multi-agent deep reinforcement learning. *Autonomous Agents and Multi-Agent Systems, 33*(6), 750–797.

Hessel, M., Silver, D., Plappert, M., Horgan, D., Modayil, J., & Doron, Y. (2018). *Learning to play in a day: Faster deep reinforcement learning by optimality tightening*. In *Proceedings of the 31st International Conference on Neural Information Processing Systems (NeurIPS 2018).*

Jiang, Z., Xu, D., & Liang, J. (2017). A deep reinforcement learning framework for the financial portfolio management problem. *arXiv preprint arXiv:1706.10059.*

Kaelbling, L. P., Littman, M. L., & Moore, A. W. (1996). Reinforcement learning: A survey. *Journal of Artificial Intelligence Research, 4*, 237–285.

Kendall, A., Hawke, J., & Cipolla, R. (2019). Learning to drive in a day. *2019 International Conference on Robotics and Automation (ICRA)*, 8248-8254.

Kober, J., Bagnell, J. A., & Peters, J. (2013). Reinforcement learning in robotics: A survey. *The International Journal of Robotics Research, 32*(11), 1238–1274.

Komorowski, M., Celi, L. A., Badawi, O., Gordon, A. C., & Faisal, A. A. (2018). The artificial intelligence clinician learns optimal treatment strategies for sepsis in intensive care. *Nature Medicine*, *24*(11), 1716–1720. PMID: 30349085

Konda, V. R., & Tsitsiklis, J. N. (2000). Actor-Critic Algorithms. *Advances in Neural Information Processing Systems*, *12*, 1008–1014.

Kormushev, P., Nenchev, D. N., Calinon, S., & Sauser, E. (2013). *Bimanual robot learning of natural interaction tasks.* In *Proceedings of the IEEE/RSJ International Conference on Intelligent Robots and Systems (IROS-13).*

Levine, S., Finn, C., Darrell, T., & Abbeel, P. (2016). End-to-end training of deep visuomotor policies. *Journal of Machine Learning Research, 17*(1), 1334–1373.

Levine, S., Kumar, A., Tucker, G., & Fu, J. (2020). Offline reinforcement learning: Tutorial, review, and perspectives on open problems. *arXiv preprint arXiv:2005.01643.*

Lipton, Z. C. (2018). The mythos of model interpretability. *arXiv preprint arXiv:1606.03490.*

Lowe, R., Wu, Y., Tamar, A., & Harb, J.. (2017). Multi-agent actor-critic for mixed cooperative-competitive environments. *Advances in Neural Information Processing Systems, 30*, 6379–6390.

Mnih, V., Kavukcuoglu, K., & Silver, D.. (2015). Human-level control through deep reinforcement learning. *Nature*, *518*(7540), 529–533. PMID: 25719670

Moody, J., & Saffell, M. (2001). Learning to trade via direct reinforcement. *IEEE Transactions on Neural Networks*, *12*(4), 875–889. PMID: 18249919

Ng, A. Y., Harada, D., & Russell, S. (1999). *Policy invariance under reward transformations: Theory and application to reward shaping*. In *Proceedings of the 16th International Conference on Machine Learning (ICML-99)*, 278-287.

Nguyen, T. T., Nguyen, N. D., & Nahavandi, S. (2020). Deep reinforcement learning for multi-agent systems: A review of challenges, solutions, and applications. *IEEE Transactions on Cybernetics*, *50*(9), 3826–3839. PMID: 32203045

Open, A. I., Akkaya, I., Andrychowicz, M., Chociej, M., ... (2019). Solving Rubik's cube with a robot hand. *arXiv preprint arXiv:1910.07113.*

Pan, S. J., & Yang, Q. (2020). A Survey on Transfer Learning. *IEEE Transactions on Knowledge and Data Engineering*, *22*(10), 1345–1359.

Pendharkar, P. C. (2018). Reinforcement learning in financial trading systems: A review. *Decision Support Systems*, *115*, 48–58.

Pomerleau, D. A. (1989). *ALVINN: An autonomous land vehicle in a neural network.* In Advances in Neural Information Processing Systems (NIPS-89), 305-313.

Puiutta, E., & Veith, E. M. (2020). Explainable reinforcement learning: A survey. *arXiv preprint arXiv:2005.06247.*

Puterman, M. L. (1994). *Markov Decision Processes: Discrete Stochastic Dynamic Programming*. Wiley-Interscience.

Russell, S., Dewey, D., & Tegmark, M. (2019). Research priorities for robust and beneficial artificial intelligence. *AI & Society*, *34*(4), 687–700.

Sallab, A. E., Abdou, M., Perot, E., & Yogamani, S. (2017). Deep reinforcement learning framework for autonomous driving. *Electronic Imaging*, *2017*(19), 70–76.

Schulman, J., Wolski, F., & Dhariwal, P.. (2017). *Proximal Policy Optimization Algorithms*. In *Proceedings of the 34th International Conference on Machine Learning (ICML-17)*, 12, 507-518.

Silver, D., Huang, A., Maddison, C. J., & Guez, A.. (2016). Mastering the game of Go with deep neural networks and tree search. *Nature*, *529*(7587), 484–489. PMID: 26819042

Sutton, R. S., & Barto, A. G. (2018). *Reinforcement learning: An introduction* (2nd ed.). MIT Press.

Sutton, R. S., McAllester, D. A., Singh, S., & Mansour, Y. (2000). *Policy Gradient Methods for Reinforcement Learning with Function Approximation.* In *Proceedings of the 12th International Conference on Neural Information Processing Systems (NIPS-00)*, 1057-1063.

Thrun, S., & Schwartz, A. (1993). *Issues in Using Function Approximation for Reinforcement Learning*. In *Proceedings of the 1993 Connectionist Models Summer School*, 255-263.

Tjoa, E., & Guan, C. (2021). A survey on explainable artificial intelligence (XAI): Toward medical AI transparency. *IEEE Transactions on Neural Networks and Learning Systems*, *32*(11), 4793–4813. PMID: 33079674

Tobin, J., Fong, R., & Ray, A.. (2017). *Domain Randomization for Transferring Deep Learning Models to New Environments*. In *Proceedings of the 2017 IEEE/RSJ International Conference on Intelligent Robots and Systems (IROS-17)*, 23-30.

Tschantz, A., Seth, A. K., & Pezzulo, G. (2020). Reinforcement learning for adaptive psychotherapy. *Trends in Cognitive Sciences*, *24*(10), 857–859.

Watkins, C. J. C. H., & Dayan, P. (1992). Q-learning. *Machine Learning*, *8*(3-4), 279–292.

Williams, R. J. (1992). Simple statistical gradient-following algorithms for connectionist reinforcement learning. *Machine Learning*, *8*(3-4), 229–256.

Yu, C., Liu, J., Ma, Y., & Zhang, W. (2021). Reinforcement learning in healthcare: A survey. *ACM Computing Surveys*, *54*(5), 1–36.

Yu, H., Zhang, X., & Zhao, D. (2020). Reinforcement learning for energy-efficient driving strategies of autonomous vehicles. *IEEE Transactions on Intelligent Transportation Systems*, *21*(8), 3397–3408.

Zeng, A., Song, S., Welker, S., & Lee, J.. (2020). Learning synergies between pushing and grasping with self-supervised deep reinforcement learning. *IEEE Robotics and Automation Letters*, *5*(2), 2562–2569.

Zhang, K., Yang, Z., & Bašić, A. (2021). Multi-agent reinforcement learning: A selective overview of theories and algorithms. *Artificial Intelligence*, *301*, 103558.

Zhang, S., Vinyals, O., Munos, R., & Bengio, Y. (2018). A study on overfitting in deep reinforcement learning. *arXiv preprint arXiv:1804.06893*.

Chapter 7
Artificial Narrow Intelligence-Based Healthcare Service Recommendation System

Sachin Sharma
https://orcid.org/0000-0002-7821-3685
Amity University Punjab, Mohali, India

ABSTRACT

The healthcare sector confronts various challenges, including the imperative to manage extensive datasets, develop innovative healthcare applications, and optimize overall delivery efficiency. This chapter proposes a unique system designed to enable users to input symptoms, receive rapid diagnoses, and access recommendations for medication and nearby hospitals, addressing the time-sensitive nature of medical diagnoses. The envisioned system capitalizes on the combined strengths of Artificial Narrow Intelligence (ANI) and cloud computing to provide swift and accurate diagnoses. ANI facilitates precise interpretation of symptoms, enhancing user experience, while cloud computing ensures seamless accessibility, allowing users to utilize the system at their convenience. The collaborative use of these technologies promises to reshape healthcare delivery, providing an efficient and accessible solution tailored to the demanding nature of the medical field.

I. INTRODUCTION

In today's rapidly evolving healthcare landscape, the discovery of new technologies and convergence of old technologies has paved the way for groundbreaking

DOI: 10.4018/979-8-3373-2008-3.ch007

innovations with the potential to enhance patient care and make medical operation efficient. ANI is a specific type of artificial intelligence in which a learning algorithm is designed to perform a single task, and any knowledge gained from performing that task will not automatically be applied to other tasks. It leverages AI technologies to establish a highly efficient system that mimics and potentially exceeds human intelligence. ANI facilitates faster decision-making since they can process and complete tasks significantly quicker than humans. As a result, it boosts productivity & efficiency of the task at hand. Cloud computing is on-demand access, via the internet, to computing resources—applications, servers (physical servers and virtual servers), data storage, development tools, networking capabilities, and more—hosted at a remote data center managed by a cloud services provider. Cloud computing has greatly changed how healthcare works. It's made it easier to get and share medical information, adjust resources as needed, save money, keep data safe, and work together. It helps doctors use data analysis, AI, and telehealth to give better care, do more research, and make healthcare more efficient overall. In simple terms, cloud computing is like a powerful tool that's making healthcare better and smarter. The fusion of cloud computing and artificial narrow intelligence (ANI) is one such groundbreaking fusion. In today's world, where data is everywhere and information keeps coming in non-stop, combining cloud computing and ANI is a powerful combination that's ready to completely change how healthcare works in many ways. One of its main advantages is that it helps healthcare providers use their resources like doctors, equipment, and time more effectively, making sure patients get the right treatment when they need it (Rawat et al., 2024). Additionally, it can improve how well treatments work by using data to give healthcare professionals better information for making decisions about patient care. During our exploration, we will see how technology can drastically change healthcare for the better, making it more personalized and efficient. This will lead to a brighter future for medicine. We hope to create something which makes the irksome task of going to the hospital and waiting hours in line simpler and less time-consuming. The healthcare sector confronts various challenges such as the requirement to gather and manage extensive data, the necessity to create and implement novel healthcare applications, and the imperative to enhance the efficiency and quality of healthcare services. The field of medicine is intricate, leading to delays in diagnosis, which can be crucial for certain patients. In situations where visiting a hospital is impractical, virtual diagnosis may prove challenging and less accurate, particularly in critical conditions. Addressing this issue is of utmost importance. The healthcare industry is facing a number of challenges including the need to collect and store large amounts of data the need to develop and deploy new healthcare applications, the need to improve the efficiency and effectiveness of healthcare delivery. Medicine is a very delicate profession; hence it takes time for the doctors to diagnose people which can create delays. This lost time can be very critical for some patients. Sometimes going to the hospital is not an option and virtual diagnosis is hard and likely to be not accurate when the patient is in a serious condition. This is a huge concern which needs to be dealt with. Artificial Narrow Intelligence (ANI) is already a transformative force in healthcare, with its application in service recommendation systems being a prime example. These systems are a class of machine learning that use data to help predict, narrow down, and find what people are looking for among an exponentially growing number of options. ANI, also known as “weak AI,” is an AI system trained for and focused on a single task. In healthcare, this translates to systems that can analyze a patient's data, such as medical history, symptoms, and lifestyle factors, to recommend specific treatments, doctors, or services. The goal is to move away from a “one-size-fits-all” approach to medicine and towards precision medicine, where care is tailored to the individual. At its core, an ANI-based healthcare service recommendation system operates by analyzing vast amounts of data to find patterns and make predictions. There are several key components that make this possible. First is data collection, which can be done through various means, including electronic health records (EHRs), patient-reported data from wearable devices, and even genomic information. This data is then processed and analyzed using various machine learning algorithms, such as collaborative filtering and content-based filtering. Collaborative filtering recommends services based on the preferences of similar users, while content-based filtering recommends services based on the characteristics of a patient's profile and the features of the services themselves. These systems continuously learn and evolve as they receive new data, making their recommendations more accurate and personalized over time. The implementation of ANI-based healthcare recommendation systems offers a multitude of benefits for both patients and healthcare providers. For patients, the most significant advantage is enhanced personalization. The system can recommend the most effective treatment plans, medications, and specialists based on an individual's unique health profile, which can lead to improved outcomes and reduced side effects. These systems can also empower patients by providing them with proactive and preventive care recommendations, helping them make more informed decisions about their health. For healthcare providers, these systems can significantly improve diagnostic accuracy and efficiency. By analyzing medical images or patient data at a speed and scale impossible for humans, ANI can assist in early disease detection, reduce medical errors, and streamline administrative tasks. This, in turn, allows doctors to focus more on patient care and less on time-consuming data analysis. The use of these systems can also lead to optimized resource allocation, ensuring that clinics and hospitals operate more efficiently and without errors. Despite the promising potential, the deployment of ANI in healthcare is not without its challenges. One of the most significant is the black box problem, where the decision-making process of the AI is not transparent or easily understood. This can be a major hurdle in a field like healthcare, where accountability and trust are paramount. Another critical challenge is data bias. If the data used to train the AI is unrepresentative or contains historical inequalities, the system may perpetuate and even amplify these biases, leading to disparities in care for certain demographic groups. The issue of data privacy and security is also a top concern, as these systems handle sensitive patient information that must be protected with the utmost care. Furthermore, challenges like the cold-start problem, where the system lacks sufficient data for new users or items, can initially limit the effectiveness of the recommendations. The future of ANI-based healthcare service recommendation systems is bright and holds immense potential. As data collection methods become more sophisticated and algorithms more advanced, these systems will likely become even more integrated into the healthcare ecosystem. The convergence of ANI with other emerging technologies, such as the Internet of Medical Things (IoMT) and wearable devices, will enable real-time health monitoring and proactive interventions. We can anticipate the development of more complex and holistic systems that not only recommend services but also assist in drug discovery, clinical trial management, and public health surveillance. The continued evolution of Explainable AI (XAI) will also be crucial, as it will help build trust and transparency by providing clear justifications for the recommendations. While the path forward requires careful navigation of ethical and regulatory issues, ANI is poised to become an indispensable tool in creating a more personalized, efficient, and equitable healthcare system for all.

II. LITERATURE SURVEY

Baker and Xiang (2023) discuss the convergence of the Internet of Things (IoT) and Artificial Intelligence (AI) has led to the development of the Artificial Intelligence of Things (AIoT), which is transforming healthcare. This paper surveys AIoT's role in creating "smarter" healthcare systems by analyzing its architecture, including sensors, communication technologies, and AI algorithms. It examines key applications like remote patient monitoring, diagnostics, and personalized medicine. The authors identify significant challenges such as data privacy and security, interoperability, and the need for robust, explainable AI models. Ultimately, the survey highlights the tremendous potential of AIoT to improve patient outcomes, enhance healthcare efficiency, and pave the way for a new era of patient-centric care, referred to as Healthcare 5.0. Gao et al. (2023) examines the use of Graph Neural Networks (GNNs) in recommender systems, highlighting their effectiveness in capturing complex user-item relationships. The paper provides a systematic review of the literature, categorizing GNN-based recommender systems based on the type of information used and the specific recommendation task. The authors discuss the key motivations for using GNNs, such as their ability to model high-order connectivity and structural properties of data. Furthermore, the survey identifies and analyzes major challenges in applying GNNs to recommender systems. These include issues with graph construction, the design of effective propagation and aggregation architectures, model optimization, and computational efficiency. The paper also explores how different GNN models address these challenges and discusses future research directions to further advance the field. Kumar et al. (2024) introduces a healthcare recommendation system that leverages Big Data Analytics (BDA) to provide personalized and accurate medical advice. It addresses the growing need for efficient healthcare solutions by analyzing vast amounts of multi-structured healthcare data, including patient records, lifestyle information, and social network activities. The system utilizes machine learning algorithms, such as Support Vector Classifier (SVC) and Random Forest (RF), to predict diseases based on symptoms and generate tailored recommendations for medications, diet, and exercise. By integrating these predictive models, the proposed system aims to enhance a patient's proactive health management, improve the accuracy of disease diagnosis, and bridge the gap between medical prediction and actionable treatment strategies. The authors validate the system's effectiveness through a case study on cardiovascular diseases, demonstrating its potential to be a scalable and efficient solution for modern healthcare.

III. HISTORICAL EVOLUTION

The historical evolution of Artificial Narrow Intelligence (ANI)-based healthcare service recommendation systems is a journey that spans several decades, from the earliest conceptual models to the sophisticated, data-driven platforms of today. This evolution can be understood as a progression through distinct phases, each marked by technological breakthroughs and a deeper understanding of how AI can be applied to the complexities of medicine.

Dawn of Expert Systems (1960s-1980s)

The roots of healthcare recommendation systems can be traced back to the development of expert systems in the 1960s and 1970s. These were some of the first practical applications of AI, designed to mimic the decision-making process of human experts by using a set of pre-programmed “if-then” rules. One of the most famous examples from this era is MYCIN, a rule-based system developed at Stanford University in the mid-1970s to diagnose and recommend treatments for bacterial infections. MYCIN was never used in clinical practice due to its rigid structure and the limited data available at the time, but it was a monumental proof of concept. It demonstrated that a computer could process symptoms and lab results to provide diagnostic and therapeutic advice with an accuracy comparable to that of human experts. Other notable expert systems of this period included CADUCEUS (INTERNIST-I), which focused on internal medicine, and CASNET for glaucoma. These early systems were a foundational step, but they were severely limited by their reliance on manually programmed rules and a lack of real-world data. They were brittle and could not handle ambiguous or complex cases outside of their narrow, defined knowledge base. The "knowledge acquisition bottleneck"—the challenge of manually codifying vast amounts of human expertise—was a major barrier to scalability and widespread adoption.

Rise of Data-Driven Approaches and Electronic Health Records (1990s-2000s)

The late 20th century saw a shift in focus from rule-based systems to data-driven approaches, driven by two key developments: the increasing power of computers and the gradual proliferation of Electronic Health Records (EHRs). As hospitals and clinics began digitizing patient information, a new kind of data source became available to AI researchers. This raw, real-world data was far richer and more nuanced than the hand-coded rules of the expert systems era. During this period, AI research in medicine began to explore early forms of machine learning. Instead of being explicitly programmed with rules, algorithms were trained to find patterns in the data. This included early forms of collaborative filtering, an algorithm that would become famous in e-commerce for recommending products based on the preferences of similar users. In healthcare, this meant algorithms could begin to recommend treatments or specialists based on the health profiles and outcomes of similar patients. The focus, however, remained largely on internal, academic research, with limited real-world clinical applications. The passage of legislation, such as the American Recovery and Reinvestment Act of 2009 in the United States, provided financial incentives for the widespread adoption of EHRs. This was a critical turning point. The resulting explosion of digital health data—including structured data like lab results and unstructured data like clinical notes—provided the fuel needed for the next wave of AI innovation. The problem was no longer a lack of data, but a need for more powerful tools to analyze it.

Machine Learning and Deep Learning Revolution (2010s-Present)

The last decade has witnessed a dramatic acceleration in the evolution of ANI-based healthcare systems, thanks to the maturation of machine learning and the rise of deep learning. With the availability of massive datasets and the development of more powerful algorithms, AI systems could now tackle tasks that were previously thought to be impossible. This period marks the true beginning of the modern healthcare recommendation system. Predictive analytics became a core capability. Systems were no longer just diagnosing; they were predicting. Using historical patient data, they could predict a patient's risk of developing a chronic disease, the likelihood of a hospital readmission, or the potential for an adverse drug reaction. This led to the development of early warning systems and preventative care recommendations. Concurrently, deep learning, particularly the use of convolutional neural networks (CNNs), revolutionized medical imaging analysis. AI systems trained on millions of medical images began to outperform human radiologists in detecting subtle signs of cancer, diabetic retinopathy, and other conditions, providing more accurate and timely diagnostic recommendations. The development of Natural Language Processing (NLP) capabilities also became a critical component. For the first time, AI could “read” and understand the vast amount of unstructured data in clinical notes, physician dictations, and discharge summaries. This allowed recommendation systems to factor in crucial information that was previously locked away in text, leading to more comprehensive and personalized recommendations. We also saw the emergence of virtual health assistants and chatbots, which used conversational AI to provide initial triage and basic health advice, recommending whether a patient should see a doctor, go to an urgent care clinic, or manage their symptoms at home. ANI-based systems are moving from being standalone tools to becoming integrated components of the healthcare workflow. They are used for everything from optimizing hospital resource allocation to recommending personalized treatment plans based on a patient's genomic data. The historical evolution of these systems reflects a journey from a handful of rigid, rule-based programs to a complex, interconnected ecosystem of intelligent applications that are fundamentally changing the practice of medicine.

IV. METHDOLOGY

This paper presents the methodology for development of medical system consists of two parts: the backend and the frontend, The frontend consists of HTML, CSS and JS which allows us to implement the interface with which the user interacts with the system. The backend consists of a Disease prediction system, a drug recommendation system and a hospital recommendation system backed by NLP which makes the entire system an interactive chatbot which imparts medical knowledge and helps the users in understanding their ailments better. Fig. 1 depicts the proposed system. Fig. 2. Illustrates the flowchart of proposed disease prediction system.

Figure 1. Proposed system

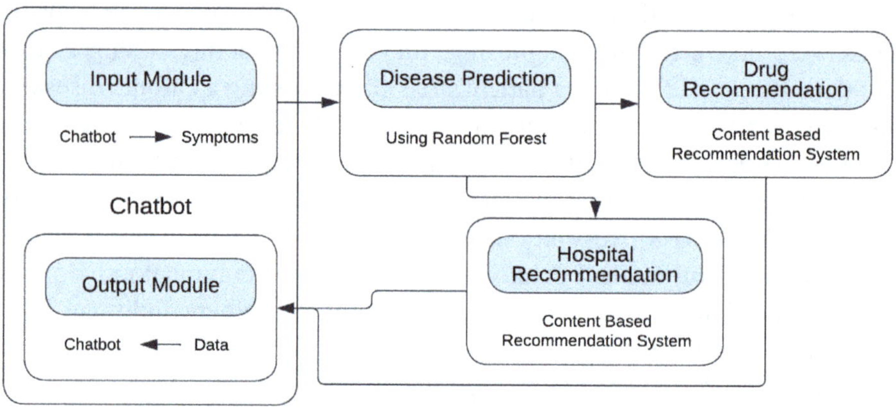

Disease prediction: This part of the system actualizes a strong machine learning demonstrate that predicts the illness a human has effectively, based on the side effects that the client has. The approach comprises the taking after:

- Gathering and cleaning the data: The dataset is obtained from Kaggle. The dataset has 132 parameters on which 42 distinctive sorts of maladies can be anticipated. This information is at that point cleaned as quality of information decides the quality of machine learning demonstrated.
- Model Building: After Gathering and Cleaning the information, the information is prepared and after bringing in Scikit-learn library, we actualize the Random Forest classifier () on this information. The quality of the model is checked by employing a confusion matrix.
- Inference: After predicting the disease utilizing Random Forest classifier algorithm that inside employments numerous choice trees to create the classification the testing information, we discover that the precision of the model is 97%.

Figure 2. Flowchart of proposed disease prediction system

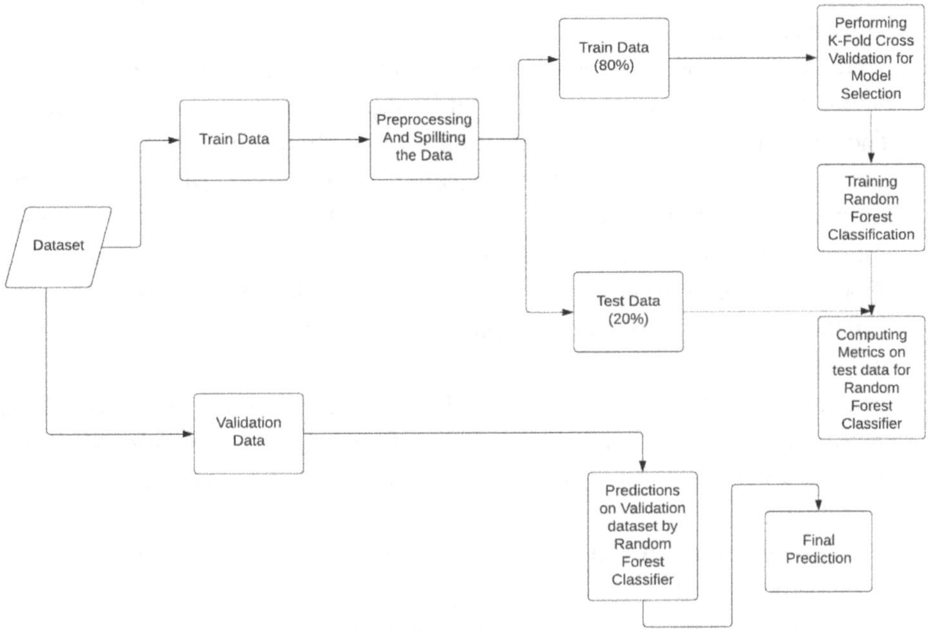

- Hospital Recommendation system: The hospital recommendation system will be a basic content-based suggestion framework utilizing a fastidiously curated dataset comprising of names, area, and other required information of different clinics over India. Content-based suggestion frameworks are a prevalent and broadly utilized approach to supply personalized proposals to clients. These frameworks are based on the thought that a user's inclinations can be anticipated based on their past interactions with things, such as their seeing and obtaining history. The objective of our content-based clinic suggestion framework is to suggest clinics to a client based on the area data given by them. Tf-IDF vectorizer and cosine likeness have been utilized in this framework.
- Drug recommendation: This fragment of the venture actualizes a deep learning how to classify drugs productively, based on quiet qualities and sedate depictions. The strategy has these taking after steps:
- Data Acquisition and Preprocessing: The dataset, sourced from 'Drug.csv', typifies significant data counting understanding socioeconomics (sexual orientation and age) and literary portrayals of drugs nearby related infections. Starting preprocessing includes encoding categorical factors and tokenizing

sedate portrayals to encourage encourage investigation. Dataset is cleansed to guarantee the quality of input information, in this manner optimizing demonstrate execution.

- Model Development: Upon information preprocessing, the successive LSTM neural arrange demonstrate is built utilizing TensorFlow and Keras libraries. The show design includes an inserting layer to change over sedate depictions into thick vector representations, taken after by an LSTM layer to capture temporal dependencies effectively. Moreover, batch normalization methods are utilized to stabilize the preparing handle. The show is prepared utilizing hyperparameter tuning methods by means of Random Search, optimizing parameters such as embedding output dimension, LSTM units, dropout rates, and learning rate.
- Evaluation and Inference: The trained model's execution is assessed utilizing measurements such as precision on the testing dataset. Expectations are made on inconspicuous sedate tests, and the coming about classification exactness is evaluated.
- NLP implementation: This technique gives a brief overview of the chatbot advancement handle, highlighting key stages from information taking care of to neural arrange preparing and client interaction.
- Data and Preprocessing: Predefined entomb and reactions are stacked from a JSON record. Each expectation is tokenized, normalized, and changed over to a "bag-of-words" representation. Special words, classes, and archives are recognized for preparing.
- Neural Network Architecture and Model Training: Neural network is outlined with input, hidden, and output layers. Fitting actuation capacities are chosen for each layer. The demonstrate is prepared utilizing bag-of-words representations and encoded names. Hyperparameters like ages and group measure are optimized.
- Chatbot Functionality: A work cleans, tokenizes, and classifies client input. Based on classification, the work recovers or creates a reaction.
- Interaction and Evaluation: The chatbot interacts with users in a continuous loop. Error handling and user criticism are consolidated for enhancement.

Fig. 3 illustrates the use case diagram.

Figure 3. Use Case Diagram

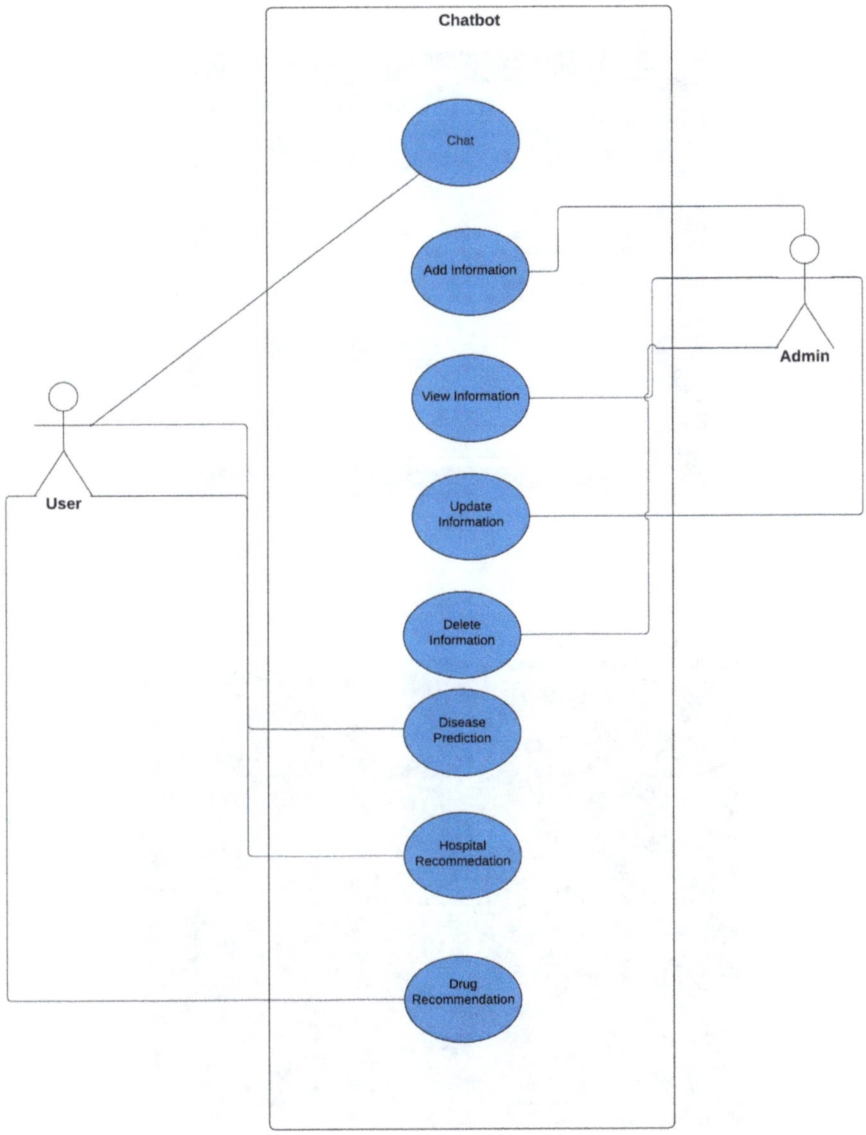

V. RESULTS

Figure 4. Chatbot Interface

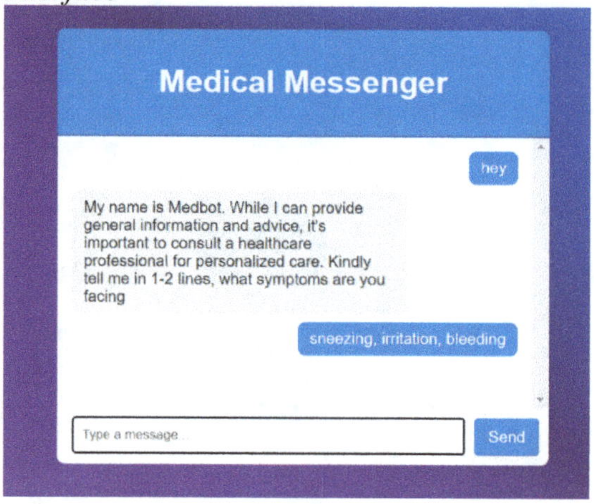

Figure 5. Results of proposed models

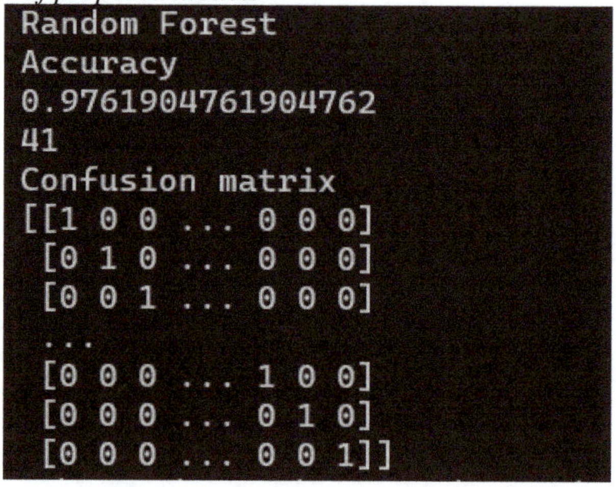

VI. IMPACT ON SOCIETY

Artificial Narrow Intelligence (ANI)-based healthcare service recommendation systems are already having a profound and multi-faceted impact on society.

While they hold immense potential for improving healthcare delivery and patient outcomes, their implementation also introduces significant economic, ethical, and social challenges that must be addressed.

- Economic Impact: The economic impact of ANI in healthcare is primarily driven by its ability to increase efficiency and reduce costs. By automating administrative tasks, such as scheduling appointments, managing patient records, and processing insurance claims, these systems free up valuable time for healthcare professionals. This allows doctors and nurses to focus more on direct patient care, potentially leading to higher job satisfaction and reduced burnout. Additionally, AI-powered systems can analyze vast datasets to identify opportunities for optimizing hospital operations, from managing bed availability to streamlining supply chains (Diksha et al., 2023). This can lead to substantial cost savings for healthcare providers and, in some cases, lower expenses for patients. Some estimates suggest that widespread AI adoption could save the U.S. healthcare system hundreds of billions of dollars annually. Beyond cost savings, ANI systems can improve accessibility to healthcare services. In areas with a shortage of medical professionals, these systems can act as a crucial first point of contact, providing initial diagnoses and recommending appropriate care pathways. This can be particularly beneficial in rural or underserved communities where a specialist might not be readily available. The rise of telemedicine, often powered by AI, allows patients to receive personalized recommendations and follow-up care from the comfort of their homes, which is a game-changer for individuals with mobility issues or those who live far from clinics.
- Ethical and Social Implications: The societal impact of ANI in healthcare is intertwined with a complex web of ethical considerations. One of the most significant concerns is data privacy and security. Healthcare recommendation systems rely on access to vast amounts of sensitive personal health information, and any data breach could have serious consequences. As these systems become more integrated, safeguarding patient data from unauthorized access or misuse is paramount. Another critical issue is algorithmic bias. If the data used to train the AI is not representative of the entire population, the system may inadvertently perpetuate or even amplify existing health disparities. For example, if a recommendation system is trained primarily on data from a specific racial or socioeconomic group, its recommendations may be less effective or even harmful for other groups (Sharma et al., 2024). This can lead to a widening of the health equity gap, where already marginalized communities receive substandard care. For this reason, it's essential that AI models are trained on diverse datasets and continuously audited for bias.

Furthermore, the integration of ANI into healthcare raises questions about patient autonomy and trust. While AI can provide a wealth of information and expert recommendations, it's crucial that patients remain in control of their own healthcare decisions. There's a risk that patients might blindly trust an AI's recommendation without fully understanding the reasoning behind it, and that doctors might become overly reliant on the technology, potentially dulling their own skills and critical thinking. Maintaining the human element in the doctor-patient relationship is vital, as it builds trust and allows for a shared decision-making process that accounts for a patient's personal values and preferences.

- Impact on the Healthcare Workforce: The introduction of AI-powered systems is also reshaping the healthcare workforce. While ANI is not expected to completely replace doctors, it will undoubtedly change their roles. By taking on repetitive, data-intensive tasks, AI allows healthcare professionals to focus on the more nuanced and empathetic aspects of their work. However, there are valid concerns about the deskilling of the workforce. If doctors become too dependent on AI for diagnosis and treatment planning, they may lose some of their diagnostic intuition and expertise over time. Additionally, the rise of AI could lead to a shift in the skills required for future healthcare professionals (Painuly & Sharma, 2024). There will be an increasing need for professionals who are not only skilled in medicine but also have a strong understanding of data analytics and AI. This will necessitate changes in medical education and training programs to prepare the next generation of doctors for a world where AI is a partner in care. The economic consequences for certain roles, such as medical transcriptionists or some administrative positions, could be significant as AI takes over more of these tasks.

VII. ADVANTAGES

Artificial Narrow Intelligence (ANI)-based healthcare service recommendation systems represent a paradigm shift in how medical care is delivered, moving away from a traditional, one-size-fits-all model towards a hyper-personalized, data-driven approach. The benefits of this transition are vast and multi-faceted, profoundly impacting patients, healthcare providers, and the healthcare ecosystem as a whole.

- Enhanced Diagnostic Accuracy and Precision: One of the most significant benefits of ANI in healthcare is its ability to dramatically improve diagnostic accuracy. These systems can analyze vast amounts of medical data—including medical images like X-rays and MRIs, patient records, and genomic information—at a speed and scale that is simply impossible for human professionals. For example, ANI algorithms trained on massive datasets of medical images can detect subtle anomalies or patterns indicative of diseases such as cancer, diabetic retinopathy, or pulmonary embolisms with a level of precision that can match or even exceed that of human experts (Agarwal & Sharma, 2024). This capability not only leads to earlier and more accurate disease detection but can also reduce the rate of misdiagnoses, a critical factor in improving patient outcomes. By providing doctors with an "AI second opinion," these systems act as powerful clinical decision support tools, helping to reduce diagnostic errors and ensuring that patients receive the correct treatment plan from the outset.

- Personalization and Improved Patient Outcomes: The cornerstone of an ANI-based recommendation system is its ability to deliver personalized medicine. By analyzing a patient's unique health profile—including their medical history, genetic makeup, lifestyle, and even environmental factors—the system can recommend a treatment plan tailored specifically to their needs. This level of personalization is crucial for chronic disease management, as it allows for dynamic adjustments to treatment plans based on real-time data from wearable devices or patient-reported information. For a patient with diabetes, for instance, an ANI system could analyze blood sugar readings, diet logs, and physical activity to suggest personalized medication adjustments or lifestyle changes (Chamoli et al., 2024). This proactive and individualized approach not only improves the effectiveness of treatment but also helps to prevent potential complications, leading to better long-term health outcomes.
- Increased Efficiency and Cost Reduction: ANI-based systems are a powerful tool for driving operational efficiency and reducing costs across the healthcare industry. These systems can automate a wide range of administrative tasks that are typically time-consuming and prone to human error. This includes everything from patient scheduling, billing, and claims processing to managing electronic health records (EHRs). By automating these processes, healthcare organizations can significantly reduce labor costs and free up staff to focus on more critical tasks. Beyond administration, ANI can optimize resource allocation within a hospital, predicting patient admissions and staffing needs to ensure that resources are used efficiently and effectively. This leads to reduced waiting times for patients and a more streamlined workflow for healthcare providers, ultimately contributing to a more sustainable and cost-effective healthcare system.
- Patient Empowerment and Proactive Care: ANI-based recommendation systems are empowering patients to take a more active role in their own health. By providing personalized health insights and proactive recommendations,

these systems help patients make more informed decisions about their well-being. This can range from simple dietary suggestions based on a patient's health goals to early warnings about potential health issues detected through continuous monitoring via wearable devices. This shift towards proactive and preventive care is vital, as it allows for interventions before a condition becomes severe, which is often less costly and more effective. Furthermore, the accessibility of these systems through mobile apps and telemedicine platforms means that patients in remote or underserved areas can receive high-quality health advice and recommendations without the need for a physical visit, bridging the gap in healthcare access.

- Acceleration of Medical Research and Drug Discovery: Beyond individual patient care, ANI is also accelerating the pace of medical research and drug discovery. By analyzing vast datasets of clinical trial information, genomic data, and scientific literature, ANI systems can identify patterns and connections that might not be apparent to human researchers. This capability can significantly shorten the time and reduce the cost associated with developing new drugs by identifying promising drug candidates, predicting their efficacy and potential side effects, and even identifying ideal candidates for clinical trials. This accelerated research and development cycle means that life-saving treatments can reach patients faster, with a higher chance of success. The benefits of Artificial Narrow Intelligence in healthcare are transformative. From enhancing diagnostic accuracy and delivering personalized medicine to improving operational efficiency and empowering patients, these systems are poised to revolutionize the way we approach health and wellness. While challenges remain, the clear advantages in terms of patient outcomes, cost reduction, and accessibility make ANI an indispensable tool for the future of healthcare.

VIII. CHALLENGES

The proliferation of Artificial Narrow Intelligence (ANI)-based healthcare service recommendation systems presents a host of formidable challenges that must be addressed to ensure their safe, equitable, and effective integration into society. While their potential benefits are undeniable, the risks associated with these systems, from a technical, ethical, and societal standpoint, are significant and require careful consideration.

- The Black Box Problem and Lack of Transparency: One of the most pressing technical and ethical challenges is the "black box" problem. Many of the most powerful and sophisticated ANI models, particularly those based on deep learning, operate in a way that is not easily understandable or transparent to human users. They make decisions and provide recommendations based on complex, non-linear relationships within vast datasets, without offering a clear, step-by-step explanation of their reasoning. In high-stakes fields like medicine, this lack of transparency is deeply problematic. When a system recommends a specific, life-altering treatment, both the patient and the physician need to understand why that recommendation was made. If a misdiagnosis occurs, or a patient's condition worsens, it is nearly impossible to audit the AI's decision-making process to determine what went wrong. This opacity erodes trust, complicates accountability, and can make it difficult to rectify errors, posing a significant barrier to widespread adoption in clinical practice. The development of Explainable AI (XAI) is an active area of research aimed at mitigating this challenge, but it is far from a solved problem.

- Algorithmic Bias and Health Disparities: A second major challenge is the risk of algorithmic bias. ANI systems are only as good as the data they are trained on, and if that data is incomplete, unrepresentative, or reflects existing societal inequalities, the AI will learn and perpetuate those biases. In healthcare, this can have dire consequences. For example, if a recommendation system is trained predominantly on data from a specific racial or socioeconomic group, its recommendations may be less accurate or even harmful for other groups (Gautam & Sharma, 2024). There have been documented cases where healthcare algorithms, trained on data reflecting historical health spending, systematically underestimated the health needs of marginalized populations, leading to reduced access to care. This risk is particularly acute in areas like dermatology, where algorithms trained on images of lighter skin tones may misdiagnose conditions in individuals with darker skin, or in cardiology, where models trained on primarily male data may fail to recognize heart attack symptoms in women. Without conscious and proactive efforts to collect diverse and representative datasets, and to continuously audit and correct for bias, ANI systems could exacerbate existing health disparities and worsen healthcare inequities.
- Data Privacy and Security Concerns: The very foundation of ANI-based healthcare systems—the access to and analysis of massive amounts of sensitive patient data—introduces significant privacy and security risks. Health information, including medical history, lab results, and genomic data, is some of the most personal and confidential data an individual possesses. A data breach of an AI system could have catastrophic consequences, leading to identity theft, discrimination, or public exposure of highly sensitive health conditions. Moreover, the sheer volume and interconnectedness of data re-

quired for these systems make them attractive targets for cybercriminals. While regulations like HIPAA in the United States and GDPR in Europe provide a framework for data protection, they were not designed specifically for the complexities of AI, where data can be used for purposes beyond its initial collection. Challenges also exist in properly anonymizing data, as sophisticated AI techniques can sometimes re-identify individuals from supposedly de-identified datasets. Ensuring robust security measures and strict privacy protocols is not just a technical requirement but an ethical imperative to maintain patient trust.

- The Problem of Over-reliance and Legal Liability: Another significant challenge is the potential for over-reliance on AI systems by healthcare professionals. While ANI is designed to be a decision-support tool, there is a risk that busy or less-experienced clinicians might blindly accept the AI's recommendations without applying their own critical judgment and experience. This can lead to a "deskilling" of the medical workforce, where human intuition and diagnostic skills atrophy from underuse. Furthermore, the question of legal liability remains largely unresolved. If an AI system makes a recommendation that leads to a negative patient outcome, who is at fault? Is it the AI developer, the hospital that implemented the system, or the doctor who accepted the recommendation? The current legal and regulatory frameworks are not equipped to handle this complexity, creating a significant barrier to widespread adoption and innovation. Establishing clear standards for accountability and a robust framework for determining liability is crucial for moving forward.
- The Cold-Start Problem and Data Quality: From a practical standpoint, two other challenges loom large: the "cold-start" problem and data quality. Recommendation systems, particularly those using collaborative filtering, struggle to provide accurate recommendations for new users or new services because they lack the necessary historical data. A new patient entering the system has no user history, and a newly developed treatment has no track record, making it difficult for the AI to provide relevant recommendations. This can be a major hurdle for new patient onboarding and the adoption of novel medical advancements (Sharma et al., 2025). Additionally, the quality of the data itself is a constant concern. Inaccurate, inconsistent, or incomplete data in electronic health records can lead to flawed analysis and incorrect recommendations. The phrase "garbage in, garbage out" is particularly relevant here; even the most advanced AI algorithms cannot overcome the limitations of poor-quality data. Ensuring data cleanliness and integrity is a monumental and ongoing task. While ANI-based healthcare service recommendation systems offer a tantalizing vision of a more efficient and personalized future,

their development and implementation are fraught with significant challenges. The lack of transparency, the risk of algorithmic bias, serious privacy and security concerns, and the unresolved issues of liability and over-reliance are all hurdles that must be overcome. Addressing these challenges requires not only technological innovation but also a commitment to ethical design, robust regulation, and a collaborative effort from technologists, healthcare providers, and policymakers to ensure these systems are developed and used in a way that truly benefits all of society.

IX. FUTURE PERSPECTIVE

The future of Artificial Narrow Intelligence (ANI)-based healthcare service recommendation systems is poised for exponential growth and transformative change, driven by advancements in technology, a growing emphasis on personalized medicine, and the need for more efficient healthcare delivery. Looking forward, these systems are expected to become more sophisticated, integrated, and capable of addressing some of the most significant challenges facing global healthcare. This future will not be a singular event, but a continuous evolution marked by several key trends and developments.

- Deeper Integration with the Internet of Medical Things (IoMT): The most immediate and impactful future development will be the deeper integration of ANI with the Internet of Medical Things (IoMT). Currently, many healthcare AI systems operate on data from a variety of sources, but the future will see a seamless, real-time flow of data from a vast network of connected medical devices, sensors, and wearables. This includes everything from smartwatches that continuously monitor heart rate and blood oxygen levels to glucose monitors, smart inhalers, and even implantable devices that track vital signs and organ function (Gautam & Sharma, 2024b). ANI will act as the intelligent brain of this network, analyzing the deluge of data generated by IoMT devices to provide real-time, proactive recommendations. This integration will enable a shift from reactive to proactive and predictive healthcare. Instead of simply recommending a treatment after a patient becomes ill, the system will be able to predict the onset of a health event—such as a diabetic episode, a cardiac arrhythmia, or a sepsis infection—before it happens. For instance, an ANI system could detect subtle changes in a patient's vital signs and activity patterns, and then issue a real-time alert to the patient and their physician, recommending specific actions or even a pre-emptive hospital visit. This not only has the potential to save lives but also to significantly reduce healthcare costs by preventing costly hospitalizations and emergency interventions. The future of these systems is a continuous, intelligent feedback loop that keeps a patient in a state of optimal health.

- The Rise of Multimodal and Generative AI: Future recommendation systems will move beyond traditional data sources like electronic health records and integrate multimodal data—combining information from medical imaging, genomic sequencing, patient-reported outcomes, and even social and environmental data. For example, a system could analyze a patient's MRI scans, their genetic risk factors, and their geographic location (which might correlate with certain environmental health risks) to provide a far more comprehensive and accurate recommendation than is possible today. Furthermore, Generative AI, a rapidly emerging field, will play a crucial role. While today's systems primarily analyze and recommend based on existing data, future generative models could create entirely new, personalized care pathways or even simulate the potential outcomes of different treatment options. A generative AI system could take a patient's complex health profile and "generate" a hypothetical treatment plan, simulating the patient's likely response and allowing doctors to fine-tune the plan before it is even initiated. This could revolutionize personalized medicine by enabling a level of foresight and predictive modeling that is currently unimaginable.
- Enhanced Personalization and Patient Engagement: The future of ANI in healthcare will place a greater emphasis on patient empowerment and engagement. Recommendation systems will become more intuitive and user-friendly, acting as a personal health coach in a way that is both informative and empathetic. Future systems will likely use conversational AI interfaces, allowing patients to interact with a "virtual health assistant" to get real-time answers to their questions, receive medication reminders, and access personalized health education. This will lead to a more collaborative model of care. Patients will be able to share their preferences, goals, and even emotional states with the AI, which will then factor this qualitative data into its recommendations. The system might suggest a treatment that is not only clinically effective but also aligns with the patient's lifestyle and personal values. This shift from a paternalistic model of care to a more collaborative one will build greater trust and compliance, leading to better long-term health management.
- Addressing Ethical Challenges Through Explainable AI (XAI) and Regulation: To achieve this vision, the future of ANI in healthcare must also address the ethical and technical challenges that currently exist. The development of Explainable AI (XAI) will be a major focus. Future systems will not only provide a recommendation but will also provide a clear, easy-to-understand rationale for it (Gupta & Sharma, 2024). This will build confi-

dence and trust among patients and clinicians, addressing the "black box" problem and ensuring that medical professionals can critically evaluate and take responsibility for the AI's suggestions. Alongside XAI, robust regulatory frameworks will evolve to govern the use of AI in medicine. Policymakers will create clear guidelines on data privacy, algorithmic bias, and accountability to ensure that these systems are safe and equitable for all populations (Pandey et al., 2024). This will include requirements for regular audits of AI models to ensure they do not perpetuate health disparities. The future will see a global effort to standardize the development and deployment of medical AI, with certifications and legal precedents that clarify liability and responsibility.

- The Evolution of the Healthcare Workforce: Finally, the future of ANI will reshape the healthcare workforce itself. Rather than replacing doctors and nurses, AI will become their indispensable partner. Future medical professionals will be trained to work with these systems, understanding how to interpret their recommendations and integrate them into their clinical practice. New roles will emerge, such as AI ethicists, data scientists for healthcare, and AI-integrated clinical specialists, who will bridge the gap between technology and medicine (Rawat et al., 2023). In this future, routine administrative tasks will be fully automated, freeing up human professionals to focus on the truly human aspects of care: empathy, compassion, and shared decision-making. The relationship between a doctor and patient will be enhanced, not diminished, by technology that handles the data-intensive work, allowing the human connection to take center stage. The future of ANI-based healthcare service recommendation systems is not just about smarter technology; it's about a smarter, more personalized, and more humane healthcare system for all.

X. CASE STUDY

Artificial Narrow Intelligence (ANI)-based healthcare service recommendation systems are no longer theoretical concepts but are actively being developed and implemented in the United States. These systems demonstrate their value through a variety of real-world case studies across different healthcare sectors, from clinical practice to patient-facing applications. Here are some notable examples.

- Mayo Clinic: One of the most prominent case studies in the U.S. comes from the Mayo Clinic, a world-renowned academic medical center. The Mayo Clinic has been a leader in applying ANI, particularly in the field of cardiology. Their collaboration with Google's AI division is a prime example of a health system and a technology company partnering to leverage vast datasets for medical breakthroughs. One of their most impactful projects involved the development of an ANI tool to screen for a weak heart pump, or low left ventricular ejection fraction. This condition, a precursor to heart failure, often goes undiagnosed because it has no obvious symptoms. The Mayo Clinic trained a deep learning model on a massive database of over 7 million electrocardiograms (ECGs) from patients. The resulting AI was able to detect the presence of a weak heart pump with an accuracy of 93%, which is more accurate than a mammogram for breast cancer detection. This ANI tool can be applied to any standard ECG, a common and low-cost test, making it a powerful and accessible screening tool for the general population. The system can now be used to screen for at-risk individuals, allowing for early intervention and a reduction in the incidence of heart failure. Beyond cardiology, the Mayo Clinic has also applied ANI to stroke detection. In emergency rooms, a computer trained to analyze CT scans can significantly reduce the time to diagnose an intracerebral hemorrhage, a type of stroke. By flagging potential issues in minutes, this AI system helps doctors make quicker decisions, which is critical for limiting brain damage and improving patient outcomes. These case studies demonstrate how ANI, by analyzing a massive volume of data, can function as a powerful clinical decision support system, providing doctors with actionable, data-driven recommendations.

- Sensely: While the Mayo Clinic's examples are heavily focused on the clinical side, companies like Sensely provide a case study of ANI in patient-facing applications. Sensely developed an AI-powered virtual nurse assistant named Molly. This AI chatbot is designed to assist patients, particularly those with chronic illnesses, by providing personalized recommendations and support. Molly's primary function is to conduct routine check-ins with patients, assess their symptoms, and provide medical advice based on standardized protocols. For example, a patient with diabetes can communicate with Molly via text or voice, and the AI will ask questions to monitor their condition and offer advice on medication management or lifestyle adjustments. The system uses natural language processing (NLP) to understand the patient's input and can even infer their emotional state. The case study of Sensely's implementation shows several key benefits:
    - Cost Reduction: The use of Molly has been shown to reduce the labor cost of patient monitoring by up to 66%, freeing up nurses to focus on patients who require in-person care.

- o 24/7 Accessibility: The AI assistant provides round-the-clock support, making healthcare more accessible for patients, particularly those with chronic conditions who need ongoing support.
- o Proactive Care: By continuously monitoring patient data, Molly can identify potential issues early and provide timely recommendations, such as advising a patient to contact their doctor based on changes in their symptoms.

This example illustrates how ANI can serve as a valuable tool for remote patient monitoring and patient engagement, making healthcare more convenient and proactive for millions of Americans.

- Google DeepMind: Google's DeepMind Health initiative, while having a significant presence in the UK, also provides an important case study with its work in the U.S. to address Acute Kidney Injury (AKI). AKI is a life-threatening condition that affects millions of Americans and is often associated with a high mortality rate. DeepMind developed an AI-powered app called Streams to help clinicians detect and manage AKI. The app analyzes a patient's electronic health record (EHR) data, including lab results and vital signs, in real-time. It then uses predictive algorithms to identify patients at a high risk of developing AKI and sends a timely alert to their medical team. This gives doctors a crucial 48-hour head start to intervene and prevent the condition from worsening. This case study highlights the power of ANI in predictive analytics and early warning systems. By sifting through a patient's data in the background, the AI can find subtle patterns that a human might miss in a fast-paced clinical environment. The use of this system has been shown to improve patient outcomes and reduce healthcare costs associated with treating the advanced stages of AKI. It also demonstrates the critical importance of secure data handling, as the partnership required a robust framework to ensure patient privacy.

China's healthcare system, facing immense pressure from a large and aging population, has become a hotbed for the development and application of Artificial Narrow Intelligence (ANI)-based healthcare service recommendation systems. The case studies from China are particularly compelling due to the country's top-down commitment to AI, a vast and digitally-savvy population, and a pressing need to bridge the gap in medical resources between urban and rural areas.

- Ping An Good Doctor: One of the most comprehensive case studies in China is from Ping An Good Doctor, a subsidiary of the insurance and financial services giant Ping An Group. Ping An Good Doctor has created a full-service, AI-driven healthcare ecosystem that combines online consultation, health management, and a vast network of physical clinics. At its core is an ANI-based recommendation system that leverages a massive database, which includes medical records, online consultation data, and a knowledge base of diseases and prescriptions. The system's primary function is to serve as an AI-powered “family doctor” for its users. When a patient enters their symptoms, the AI uses natural language processing (NLP) to understand the query and a deep learning model to analyze the symptoms. It then provides an initial diagnosis and a recommendation on the next steps, which could be anything from self-care advice to a recommendation to see a specialist or go to a specific hospital. The system's accuracy in assisting with initial inquiries has been reported to be approximately 98%, and it has handled millions of consultation requests per day. The case study of Ping An Good Doctor highlights several key aspects of ANI's impact in China:

- Bridging the Resource Gap: By providing a high-quality initial consultation service, the system helps filter out non-urgent cases from the overstretched hospital system. It directs patients to the appropriate level of care, preventing the unnecessary over-crowding of top-tier hospitals and reducing the burden on their specialists.
- Integrated Ecosystem: The system is not a standalone tool but is seamlessly integrated with Ping An's other services, including insurance. This allows for a closed-loop system where the AI can help with a diagnosis, recommend a specific hospital or doctor, and even assist with insurance claims.
- 24/7 Accessibility: The platform provides round-the-clock medical advice, which is a game-changer for people in rural or remote areas who may not have immediate access to a doctor. This has led to a significant improvement in healthcare accessibility across the country.

- Tencent's “AI Doctor” and Diagnostic Support: Another major player in China's AI healthcare landscape is Tencent, a technology conglomerate. Tencent's AI Medical Labs have developed a number of tools, but one of the most notable is their “Miying” ( ) AI-powered diagnostic system. Miying is a set of AI tools that assist doctors in a variety of clinical scenarios, from medical imaging to disease risk prediction. A compelling case study comes from their work in cancer screening. Miying was trained on millions of medical images, including CT scans and endoscopies, to identify early signs of a variety of cancers, such as esophageal, colorectal, and lung cancer. In one instance, the system was able to detect suspicious lesions in medical images with a high degree of accuracy, which could easily be missed by the human eye. The AI provides a recommendation by highlighting the suspicious areas for a doctor's review, acting as an indispensable second opinion. This helps to reduce the rate of misdiagnosis and ensures that patients receive timely treatment.

  - o Complementing, Not Replacing, Doctors: Miying is a prime example of an ANI system that is designed to be a clinical decision support tool. It is not meant to replace doctors but to augment their capabilities, allowing them to focus on complex cases and patient care.
  - o Focus on Early Detection: By excelling at pattern recognition, these systems can significantly improve the early detection of diseases, which is a crucial factor in improving patient survival rates.
  - o Scalability: The ability of these systems to analyze vast numbers of medical images and patient records means that high-quality diagnostic assistance can be scaled to a large population, addressing the shortage of specialized medical professionals like radiologists.

- Tsinghua University's AI Agent Hospital: Perhaps the most ambitious case study in China is the Tsinghua University's "AI Agent Hospital," launched in 2024. This is a groundbreaking project that moves beyond a single application to create an entire virtual hospital ecosystem powered by AI. It features 42 AI-powered "doctors" across 21 different specialties. The system can replicate an entire clinical workflow, from initial consultation and diagnosis to treatment recommendations and follow-up care. The "hospital" operates on a large language model (LLM) and is trained on vast medical literature and millions of simulated patient cases. It can "treat" up to 10,000 virtual patients in a matter of days, a feat that would take human doctors years to accomplish. This allows the AI models to be refined and evolved rapidly, improving their diagnostic accuracy and treatment recommendations. This case study is a blueprint for the future and reveals:
- Holistic System Design: It's not just a recommendation engine; it's an entire, end-to-end healthcare service system. This approach aims to address systemic inefficiencies and provide a seamless patient journey.
- Role in Medical Education: The "Agent Hospital" serves as a powerful educational tool for medical students and a testing ground for new clinical protocols, allowing for a safer and more rapid development of healthcare solutions.
- Integration of LLMs: The use of LLMs in a healthcare context is a major step forward, as it allows the AI to "think" and communicate in a more humanlike way, making the patient experience more intuitive and conversational.

India presents a compelling and unique case study for the application of Artificial Narrow Intelligence (ANI)-based healthcare service recommendation systems.

Faced with a massive population, a significant urban-rural healthcare divide, and a shortage of specialist doctors, India has become a fertile ground for AI innovation aimed at democratizing access to quality care. The case studies below highlight how various players, from large institutions to nimble startups, are leveraging ANI to address these challenges.

- Aravind Eye Care System: The Aravind Eye Care System is globally renowned for its high-volume, low-cost model of treating preventable blindness. As a case study for ANI, its collaboration with Google and a number of other academic institutions stands out. The challenge for Aravind was how to screen millions of people, particularly in rural areas, for diabetic retinopathy, a condition that can lead to blindness and often shows no symptoms in its early stages. The shortage of qualified ophthalmologists made it impossible to manually screen every person at risk. To solve this, a deep learning model was trained on a massive dataset of retinal images from patients in India and around the world. The resulting AI algorithm can analyze a retinal scan and accurately identify signs of diabetic retinopathy with an accuracy of 97.5%, rivaling that of a human ophthalmologist. The system provides a recommendation on whether a patient has the condition and the severity, which helps in triaging patients. This ANI-based system is now being deployed in remote villages through mobile screening vans. A technician can take a picture of the patient's retina, and the AI provides a diagnosis on the spot, recommending whether the patient needs to visit a specialist at a hospital for further treatment. This not only makes screenings more accessible and cost-effective but also helps doctors prioritize the most urgent cases, effectively turning a time-consuming diagnostic task into a quick, scalable screening process.
- Qure.ai: Qure.ai, a Mumbai-based startup, is another prime example of ANI's impact on healthcare in India. Their AI-powered solutions are designed to address the shortage of radiologists and the high cost of medical imaging. One of their flagship products is an AI platform that can read medical images like CT scans and chest X-rays. A key case study involves its use in tuberculosis (TB) screening. TB remains a major public health challenge in India. Qure.ai's AI tool was trained on millions of chest X-rays to accurately detect abnormalities indicative of TB. The system can provide a report in a matter of seconds, flagging suspected cases for a radiologist's review. This capability is particularly impactful in remote clinics and rural hospitals where access to a specialized radiologist is limited or non-existent. The AI provides a crucial diagnostic recommendation, allowing a local doctor to make a quick and informed decision. Similarly, in emergency settings, their AI can analyze head CT scans to detect intracranial hemorrhages and other abnormalities, provid-

ing a timely alert to physicians. This is a life-saving application, as prompt diagnosis of a stroke is critical for patient outcomes. The success of Qure.ai demonstrates how ANI, by automating the initial analysis of medical images, can help bridge the expert talent gap and accelerate the diagnostic process across a country with diverse and often underserved populations.

- Niramai: Niramai Health Analytix, based in Bangalore, provides a compelling case study on using ANI for non-invasive breast cancer screening. Their technology, called Thermalytix, uses a high-resolution thermal camera to capture thermal images of a woman's breast. The underlying premise is that cancerous tumors, being metabolically active, emit more heat than normal tissue. The ANI-based system then analyzes these thermal images using machine learning algorithms to detect subtle, early-stage signs of cancer. The key benefit of this recommendation system is its non-invasive nature and its ability to detect early-stage cancer in younger women, for whom traditional mammography is often less effective. The system provides a risk score recommendation, helping to triage patients for further investigation by a doctor. This technology is particularly well-suited for the Indian context, as it is radiation-free, painless, and can be used in a mobile setting. It helps in the early detection of a disease that is a significant health concern for Indian women, especially in a country where awareness and access to regular screenings are not widespread.
- HealthifyMe: Moving beyond diagnostics, Indian startups are also leveraging ANI for personalized health and wellness. HealthifyMe is a leading example, offering a recommendation system that helps users achieve their fitness and weight loss goals. The platform uses a combination of data from user-reported food intake, fitness trackers, and an AI nutritionist named "Ria". Ria acts as an intelligent assistant, providing personalized diet and exercise recommendations based on the user's goals, daily activity, and dietary habits. It can, for instance, analyze a picture of a meal, identify the food items, and recommend a healthier alternative or a different portion size. The system also recommends workout routines and tracks progress, offering real-time feedback. While not a medical service in the traditional sense, this type of ANI is a powerful tool for preventative healthcare, helping to manage and mitigate lifestyle diseases like obesity, diabetes, and heart disease, which are on the rise in India.

XI. CONCLUSION

This proposed technique illustrates the execution of Random Forest, LSTM and Cosine Likeness models for disease detection, drug recommendation and Hospital recommendation, individually. By applying appropriate information preprocessing procedures and carefully tuning hyperparameters, all models can accomplish tall exactness and generalizability. The execution of NLP within the project makes it exceptionally progressed and able to reply to different restorative related questions. The extend is conveyed on a cloud stage, making it accessible to distinctive clients. The advance investigation seems to investigate consolidating extra information sources and progressing profound learning procedures to move forward with disease discovery and drug recommendation accuracy. Future work on this venture seem lead to speedier therapeutic determination of diseases, in this way making the lives of the specialists simpler by lessening their workload.

REFERENCES

Agarwal, J., & Sharma, S. (2024). Artificial Intelligence enabled cognitive computer-centered digital analysis model for examination of the children's mental health. *Evolutionary Intelligence*, *17*(5–6), 3675–3685. DOI: 10.1007/s12065-024-00951-6

Baker, S., & Xiang, W. (2023). Artificial Intelligence of Things for Smarter Healthcare: A survey of advancements, challenges, and opportunities. *IEEE Communications Surveys and Tutorials*, *25*(2), 1261–1293. DOI: 10.1109/comst.2023.3256323

Chamoli, A., Kirsali, A., & Sharma, S. (2024). Cyber Attack Prevention Method for Enhanced Privacy of Patients Digital Healthcare Data in Smart Hospitals. In 2024 7th International Conference on Circuit Power and Computing Technologies (ICCPCT), 2, 54–59. https://doi.org/DOI: 10.1109/iccpct61902.2024.10672954

Diksha, N., Verma, A. K., Bhadula, S., & Sharma, S. (2023). Artificial Intelligence Enabled Disease Prediction System in Healthcare Industry. In *2023 IEEE International Conference on Blockchain and Distributed Systems Security (ICBDS)*, 1–6. https://doi.org/DOI: 10.1109/icbds58040.2023.10346275

Gao, C., Zheng, Y., Li, N., Li, Y., Qin, Y., Piao, J., Quan, Y., Chang, J., Jin, D., He, X., & Li, Y. (2023). A survey of Graph Neural networks for recommender Systems: Challenges, methods, and directions. *ACM Transactions on Recommender Systems*, *1*(1), 1–51. DOI: 10.1145/3568022

Gautam, A., & Sharma, S. (2024). Artificial Narrow Intelligence Inspired Neuromorphic Computing for Logic Operations in Healthcare Appliances. In 2024 7th International Conference on Circuit Power and Computing Technologies (ICCPCT), 714–719. https://doi.org/DOI: 10.1109/iccpct61902.2024.10672744

Gautam, A., & Sharma, S. (2024b). Artificial Narrow Intelligence Inspired Neuromorphic Computing for Logic Operations in Healthcare Appliances. In 2024 7th International Conference on Circuit Power and Computing Technologies (ICCPCT), 714–719. https://doi.org/DOI: 10.1109/iccpct61902.2024.10672744

Gupta, A., & Sharma, S. (2024). Deep Learning Inspired Biomarker Diagnostic Enabled Heart Health Monitoring System for Cardiac Arrest Detection. In *2024 International Conference on Emerging Technologies and Innovation for Sustainability (EmergIN)*, 13–17. https://doi.org/DOI: 10.1109/emergin63207.2024.10960916

Kumar, M. S., Vellela, S. S., Rao, G. R., Srinivas, B. R., & Javvadi, S. SyamsundaraRao, T., & Kumar, K. K. (2024). An Interactive Healthcare Recommendation System Using Big Data Analytics. In 2024 3rd International Conference for Advancement in Technology (ICONAT), 1–6. https://doi.org/DOI: 10.1109/iconat61936.2024.10774650

Painuly, S., & Sharma, S. (2024). Natural Language Processing Techniques for e-Healthcare Supply Chain Management System. In *2024 International Conference on Emerging Systems and Intelligent Computing (ESIC)*, 11–16. https://doi.org/DOI: 10.1109/esic60604.2024.10481580

Pandey, C., Sharma, S., & Bhadula, S. (2024). Artificial Intelligence Technique in Next Generation Healthcare Systems. In *2024 IEEE International Conference on Communication, Computing and Signal Processing (IICCCS)*, 1–6. https://doi.org/DOI: 10.1109/iicccs61609.2024.10763570

Rawat, R., Goyal, H. R., & Sharma, S. (2023). Artificial narrow Intelligence techniques in Intelligent Digital Financial Inclusion System for Digital Society. 2021 5th International Conference on Information Systems and Computer Networks (ISCON), 1–5. https://doi.org/DOI: 10.1109/iscon57294.2023.10112133

Rawat, R., Goyal, H. R., & Sharma, S. (2024). Hofstede's Cultural Dimension Driven Artificial Narrow Intelligence IDFIS for Industry 5.0 Empowered Digital Society. *Recent Patents on Engineering*, *19*. Advance online publication. DOI: 10.2174/0118722121334543241001050846

Sharma, S., Tyagi, R., & Mohan, S. (2024). Edge Intelligence Decentralized Blockchain-Based Internet of Things (B-IoT) for sustainable healthcare. In Chapman and Hall/CRC eBooks (pp. 109–124). https://doi.org/DOI: 10.1201/9781003407096-7

Sharma, S., Tyagi, R., & Mohan, S. (2025). Blockchain-Based Security and Privacy in Digital Healthcare Recommender Systems. In In Healthcare Recommender Systems (pp. 221–237). https://doi.org/DOI: 10.1007/978-3-031-80056-6_10

Chapter 8
Natural Language Processing (NLP) for Industry Applications Sentiment Analysis for Customer Feedback

Wasswa Shafik
https://orcid.org/0000-0002-9320-3186
Dig Connectivity Research Laboratory (DCRLab), Uganda

ABSTRACT

Natural Language Processing (NLP) is revolutionizing industry applications by enabling advanced analysis and understanding of textual data. Sentiment analysis, a key NLP technique, plays a crucial role in deriving actionable insights from customer feedback across various sectors. This study explores the application of sentiment analysis in processing customer reviews, surveys, and social media interactions to identify patterns, gauge satisfaction levels, and inform decision-making. We examine methodologies ranging from lexicon-based approaches to cutting-edge machine learning and deep learning models, highlighting their efficacy and challenges in real-world scenarios. Emphasis is placed on handling multilingual data, mitigating biases, and improving sentiment detection accuracy in diverse cultural contexts. Integrating sentiment analysis with industry processes, businesses can enhance customer experience, drive product innovation, and maintain a competitive edge. This work underscores the transformative potential of NLP in harnessing the voice of the customer for strategic advantage.

DOI: 10.4018/979-8-3373-2008-3.ch008

1 INTRODUCTION

Natural Language Processing (NLP) is commonly used in industries as an advanced technique to improve customer service and satisfaction in enterprises by providing analysis of large-scale customer feedback data. However, studies on its implementation in the industry have not received much attention in the field of information processing. As a result, in this research, the fine-tuned model with a small set of task-specific data was used to conduct an analysis of the sentiment classification of the provided customer satisfaction data, as well as the detection of specific comments on interested topics (Jain & Mitra, 2023). The experimental results proved the feasibility of the analysis. Furthermore, the use of a deep transformer model helped to implement a more accurate and iteratively complex analysis of large-scale customer feedback data. The performance of this research was proven to reach a new record using such small data. The use of fewer than 10,000 labeled customer satisfaction data for fine-tuning the model reached an accuracy of 94.8% on the supervised sentiment analysis task that contains five levels of sentiment annotation, and it was able to detect some task-related comments in the assumed different experimental scenarios for the performance of different enterprise teams (M. Gupta et al., 2023). The different experimental scenarios were discussed in the results.

NLP stands for natural language processing. It refers to the process by which machines and algorithms are taught to understand and process human language. This development has come as part of AI, enhanced through the data explosion. NLP stands to be much more advanced, has a broader scope, and has diversified applications. It is slowly replacing the need for traditional data entry and call centers. Ambiguous language might be a part of your day, but it is no longer a challenge for machines. It not only breaks and segments data but also converts it into an easy-to-understand format while maintaining the flow and context (Shafik, 2023b, 2024a). As a business, this can be very advantageous. It means you can study every section, executive summary, and conclusion and build your strategy accordingly without the fear of missing an important part of the report. These small details can often make a significant difference in the direction of your company. This prediction can only be made from understanding and analyzing data properly. In an age where quality management has been combined with AI and robotics, NLP is a game-changer. Many other industries are capable of benefiting from this widespread technology (Gayki et al., 2023). The following section includes insights on applications and solutions by industries.

Structured data are usually quantitative values related to operational information that is neatly organized in tables and able to be analyzed using statistical and analytical methods. On the other hand, unstructured data are qualitative and pertain to a variety of different types of relations. Unstructured data can contain a tremendous amount of information but are typically much more difficult to handle because they are not as easily organized and are more difficult to interpret. However, they are still highly important due to the value of their insights, which companies can extract that can be invaluable and highly advantageous (Bux Talpur & Huang, 2019). Over 50% of the unstructured data that companies possess is in textual form. This textual data can hold a breadth of information for problems that can appear in business in areas such as the extraction of meaningful facts, idea association, classification, categorization, clustering, relevance assessment, opinion generation, and sentiment analysis (Shafik, 2024b). Until recently, regardless of great advances in machine learning, the codification of natural language was no simple task. However, the last decade has seen significant advances in data resources, NLP methods, and many developments in machine learning and deep learning models, focused on different and more complex tasks, were specifically created and also adapted for NLP tasks (Khatri, 2023).

Figure 1. Natural Language Processing

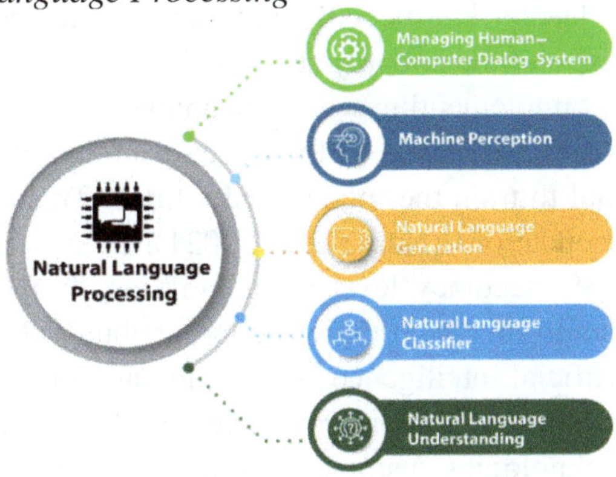

In general, many NLP sub-techniques are categorized into two repositories of NLP techniques: linguistic knowledge-based and statistical-based techniques with aspects as presented in Figure 1. These two categories are used interchangeably to achieve the desired output; they are even used in combination with each other. For example, in the POS tagging process, we can use linguistic knowledge to build grammar rules to classify words as nouns or verbs. These rules can also be utilized to identify the noun or verb in the system and to scan the surrounding words to classify them (Wang, 2024). On the other hand, we can use statistical techniques to calculate the probability of each word being a certain grammatical category based on the observed frequency of that word in the specific documents or our corpus. Then, by multiplying each word's probability with other probabilities, we can develop the most likely sequence of grammatical tags in the document. There are many NLP algorithms utilized to achieve specific tasks or objectives. Due to the wide array of NLP algorithms, these algorithms can themselves be applied in several specialized areas. In terms of specialized NLP techniques, a comprehensive list includes the NLP algorithms, concepts, and applications developed by various groups (Shafik et al., 2024). All applications are within knowledge extraction, information retrieval and question answering, coreference, tokenization, sentence splitting, part-of-speech tagging, named entity recognition, constituency parsing, dependency parsing, semantic role labeling, coreference and similarity, non-English language processing, and machine learning training (Gayki et al., 2023).

2 UNDERSTANDING SENTIMENT ANALYSIS

This section discusses how to implement sentiment analysis for competitive advantage using Python. It focuses on the practical implementation of sentiment analysis for customer feedback, especially on financial products. The chapter concludes with a checklist on how to apply sentiment analysis for customer feedback in a structured way. By implementing sentiment analysis on customer feedback, the model showed better accuracy levels, a 30% increase compared to using techniques other than multinomial to train the model, and a lift in Treasury rating and asset management recommendations (Nufus et al., 2021). Moreover, support has been observed, showing 58% accuracy levels in identifying disappointment and 86% accuracy levels in identifying multidimensional attributes. NLP is a subfield of computer science, artificial intelligence, and computational linguistics concerned with the interactions between computers and human languages. It provides ease of interaction with technologies customers use and, therefore, increases customer adoption of technologies. With the exponential growth of unstructured data, the possibilities of using NLP to transform businesses across different industries are endless (Keivandarian & Carvalho, 2023). Businesses quickly adopted NLP for customer service inquiries, whether submitted via email, social media, chat, or voice.

2.1 Definition and Importance of Sentiment Analysis

In this ever-changing market and competition structure, understanding customer behaviors and ideas has become indispensable. While companies do not have a chance to understand and analyze the increasing number of feedback and comments from customers with manual research, natural language processing, especially sentiment analysis mechanisms, has started to be used as a critical tool to guide companies in estimating the success of their performed activities. Sentiment analysis is applied as a language processing technique used to automatically determine emotions conveyed in sentiment about the sentence or text based on public opinion (Tarnowska & Ras, 2019). In this study, firstly, general information is provided about natural language processing and popular NLP techniques are analyzed. Then, a detailed tutorial for business applications is elaborated via sample coding with real-time, readily available usage data. Sentiment analysis in the customer satisfaction field is a sub-discipline of document-level subjectivity, where users give scores based on different conditions. For example, positive, negative, and neutral scores within the range of one to five. The main purpose of it is not just to determine customer satisfaction or dissatisfaction but to help companies determine customers' emotional views, feelings, or ideas about a product, service, company, brand, or topic. According to these emotional expressions, companies can get a chance to ensure customer satisfaction by developing strategies according to customers' ideas and managing the weak points (Kamal & Himel, 2023). In this framework, rather than determining the general concept of the messages, it is an implementation that business units can understand sentences, feelings, and issues that need to be eliminated.

2.2 Types of Sentiment Analysis

The main goal of this chapter is to provide an in-depth overview and step-by-step guide to sentiment analysis for customer feedback with Python and NLP. We aim to facilitate the use of these resources for technical business analysts who, without having much linguistic or technical knowledge, are working on getting insights from the vast source of customer comments from various survey data sources. This guide would shed some light on the use of the natural language processing framework, which includes functions such as tokenization, a bag of words, lemmatization, and classification models like the famous Naive Bayes classifier or support vector machine (Tuama et al., 2023). Sentiment analysis is a natural language processing technique that determines the attitude conveyed in the text. Are the statements or comments expressing any positive, negative, or neutral opinions or emotions? The terms sentiment analysis and opinion mining can be used interchangeably. Depending on the goals, there can be several sub-tasks for sentiment analysis. The first step of doing meaningful sentiment analysis on text data is the same as for any NLP application. In this chapter, we will consider both the case of sorted-out annotations where the sentiments are already indicated and the unsupervised version of sentiment analysis. Prior to applying any classification technique, it is important to create the label for the supervised training set (Hung, 2023). Training a machine learning model without labels is similar to asking a baby to execute a task without any knowledge of what the desired outcome is supposed to look like.

3 DATA COLLECTION AND PREPROCESSING FOR SENTIMENT ANALYSIS

Data continues to grow at a faster rate than ever before. Businesses and enterprises are collecting, storing, and analyzing this profusion of data at a staggering pace. One prominent form of data relevant to consumer product companies is consumer feedback via various free-text sources. Natural Language Processing can help convert free-text data into actionable insights by allowing brands to gather, manage, and analyze these sources all over the world at a scale that was previously impossible. In this chapter, we aim to show organizations how they can realize these benefits (Khan & Fatima, 2023). In particular, we explain the major steps in applying NLP to determine sentiment from customer feedback and provide practical guidance. We also provide working examples using topic-specific datasets. To apply sentiment analysis in practice, one naturally has several steps to execute beforehand. In general, the major steps include gathering customer feedback, preprocessing dirty natural language, using NLP to supply clean natural language, labeling outputs to distinguish sentiment, and applying relevant models. Given unstructured, crowd-sourced textual data, it is essential to master the tasks involved in order to determine sentiment efficiently and accurately, as sampled applications are presented in Figure 2. Without thorough execution of these steps, an analysis project will fall short of meeting business expectations (Badia & Mohammed, 2019). Moreover, as we walk through this process, avoid common pitfalls, and offer examples, you will learn to navigate around potential issues with your datasets with ease.

Figure 2. Applications of Natural Language Processing

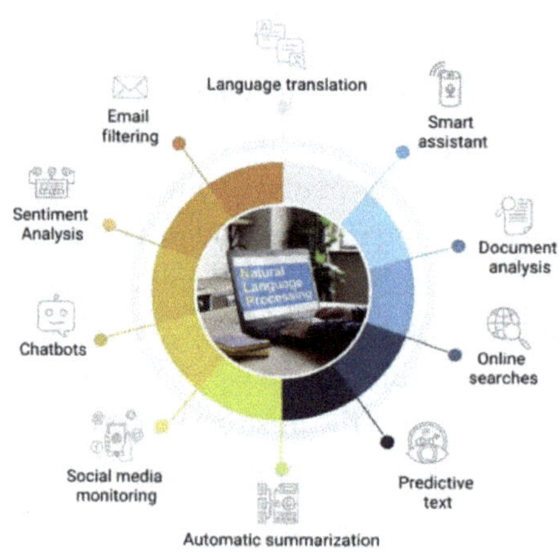

3.1 Sources of Customer Feedback Data

Customer feedback data is usually available in abundance within companies. This is because, in order to make significant improvements in products or services, companies need to gauge the satisfaction levels of their clientele. By understanding whether customers are content with an item or a set of services, these organizations can then improve sales through making the necessary adjustments. As a result, the data used by companies to understand public perceptions of certain products or services usually takes the form of either rating scale data or free text data (Singh et al., 2017). The data is collected from a variety of sources, such as social media comments, feedback forms, or reviews, among other sources. Social media comments usually contain the opinions of many and are a quick way to gather vast amounts of feedback data, whereas feedback forms and reviews usually contain more detailed information on a customer's opinion. The scope of this paper will focus only on the available NLP toolkit exclusively for free text data before ending with the applications of the available NLP toolkit to customer feedback data. However, below is a brief introduction to some of the techniques used to deal with rating scale data (Vemulapalli & Peddi, 2023). These techniques have proven to be very useful when analyzing these forms of customer feedback data.

3.2 Text Cleaning and Preprocessing Techniques

Text cleaning refers to the process of parsing or removing characters that should not be present, such as HTML tags, emojis, special characters, and numerics that are not words, along with other unnecessary elements. These can be removed by applying patterns or expressions. Preprocessing text data helps in obtaining better results from customer feedback for any NLP project. There are a variety of commonly used preprocessing methods and techniques that companies use to improve the accuracy of their text data (Al Omari, 2022). When it comes to improving sentiment analysis results, implementing the right combination of data-prepping methods is key. There are many strategies available for data preprocessing. Some specific methods that companies use most often include stemming, removing stop words, lowercase conversion, and lemmatization. Lemmatization and stemming are text normalization techniques that normalize text data; they are used to convert high-dimensional data to low-dimensional data. Both techniques are frequently implemented by companies when they create an NLP project to address the problem of lexical variation (Ibrahim & Salim, 2016).

4 SUPERVISED AND UNSUPERVISED LEARNING MODELS FOR SENTIMENT ANALYSIS

As shown in the previous discussion, we can execute sentiment analysis with a variety of different methods. However, extracting meaning from a large corpus of customer feedback is a complex task, and many NLP text preprocessing methods are commonly used to facilitate the process (Shafik, 2025). For starters, sentiment analysis uses supervised machine learning algorithms like convolutional neural networks, recurrent neural networks, and long short-term memory as the state of the art. To train these neural networks, vast labeled datasets are commonly used (Rezapour, 2021). Other than neural networks, random forests, naive Bayes, and support vector machines are all widely used supervised learning techniques that require a pre-annotated dataset, which is a factor that sets the attributes of an input text to the output sentiment classification. Most supervised models follow the generic input function. This involves tokenizing the input text into a word vector and then feeding the word vector into a preceding RNN or other models. Optimal choices for modeling and preprocessing text may vary depending on the types of records in the feedback corpus, the actual dataset distribution of the feedback data, and the availability of sentiment-aware word embeddings (Saad, 2020).

4.1 Supervised Learning

A highly efficient way to solve a task would be to build a perfectly certified robot that could complete any task. A much more efficient approach is supervised learning. It saves labor and resources, and the performance is extremely good. The comparison of both means can be emphasized by saying that supervised learning stands on the shoulders of reinforcement learning. Supervised learning, combined with its friendly environments for deep learning, is making an amazing contribution to our society that it won't be saturated. The benefit of supervised learning is tremendous: it saves a lot of human knowledge, skills, and resources; it makes the computer perform very well; it reduces the chance of error to a very low level (Londhe & Rao, 2022). The reason for this is that supervision provides necessary knowledge and guidance to the system. Without a teacher, a student can make different types of mistakes, and only by being corrected can the student avoid the mistakes the next time. When the task has continuous numbers as outcomes, the learning task is referred to as regression. If the outcomes are binary, the task is referred to as binary classification. If the outcomes fall into multi-categorical numbers, the task is referred to as multi-label classification (Vairamani & Nayyar, 2023). In this project and proposal, we are going to focus on the application of sentiment analysis for the analysis of sentiment from the body of natural language using Python and Python libraries.

4.2 Unsupervised Learning

Imagine I have given you a fruit in an unlabelled manner and then ask you which type of fruit this is, and you say apple because you have eaten this type of fruit before, so you recognized it with its features. This is basically your learning. Unsupervised learning is a similar type of learning in which you don't have labels, as there is no tutoring; only feedback is given. For every input, you do not have any corresponding output variable. When given data, we try to find some structure in the input data. The most common unsupervised learning task is called clustering, in which data is automatically placed into pre-determined groups. For example, clustering algorithms can be used to cluster together a set of documents, find groups of people who have similar purchasing behavior or identify similar objects or items (Purwandari et al., 2023). The machine learning algorithm is given a dataset that lacks labels. It partitions a set of objects into clusters, where each object belongs to a cluster with the nearest mean. These objects will be combined into the same cluster. The number of clusters is the free parameter that controls the granularity of the resulting clustering. In other words, the free parameter limits the clusters and thus controls the minimum scale at which the algorithm will represent structures. Unsupervised learning is an important method of discovering useful or interesting patterns in data. It is most commonly used for exploratory, descriptive, and explanatory purposes. Unsupervised learning is used in practical cases, i.e., market segmentation, discovering features in an input, and feature learning. For example, if you have a dataset that contains the heights and weights of people, then with the help of unsupervised learning, you can cluster people into different groups based on height and weight (Ospanova et al., 2022). Then, according to the group or cluster, you can decide which classification or regression algorithm you want to use, depending on the group or cluster of the data, amidst NLP tasks, as illustrated in Figure 3

Figure 3. Natural Language Processing

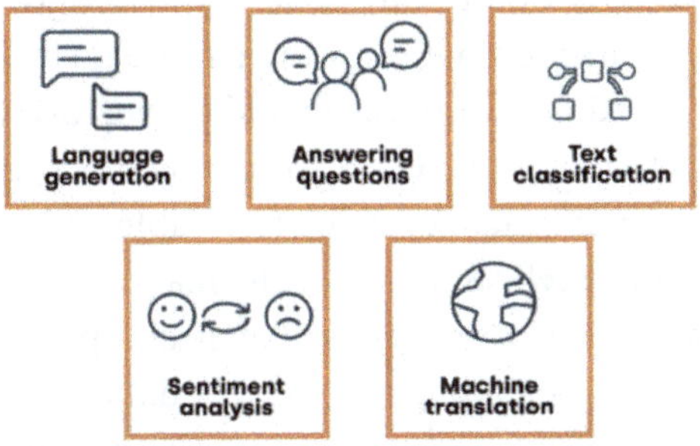

5 FEATURE ENGINEERING AND SELECTION TECHNIQUES

Feature engineering is a key step in any predictive modeling exercise that involves learning from complex, large-scale, high-dimensional, and unstructured data. In the context of text analytics or sentiment analysis, it is particularly important because text data are almost always highly unstructured and, therefore, a number of features and feature selection techniques need to be applied in order to ensure that the most appropriate numerical method of pattern recognition is taken when creating a predictive model. This chapter describes the process of semantics in terms of feature engineering that is concerned with converting the raw elements of the text, such as words or phrases, into appropriate sequences of numerical values in order to identify the relevant features most representative of the dimensions of sentiment (Bharathi et al., 2023). There are many ways in which textual semantic data can be transformed into more powerful feature vectors for their use in the context of data analytics through machine learning principles. For example, a basic technique of counting words or generating the term frequency-inverse document in order to derive feature vectors of words can be used. Then, other types of structure beyond the words themselves, such as bigrams and trigrams taken from a data corpus, can also improve the acquired quality of the feature vectors and, with it, the performance of the derived sentiment model (Rajeswari & Kumar, 2019). Therefore, part-of-speech attributed to words in a sentence can also be added to the feature vectors in order to add more useful information, particularly with respect to the sentiment.

5.1 N-grams and Bag-of-Words Representation

Word skips bi-grams addition. N-grams can make certain sentence structures or relationships more comprehensible. In terms of bigrams or word pairs, too often, we miss meanings by using simple bigrams. For example, "not good" and "poor experience" are two common bigrams specifically indicating customers' dissatisfaction, but "not a good experience" is quite different from "not good experience." So, in previous analysis, these pairs would appear to be more positive. By adding in word skip bi-grams, the two-word pair bigrams would be vectorized as "not_good" and "a_experience." Thanks to that, the correct word may more likely be generated (Ng et al., 2023). We still pay attention to creating a suitable and general bigrams list for all texts within the domain. Rich semantic vectorization has been found necessary. What is challenging with bag-of-words is that it completely loses the syntactic structures and the underlying meanings of the text data. Moreover, even with stop words removed from the dictionary, word frequencies are still used to represent the relationship between each word and the entire vocabulary; the availability of correct homonyms would naturally affect outcomes (Marwat et al., 2022). For example, "irritated feeling" or "irritated due" was found in a misclassified dataset aiming at identifying affirmative messages or adversative messages, which obviously express customers' nervousness or admiration rather than an affirmative one. We cannot easily define a set of rules or grammar to express, and some direct country names and population numbers may be misleading or transferable without reasonable and standard contexts. The number of n-grams and their occurrence order is unpleasant to describe, which inhibits subjects from leaving a human-recognizable term for the correct meaning we have discovered through pre-classification in a broader domain and the existing historical marketing teams recognized (López Condori & Gonzales Saji, 2021).

5.2 TF-IDF and Word Embeddings

Normally, techniques such as a count function on the number of times a term appears in a document over the total number of documents would lead to what is known as Bag of Words representation. In such a representation, similar words such as "good" and "better" may appear to be unrelated. This would mean that the features can be quite specific and possibly include stopwords (non-descriptive words such as "a," "in," and "the"). Nevertheless, a better method of representing a collection of documents is the term frequency-inverse document frequency vectorizer, abbreviated to TF-IDF (Sharma et al., 2023). This method normalizes word frequency by considering that frequently appearing words in most documents are less meaningful. However, TF-IDF has a few shortcomings. The method implies that words with a semantic relationship have their vectors aligned in the same direction when this is often not the case. Additionally, because the vector space is high-dimensional, this method leads to unsatisfactory performance when using conventional machine learning algorithms. Consequently, natural language processing practitioners have turned towards the method of word embeddings, where the algorithms have been trained to understand the interconnections between words (Van Le & Huh, 2021). One of the most famous machine learning models for word embeddings is an algorithm known as Word2Vec. Word2Vec assumes that context, referenced by the neighboring words of a target word, is all that is needed to understand the meaning of the word. When every word is treated as a different, peculiar particle, it would be like every word in a sentence is a different picture in which the word appears. A connectionist model such as Word2Vec would take into account neighboring words for all of the images, allowing the model to understand each word while also estimating probabilities of the appearance of the neighboring words (Karamouzas et al., 2022; Srinivas et al., 2023).

6 DEEP LEARNING APPROACHES FOR SENTIMENT ANALYSIS

In this section, we will analyze different deep-learning models for sentiment analysis. Deep learning strategies used for sentiment analysis are known as bidirectional neural networks, convolutional neural networks, recurrent neural networks, hybrid neural networks, and transfer learning applied to deep neural networks. Bidirectional neural networks have been extensively used in natural language processing scenarios, capturing the relationships between words. These types of networks propagate information from both the forward and the backward directions of the data at the same time (al Harshit Sharma, 2024). The use of a bidirectional neural network has significantly improved the performance of classifiers in sentiment analysis compared to the forward or backward models when it comes to capturing details that influence the final result. These are especially useful in tasks that require reading and understanding the entirety of an input sequence. Considering that sentiment is learned not only by words but also by their relationship within a text, models like bidirectional neural networks seem ideal (Aguilar-Moreno et al., 2024).

6.1 Recurrent Neural Networks (RNNs)

Probably the most recognizable deep learning architecture for sequential data is the Recurrent Neural Network (RNN). It uses loops to incorporate information from previous sequence steps. It can be considered to reflect temporal ordering. RNN, for sentences of sequential ordering in words, can be the most frequently used network for sequential data like sequences of stock data, time series, sentiment analysis, etc. Due to its control of computation time, its architecture can be complex, with many computational layers using the same weights (Ajmeera & Kamakshi, 2024). However, training them, particularly for data with long sequential lengths, becomes difficult as the length of data training goes into a long chain of function applications, which makes the network vulnerable to vanishing or exploding gradients for large chain lengths. To address this issue, Long Short-Term Memory (LSTM) and, more recently, Gated Recurrent Unit (GRU) have their gates to control their memory when dealing with long sequences, very long sequence training tasks, and noisy or grained temporal data pruning (P. Gupta et al., 2021).

6.2 Convolutional Neural Networks (CNNs)

In the 21st century, CNNs have dominated various computer vision competitions in tasks such as image classification, image segmentation, action recognition, facial recognition, and more that solve end-to-end pipeline system problems. Despite conventional fully connected networks, which are not in favor of recognizing patterns in spatial hierarchies due to their limitations in resolving global compositions, the geometry of patterns' spatial relatedness, and memory of weights, CNNs process and assemble them efficiently and effectively through localized layers only without compromising connectivity and with much fewer parameters to train (Aliwy et al., 2022). CNNs downsize the feature output size, decreasing the internal redundancy of training data and requiring much fewer parameters that demand fewer computational resources to train. To ease and regularize the training of CNNs with deep layers, parameters are sparsely connected and shared intensively, allowing them to have the same underlying weight while being adjusted to create several feature maps for each layer. The use of rectified linear units as CNNs' outputs can resolve the vanishing gradient problem owing to an accelerated calculation approach by the use of dropout as a means of regularization to prevent overfitting, especially for small-sized CNNs, which are actually large networks when trained end-to-end (Poncelas et al., 2020).

7 EVALUATING SENTIMENT ANALYSIS MODELS

Sentiment analysis is a critical application of natural language processing (NLP) relating to the assessment and categorization of subjective opinions contained in raw text data. It can be important to organizations and businesses by helping them analyze and comprehend the sentiments and emotions circulating about their products in the minds of the public in the form of reviews, feedback, and customer conversations. Inadequate sentiment analysis can hinder the decision-making processes of businesses. It is, therefore, important that only high-precision sentiment analysis models are deployed on the manufacturing floor or in business (K, 2020). However, the performance of these models largely depends on the features of the algorithms adopted to accomplish the analysis. Consequently, the evaluation procedure of sentiment analysis models should take into account what kind of data the model will be exposed to in practice and what specifically the model is designed to achieve. In sentiment analysis implementation, classification tasks are more often than not used. However, due to the ambiguous nature of emphasis quantities and locations, it is unrealistic to really want the pinpointed locations where negative or positive words are present in a knowledge base (C & Vadivu, 2021). Therefore, the task is simplified into three activities that produce categorical labels, and then assessments are performed. These activities include categorizing full documents into selected levels of affirmative, neutral, or negative labels, categorizing categories of aspect-based features in the text to identify their relevance as opinion holders, and discerning the sentiments or connotations of opinion providers within the content. However, to use these categorizing rules, the sentiment analysis functions must be succinct and flexible enough for automatic performance (Kadu et al., 2022). This characterizes the full content categorizing task and provides a baseline research description with a proposed framework and state-of-the-art capabilities:

- F1 Score: The F1 score is the weighted average of precision and recall. The best value the F1 score can take is 1, and the worst is 0. It is a good way to show that a class is correctly classified. It also provides a single measure for data-based classification. The F1 score is a measure that combines the effectiveness of the classifier for all the classes in the classification.
- Hamming Loss: Hamming loss is used to measure the mismatches between two datasets. A smaller loss is perfectly incremental. To find the Hamming loss, it is necessary to count the number of label mismatches and divide by the total number of label occurrences.
- Jaccard Similarity: Similar to the F1 score, Jaccard similarity is defined by how many objects are in both sets accurately. The average value of Jaccard for each class will be treated.
- Log Loss: Log loss is used to evaluate classification where the label has a probability of the model.
- Matthews Correlation Coefficient: Matthews correlation coefficient is a quality metric that uses all four results of a binary classification to determine the accuracy of a model. On the basis of the truth, positive predictive value, negative predictive value, sensitivity, and specificity of a model, it is considered to be more reliable compared to the F1 score and accuracy score.
- Precision: Precision is the ratio of the number of true positives to the total number of instances. A class is considered problematic if it has a high score. It is important for two groups whose truth is poor and one whose accuracy is high.
- Recall: Recall is the ratio of the number of true positives to the total number of instances, and it indicates which node should be taken as the real value. Recall may be more important than precision for a group with low accuracy and higher accuracy.
- True Positive Rate (TPR) and False Positive Rate (FPR): TPR and FPR are rates considered defective or the number of good isolates based on the number of good isolates for TPR and FPR. The receiver operating characteristic, or ROC for short, is a graph that indicates the true positive rate versus the false positive rate at various thresholds. Generally, precision or threshold is needed, both important measures of the quality of a classifier.

8 CHALLENGES AND LIMITATIONS IN SENTIMENT ANALYSIS

Challenges often encountered by researchers in sentiment analysis are the presence of noisy text, the presence of subjectivity and sentiment ambiguity for a particular context and language, the influence of negations in sentences, the fluctuations of sentiment distribution in a particular context of study, and how sentiment varies with time, as well as conflicts in the sentiment prediction between sentiment lexicons (Keivandarian & Carvalho, 2023). Additionally, limitations to the current sentiment analysis include the reliance on the availability of software and data for use in sentiment analysis, the lack of a universal agreement on the emotional words considered, the classification of emotional words into their polarities - positive or negative, and difficulties in sentiment prediction in natural language. Of these challenges and limitations, subjectivity can be considered one of the most significant problems in natural language text analysis. This subjectivity problem occurs when a person's opinion is viewed and interpreted differently by different people (Khatri, 2023). Essentially, the sentiment behind the sentence needs the context of words near the given word, and the presence of language and sentimental ambiguity, therefore, confuses the application of sentiment analysis.

8.1 Ambiguity and Sarcasm in Texts

One of the most dominant features in texts is the existence of ambiguity. Humor, for example, has for a long time been a special focus of study where misunderstanding context or semantics often has an entertaining consequence. However, the misinterpretation of sarcasm can lead to various problems, which in business may have a negative impact. In larger organizations, especially public limited companies, a small misinterpretation may lead to huge losses in terms of millions of consumers (C & Vadivu, 2021; Shafik, 2023a). Therefore, when using sentiment analysis, we can choose to either preserve the sarcastic information, helping with direct human understanding or neutralize it. Sarcasm is viewed as a primary form of verbal irony but often contains a note of bitterness or hostility. It's no wonder that sarcasm is considered one of the language's greatest inventions ever due to the value of its underlying criticism and humor. One common understanding of sarcasm is the idea that the speaker is saying something opposite to its underlying belief or literal meaning (Shafik, 2024a). The difference between verbal irony, sarcasm, and satire may revolve around the various intentions of the speaker, the speaker's tone, or both. Sarcasm, if positive and not hurting anyone, may be retained in a sentiment analysis process, because sentiment words considered might have an opposing meaning; sentiment classification is not clear. Non-conflict or positive sarcasm can involve exhortation and cheerfulness, or it may be related to verbal appreciation, humility, and friendliness. Documents using positive sarcasm were interpreted as being positive, but at the moment, we cannot detect that; we would leave sarcasm as sarcasm (Hidayatullah et al., 2023).

8.2 Domain-Specific Challenges

Domain-specific features include complex and ambiguous expressions of sentiments, idiomatic expressions, abbreviations, and internet slang. For instance, among e-commerce platforms, abbreviations such as "JD," Taobao, "Jingdong," and "Botu," as well as "Seckill," and top-level domains of e-commerce enable fine-grained sentiment analyses of the distinct features. Second, samples of semantically similar sentences are very imbalanced, with large numbers of similar sentiment polarities, making it difficult for system models to converge (Khatri, 2023). For instance, reviews with relatively high scores receive the labels of negative or lower sentiment scores at a smaller proportion, thereby leading to imbalanced classes. To enhance a model's generalizability in handling the natural language features in specific industries, optimal lexical resources and sentiment-conversion tools are required. Suggestions for consumer electronics analysis are described in more detail (Marwat et al., 2022):

(i) using sentiment dictionaries with extensive coverage and high-quality sentiment labels to achieve high-precision sentiment extraction from the sentence;
(ii) using adjectives and adverbs as preparatory work, given their ability to express fine-grained emotional content and their importance in sentiment scoring.

When considering how to separate different consumer perspectives and product attributes, taking into account their most essential needs, the optimal sentiment dictionary and the sentiment lexicon can be obtained.

9 REAL-WORLD APPLICATIONS OF SENTIMENT ANALYSIS

Real-world applications of sentiment analysis for handling large volumes of customer feedback are quite diverse.

9.1 Sampled Real World Application

To elaborate, we will use a few cases that have been developed for Fortune 500 companies.

9.1.1 Enterprise Software Provider

An enterprise software provider was struggling with their customer feedback collection process. They managed numerous incoming support calls and emails, which were then dispersed across multiple support teams. The inconsistency of tagging led to a 10% insertion error into their CRM system. In order to address this issue, the provider used expertise in creating an NLP model that would distinguish between satisfied and unsatisfied clients; this included the negative or positive consequences of their recent interactions. The company also wanted to identify client references and apply specific comments to support calls and emails (Badia & Mohammed, 2019). Ultimately, the NLP engine was able to increase their case level predictions to 78% and subsequently highly correlate with the customer satisfaction survey results.

9.1.2 Multinational Lodging Company

A major lodging company was undergoing a renovation of its outdated reservation system. To efficiently collect feedback, the company devised a process that was able to score customer complaints, recommendations, and positively toned feedback. A model was built that returned a 65% correlation between internal and public communication. This enabled the company to achieve insight into the customer sentiment history, recognizing that their greatest benefits would come from utilizing predictive customer sentiment behavior (Vairamani & Nayyar, 2023).

9.1.3 Large Software Company

One of the largest cloud-based enterprise software companies worldwide hosts events for multiple product lines each year. Large-scale customer events typically result in varying types of feedback, which a live human agent generally handles. The company wanted to increase its contact with customers to present less customized solutions that are now operationalized. The NLP model analyzed live agents, service calls, and social trial messages that human agents had labeled over the previous four years (Bharathi et al., 2023; Rajeswari & Kumar, 2019). The NLP engine significantly improved sub-classification and base-level classification.

9.1.4 SolidWorks – Dassault Systèmes

Dassault Systèmes' software SolidWorks is a 3D CAD program for engineers, which enables them to create, edit, and review designs. The client was most interested in open workflows, enabling them to identify the steps required to close a complaint. Therefore, a classifier was introduced that recognized distinct transactional tones, recommendations, and subjects. Through the NLP model, they were able to classify product-specific text and, in doing so, recommend the appropriate action for different requests coming through their customer support and partner channels (al Harshit Sharma, 2024; Karamouzas et al., 2022).

9.2 Customer Feedback Analysis in E-Commerce

Customer feedback analysis has become increasingly important in e-commerce. With the increase in the number of customers and the daily operations of the store, the mechanism of mail order cannot effectively grasp the real-time feedback information of the store. The implementation of NLP technology to analyze appraisals and improve deficiencies can greatly enhance customer experience and overall sales in the store. The rapid development of big data processing technology and the popularity of neural networks have made natural language understanding models much more powerful than before, and it has become more practical to use neural networks to perform natural language processing tasks, including the recognition of emotions in sentences, with high accuracy (Ajmeera & Kamakshi, 2024; P. Gupta et al., 2021). Through sentiment analysis, stores can more quickly, accurately, and effectively detect positive and negative sentiment in customer feedback and respond promptly. We used top sellers' data and collected samples with good, neutral, and bad comments on the 20 most popular items. We also constructed a model, applied the 5 most popular, and tested natural language processing models for sentiment analysis to study their differences and effectiveness. Then, we designed and built a simple API to display our results on intelligent feedback for the seller (Kadu et al., 2022). We found that one model works best on a specific dataset, and the performance of other models is not ideal. Moreover, the evaluation results on the top sellers are different from the results of the other dataset. One model turns out to be the best-performing, followed by others. Because the feedback data in top sellers is from an online store, we need to limit the length of the submitted feedback, so shorter feedback is expected. This will impact the experimental results (Karamouzas et al., 2022; Van Le & Huh, 2021). Concerning the subjective feelings of users, the models can be easily integrated into the final application.

9.3 Brand Reputation Management

The way you manage your brand's reputation is essential in obtaining and retaining customers. Your reputation dictates how well your brand is perceived and the types of customers you attract. A business that has a positive, strong reputation is very attractive to customers who are considering patronizing the business. In contrast, a business that has a negative, weak reputation is very unattractive to potential patrons who would rather avoid doing business with an uncertain business and take their business elsewhere. Loyal customer attrition is dependent on both brand sentiment as well as the strength of brand loyalty (P. Gupta et al., 2021). The reputational score of a brand also weighs heavily on considerations of new customer acquisition. Consumers and prospective job candidates are frequently leery of investing their time and money in an organization that is easily whittled by bad news. Model output from custom-trained customer feedback NLP models will frequently contribute to brand reputation management by providing insights into prevalent service quality themes that are driving unflattering or dissonant customer sentiments. Such insights may reveal brand-enhancing trends or problem areas at specific service delivery locations, at certain times of day or days of the week, or assist with situational analysis related to broader organizational change (Vemulapalli & Peddi, 2023). A discerning analysis of unanticipated negative comments made by customers about aspects of your operations that fall outside normal service delivery might alert you to violations of laws, regulations, or company policies or procedures that are endangering your brand reputation.

9.4 Sentiment Analysis in Social Media Posts

Social media has been closely linked with public sentiment and opinions, and researchers realize that mining opinions from social media data is critical in many aspects. The influence of social media has been seen in various fields, such as predicting public opinion and election results. Moreover, many enterprises also consider sentiment analysis as a critical part of customer management in order to grasp customers' preferences and emotions intuitively and to guide their business strategies (Ibrahim & Salim, 2016). Sentiment analysis on social media text is primarily performed using feature-oriented machine learning models, where both unigram and bigram features are generally used due to the prevalence of the bag-of-words model. Furthermore, Convolutional Neural Networks can learn higher-level abstractions by adopting word embeddings, and Recurrent Neural Networks are well-suited to handling sequential data. Although those feature-oriented models have performed well on standard sentiment classification benchmarks, they have not yet provided outstanding performance on noisy social media data because of the short texts, code-switch mismatch between different languages, informal expression, misspellings, typos, anomalies, truncated sentences, and varied usage of words (Al-Shukrawi et al., 2023; Vairamani & Nayyar, 2023). Sentiment analysis methods combine human language processing and machine learning to study free-text surveys. First, text data cleaning is performed, including generalization, stemming, and removal of stop-words and punctuation. This is intended to reduce the variability and complexity of language usage. After the text has been cleaned, the word length is mapped to a feature vector, and frequent words that may dominate sentiment polarity scores are removed using the term frequency-inverse document frequency or the Chi-squared feature selection method. Finally, the sentiment polarity scores in the training data are used to train the models (Hung, 2023; Saad, 2020). In a practical application, a significant portion of user sentiment appears as a mixture of praise and complaints; a smaller percentage is neutral, and the remaining texts are commercial messages depicting product usage.

10 ETHICAL CONSIDERATIONS IN SENTIMENT ANALYSIS

An automated process will not consider the depth of the process or the accuracy to be implemented with the technology and the consequences of the application. Demographic imbalance can cause problems, which include systematic error biases for specific groups and unforeseen outcomes for marginalized groups. A methodology that utilizes natural language data for a language model that improves the generation of human-like language when conversing is called a large language model.

10.1 Bias and Fairness in NLP Models

Modern NLP systems have access to a large amount of historical data and, therefore, have the potential to make decisions based on potentially biased or non-representative training data. If not managed with care, these models can inadvertently pick up or perpetuate human biases, amplifying societal imbalances. This is because the training sets that NLP models use do not come from a vacuum; instead, they are mostly drawn from real-world data. Anything represented in this space by people will be biased, making it even more challenging to ensure these systems are free of such flaws (Purwandari et al., 2023; Rajeswari & Kumar, 2019). It should be noted that bias is not inherently harmful. It is only an issue if it amplifies societal imbalances or if it leads to unfair or unethical behavior. For example, a biased model that provides a more accurate prediction within some specific demographic is still a helpful AI tool. It is trained to be biased to minimize generalization errors. However, suppose this means some demographics are suffering unfair harm from the model's behavior. In that case, this can be classified as a form of ethical bias, which is a problem in many real-world applications, including advertising, lending, hiring, marketing, and public opinion. As such, this issue has received a significant amount of attention, originating from various fields, including law, sociology, critical race theory, artificial intelligence, and especially data ethics (Marwat et al., 2022; Ng et al., 2023).

10.2 Privacy and Data Protection Concerns

Regardless of the company, the processing of sensitive customer data will usually lead to much stricter restrictions regarding the processing of personal data or confidential corporate information, which affects all activities. The first thing is to check that the data obtained complies with the privacy laws and the company's internal regulations, as data can be prone to accidental leakage of sensitive information. The migration of data from one location to another generally means the promotion of data, and so it is important to ensure that the compliance of regulations is monitored (Jain & Mitra, 2023). Techniques include the localization of service providers, methodologies with better control of personal and confidential information, and an indication of things like data retention policies. Security and privacy properties must be maintained regardless of the technical mechanisms such as partitioning, storage, storage of redundant encryption keys, and cryptographic encryption used to implement these properties that otherwise would not have them in a situation where the applications are executed directly on local physical or virtual machines. Data security can also be used effectively in the cloud. Utilizing these models to develop bias models includes two methods (Ng et al., 2023; Rajeswari & Kumar, 2019). Reducing bias mitigates the effects of sensitive determining factors prior to analyzing concepts. Additionally, in identifying and correcting these distributions, post-processing recalibrates bias scores.

10.3 Automated Language Model Construction

With the advances in automated language model construction, ethics in robotics have been recognized by academia as an existential threat to the machine learning community. To improve and maintain vigilance for ethical compliance, all classifications of natural language understanding or statistical models that find meaning in language data need to be designed and evaluated comprehensively. This modeling can be categorized considering the process through which data is handled and the outcomes of bias modeling, as well as comments from data sources. Bias reduction methods include fairness through aware response generation and data debiasing from online gathering by diverse groups (P. Gupta et al., 2021; Srinivas et al., 2023). Accelerated investment in construction decisions about these new capabilities allows for the appropriateness of new models before the actual deployment of technology that incorporates predictive methods. Large data in which context plays an active role is especially susceptible to problems from problematic user benefits. The current research has reviewed various fairness concerns in NLP models, encompassing data collection and annotation, training, learning the NLP model, deployment, and usage. To tackle model fairness comprehensively, several works propose to target both the training data and the model, while additional approaches suggest applying different processes to specific NLP models (Bux Talpur & Huang, 2019; C & Vadivu, 2021). The approaches include customizing an NLP model from scratch to have a particular fairness property, performing preprocessing for other techniques, using adversarial learning, and minimizing various bias-utility trade-offs. Surprisingly, researchers indicate that most NLP literature on bias and fairness proposes algorithms and theories, but fewer demonstrate work addressing real-world problems in a deployed NLP model or production application of NLP. Considering the expanding utilization of NLP beyond research and the likelihood of an adverse impact if carelessly employed, crafting a process to generate, use, and deploy these models necessitates thorough development and quality assurance processes to detect and mitigate a wide array of unwanted biases (Kadu et al., 2022; Kamal & Himel, 2023). One facet of specific concern entails ethical considerations regarding the accuracy and fairness of these models, as these could potentially influence decisions across different industries, thereby directing the course of action for multiple entities within the global business landscape.

11 FUTURE TRENDS AND INNOVATIONS IN SENTIMENT ANALYSIS

Three major future trends are expected for sentiment analysis, which is expected to optimize the system better and make it more accurate. Discrepancies originating from spelling errors and informal and casual texts written by users on web pages are glaring linguistic features of low-serious language.

11.1 Aspect-based Opinion Interest Device

Many of the DIY or toolkit versions poorly remedy these common issues, so the correctness and accuracy of their sentiment examination components are affected. These crises are exacerbated in many non-English languages by errors among a wider linguistic range, such as multiple 2-byte Unicode code points. The trend is that people will automatically be able to build a highly delicate aspect-based opinion interest device. Sentiment estimates can be calculated by helping each attribute to direct sentiment examination to the target entity and target attribute of interest (Gayki et al., 2023; Wang, 2024). The second evolution is that the available sentiment assessment instruments will expand. More sentiment evaluation instruments, intelligence investigation tools, and several free sentiment valence instruments like lexicons and classifications will be available. These frameworks can be substituted or used for past annotation strategies by experts to accelerate the overall process of determining sentiment. Inquiry through the examination of consultation data will become a common strategy for expansive devices across all industries through the cumulative use of open tools. Many traditional industries usually have fewer truthful consultation data in the beginning. One can consult the chatbot unit on any desired website that is ready to request real-time sentiment results without needing past data annotations. The input consultation can be the domain and the set of relations (Al-Shukrawi et al., 2023; Ospanova et al., 2022). The task of the device is to scrape consultation from the chat website, possess data annotations and elective conversion, and then produce the required sentiment examination tools.

11.2 Deep Learning Advancement

Deep learning is a family of unsupervised feature learning algorithms. Deep learning is not appropriate for every machine learning project. However, in certain high-impact settings, like computer vision and speech recognition, deep learning models have been able to outperform other types of models both practically and on statistical benchmarks. Notable deep learning methods include neural networks, matrix factorization, and recursive autoencoders. One example of a deep learning approach is a popular unsupervised learning algorithm that learns the structure of word representations in similar contexts and can be used to create word embedding vectors (Vemulapalli & Peddi, 2023). The deep learning architecture determines how hidden layers are interconnected and how complex features are defined by the structure of the network, making this family of methods less exposed to the main disadvantage of machine learning classification models. Textual data are essentially sequences, and it is important to have a model that is able to understand not just singular words but the relationships between them. Because of this, some of the deep learning models most applied to NLP problems take sequences of single tokens as input and produce a sequence of tokens as output (Londhe & Rao, 2022). These sequence-to-sequence learning models address many NLP problems and challenges, and one example of such a model is architecture. Other models in this family are more focused on extracting features to representations, constructing and using statistical relationships at multiple levels of abstraction, or extracting contextual information from long sequences of text. Some general models of this type are used for building models that are able to address a wide range of NLP tasks (Jain & Mitra, 2023).

11.3 Explainable AI in NLP

Explainable AI for Natural Language Processing is an essential part of ensuring the model's comprehension is aligned with our understanding. NLP and our ability to model a text can be quite complex and challenging to ensure that we fully understand. This leads to a drastic impact on transparency since the motivations behind a decision made by a model that involves text could often be hidden, creating a highly nontrivial direction from which the decision originates. It could make the decision unintuitive and seemingly arbitrary (Singh et al., 2017). Therefore, explainable AI becomes relevant in this matter since it helps interface between our understanding and the internal mechanics of the model. Consider an industrial application in which a deep learning model is built for analyzing the vast amount of customer feedback received by the company, which was previously manually reviewed and required several hours of work per week. The model was found to be delivering unsatisfactory performance due to providing outputs that are not accountable. Adding explainable AI to the neural networks increases the accountability of the model and significantly reduces the issues to some believable reasoning (Jain & Mitra, 2023; Khan & Fatima, 2023). NLP models often depend on attention mechanism-related features that play a relevant role in explaining model behavior and the input for it, demonstrating a substantial depth in human knowledge. They conclude by stating that to achieve alignment between our understanding and the model's comprehension, we first need to understand the data and the possible training process involved in training the model. After this, we would be in a better position to understand the holistic approach used to select decision-support models for NLP. The domain of Customer Satisfaction Analysis is vast and knowledge-intensive, complementing the market's demand with a light review of how decision support tools based on text mining and sentiment analysis have been created over the years to support the understanding of customer feedback (Rajeswari & Kumar, 2019; Sharma et al., 2023). Despite the encouraging results, several issues remain to be addressed while firms are rushing to adopt decision-support tools.

12 CONCLUSION

Despite the significant progress that the NLP field, especially sentiment analysis, has made over the years, much remains to be done. Customer feedback is rich, immensely diverse, informal, and often given in many different languages and writing styles. The complexity of such data makes a reliable translation, transformation, normalization, or preprocessing of the text, as well as the efficient extraction of actionable implications from such enormous amounts of feedback, a very complex task. Cumbersome linguistic complexity is something most NLP systems are not yet able to handle with the required rigor. Furthermore, a lack of labeled data, access to unused or protected data, and losing important meanings in transformation steps should be undesirable and important obstacles for analyzing languages where reliable NLP models are not yet available and for creating NLP tools or for applying models in new domains. Although NLP has developed robust benchmarks on well-known tasks, the challenges at the enterprise level are still significant. The use of less advanced tools can be disappointing to the organizational user or can even misinterpret the analyses. Does your work really live up to your standards? Is the oversimplification in the workflow worth the investment? NLP cannot effectively refine views from scaling large data to customers if so. As a result of the pandemic, NLP relevance in CX and many domains has rapidly increased. However, observed technologies are no silver bullet. Technical NLP decisions, including those related to quality, ethics, transparency, and collaboration risks and challenges, call for careful consideration and critical judgment. That being said, successful NLP insights for sentiment analysis tragically confirm that the key to intelligent decision-making in market insights or customer feedback is not to be insufficiently bold. Highly scalable, lean NLP pipelines can offer clear advantages for businesses, but we argue that trade-offs and capability must be made critically and questions wisely when building, calibrating, and applying such systems.

REFERENCES

Aguilar-Moreno, J. A., Palos-Sanchez, P. R., & Pozo-Barajas, R. (2024). Sentiment analysis to support business decision-making. A bibliometric study. In *AIMS Mathematics* (Vol. 9, Issue 2). https://doi.org/DOI: 10.3934/math.2024215

Ajmeera, N., & Kamakshi, P. (2024). Hamiltonian deep neural network fostered sentiment analysis approach on product reviews. *Signal, Image and Video Processing*, *18*(4). Advance online publication. DOI: 10.1007/s11760-024-03014-6

al Harshit Sharma, E. (2024). Statistical Analysis and Accuracy Assessment of Improved Machine Learning Based Opinion Mining Framework. *Advances in Nonlinear Variational Inequalities*, *27*(1). Advance online publication. DOI: 10.52783/anvi.v27.322

Al Omari, M. (2022). OCLAR: Logistic regression optimisation for Arabic customers' reviews. *International Journal of Business Intelligence and Data Mining*, *20*(3). Advance online publication. DOI: 10.1504/IJBIDM.2022.122177

Al-Shukrawi, A. A. H., Jamil, L. S., Alzuabidi, I. A., Al-Gamal, A. S., Noah, S. A. M., Hasan, M. K., Al-Ghuribi, S. M., Aliyu, R., Jabal, Z. K., & Ahmed, A. A. (2023). Opinion Mining in Arabic Extremism Texts: A Systematic Literature Review. *AlKadhum Journal of Science*, *1*(2). Advance online publication. DOI: 10.61710/akjs.v1i2.60

Aliwy, A. H., Abbas, A. R., & Hadi, M. J. (2022). Key Challenges and Proposed Solutions to Design Sentiment Analysis System. *International Journal of Intelligent Engineering and Systems*, *15*(4). Advance online publication. DOI: 10.22266/ijies2022.0831.24

Badia, K., & Mohammed, B. S. (2019). Multilingual sentiments analysis to improve the quality of services provided by Algerian telephone operator. *CEUR Workshop Proceedings*, •••, 2351.

Bharathi, R., Bhavani, R., & Priya, R. (2023). Leveraging Deep Learning Models for Automated Aspect Based Sentiment Analysis and Classification. *SSRG International Journal of Electrical and Electronics Engineering*, *10*(5). Advance online publication. DOI: 10.14445/23488379/IJEEE-V10I5P111

Bux Talpur, D., & Huang, G. (2019). Words segmentation-based scheme for implicit aspect identification for sentiments analysis in english text. *International Journal of Advanced Computer Science and Applications*, *10*(12). Advance online publication. DOI: 10.14569/ijacsa.2019.0101204

C, S., & Vadivu, G. (2021). Fine grained sentiment polarity classification using augmented knowledge sequence-attention mechanism. *Microprocessors and Microsystems, 81*. https://doi.org/DOI: 10.1016/j.micpro.2020.103365

Gayki, Miss. Y., Chatke, Mr. P., Nandane, Miss. R., Shinde, Mr. U., Ghugare, Mr. M., Rathod, P., & Pardey, Prof. M. (2023). A Survey on "Sentiment Analysis of E-commerce Website's Reviews.". *International Journal for Research in Applied Science and Engineering Technology*, *11*(10). Advance online publication. DOI: 10.22214/ijraset.2023.56255

Gupta, M., Kushwaha, A. S., Sinha, A., Singh, P., & Kumar, R. (2023). Multi-Class Sentiment Analysis of Hindi Textual Data. *2023 IEEE 20th India Council International Conference, INDICON 2023*. https://doi.org/DOI: 10.1109/INDICON59947.2023.10440890

Gupta, P., Mehlawat, M. K., Khaitan, A., & Pedrycz, W. (2021). Sentiment Analysis for Driver Selection in Fuzzy Capacitated Vehicle Routing Problem with Simultaneous Pick-Up and Drop in Shared Transportation. *IEEE Transactions on Fuzzy Systems*, *29*(5). Advance online publication. DOI: 10.1109/TFUZZ.2020.2970834

Hidayatullah, A. F., Kalinaki, K., Aslam, M. M., Zakari, R. Y., & Shafik, W. (2023). Fine-Tuning BERT-Based Models for Negative Content Identification on Indonesian Tweets. *ICITDA 2023 - Proceedings of the 2023 8th International Conference on Information Technology and Digital Applications*. https://doi.org/DOI: 10.1109/ICITDA60835.2023.10427046

Hung, B. T. (2023). Joining Aspect Detection and Opinion Target Expression Based on Multi-Deep Learning Models. In *Springer Series in Reliability Engineering*. https://doi.org/DOI: 10.1007/978-3-031-21232-1_4

Ibrahim, M. A., & Salim, N. (2016). Aspect Oriented Sentiment Analysis Model of Arabic Tweets. [IJCS T]. *International Journal of Computer Science Trends and Technology*, *4*(4).

Jain, V., & Mitra, A. (2023). Development and application of machine learning algorithms for sentiment analysis in digital manufacturing: A pathway for enhanced customer feedback. In *Emerging Technologies in Digital Manufacturing and Smart Factories*. https://doi.org/DOI: 10.4018/979-8-3693-0920-9.ch002

K, G. (2020). Supervised Machine Learning algorithm using Sentiment Analysis based on customer feedback for smart phone product. *International Journal of Emerging Trends in Engineering Research, 8*(8). https://doi.org/DOI: 10.30534/ijeter/2020/67882020

Kadu, Mr. L., Deshpande, Dr. M., & Pawar, Dr. V. (2022). Survey of Deep Learning Approaches for Twitter Text Classification. *International Journal of Advanced Engineering Research and Science, 9*(12). Advance online publication. DOI: 10.22161/ijaers.912.12

Kamal, M., & Himel, A. S. (2023). Redefining Modern Marketing: An Analysis of AI and NLP's Influence on Consumer Engagement, Strategy, and Beyond. *Eigenpub Review of Science and Technology, 7*(1).

Karamouzas, D., Mademlis, I., & Pitas, I. (2022). Neural Knowledge Transfer for Sentiment Analysis in Texts with Figurative Language. *IEEE International Workshop on Machine Learning for Signal Processing, MLSP, 2022-August*. https://doi.org/DOI: 10.1109/MLSP55214.2022.9943314

Keivandarian, N., & Carvalho, M. (2023). A Survey on Sentiment Classification Methods and Challenges. *Proceedings of the International Florida Artificial Intelligence Research Society Conference, FLAIRS, 36*. https://doi.org/DOI: 10.32473/flairs.36.133314

Khan, H. F., & Fatima, N. (2023). Analyzing Customer Sentiment in Drug Reviews Using Natural Language Processing. *2023 7th International Conference on Electronics, Materials Engineering and Nano-Technology, IEMENTech 2023*. https://doi.org/DOI: 10.1109/IEMENTech60402.2023.10423529

Khatri, M. R. (2023). Integration of Natural Language Processing, Self-Service Platforms, Predictive Maintenance, and Prescriptive Analytics for Cost Reduction, Personalization, and Real-Time Insights Customer Service and Operational Efficiency. *International Journal of Information and Cybersecurity, 7*(9).

Londhe, A., & Rao, P. V. R. D. P. (2022). Dynamic Classification of Sentiments from Restaurant Reviews Using Novel Fuzzy-Encoded LSTM. In *International Journal on Recent and Innovation Trends in Computing and Communication* (Vol. 10, Issue 9). https://doi.org/DOI: 10.17762/ijritcc.v10i9.5714

López Condori, J. J., & Gonzales Saji, F. O. (2021). Análisis de sentimiento de comentarios en español en Google Play Store usando BERT. *Ingeniare. Revista Chilena de Ingeniería, 29*(3). Advance online publication. DOI: 10.4067/s0718-33052021000300557

Marwat, M. I., Khan, J. A., Dahman Alshehri, M., & Ali, M. A., Hizbullah, Ali, H., & Assam, M. (2022). Sentiment Analysis of Product Reviews to Identify Deceptive Rating Information in Social Media: A SentiDeceptive Approach. *KSII Transactions on Internet and Information Systems, 16*(3). Advance online publication. DOI: 10.3837/tiis.2022.03.005

Ng, J. X., Lim, K. M., Lee, C. P., Lim, Q. Z., Ooi, E. K. H., & Loh, N. K. N. (2023). Sentiment Analysis Using Learning-based Approaches: A Comparative Study. *2023 11th International Conference on Information and Communication Technology, ICoICT 2023, 2023-August*. https://doi.org/DOI: 10.1109/ICoICT58202.2023.10262604

Nufus, G. K., Mustafid, M., & Gernowo, dan R. (2021). Sentiment Analysis for Video on Demand Application User Satisfaction with Long Short Term Memory Model. *E3S Web of Conferences, 317*. https://doi.org/DOI: 10.1051/e3sconf/202131705031

Ospanova, A., Pandharinath Patil, H., Arun Parekh, P., Rajendra Patil, T., & Santosh Gangatire, P. (2022). Sentiment Analysis of Text Feedback. *Article in International Journal of Innovative Research in Science Engineering and Technology.*

Poncelas, A., Lohar, P., Way, A., & Hadley, J. (2020). The Impact of Indirect Machine Translation on Sentiment Classification. *AMTA 2020 - 14th Conference of the Association for Machine Translation in the Americas, Proceedings, 1.*

Purwandari, K., Wulandari, A., Maretta, N. T., Regina, S., & Vincent. (2023). Implementation of AI Model for Sentiment Analysis of Pharmaceutical Products. *ICCA 2023 - 2023 5th International Conference on Computer and Applications, Proceedings*. https://doi.org/DOI: 10.1109/ICCA59364.2023.10401475

Rajeswari, S., & Kumar, T. P. (2019). Sentiment analysis over high dimensional data sets using advanced data engineering techniques. *Journal of Advanced Research in Dynamical and Control Systems, 11*(4 Special Issue).

Rezapour, M. (2021). Sentiment classification of skewed shoppers' reviews using machine learning techniques, examining the textual features. *Engineering Reports, 3*(1). Advance online publication. DOI: 10.1002/eng2.12280

Saad, A. I. (2020). Opinion Mining on US Airline Twitter Data Using Machine Learning Techniques. *16th International Computer Engineering Conference, ICENCO 2020*. https://doi.org/DOI: 10.1109/ICENCO49778.2020.9357390

Shafik, W. (2023a). *A Comprehensive Cybersecurity Framework for Present and Future Global Information Technology Organizations*. https://doi.org/DOI: 10.4018/978-1-6684-9018-1.ch002

Shafik, W. (2023b). Introduction to ChatGPT. In *Advanced Applications of Generative AI and Natural Language Processing Models*. https://doi.org/DOI: 10.4018/9798369305027.ch001

Shafik, W. (2024a). Data Privacy and Security Safeguarding Customer Information in ChatGPT Systems. In *Revolutionizing the Service Industry Wth OpenAI Models* (pp. 52–86). IGI Global., DOI: 10.4018/979-8-3693-1239-1.ch003

Shafik, W. (2024b). Deep Learning Impacts in the Field of Artificial Intelligence. In *Deep Learning Concepts in Operations Research* (pp. 9–26). Auerbach Publications., DOI: 10.1201/9781003433309-2

Shafik, W. (2025). *Technology as a Catalyst for Achieving the Sustainable Development Goals (SDGs)* (pp. 3–39). https://doi.org/DOI: 10.1007/978-981-96-7299-8_1

Shafik, W., Kalinaki, K., Fahim, K. E., & Adam, M. (2024). Safeguarding Data Privacy and Security in Federated Learning Systems. In *Federated Deep Learning for Healthcare* (pp. 170–190). CRC Press., DOI: 10.1201/9781032694870-13

Sharma, S., Jain, A., Ramola, B., Ravindar, B., Al-Taee, M., & Alazzam, M. B. (2023). Implementation of Natural Language Processing for sentiment Analysis. *2023 3rd International Conference on Advance Computing and Innovative Technologies in Engineering, ICACITE 2023*. https://doi.org/DOI: 10.1109/ICACITE57410.2023.10182452

Singh, B., Kushwaha, N., & Vyas, O. P. (2017). An interpretation of sentiment analysis for enrichment of Business Intelligence. *IEEE Region 10 Annual International Conference, Proceedings/TENCON*. https://doi.org/DOI: 10.1109/TENCON.2016.7847950

Srinivas, P. V. V. S., Gayathri, K., & Bhavitha, K., Jahnavi, & Sarath, K. D. (2023). BLIP-NLP Model for Sentiment Analysis. *Proceedings of the 2nd International Conference on Edge Computing and Applications, ICECAA 2023*. https://doi.org/DOI: 10.1109/ICECAA58104.2023.10212253

Tarnowska, K. A., & Ras, Z. W. (2019). Sentiment analysis of customer data. *Web Intelligence*, *17*(4). Advance online publication. DOI: 10.3233/WEB-190423

Tuama, M. H., Mashloosh, W. M., Albehadili, H. M., Alazzawi, M., & Al-shareeda, M. A. (2023). Beyond Polarity: The Potential Applications and Impacts of Sentiment Analysis and Emotion Detection. *AlKadhum Journal of Science*, *1*(2). Advance online publication. DOI: 10.61710/akjs.v1i2.51

Vairamani, A. D., & Nayyar, A. (2023). Decoding product sentiments: Unraveling reviews with explainable analysis using Hugging-Face transformer. In *XAI Based Intelligent Systems for Society 5.0*. https://doi.org/DOI: 10.1016/B978-0-323-95315-3.00003-6

Van Le, N. B., & Huh, J. H. (2021). Applying sentiment product reviews and visualization for bi systems in vietnamese e-commerce website: Focusing on vietnamese context. *Electronics (Switzerland)*, *10*(20). Advance online publication. DOI: 10.3390/electronics10202481

Vemulapalli, A., & Peddi, A. (2023). A Comparative Study of Twitfeel and Transformer-Based Techniques for the Analysis of Text Data for Sentiment Classification. *Proceedings of International Conference on Contemporary Computing and Informatics, IC3I 2023*. https://doi.org/DOI: 10.1109/IC3I59117.2023.10397647

Wang, H. (2024). An Overview of the Application of Convolutional Neural Networks inSentiment Analysis. *Science and Technology of Engineering. Chemistry and Environmental Protection, 1*(5). Advance online publication. DOI: 10.61173/t4sg2v25

KEY TERMS AND DEFINITIONS

Artificial Intelligence: The multidisciplinary field of computer science aimed at creating systems capable of performing tasks that typically require human intelligence, such as reasoning, perception, and decision-making.

Big Data: The vast and complex datasets characterized by high volume, velocity, and variety, which require advanced computational techniques for storage, processing, and analysis.

Business Intelligence: Business Intelligence refers to the systematic process of collecting, analyzing, and visualizing organizational data to support strategic decision-making and performance optimization.

Customer Experience: Customer Experience encompasses the holistic perception and interactions a customer has with a company across all touchpoints, shaping satisfaction and loyalty.

Customer Feedback: Customer Feedback is the evaluative information provided by consumers regarding products, services, or interactions, which organizations use to enhance quality and responsiveness.

Customer Relationship Management: A strategic approach supported by digital tools that integrates data and interactions to optimize customer engagement, satisfaction, and retention.

Data Mining: The computational practice of discovering hidden patterns, correlations, and knowledge from large datasets through statistical, machine learning, and algorithmic methods.

Data-Driven Insights: Data-Driven Insights are actionable conclusions derived from rigorous data analysis that inform evidence-based strategies and organizational decisions.

Machine Learning: A subset of artificial intelligence that enables systems to autonomously learn from data patterns and improve predictive or classificatory performance without explicit programming.

Natural Language Processing: An interdisciplinary field of computer science and linguistics focused on enabling machines to understand, interpret, and generate human language.

Opinion Mining: Opinion Mining, often termed sentiment mining, is the computational technique of identifying and extracting subjective information such as attitudes, evaluations, and emotions from textual data.

Predictive Analytics: Predictive Analytics is the use of statistical models, machine learning, and historical data to forecast future trends, behaviors, and outcomes in decision-making contexts.

Sentiment Analysis: Sentiment Analysis is the methodological process of determining the polarity and intensity of emotions or opinions expressed in text, typically classified as positive, negative, or neutral.

Text Analytics: The application of computational methods to extract meaningful patterns, structures, and knowledge from large volumes of unstructured textual data.

Chapter 9

Modern Teaching Using AR/VR Powered by the Metaverse

Kashvi Chaturvedi
https://orcid.org/0009-0005-3192-3400
Ajeenkya D.Y. Patil University, India

Sunil Sankathala
https://orcid.org/0009-0004-7809-7647
Ajeenkya D.Y. Patil University, India

Pooja Dehankar
Ajeenkya D.Y. Patil School of Engineering, India

Atharva Haresh Saraf
https://orcid.org/0009-0006-3842-5508
Ajeenkya D.Y. Patil University, India

Aditya Shrivastav
https://orcid.org/0009-0000-8461-8171
Ajeenkya D.Y. Patil University, India

Susanta Das
https://orcid.org/0000-0002-9314-3988
Ajeenkya D.Y. Patil University, India

ABSTRACT

The learning process can be improved by integrating simulation, modeling, and analytical tools into the Metaverse. Virtual worlds, lifelike simulations, and worldwide cooperation in the Metaverse can all be combined to improve the creation of more efficient and interesting teaching strategies, which will eventually better prepare students for the difficulties that the engineering field will present in the future. Exam security and reliability are further guaranteed by the Metaverse's technological capabilities, which enhance assessment dependability by integrating biometric identification and real-time monitoring. The chapter focuses on Advantages as well as difficulties of integrating metaverse-based teaching tools. The chapter discusses revolutionary potential of augmented reality/virtual reality (AR/VR) technology in

DOI: 10.4018/979-8-3373-2008-3.ch009

the metaverse for contemporary education. Real-world uses of modern teaching using AR/VR powered by the metaverse along with prospective future uses of the metaverse in the classroom is also explored in this chapter.

1. INTRODUCTION

Metaverse talk about vastly networked virtual setting that lets users to communicate instantly with digital things and each other, going beyond standalone virtual reality experiences and online multiplayer games. Since smartphones were created, it is anticipated to be one of the most significant technology disruptions to our daily lives. By creating a smooth user-computer interaction (HCI), an interactive interface which is both dependable and simple to use can be created. The current state of application of the underlying technologies of the metaverse, such as blockchain, virtual technology, fifth-generation (5G) connectivity, HCI, and three-dimensional (3D) reconstruction, is studied and described using the preferred reporting items for systematic reviews and meta-analyses (PRISMA) principles (Rahul et al., 2025).

Metaverse, is persistent and ever-present habitat that mixes digital virtuality with physical reality. Its foundation is convergence of technologies that enable multimodal interactions with virtual environments, humans, and digital objects. Thus, in permanent multiuser systems, the Metaverse is a networked, social, and immersive environment. It makes real-time embodied user communication seamless and allows for dynamic interactions with digital things. In its initial version, it was a network of virtual worlds with teleportation capabilities for avatars. The modern version of the Metaverse includes social, immersive virtual reality platforms that work with open game worlds, AR collaboration spaces, and massively multiplayer online video games (Mystakidis, 2022).

Virtual reality (VR) and augmented reality (AR) are transforming education by offering captivating learning settings that are interactive and immersive. In a number of domains, such as STEM, medicine, language learning, and special education, both technologies provide improved retention and skill development. However, obstacles like as exorbitant expenses, technological limitations, and ethical considerations restrict their uptake. For AR and VR to be used effectively, educators, legislators, and corporate executives must work together to create educational frameworks, facilitate access, and provide teacher preparation programs. The disruptive potential of AR and VR in education is examined, particularly in relation to its application in individualized and immersive learning. It highlights how industry and academia must work together to innovate, create educational content, and increase access to these technologies (Thangavel, 2025).

Natural Language Processing (NLP) and Artificial Intelligence (AI) are rapidly revolutionizing interactive learning through metaverse. Intelligent tutors that offer real-time feedback and adaptive learning experiences have been made possible by recent developments in Large Language Models (LLMs) (Alonso-Fernandez et al., 2024; Yang et al., 2024). AI-powered avatars, can create individualized learning pathways by interpreting speech, gestures, and emotions. Through this integration, immersive platforms based on AR and VR are guaranteed to transform into dynamic, AI-powered intelligent learning ecosystems (Wu et al., 2023).

Fast computers and networks, wearable technology, and sensor technologies have all contributed to the growing popularity of the Edu-Metaverse. As a result, Edu-Metaverse research is becoming a hot issue. In addition to providing additional experiential learning chances for experiencing, investigating, learning, and practicing in challenging, varied, and authentic tasks and contexts that are not available in the actual world, the Edu-Metaverse enables students to feel the presence of learning. Additionally, they are permitted to work, communicate, and cooperate with individuals they rarely encounter in the actual world. Barriers related to time, location, expense, risks, or tangible materials can be overcome in the Edu-Metaverse (Chen et al., 2023).

Besides, wearable technology and AI analytics increase the Edu-Metaverse's capacity to personalize learning. For example, machine learning (ML) algorithms can be connected to biosensors and eye-tracking wearables to monitor student engagement, tension, or exhaustion and offer adaptive responses (Alves et al., 2024). In order to guarantee that students have a customized and responsive educational experience, AI-enabled technologies adjust the course material or suggest breaks. The general trend of moving away from a one-size-fits-all strategy and toward highly customized strategies aided by metaverse technology is consistent with these personalized learning pathways (Razaque et al., 2024).

Because of its potential to completely transform online communication, teamwork, education, and employment, many people call metaverse, virtual shared environment that blends virtual and augmented reality technologies, "Internet of the future." However, there is a lack of empirical data to assess its educational efficacy, despite its promise strategic and corporate applications. This qualitative study looked at the benefits and drawbacks of the It's challenging to identify the best practices and rules for using it in the classroom. However, we may begin to gather evidence and pinpoint workable strategies for metaverse-based teaching and learning initiatives by gathering participant input, tracking progress over time, analyzing usage and engagement data, and assessing learning outcomes. With this data, educators may use Metaverse to make well-informed decisions that will optimize learning outcomes and foster creative teaching strategies. Institutions of higher learning must develop guidelines to guarantee the ethical and responsible use of the Metaverse in the future and put in place safeguards for the security, privacy, and welfare of students, employees, and other participants in metaverse-based learning settings (Onu et al., 2024).

One cutting-edge technology that has the potential to completely transform modern urban living is the Metaverse of Things (MoT). It includes, among other things, infrastructure management, sustainability, urban planning, and public engagement. MoT combines metaverse technology with the Internet of Things (IoT). The ultimate goal is to create extremely immersive, interactive, and networked virtual environments that are as close to reality as possible. Several aspects of urban living are improved by the Internet of Things (IoT), which uses digital technologies like virtual reality (VR), augmented reality (AR), and others to collect data, improve communication, and automate some tasks (Alam, 2024).

A Triad of Visual Digital Innovation (TVDI), the use of emerging technologies in higher education is revolutionizing teaching procedures, especially in global collaborative projects. Teaching experiences using various technologies were created during the COVID-19 epidemic (2020–2022) in order to engage students who completed their education electronically. The use of the trio rose significantly at the conclusion of the imprisonment. The absence of particular approaches that successfully incorporate these technologies in a multicultural and sustainable setting is still a problem, though. The examples show how TVDI can enhance professional teaching-learning experiences in creative areas, which can encourage increased motivation, immersion, and even cross-border cooperation. The results indicate that other educational contexts and initiatives that want to include TDVI to address regional and worldwide issues can adopt and duplicate the educational innovations and approaches created (Acuna et al., 2024).

2. REAL-WORLD USES

The study of morphology could undergo a radical change due to emerging technologies like virtual and augmented reality (VR/AR). A new digital world has been made possible by contemporary imaging techniques which allow researchers to exchange and thoroughly examine morphological data online. However, because a computer screen is used to display this digital data, it may still be challenging to comprehend and challenging to use. In addition to offering a more immersive experience and more opportunities for exploration, VR/AR technologies help close the gap between analog and digital by displaying 3D data to users in a manner that is very similar to how they would interact with real anatomy (Cieri et al., 2021).

There are numerous uses for augmented reality in range of businesses, comprising education and recreation. Since the majority of people own a mobile device that can support the graphic rendering systems needed for augmented reality projects, the last ten years of continuously evolving technology have significantly increased the viability of these projects. Since many other disciplines of research are now branching out into how augmented reality might be applied in schools, education in particular has profited from these technological advancements. Nevertheless, remarkably little study has been done on the use of augmented reality to improve Holocaust education's impact or delivery (Challenor & Ma, 2019).

In higher education, virtual representations are frequently employed to depict simulations or develop models. However, a lot of students struggle to understand mechanical systems, whether they are presented in 3D CAD specification or a 2D design plan. For this reason, we use real system changes linked to different representations, particularly for students who are not tech-savvy. The challenge of connecting a representation to the actual system can be addressed by augmented reality. Since mechanical design pedagogy has not previously made use of augmented reality, assessing the technology's potential to improve mechanism comprehension was a difficulty. An electromechanical mechanism has been subjected to an augmented reality scenario. It facilitates component and location identification, mechanism exploration, and, for example, the easier identification of the transmission power flow or kinematic chain. The students utilized a tablet and HoloLens glasses, two distinct interfaces, each with unique benefits (Scaravetti & Doroszewski, 2019).

The design and assessment of an AR alphabet book—a book that uses augmented reality to teach preschoolers the alphabet—are covered. With the help of the pattern markers as an interaction tool, kids could enjoyably and interactively observe the superimposed virtual alphabet when paired with a computer and camera. Teaching young children can often be challenging since their attention spans are shorter than those of the elderly, making it harder for them to concentrate. Introducing engaging and interactive learning could attract students' attention and improve instruction for younger students. Play, singing, dancing, theater, etc were all key components of fun-learning. Studies have demonstrated that enjoyable learning also improves a user's memorization and comprehension skills. One method of teaching kids the alphabet is through flashcards. Flashcards' tactile format encourages involvement during the learning process, which may lead to more enjoyable learning. However, by utilizing augmented reality technology, flash cards' potential could be further enhanced. Therefore, as AR offers rich media learning, promoting its use could include fun learning (Rambli et al., 2013).

3. ADVANTAGES OF INTEGRATING METAVERSE-BASED TEACHING TOOLS

The integration of generative AI (Gen-AI) and LLM-powered systems into immersive metaverse classrooms offers another noteworthy benefit. Research indicates that AI-powered conversational agents integrated into AR/VR settings can improve professional and soft skills training by simulating interviews, offering formative evaluations, and providing immediate, tailored feedback (Zhao et al., 2024; Wu et al., 2023). NLP-enabled Intelligent Tutoring Systems (ITS) provide natural interaction between students and avatars, promoting learning in a variety of fields, such as language instruction, STEM, and healthcare (Alonso-Fernandez et al., 2024). When compared to static VR content alone, these solutions show how AI-enhanced personalization rapidly improves student autonomy, motivation, and retention.

In the past, professional education persisted throughout the third industrial revolution and all subsequent ones. Not only has the half-life of relevant knowledge decreased the pace of knowledge increasing has also accelerated from lifetimes to months during those revolutions.. Will we be able to adapt to that speed? With the outdated, one-size-fits-all Prussian educational approach, how can we learn everything we need to know? Professionals must transition between many work situations, so we should fundamentally restructure educational system. New system needs to be tailored to each person's unique learning preferences and skill set. For new personalized learning system to evolve in its symbiotic relationship with humans, it must be sufficiently flexible and engaging. We should think about coexisting with memetic symbiosis autonomous cognitive systems—specifically, digital twins—in order for it to occur (Kinsner, 2021).

Business game-based learning (GBL) must be in line with training and development learning objectives and results, and it must make it abundantly evident that learning can be assessed and accomplished. Serious gaming experiences encourage a mindset of accepting the challenge, a drive for success, and constant innovation through participant commitments, all of which support human growth and transformation. The participant is forced to experience an immersive environment through simulations. Lastly, the term "gamification" refers to a group of methods that can be utilized to enhance educational and professional activities. Both corporate LTD (Learning, Training, and Development) and higher education instruction are being severely disturbed. More experiential learning—the kind of learning sparked by serious games, simulations, immersive learning environments, and gamification—is needed in light of the innovations in education (Ahmed & Sutton, 2017).

In the United States (US), all colleges and universities are finding innovative methods to improve learning and reach new student communities. However, new technologies are a huge financial burden for the majority of institutions. The majority of schools have merely attached new technologies to fixed teachers, fixed facilities, and inflexible ideas about classroom education. In these situations, rather than being a solution, technology contributes to the issue of growing expenses (Twigg, 2005).

In recent years, digital twins have drawn a lot of interest and become a trendy term. Large-scale data collection, analysis, and processing have become simpler and more affordable with the development of technologies. This has made it possible to develop and use digital twins more widely. Data-driven information and insightful insights are provided by digital twins to aid in decision-making. They assist reduce the risks and uncertainties related to decision-making processes by allowing businesses to test various methods, simulate scenarios, and evaluate effects of changes before putting them into practice. The academic community has also been impacted by technological advancements, and initiatives are underway to create Digital Twins for a range of educational purposes, such as assisting with administrative, research, and teaching procedures. As technology advances, new and innovative applications are likely to emerge, altering numerous aspects of academic administration, research, teaching, and learning (Chande, 2024).

Digital technologies offer an unmatched chance to upend long-standing educational paradigms as they develop further. A dynamic and engaging medium for teaching sustainability, virtual worlds close the gap between theoretical understanding and practical application. These risk-free interactive settings allow students to engage with complex ecological systems and sustainability challenges, facilitating study and experimentation that would be unfeasible or impracticable in the actual world. Adventure worlds allow children to learn through exploration in a narrative setting through missions that are fueled by stories. Open-ended, sandbox-like settings where creativity and imagination are valued highly are offered by creative worlds (Damaševičius & Sidekerskienė, 2024).

By creating digital twins of their pupils, teachers can keep an eye on their development, understand how they learn, and modify curriculum to meet the needs of every learner. This makes it easier to provide customized feedback and enhance learning results (Wang et al., 2023). Digital twins can streamline campus operations, such as energy management, security, and maintenance. As a result, learning environments are enhanced and resources are used more efficiently (Rathore et al., 2021). Digital twins of classroom settings can be used to create engaging remote studying experiences. Students can interact with educational materials, participate in group activities, and interact with virtual classrooms, claim Sylvester et al. (2023). Researchers can test novel concepts and technologies in a virtual environment by analyzing educational methods and results using digital twins before implementing them in the real world (Zhang, 2017). Students' interest and engagement can be raised in the classroom through interaction and immersion. Students can experiment and practice in a risk-free online setting. Effectively managing digital and physical resources through data-driven insights. Experiences in education that are especially created to satisfy each learner's requirements and preferred method of learning. The ability to regularly and high-quality teach more students, particularly those in underprivileged or remote areas (Ayoade et al., 2022).

4. DIFFICULTIES OF INTEGRATING METAVERSE-BASED TEACHING TOOLS

Many educational institutions find it challenging to implement VR because of the high initial costs associated with both software and hardware (such as powerful computers and VR headsets) (Cook et al., 2019). Compatibility issues, software bugs, and poor internet access can all interfere with learning and reduce user interest (Sarrab et al., 2016). There is a digital divide and unequal access to metaverse-based learning since some kids do not have the required technology at home or in school (Sripan & Jeerapattanatorn, 2025). There are a lot of teachers and students who are not equipped to use the metaverse's immersive and interactive features (Stanoevska-Slabeva, 2022). It takes specific expertise in 3D modeling, virtual environment design, and interactive story development to create interesting and useful educational content for the metaverse (Lo & Tsai, 2022). It is essential to make sure that the material is not only interesting but also pedagogically solid and pertinent to the curriculum (Davis & Krajcik, 2005). Since 2021, metaverse refers to new form of cyberspace, has gained popularity. There are numerous definitions of Meterverse and attempts to establish a formal standard or definition. But it was difficult for these definitions to be accepted by everyone. We outline four essential features of the Metaverse—socialization, immersive interaction, genuine world-building, and expandability—instead of offering a precise description. These features not only make the Metaverse a unique and amazing virtual environment, but they also expose it to all security and privacy threats, including phishing, data injection, eavesdropping, illegal access, personal information leakage, compromised authentication, insecure design, and more (Huang et al., 2023). With effects on users worldwide and a variety of behavioral, social, and psychological repercussions, digital addiction has grown to be a serious public health concern. Examined are national laws, international initiatives, and existing legal structures to address this expanding issue. Playtime limits, age restrictions, and content prohibitions are just a few of the laws that have been implemented in some nations to combat digital addiction. The goal of these initiatives is to lessen the negative habits linked to excessive internet use, especially in susceptible groups like teenagers. The ethical conundrums surrounding the regulation of digital addiction are examined, including the possibility of governmental overreach, freedom of expression, and privacy rights (Carter & Johnson, 2023). The Metaverse's creative potential for knowledge work has primarily been investigated in relation to its capacity to improve remote collaboration. By explicitly isolating their virtual workplace from their actual environment, knowledge workers can proactively protect themselves against typical distractions in public, private, or collaborative settings. Knowledge workers must be aware of and capable of customizing technological affordances to maximize work outcomes, while Metaverse apps may potentially provide new sources of distraction. Instead of replicating traditional corporate offices in the Metaverse and their typical distractions, we should use its potential to supplement, change, or replace traditional work environments, according to a theoretical model of virtual workplace distraction management that is informed by these findings (Marx et al., 2025). Interest in the concept of the metaverse has increased as a result of the COVID-19 pandemic's restrictions forcing many people to seek out alternative training and educational possibilities. The metaverse, which combines the virtual and real worlds to create a highly immersive experience, is seen as the next generation of the Internet. It should come as no surprise that next-generation training and education systems are interested in ways to incorporate themselves into metaverse settings. Participants are specifically seeking more flexible and interactive training that yet maintains a high standard of instructional content and engaging workflows (Yilmaz et al., 2023). Simplifying school plant management is a revolutionary strategy that transforms educational institutions by making the most of resources, improving classroom environments, and enabling children to flourish. Asset, maintenance, facilities, financial and human resources management are all crucial areas that require development. Implementing integrated management systems, embracing technology-based solutions, outsourcing non-core operations, increasing capacity and training, and tracking and evaluating performance are all ways to streamline school plant administration. By adopting these cutting-edge strategies, schools can reap numerous advantages, such as enhanced decision-making, cost savings, increased efficiency, and better service delivery. Resources can be redirected by schools to support their primary goal of offering top-notch instruction and support services. Students, faculty, and the larger community will all gain from improved educational experiences and results, which will have significant benefits (Ebom-Jebose, 2025). However, pessimism endures due to worries that enthusiasm would surpass scientific advancement. According to a CoinMarketCap report (published in February 2023) that lists over 240 distinct Metaverse initiatives, interoperability is a major barrier. Even though its significance is well acknowledged, there is still a dearth of systematic study on interoperability (Yang et al., 2025). One of the most popular study topics nowadays is the metaverse, which allows people to interact, learn, and work together in a networked, three-dimensional, immersive virtual environment. The metaverse is the perfect model for jobs involving education, training, and skill development because of its rich multimedia streaming capabilities and immersive user experience with fast communication (Jagatheesaperumal et al., 2024). Platformization is the term for this process, which has led to the emergence of platform society, a phenomenon in which platforms have permeated metropolitan cultures. A recent example of platformization is the Metaverse, a global platform project launched by Meta (formerly Facebook), a globally running platform organization (Allam et al., 2022).

5. REVOLUTIONARY POTENTIAL OF AR/VR TECHNOLOGY IN THE METAVERSE FOR CONTEMPORARY EDUCATION

New possibilities for creating dynamic, captivating educational experiences are being presented by three-dimensional virtual world environments. These virtual worlds are special because they let users engage with other people via their avatars and with items in the surroundings, enabling them to create experiences that might not be feasible in the actual world (Eschenbrenner et al., 2008; Squire, 2010; Van Dam et al., 2002). Computer-assisted learning items, such as educational computer games, are an increasingly popular educational approach. Since the digital world has changed over the past several decades, students of the current age expect technology to be used to enhance their education. As a result, old passive learning approaches must be replaced with active, multimodal, experimental learning approaches (Rondon et al., 2013). The vast collection of diverse technologies known as the Edu-Metaverse has sparked a significant and unprecedented shift in the field of education. The emergence of AI-enabled agents, immersive educational scenarios that can speed up learning and skill acquisition, and embodied and multimodal engagement are some of the Edu-Metaverse features that have brought about this shift. Unlike traditional classroom teaching models, smart education is a collaborative and visual model that uses the latest AI technologies to achieve a learning outcome. However, the question that must be considered is how to develop an intelligent educational model that makes use of the Edu-Metaverse to enhance student learning outcomes. A smart teaching environment, multimodal teaching resources, AI-enabled evaluation, and smart pedagogy in the context of Edu-Metaverse should all be highlighted in such a paradigm (Shu & Gu, 2023). In order to provide fair, inclusive, and high-quality education in all schools, it is important to address children' learning difficulties. The contemporary educational environment demands a comprehensive strategy that benefits all students, even while special education programs are in place to meet the needs of students with a variety of learning challenges. Illuminating four crucial elements that are necessary to fostering an inclusive learning environment is the main goal. Since education is a basic human right and every student should have an equal chance to study and succeed, it highlights the significance of educational equity (Barnard & Henn, 2023). There is disagreement over whether education actually promotes social justice and equity as claimed. Regardless of the debate's conclusion, education has a better chance of surviving this process if it is provided through a national system and through schools that are truly inclusive—welcoming diversity and difference, working to uphold the right to a high-quality education, and focusing on both out-of-school and in-school but unlearning children. However, a significant portion of children in many educational systems continue to fall short of the minimum required levels of learning, typically due to discriminatory practices, negligence, or a lack of resources and information about the individuals who are excluded, their residences, and the reasons for their absences from school (Shaeffer, 2019). In the context of the metaverse, virtual reality (VR) and augmented reality (AR) technologies have a big impact on how people will connect with each other, learn, and work in the future. AR and VR has transformed way all work by facilitating virtual offices and remote collaboration, as well as improving training opportunities for a variety of professions. These technologies' potential to increase output, cut expenses, and foster a more sustainable workplace is examined. revolutionary potential of AR and VR in the field of education, where it is described how immersive learning environments encouraged greater comprehension, increased student engagement, and enabled individualized learning routes. Highlighted are cutting-edge applications that have revolutionized teaching and learning, including collaborative learning environments, simulation-based training, and virtual field trips (Kuleto et al., 2024). Through the use of Student-Centered Active Learning, student groups produced their own virtual reality content, fostering critical thinking and problem-solving skills, communication, collaboration, and computer-information literacy (Wu et al., 2023). Number of obstacles might prevent them from being widely used in settings with limited resources, particularly in poor nations. These include societal opposition to new technology, exorbitant expenses, a lack of locally relevant material, inadequate teacher preparation, and infrastructure constraints. AR and VR in educational is complicated by institutional and governmental impediments, technological limits, and equality concerns. Therefore, a plan to overcome them is required. Cost-sharing schemes, content localization, teacher professional development, and the creation of scalable, affordable solutions are a few possible remedies (Mondal & Mondal, 2025).

The avatar is the player character's digital representation in the metaverse. Avatar realism has significantly increased with use of real-time tracking, identification, or simulation technology. Teachers and students can add features to their avatars by customizing them (such skin tone, gender, and style sense) more or less like themselves. For example, Zhao et al. (2022) pointed out that information such as avatar learners' facial emotions and motions can be captured and dynamically exhibited by scanning users' physical appearance. Avatars can also be shared and manipulated by users via real-time tracking, controls, or sensors (Genay et al., 2021).

The shift to a digital environment, which allows for consistent services to be provided regardless of physical location or other circumstances, has been speeded up by global Covid-19 pandemic. Perhaps most representative embodiment of this trend is the Metaverse. The open Metaverse framework is a suitable and sensible design option to accommodate many virtual world instances and platforms. Achieving technical completeness in each of the open Metaverse's building blocks is essential because the framework's development is still in its very early stages. Extensive standardized studies on the open Metaverse framework are necessary and essential given the Metaverse's future growth and dissemination (Kang, 2021). eXtended Reality (XR) technologies, which are characterized as virtual reality, augmented reality, and mixed reality, offer a potentially elegant answer to the COVID-19 pandemic, which forced humanity to consider new ways of functioning internationally without physically being present with other people. To solve practical issues in data processing, mental health, training, simulation, and disease progression research, commercial and academic teams are looking into XR solutions. Previously, XR solutions were believed to be mostly for gaming. Large companies like Microsoft and Meta have lately declared their intention to create a new paradigm for interacting with the digital world, called the Metaverse (Taylor and Soneji, 2022). According to Park and Kim (2022), the current Metaverse is based on the social value of Generation Z that online and offline selves are the same, in contrast to earlier studies on the Metaverse that were based on Second Life. The development of deep learning-based high-precision recognition and natural generation models has strengthened the Metaverse in a number of ways, from always-on mobile access to virtual currency-based connectivity with reality. A modern definition of the Metaverse that differs from the one that existed in the past is necessary due to the incorporation of improved social activities and neural-net techniques.

6. PROSPECTIVE FUTURE USES OF THE METAVERSE IN THE CLASSROOM

In future, LLMs and ML-driven personalization are expected to merge with AI-powered metaverse platforms to provide “self-driving classrooms.” These settings will use Gen-AI to produce educational content collaboratively, continuously assess student behavior, and modify learning materials in real time (Jin et al., 2024). These advancements signal a shift toward self-sufficient, AI-powered metaverse ecosystems where individualized instruction is both predictive and reactive, foreseeing the requirements of students before they materialize. The scalability and durability of

AI-embedded immersive education are demonstrated by recent research on gamified collaborative AI platforms such as "LearningverseVR," which are consistent with this goal (Ahmed et al., 2024).

The immersive virtual world known as the metaverse, which allows users to participate in digital activities, has the potential to completely transform education. The Unified Theory of Acceptance and Use of Metaverse Technology (UTAUMT), an enhanced model, is offered to help decision-makers and educators. Metaverse hedonic motivation (MHM), metaverse price value (MPC), metaverse self-efficacy (MSE), metaverse facilitating conditions (MFC), metaverse performance expectancy (MPE), metaverse effort expectancy (MEE), and metaverse social influence (MSI) are just a few of the many elements that make up the UTAUMT. A questionnaire that participants self-administered was used to evaluate these criteria. The results show a significant impact of MEE, MSI, MFC, MSE, and MBI on the educational metaverse MUB. Adding elements unique to the metaverse to the technology acceptance framework is one theoretical contribution of the extended UTAUMT model. The integration of the metaverse, user training, and assistance are the main management implications that aim to increase the adoption rate (Nguyen et al., 2024).

7. ANALYSIS

Following figures, Figure 1, Figure 2, and Figure 3, represent bibliometric analysis on "Modern teaching using AR/VR powered by the metaverse" which is made using VOSviewer and data regarding this has been taken from lens for the year ranging from 2005 to 2025. The map shows how incorporating VR, AR, and metaverse technology into education is growing across disciplinary boundaries. Each figure shows different aspects on the topic, starting with keyword connection, moving on to research focus on these keywords over a period of time and finally representing its density visualization.

Using term clustering, Figure 1 displays a co-occurrence network map that illustrates the intellectual structure of the AR and VR research landscape. Every node stands for a keyword, and the connections across nodes show how frequently certain keywords occur together in academic works. While colors indicate groups of related concepts that frequently occur together in the literature, node size corresponds to the term's frequency.

Keywords like "metaverse," "artificial intelligence," "education," and "healthcare" are prominent in the center and most dominating cluster, indicating that AR/VR technologies are frequently investigated in conjunction with interdisciplinary fields. As an illustration of the pedagogical shift brought about by immersive technologies, the term "education" is closely associated with subtopics such as distant learning, gamification, digital literacy, and simulation. Similar to this, phrases like telemedicine, dementia, cognition/physiology, and medical education indicate the expanding use of AR/VR in patient care and medical education.

Figure 1. Bibliometric Analysis on Modern teaching using AR/VR powered by the metaverse using VOSviewer and data from Lens

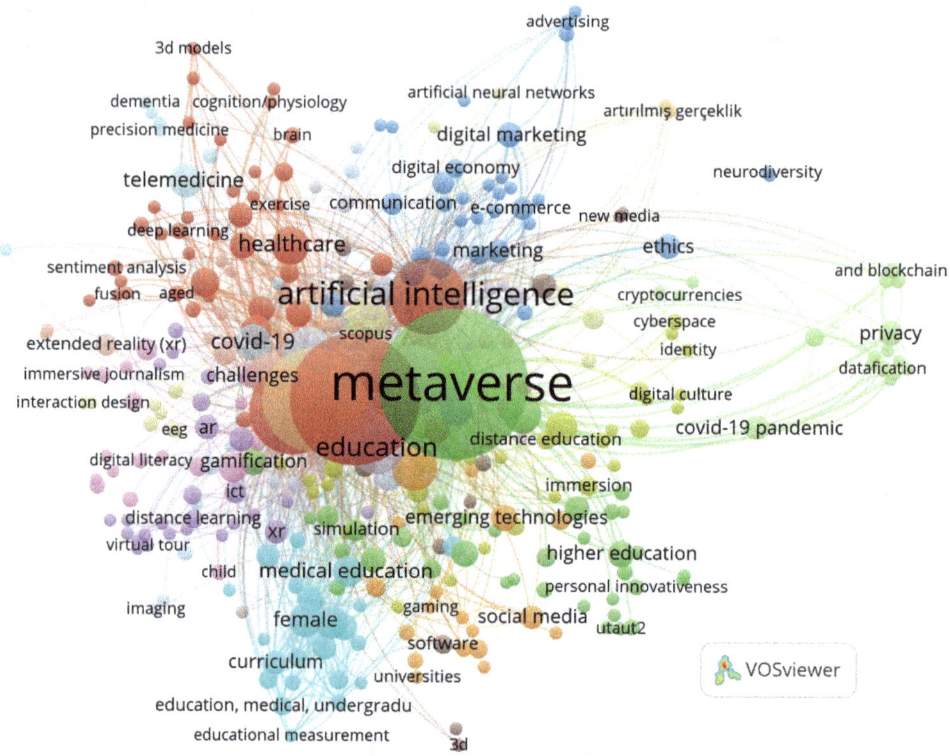

(VOSviewer; Lens.org)

Additionally, clusters clearly distinguish different areas of research focus. The integration of AR/VR with consumer behavior analysis and virtual shopping environments is the focus of one notable cluster that revolves on digital marketing, e-commerce, and artificial neural networks. The growing worries about digital identity and personal data in virtual spaces are highlighted by another cluster that connects privacy, cybersecurity, and datafication.

All things considered, the figure offers a thorough mapping of research on AR and VR, demonstrating that these disciplines are now intricately entwined with larger societal, ethical, educational, and healthcare systems rather than existing as separate technological entities.

Figure 2. Bibliometric Analysis on Modern teaching using AR/VR powered by the metaverse over a period of time using VOSviewer and data from Lens

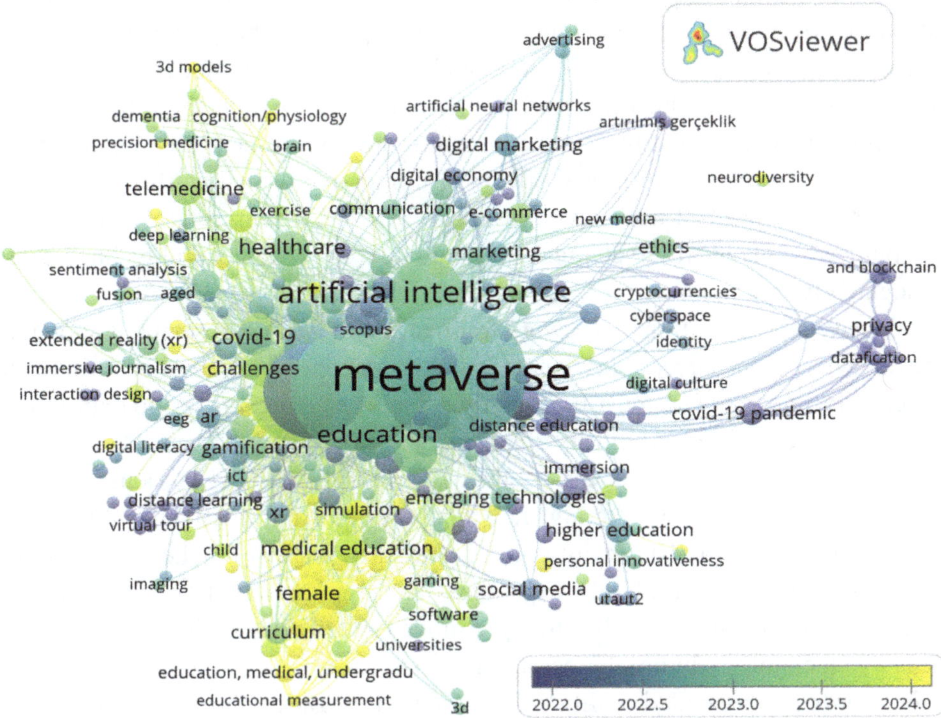

(VOSviewer; Lens.org)

A temporal overlay picture of the development of research themes in AR and VR from 2005 to 2025 is provided in Figure 2. The color gradient, which goes from blue for earlier years to yellow for more current ones, makes it easier to see how some terms become more popular over time.

An early concentration on virtual environments and their commercial applications is reflected in the blue and green hues of the early research themes, which encompass fundamental ideas like virtual tours, digital culture, cyberspace, and e-commerce. During these early years, AR and VR technologies were mainly experimental and mainly investigated for online gaming and engagement.

The emergence of terms like COVID-19, telemedicine, distance learning, and extended reality (XR) signals a move toward applied research in response to global issues as the timeline moves toward green and yellow hues. Immersion technology for remote communication, healing, and education have become more popular as a result of the pandemic. More modern concepts like gamification, digital marketing, and personal innovativeness point to a more widespread adoption of these technologies in institutional procedures and daily life.

As shown by its vivid yellow color, one noteworthy trend is the recent shift of "education" from a supporting theme to a primary phrase. This points to a growing interest in the ways that AR and VR might change pedagogy, especially in curriculum design, medical education, and higher education. At the same time, issues like identity, privacy, and ethics are becoming more important, indicating a greater understanding of the sociopolitical effects of immersive virtual worlds.

As a result, Figure 2 not only shows how AR/VR research has evolved over time, but it also places these changes in the context of more general technological and social advancements.

A density representation of keyword frequencies in AR/VR research is shown in Figure 3, where blue/purple areas denote low-density zones and yellow spots indicate high-density regions. The most thoroughly researched concepts in the dataset can be easily found with the aid of this graphic.

The term "metaverse" is at the center of the map, encircled by dense clusters of terms such as digital marketing, healthcare, education, artificial intelligence, and medical education. The main areas of scholarly interest for the past 20 years are indicated by these vivid yellow patches. The importance of "healthcare" and "education" further supports the strategic move toward real-world applications of immersive technology in human-centered domains.

Keywords like extended reality (XR), simulation, gamification, and new technologies are found in medium-density zones in green, indicating that although these are significant themes, they are still in a comparatively exploratory stage in relation to the main themes. Peripheral concepts such as datafication, cyberspace, and neurodiversity, on the other hand, emerge in cooler hues, suggesting a limited but expanding level of scholarly participation.

Figure 3. Bibliometric Analysis of density of Modern teaching using AR/VR powered by the metaverse over a period of time using VOSviewer and data from Lens

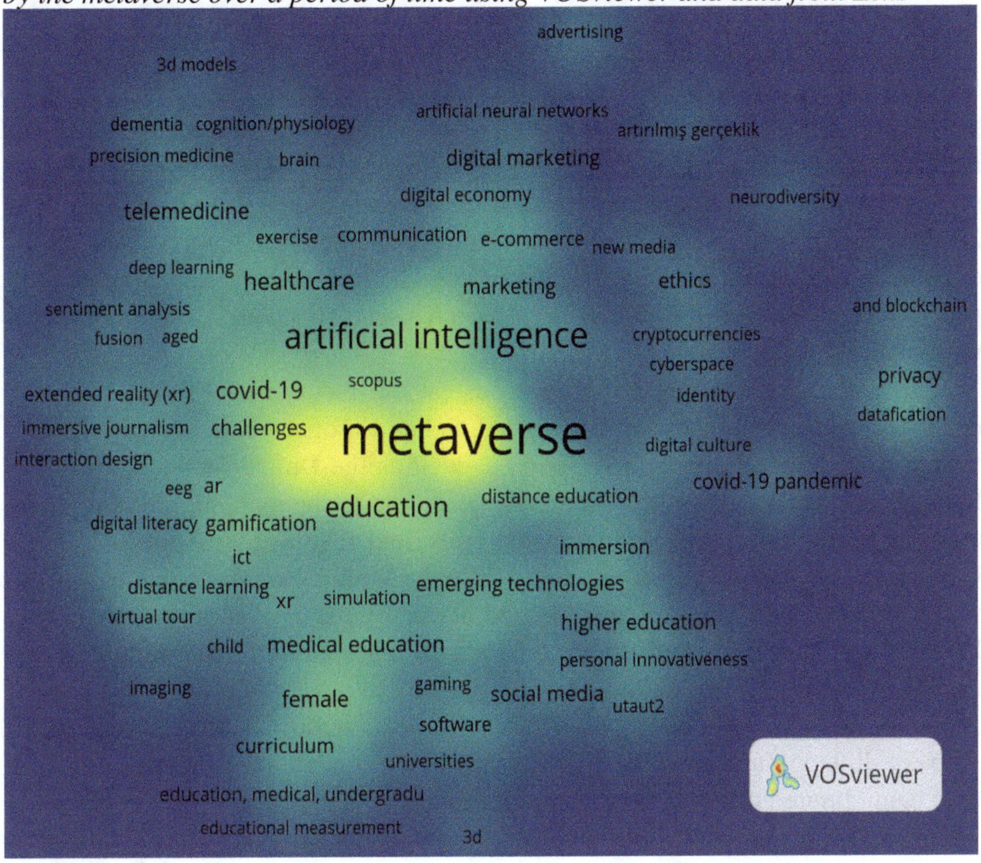

(VOSviewer; Lens.org)

The saturation of study fields can be intuitively understood thanks to this heatmap-like representation. For instance, although areas such as marketing and the digital economy have already been extensively studied, topics like identity, ethics, and digital culture present chances for further in-depth research in the future, particularly as AR/VR technologies proliferate and become more ingrained in daily life.

A word cloud of terms derived from the dataset, same as used for bibliometric analysis, is shown in Figure 4, offering a clear visual representation of the most important research ideas in the area. The common use of terms like "metaverse," "virtual reality," "augmented reality," "education," and "artificial intelligence" underscores their importance in the field. Emerging intersections of immersive technologies with AI-driven educational paradigms are reflected in buzzwords like "gamification," "digital twins," "machine learning," "NLP," and "personalized learning." Each keyword's relative magnitude shows how frequently it occurs, providing a clear picture of the distribution of thematic priorities across domains in metaverse-related education research.

The publication trend over time is shown in Figure 5, which shows a slow but consistent increase from 2005 to 2019 before an exponential increase in output starting in 2020. The COVID-19 epidemic, which sped up interest in immersive learning, remote learning, and digital transformation, coupled with this dramatic rise. Research on AR/VR, AI, and metaverse education appears to have peaked in 2022 and 2024, which is consistent with the global movement to incorporate cutting-edge technologies into instruction and training. The pattern suggests that within the past five years, the subject has developed from a specialized area of interest into a major area of study.

The global distribution of publications on the metaverse, AR/VR, and AI-enhanced education is shown in Figure 6. Leading European nations including the United Kingdom, Germany, and Spain, as well as the United States, China, and India, have donated the most documents, according to the map, highlighting their crucial contributions to the development of this field of study (data from Lens.org). Increasing activity is also seen in regions like the Middle East and Southeast Asia, which reflects rising interest in and funding for immersive learning technology. Even though their contributions are relatively smaller, those from South America and Africa show how this field is becoming more and more global. This geographic analysis highlights how research on AI-driven metaverse education is expanding globally, linking various educational contexts and innovation ecosystems, rather than being limited to a few technology hotspots.

Figure 4. Word Cloud of Keywords from Various Papers

Figure 5. Area Chart Depicting Publication Trend over Time

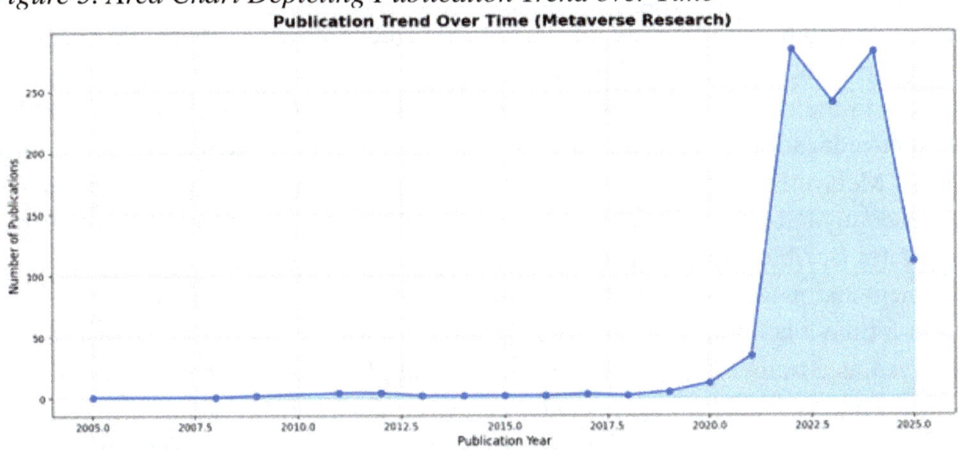

Figure 6. World Graph of Countries' Contributions in the Field

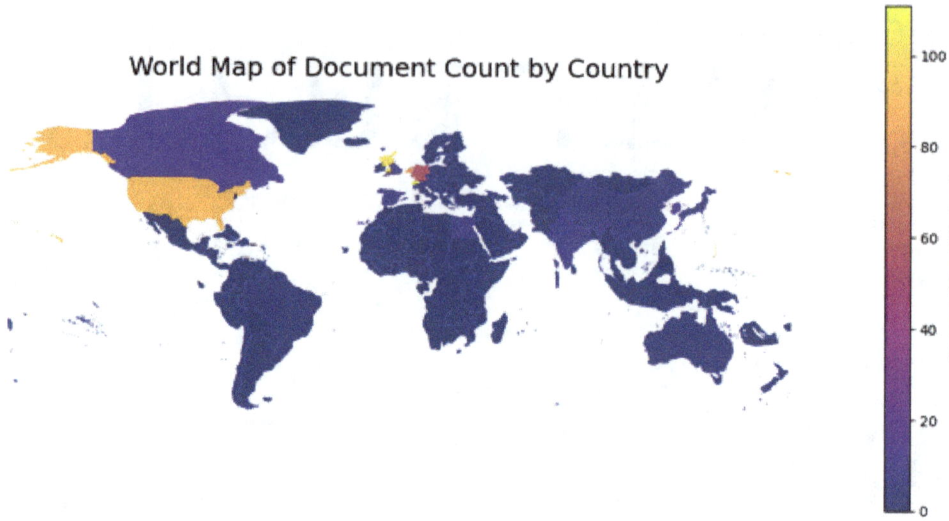

8. CONCLUSION

The metaverse has the power to revolutionize education. Higher levels of engagement and improved learning outcomes are possible results of the metaverse. Future education will be significantly impacted by this technology. As the world becomes more digital, acquiring new skills and adapting to new technology are essential for success in the twenty-first century. The Metaverse is the next evolution of virtual reality in education. Further research is necessary to identify the optimal conditions for the Metaverse's efficacy, as not all courses and students can profit from its use for teaching and learning. Future research should look at how well the Metaverse facilitates flexible and tailored learning, which enables students to engage in more pertinent and meaningful learning activities and study at their own pace.

In a time when many advanced technologies have matured, the metaverse has emerged as a transformative force that is altering how we engage with the digital world. The metaverse, a huge, networked digital environment where users engage with one another through avatars, is predicted to be the next Internet. It offers a sneak peek at a time when it will be difficult to distinguish between the real and virtual worlds. By creating new opportunities for engagement and immersive learning, the Metaverse has the potential to fundamentally alter a number of industries, most notably education, as we investigate this cutting-edge cosmos. By doing thus, it addresses the larger global issues embodied in Sustainable Development Goal 4-Quality Education, in addition to promoting cooperative learning opportunities.

REFERENCES

Acuna, A., Juarez, A., & Vazquez, R. (2024, October). Educational innovations supported by AI, VR, AR and metaverse technologies. In *2024 International Conference on Artificial Intelligence, Metaverse and Cybersecurity (ICAMAC)* (pp. 1-7). IEEE.

Ahmed, A., & Sutton, M. J. (2017). Gamification, serious games, simulations, and immersive learning environments in knowledge management initiatives. *World Journal of Science. Technology and Sustainable Development*, *14*(2/3), 78–83.

Ahmed, S., Zhao, Y., & Chen, X. (2024). AI-enhanced interview simulation in the metaverse: Transforming professional skills training through VR and generative conversational AI (ITEM). *Computers and Education: Artificial Intelligence*, *5*(2), 100123. DOI: 10.1016/j.caeai.2024.100123

Alam, T. (2024). Metaverse of Things (MoT) applications for revolutionizing urban living in smart cities. *Smart Cities*, *7*(5), 2466–2494.

Allam, Z., Sharifi, A., Bibri, S. E., Jones, D. S., & Krogstie, J. (2022). The metaverse as a virtual form of smart cities: Opportunities and challenges for environmental, economic, and social sustainability in urban futures. *Smart Cities*, *5*(3), 771–801.

Alonso-Fernandez, C., Guzman, F., & Yang, J. (2024). Integrating artificial intelligence and extended reality in language education: A systematic literature review (2017–2024). *Education Sciences*, *15*(8), 1066. DOI: 10.3390/educsci15081066

Alves, M., Borges, A., & Lima, R. (2024). Integrating AI-driven wearable metaverse technologies into ubiquitous blended learning. *Education Sciences*, *15*(7), 900. DOI: 10.3390/educsci15070900

Ayoade, I., Adedigba, A., Adeyemi, O. A., Adeaga, O. A., & Akanbi, O. (2022). Trends and prospects of digital twin technologies: A review. *Quantum journal of engineering, science and technology, 3*(4), 11-24.

Barnard, R. W., & Henn, R. H. (2023). Overcoming learning obstacles: Strategies for supporting students with diverse needs. *OAlib*, *10*(8), 1–14.

Carter, W., & Johnson, E. (2023). Legal responses to digital addiction: Regulating online gaming, social media, and virtual reality for public health and safety. *Legal Studies in Digital Age*, *2*(2), 24–36.

Challenor, J., & Ma, M. (2019). A review of augmented reality applications for history education and heritage visualisation. *Multimodal Technologies and Interaction*, *3*(2), 39.

Chande, S. V. (2024). An Exploratory view of Application of Digital Twin Technology in Education. *International Journal of Advanced Trends in Computer Science and Engineering, 13*(2).

Chen, X., Zou, D., Xie, H., & Wang, F. L. (2023). Metaverse in education: Contributors, cooperations, and research themes. *IEEE Transactions on Learning Technologies, 16*(6), 1111–1129.

Cieri, R. L., Turner, M. L., Carney, R. M., Falkingham, P. L., Kirk, A. M., Wang, T., Jensen, B., Novotny, J., Tveite, J., Gatesy, S. M., & Farmer, C. G. (2021). Virtual and augmented reality: New tools for visualizing, analyzing, and communicating complex morphology. *Journal of Morphology, 282*(12), 1785–1800. PMID: 34689352

Cook, M., Lischer-Katz, Z., Hall, N., Hardesty, J., Johnson, J., McDonald, R., & Carlisle, T. (2019). Challenges and strategies for educational virtual reality: Results of an expert-led forum on 3D/VR technologies across academic institutions. *Information Technology and Libraries, 38*(4), 25–48.

Damaševičius, R., & Sidekerskienė, T. (2024). Virtual worlds for learning in metaverse: A narrative review. *Sustainability, 16*(5), 2032.

Davis, E. A., & Krajcik, J. S. (2005). Designing educative curriculum materials to promote teacher learning. *Educational Researcher, 34*(3), 3–14.

Ebom-Jebose, A. (2025). Streamlining School Plant Management: A Transformative Approach for Educational Institutions. *Int'l Journal of Education Research and Scientific Development, 7*(1), 101–114.

Eschenbrenner, B., Nah, F. F. H., & Siau, K. (2008). 3-D virtual worlds in education: Applications, benefits, issues, and opportunities. [JDM]. *Journal of Database Management, 19*(4), 91–110.

Genay, A., Lécuyer, A., & Hachet, M. (2021). Being an avatar "for real": A survey on virtual embodiment in augmented reality. *IEEE Transactions on Visualization and Computer Graphics, 28*(12), 5071–5090. PMID: 34310309

Huang, Y., Li, Y. J., & Cai, Z. (2023). Security and privacy in metaverse: A comprehensive survey. *Big Data Mining and Analytics, 6*(2), 234–247.

Jagatheesaperumal, S. K., Ahmad, K., Al-Fuqaha, A., & Qadir, J. (2024). Advancing education through extended reality and internet of everything enabled metaverses: Applications, challenges, and open issues. *IEEE Transactions on Learning Technologies, 17*, 1120–1139.

Jin, Y., Sun, Z., & Park, H. (2024). Developing an immersive game-based learning platform with generative AI and VR technologies: LearningverseVR. *Computers and Education: X Reality, 5*(1), 100019. https://doi.org/DOI: 10.1016/j.cexr.2024.100019

Kang, Y. M. (2021). Metaverse framework and building block. *Journal of the Korea Institute of Information and Communication Engineering, 25*(9), 1263–1266.

Kinsner, W. (2021, September). Digital twins for personalized education and lifelong learning. In *2021 IEEE Canadian conference on electrical and computer engineering (CCECE)* (pp. 1-6). IEEE.

Kuleto, V., Ilić, M. P., Ranković, M., Radaković, M., & Simović, A. (2024). Augmented and virtual reality in the metaverse context: the impact on the future of work, education, and social interaction. In *Augmented and virtual reality in the metaverse* (pp. 3–24). Springer Nature Switzerland.

Lens.org

Lo, S. C., & Tsai, H. H. (2022). Design of 3D virtual reality in the metaverse for environmental conservation education based on cognitive theory. *Sensors (Basel), 22*(21), 8329. PMID: 36366028

Marx, J., Mirbabaie, M., & Rieskamp, J. (2025). Working from the Metaverse: A distraction management perspective. *Journal of Management Information Systems, 42*(1), 206–237.

Mondal, H., & Mondal, S. (2025). Adopting augmented reality and virtual reality in medical education in resource-limited settings: Constraints and the way forward. *Advances in Physiology Education, 49*(2), 503–507. PMID: 40136005

Mystakidis, S. (2022). Metaverse. *Encyclopedia, 2*(1), 486–497.

Nguyen, A. H. D., Le, T. T., Dang, T. Q., & Nguyen, L. T. (2024). Understanding metaverse adoption in education: The extended UTAUMT model. *Heliyon, 10*(19). PMID: 39416817

Onu, P., Pradhan, A., & Mbohwa, C. (2024). Potential to use metaverse for future teaching and learning. *Education and Information Technologies, 29*(7), 8893–8924.

Park, S. M., & Kim, Y. G. (2022). A metaverse: Taxonomy, components, applications, and open challenges. *IEEE Access : Practical Innovations, Open Solutions, 10*, 4209–4251.

Rahul, D., George, S., & Amritha, P. S. (2025). Metaverse-Powered Human–Computer Interactions and Applications. In *Applying Metaverse Technologies to Human-Computer Interaction for Healthcare* (pp. 38–55). Auerbach Publications.

Rambli, D. R. A., Matcha, W., & Sulaiman, S. (2013). Fun learning with AR alphabet book for preschool children. *Procedia Computer Science*, *25*, 211–219.

Rathore, M. M., Shah, S. A., Shukla, D., Bentafat, E., & Bakiras, S. (2021). The role of ai, machine learning, and big data in digital twinning: A systematic literature review, challenges, and opportunities. *IEEE Access : Practical Innovations, Open Solutions*, *9*, 32030–32052.

Razaque, A., Khan, M., & Alghamdi, M. (2024). Personalization of the learning path within an augmented reality spatial ability training application based on fuzzy weights. *Sensors (Basel)*, *22*(18), 7059. DOI: 10.3390/s22187059 PMID: 36146410

Rondon, S., Sassi, F. C., & Furquim de Andrade, C. R. (2013). Computer game-based and traditional learning method: A comparison regarding students' knowledge retention. *BMC Medical Education*, *13*(1), 30. PMID: 23442203

Sarrab, M., Elbasir, M., & Alnaeli, S. (2016). Towards a quality model of technical aspects for mobile learning services: An empirical investigation. *Computers in Human Behavior*, *55*, 100–112.

Scaravetti, D., & Doroszewski, D. (2019). Augmented Reality experiment in higher education, for complex system appropriation in mechanical design. *Procedia CIRP*, *84*, 197–202.

Shaeffer, S. (2019). Inclusive education: A prerequisite for equity and social justice. *Asia Pacific Education Review*, *20*(2), 181–192.

Shu, X., & Gu, X. (2023). An empirical study of A smart education model enabled by the edu-metaverse to enhance better learning outcomes for students. *Systems*, *11*(2), 75.

Squire, K. (2010). From information to experience: Place-based augmented reality games as a model for learning in a globally networked society. *Teachers College Record*, *112*(10), 2565–2602.

Sripan, T., & Jeerapattanatorn, P. (2025). Metaverse-based learning: A comprehensive review of current trends, challenges, and future implications. *Contemporary Educational Technology*, *17*(3), ep584.

Stanoevska-Slabeva, K. (2022). Opportunities and challenges of metaverse for education: a literature review. *Edulearn22 Proceedings*, 10401-10410.

Sylvester, A., Mines, R., David, R., & Campbell-Meier, J. (2023, January). Conceptualization of digital twins in an education services environment: A straw man proposal. In *Proceedings of the 56th Hawaii international conference on system sciences*.

Taylor, S., & Soneji, S. (2022). Bioinformatics and the metaverse: Are we ready? *Frontiers in Bioinformatics*, *2*, 863676. PMID: 36304263

Thangavel, S. (2025). Revolutionizing Education Through Augmented Reality (AR) and Virtual Reality (VR): Innovations, Challenges and Future Prospects. *Challenges and Future Prospects (March 03, 2025).*

Twigg, C. A. (2005). Improving learning and reducing costs for online learning. In *Encyclopedia of distance learning* (pp. 1054–1060). IGI Global Scientific Publishing.

Van Dam, A., Laidlaw, D. H., & Simpson, R. M. (2002). Experiments in immersive virtual reality for scientific visualization. *Computers & Graphics*, *26*(4), 535–555.

VOSviewer. https://www.vosviewer.com/

Wang, M., Bi, X., & Liu, F. (2023). Research on digital twin technology and application in campus. *The frontiers of society, science and technology, 5*(5), 118-123.

Wu, W. C. V., Manabe, K., Marek, M. W., & Shu, Y. (2023). Enhancing 21st-century competencies via virtual reality digital content creation. *Journal of Research on Technology in Education*, *55*(3), 388–410. DOI: 10.1080/15391523.2021.2024049

Wu, W. C. V., Manabe, K., Marek, M. W., & Shu, Y. (2023). Enhancing 21st-century competencies via virtual reality digital content creation. *Journal of Research on Technology in Education*, *55*(3), 388–410.

Yang, C., Liu, F., & Huang, Z. (2024). Application of artificial intelligence and virtual reality in soft skills training with modeled personality. *Applied Sciences (Basel, Switzerland)*, *15*(16), 9067. DOI: 10.3390/app15169067

Yang, L., Ni, S. T., Wang, Y., Yu, A., Lee, J. A., & Hui, P. (2025). Interoperability of the metaverse: A digital ecosystem perspective review. *IEEE Engineering Management Review*.

Yilmaz, M., O'farrell, E., & Clarke, P. (2023). Examining the training and education potential of the metaverse: Results from an empirical study of next generation SAFe training. *Journal of Software (Malden, MA)*, *35*(9), e2531.

Zhang, H. (2017). The digital twin: Data driven simulations innovate the manufacturing process. *White paper for DXC technology*, 14-17.

Zhao, L., Chen, S., & Fang, X. (2024). The implementation of the cognitive theory of multimedia learning in the design and evaluation of an AI educational video assistant utilizing LLMs. *Heliyon*, *10*(4), e19326. DOI: 10.1016/j.heliyon.2024.e19326

Zhao, Y., Jiang, J., Chen, Y., Liu, R., Yang, Y., Xue, X., & Chen, S. (2022). Metaverse: Perspectives from graphics, interactions and visualization. *Visual Informatics*, *6*(1), 56–67.

ADDITIONAL READING

AR VR in Education: Paving the way towards Great Learning. Appventurez. Retrieved 2025, from https://www.appventurez.com/blog/role-of-ar-vr-in-education-sector#:~:text=How%20AR%20can%20help%20in,rather%20than%20just%20presenting%20facts

Levashova, E. (2024). The Value of AR and VR in Education: An Educator's Perspective. *zSpace Blog*. Retrieved 2025, from https://blog.zspace.com/the-value-of-augmented-reality-and-virtual-reality-in-education-a-perspective-from-an-experienced-educator#:~:text=Accessibility:%20AR/VR%20democratizes%20education.%20Students%20in%20remote,of%20reach.%20Equity%20in%20education%20becomes%20achievable

Mohamadelbarraj. (2025, July 28). *What is the Metaverse and Its Role in Education*. BSBI. Retrieved 2025, from https://www.berlinsbi.com/blog/what-is-the-metaverse-and-its-role-in-education

Yasmina. (2024). *Virtual and augmented reality in education*. Beyond by Esade. Retrieved 2025, from https://www.esade.edu/beyond/en/virtual-reality-augmented-reality-education/#:~:text=These%20technologies%20not%20only%20have,providing%20visual%20and%20practical%20representations

KEY TERMS AND DEFINITIONS

Metaverse: The overarching concept of a persistent, shared, 3D virtual world where users can interact, learn, and collaborate.

Augmented Reality (AR): Overlaying digital content onto the real world, enhancing the learning experience with interactive elements and visualizations.

Virtual Reality (VR): Creating fully immersive digital environments where users can interact with simulations and explore virtual spaces.

Immersive Learning: Learning experiences that fully engage the user's senses, creating a more memorable and effective learning environment.

Experiential Learning: Learning through hands-on activities and simulations, allowing students to apply knowledge and develop practical skills.

Personalized Learning: Tailoring educational content and experiences to meet the specific needs and learning styles of individual students.

3D Visualization: Using 3D models and simulations to represent complex concepts and objects, making them easier to understand and visualize.

Simulations: Creating virtual environments that mimic real-world scenarios, allowing students to practice skills and make decisions in a safe and controlled setting.

Digital Twins: Creating virtual representations of physical objects or systems, which can be used for training, maintenance, and design purposes.

Edu-Metaverse: A specific term referring to the application of metaverse technologies in the field of education.

Compilation of References

Achiam, J., Fischer, I., & Pinto, L.. (2017). *Constrained Policy Optimization.* In *Proceedings of the 34th International Conference on Machine Learning (ICML-17)*, 288-297.

Acuna, A., Juarez, A., & Vazquez, R. (2024, October). Educational innovations supported by AI, VR, AR and metaverse technologies. In *2024 International Conference on Artificial Intelligence, Metaverse and Cybersecurity (ICAMAC)* (pp. 1-7). IEEE.

Agarwal, J., & Sharma, S. (2024). Artificial Intelligence enabled cognitive computer-centered digital analysis model for examination of the children's mental health. *Evolutionary Intelligence*, *17*(5–6), 3675–3685. DOI: 10.1007/s12065-024-00951-6

Aguilar-Moreno, J. A., Palos-Sanchez, P. R., & Pozo-Barajas, R. (2024). Sentiment analysis to support business decision-making. A bibliometric study. In *AIMS Mathematics* (Vol. 9, Issue 2). https://doi.org/DOI: 10.3934/math.2024215

Ahmad, M., Yaramic, I., & Roy, T. D. (2023). Creating trustworthy LLMs: Dealing with hallucinations in healthcare AI.

Ahmad, N., Mamatjan, E., Wali, T., & Mamatjan, Y. (2024). The Development of CanPrompt Strategy in Large Language Models for Cancer Care. *21st IEEE Conference on Computational Intelligence in Bioinformatics and Computational Biology, CIBCB 2024*. https://doi.org/DOI: 10.1109/CIBCB58642.2024.10702147

Ahmed, A., & Sutton, M. J. (2017). Gamification, serious games, simulations, and immersive learning environments in knowledge management initiatives. *World Journal of Science. Technology and Sustainable Development*, *14*(2/3), 78–83.

Ahmed, S., Zhao, Y., & Chen, X. (2024). AI-enhanced interview simulation in the metaverse: Transforming professional skills training through VR and generative conversational AI (ITEM). *Computers and Education: Artificial Intelligence*, *5*(2), 100123. DOI: 10.1016/j.caeai.2024.100123

Ajmeera, N., & Kamakshi, P. (2024). Hamiltonian deep neural network fostered sentiment analysis approach on product reviews. *Signal, Image and Video Processing, 18*(4). Advance online publication. DOI: 10.1007/s11760-024-03014-6

Akhtar, M. A. K., Kumar, M., & Nayyar, A. (2024). The Role of Human-Centered Design in Developing Explainable AI. In *Towards Ethical and Socially Responsible Explainable AI: Challenges and Opportunities* (pp. 99–126). Springer Nature Switzerland.

al Harshit Sharma, E. (2024). Statistical Analysis and Accuracy Assessment of Improved Machine Learning Based Opinion Mining Framework. *Advances in Nonlinear Variational Inequalities, 27*(1). Advance online publication. DOI: 10.52783/anvi.v27.322

Al Omari, M. (2022). OCLAR: Logistic regression optimisation for Arabic customers' reviews. *International Journal of Business Intelligence and Data Mining, 20*(3). Advance online publication. DOI: 10.1504/IJBIDM.2022.122177

Alam, T. (2024). Metaverse of Things (MoT) applications for revolutionizing urban living in smart cities. *Smart Cities, 7*(5), 2466–2494.

Al-Chaer, E. D. (2024). Intelligence Amplified: Exploring the Future of Higher Education in the AI Age. In *Higher Education in the Arab World: Digital Transformation* (pp. 13–35). Springer Nature Switzerland.

AlDhaen, F. S. (2025). AI-powered transformation of healthcare: Enhancing patient safety through AI interventions with the mediating role of operational efficiency and moderating role of digital competence-insights from the gulf Cooperation Council region. *Healthcare (Basel), 13*(6). PMID: 40150463

Aldoseri, A., Al-Khalifa, K. N., & Hamouda, A. M. (2024). AI-powered innovation in digital transformation: Key pillars and industry impact. *Sustainability, 16*(5), 1790.

Aliwy, A. H., Abbas, A. R., & Hadi, M. J. (2022). Key Challenges and Proposed Solutions to Design Sentiment Analysis System. *International Journal of Intelligent Engineering and Systems, 15*(4). Advance online publication. DOI: 10.22266/ijies2022.0831.24

Alkalbani, A. M., Alrawahi, A. S., Salah, A., Haghighi, V., Zhang, Y., Alkindi, S., & Sheng, Q. Z. (2024). A systematic review of Large Language Models in medical specialties: Applications, challenges and future directions. In *Research Square*.

Allam, Z., Sharifi, A., Bibri, S. E., Jones, D. S., & Krogstie, J. (2022). The metaverse as a virtual form of smart cities: Opportunities and challenges for environmental, economic, and social sustainability in urban futures. *Smart Cities, 5*(3), 771–801.

Alonso-Fernandez, C., Guzman, F., & Yang, J. (2024). Integrating artificial intelligence and extended reality in language education: A systematic literature review (2017–2024). *Education Sciences, 15*(8), 1066. DOI: 10.3390/educsci15081066

Al-Shukrawi, A. A. H., Jamil, L. S., Alzuabidi, I. A., Al-Gamal, A. S., Noah, S. A. M., Hasan, M. K., Al-Ghuribi, S. M., Aliyu, R., Jabal, Z. K., & Ahmed, A. A. (2023). Opinion Mining in Arabic Extremism Texts: A Systematic Literature Review. *AlKadhum Journal of Science, 1*(2). Advance online publication. DOI: 10.61710/akjs.v1i2.60

Alves, M., Borges, A., & Lima, R. (2024). Integrating AI-driven wearable metaverse technologies into ubiquitous blended learning. *Education Sciences, 15*(7), 900. DOI: 10.3390/educsci15070900

Amodei, D., Olah, C., Steinhardt, J., Christiano, P., ... (2016). Concrete problems in AI safety. *arXiv preprint arXiv:1606.06565.*

Arievitch, I. M. (2020). Reprint of: The vision of Developmental Teaching and Learning and Bloom's Taxonomy of educational objectives. *Learning, Culture and Social Interaction, 27*, 100473.

Arslan, M., Munawar, S., & Cruz, C. (2024). Sustainable Digitalization of Business with Multi-Agent RAG and LLM. In F. J. (Ed.), *Procedia Computer Science* (Vol. 246, Issue C, pp. 4722 – 4731). Elsevier B.V. https://doi.org/DOI: 10.1016/j.procs.2024.09.337

Astra DB Serverless. (2025). Retrieved from https://docs.datastax.com/en/astra-db-serverless/faqs.html

Astra DB Serverless. (2025). Retrieved from https://docs.datastax.com/en/astra-db-serverless/get-started/astra-db-introduction.html#connect-and-integrate

Athul, S., Saxena, A., Mahajan, J., Panikulangara, L., Kulkarni, S., & Bang, D. S. (2024). LegalMind System and the LLM-based Legal Judgment Query System. *TQCEBT 2024 - 2nd IEEE International Conference on Trends in Quantum Computing and Emerging Business Technologies 2024*. https://doi.org/DOI: 10.1109/TQCEBT59414.2024.10545179

Ayoade, I., Adedigba, A., Adeyemi, O. A., Adeaga, O. A., & Akanbi, O. (2022). Trends and prospects of digital twin technologies: A review. *Quantum journal of engineering, science and technology, 3*(4), 11-24.

Badia, K., & Mohammed, B. S. (2019). Multilingual sentiments analysis to improve the quality of services provided by Algerian telephone operator. *CEUR Workshop Proceedings*, •••, 2351.

Baker, S., & Xiang, W. (2023). Artificial Intelligence of Things for Smarter Healthcare: A survey of advancements, challenges, and opportunities. *IEEE Communications Surveys and Tutorials*, *25*(2), 1261–1293. DOI: 10.1109/comst.2023.3256323

Barbieri, C., Neri, L., Stuard, S., & Mari, F., & Mart\'\in-Guerrero, J. D. (2023). From electronic health records to clinical management systems: How the digital transformation can support healthcare services. *Clinical Kidney Journal*, *16*(11), 1878–1884. PMID: 37915897

Barnard, R. W., & Henn, R. H. (2023). Overcoming learning obstacles: Strategies for supporting students with diverse needs. *OAlib*, *10*(8), 1–14.

Baškarada, S., Watson, J., & Cromarty, J. (2017). Balancing transactional and transformational leadership. *The International Journal of Organizational Analysis*, *25*(3), 506–515.

Bates, B. (2023). Learning theories simplified:... and how to apply them to teaching.

Bellman, R. (1957). *Dynamic Programming*. Princeton University Press.

Bengio, Y., Louradour, J., Collobert, R., & Weston, J. (2009). Curriculum learning. *Proceedings of the 26th International Conference on Machine Learning*, 41-48.

Bernacki, M. L., Greene, M. J., & Lobczowski, N. G. (2021). A systematic review of research on personalized learning: Personalized by whom, to what, how, and for what purpose (s)? *Educational Psychology Review*, *33*(4), 1675–1715.

Bharathi, R., Bhavani, R., & Priya, R. (2023). Leveraging Deep Learning Models for Automated Aspect Based Sentiment Analysis and Classification. *SSRG International Journal of Electrical and Electronics Engineering*, *10*(5). Advance online publication. DOI: 10.14445/23488379/IJEEE-V10I5P111

Boddington, P. (2017). *Towards a code of ethics for artificial intelligence*. Springer.

Bonneau, J., Herley, C., Van Oorschot, P. C., & Stajano, F. (2015). The quest to replace passwords: A framework for comparative evaluation of Web authentication schemes. *IEEE Symposium on Security and Privacy*, 553–567.

Bowen, J. A., & Watson, C. E. (2024). *Teaching with AI: A practical guide to a new era of human learning*. JHU Press.

Brass, J., & Lynch, T. L. (2020). Personalized learning: A history of the present. *Journal of Curriculum Theorizing*, *35*(2).

Brøgger, K., Brøgger, K., & Janssen. (2019). Governing through standards: The faceless masters of higher education. Germany: Springer International Publishing.

Bryson, J. J. (2018). The artificial intelligence debate: Why AI needs regulation. *Nature, 563*(7733), 456–458.

Buckley, W. (2017). Society as a complex adaptive system. In *Systems research for behavioral science* (pp. 490–513). Routledge.

Buolamwini, J., & Gebru, T. (2018). Gender shades: Intersectional accuracy disparities in commercial gender classification. *Proceedings of Machine Learning Research, 81*, 77–91.

Busch, F., Hoffmann, L., Rueger, C., van Dijk, E. H. C., Kader, R., Ortiz-Prado, E., Makowski, M. R., Saba, L., Hadamitzky, M., Kather, J. N., Truhn, D., Cuocolo, R., Adams, L. C., & Bressem, K. K. (2024). Systematic review of large language models for patient care: Current applications and challenges. In *bioRxiv*.

Bux Talpur, D., & Huang, G. (2019). Words segmentation-based scheme for implicit aspect identification for sentiments analysis in english text. *International Journal of Advanced Computer Science and Applications, 10*(12). Advance online publication. DOI: 10.14569/ijacsa.2019.0101204

C, S., & Vadivu, G. (2021). Fine grained sentiment polarity classification using augmented knowledge sequence-attention mechanism. *Microprocessors and Microsystems, 81*. https://doi.org/DOI: 10.1016/j.micpro.2020.103365

Cairney, T. H. (2018). *Pedagogy and Education for Life: A Christian reframing of teaching, learning, and formation.* Wipf and Stock Publishers.

California State Legislature. (2018). California Consumer Privacy Act (CCPA). https://leginfo.legislature.ca.gov/faces/billTextClient.xhtml?bill_id=201720180AB375

Cardoso, R. C., & Ferrando, A. (2021). A Review of Agent-Based Programming for Multi-Agent Systems. *Computers, 10*(2), 16. DOI: 10.3390/computers10020016

Carter, W., & Johnson, E. (2023). Legal responses to digital addiction: Regulating online gaming, social media, and virtual reality for public health and safety. *Legal Studies in Digital Age, 2*(2), 24–36.

Challenor, J., & Ma, M. (2019). A review of augmented reality applications for history education and heritage visualisation. *Multimodal Technologies and Interaction, 3*(2), 39.

Chamoli, A., Kirsali, A., & Sharma, S. (2024). Cyber Attack Prevention Method for Enhanced Privacy of Patients Digital Healthcare Data in Smart Hospitals. In 2024 7th International Conference on Circuit Power and Computing Technologies (ICCPCT), 2, 54–59. https://doi.org/DOI: 10.1109/iccpct61902.2024.10672954

Chande, S. V. (2024). An Exploratory view of Application of Digital Twin Technology in Education. *International Journal of Advanced Trends in Computer Science and Engineering*, *13*(2).

Chan, K. S., & Zary, N. (2019). Applications and challenges of implementing artificial intelligence in medical education: Integrative review. *JMIR Medical Education*, *5*(1), e13930. PMID: 31199295

Chen Gao, X. L. (2024). Large language models empowered agent-based modeling and simulation: A survey and perspectives. *Humanities & Social Sciences Communications*.

Chen, H., Zhang, L., & Wang, J. (2021). Quantum computing for biometric authentication: Challenges and opportunities. *IEEE Transactions on Information Forensics and Security*, *16*, 3120–3135.

Chen, X., Zou, D., Xie, H., & Wang, F. L. (2023). Metaverse in education: Contributors, cooperations, and research themes. *IEEE Transactions on Learning Technologies*, *16*(6), 1111–1129.

Chow, Y., Poupart, P., & Van den Broeck, G. (2018). *Risk-Sensitive Reinforcement Learning*. In *Proceedings of the 35th International Conference on Machine Learning (ICML-18)*, 811-819.

Cieri, R. L., Turner, M. L., Carney, R. M., Falkingham, P. L., Kirk, A. M., Wang, T., Jensen, B., Novotny, J., Tveite, J., Gatesy, S. M., & Farmer, C. G. (2021). Virtual and augmented reality: New tools for visualizing, analyzing, and communicating complex morphology. *Journal of Morphology*, *282*(12), 1785–1800. PMID: 34689352

Cobbe, K., Klimov, O., Hesse, C., Kim, T., & Schulman, J. (2019). Quantifying generalization in reinforcement learning. *International Conference on Machine Learning*.

Cook, M., Lischer-Katz, Z., Hall, N., Hardesty, J., Johnson, J., McDonald, R., & Carlisle, T. (2019). Challenges and strategies for educational virtual reality: Results of an expert-led forum on 3D/VR technologies across academic institutions. *Information Technology and Libraries*, *38*(4), 25–48.

Coombs, C., Hislop, D., Taneva, S. K., & Barnard, S. (2020). The strategic impacts of intelligent automation for knowledge and service work: An interdisciplinary review. *The Journal of Strategic Information Systems*, *29*(4), 101600. DOI: 10.1016/j.jsis.2020.101600

Damaševičius, R., & Sidekerskienė, T. (2024). Virtual worlds for learning in metaverse: A narrative review. *Sustainability*, *16*(5), 2032.

Das, D. R., Satpathy, I., & Patnaik, B. C. M. (2023). AI-enabled healthcare service. In *AI and IoT-Based Technologies for Precision Medicine* (pp. 108–120). IGI Global.

DataStax. (2025). *Astra DB for Generative AI app Creation & Development*. DataStax. https://www.datastax.com/products/datastax-astra

DataStax. (2025b). *Langflow: Visual low-code AI app builder for agents and Rag*. DataStax. https://www.datastax.com/products/langflow

Davis, E. A., & Krajcik, J. S. (2005). Designing educative curriculum materials to promote teacher learning. *Educational Researcher, 34*(3), 3–14.

Daw, N. D., Niv, Y., & Dayan, P. (2006). Corticostriatal circuits and the computation of time. *Psychological Review, 113*(4), 167–177.

Deisenroth, M. P., & Rasmussen, C. E. (2011). *PILCO: A model-based and data-efficient approach to policy search*. In *Proceedings of the 28th International Conference on Machine Learning (ICML-11)*, 465-472.

Deng, J., Guo, J., & Zafeiriou, S. (2019). ArcFace: Additive angular margin loss for deep face recognition. *IEEE Transactions on Biometrics, Behavior, and Identity Science, 42*(5), 1283–1295.

Dhaduk, H. (2023, May). *What is an AI Agent? Characteristics, Advantages, Challenges, Applications*. Retrieved from https://www.simform.com/blog/ai-agent/

Diksha, N., Verma, A. K., Bhadula, S., & Sharma, S. (2023). Artificial Intelligence Enabled Disease Prediction System in Healthcare Industry. In *2023 IEEE International Conference on Blockchain and Distributed Systems Security (ICBDS)*, 1–6. https://doi.org/DOI: 10.1109/icbds58040.2023.10346275

Dong, J. J., Hwang, W. Y., Shadiev, R., & Chen, G. Y. (2017). Pausing the classroom lecture: The use of clickers to facilitate student engagement. *Active Learning in Higher Education, 18*(2), 157–172.

Doshi-Velez, F., & Kim, B. (2017). Towards a rigorous science of interpretable machine learning. *arXiv preprint arXiv:1702.08608*.

Ebom-Jebose, A. (2025). Streamlining School Plant Management: A Transformative Approach for Educational Institutions. *Int'l Journal of Education Research and Scientific Development, 7*(1), 101–114.

Eckrich, J., Ellinger, J., Cox, A., Stein, J., Ritter, M., Blaikie, A., Kuhn, S., & Buhr, C. R. (2024). Urology consultants versus large language models: Potentials and hazards for medical advice in urology. *BJUI Compass, 5*(5), 438–444. PMID: 38751951

Eschenbrenner, B., Nah, F. F. H., & Siau, K. (2008). 3-D virtual worlds in education: Applications, benefits, issues, and opportunities. [JDM]. *Journal of Database Management, 19*(4), 91–110.

European Parliament. (2016). General Data Protection Regulation (GDPR). https://eur-lex.europa.eu/eli/reg/2016/679/oj

Fahmi, F., Suhendro, D. K., & Wardoyo, R. (2022). Reinforcement learning for personalized insulin dosing in diabetes management. *Journal of Biomedical Informatics, 130*, 104107.

Fan, S., Ilk, N., Kumar, A., Xu, R., & Zhao, J. L. (2024). Blockchain as a trust machine: From disillusionment to enlightenment in the era of generative AI. *Decision Support Systems, 182*. Advance online publication. DOI: 10.1016/j.dss.2024.114251

Farebrother, J., Machado, M. C., & Bowling, M. (2018). Generalization and regularization in DQN. *arXiv preprint arXiv:1810.00123.*

Fatima, I., Grover, V., Raza Khan, I., Ahmad, N., & Yadav, A. (2023). Artificial intelligence in medical filed. *EAI Endorsed Transactions on Pervasive Health and Technology*, •••, 9.

Finn, C., Abbeel, P., & Levine, S. (2017). Model-agnostic meta-learning for fast adaptation of deep networks. *Proceedings of the 34th International Conference on Machine Learning*, 1126-1135.

Fischer, T. (2018). Reinforcement learning in financial markets – A survey. *Journal of Economic Dynamics & Control, 91*, 113–129.

Florêncio, D., & Herley, C. (2019). A large-scale study of Web password habits. *Proceedings of the 16th International Conference on World Wide Web*, 657-666.

Fuchs, A., Trachsel, T., Weiger, R., & Eggmann, F. (2023). ChatGPT's performance in dentistry and allergyimmunology assessments: A comparative study. *Swiss Dental Journal, 134*(2), 1–17. PMID: 38726506

Galbally, J., Marcel, S., & Fierrez, J. (2020). Biometric antispoofing techniques: Challenges and solutions. *IEEE Transactions on Biometrics, Behavior, and Identity Science, 2*(3), 168–180.

Gao, C., Zheng, Y., Li, N., Li, Y., Qin, Y., Piao, J., Quan, Y., Chang, J., Jin, D., He, X., & Li, Y. (2023). A survey of Graph Neural networks for recommender Systems: Challenges, methods, and directions. *ACM Transactions on Recommender Systems, 1*(1), 1–51. DOI: 10.1145/3568022

Gao, Y., Huang, H., & Liu, Y. (2022). Reinforcement learning for traffic signal control and route optimization. *Transportation Research Part C, Emerging Technologies*, *140*, 103754.

Gao, Y., Li, R., & Croxford, E., Caskey John and Patterson, B. W., Churpek, M., Miller Timothy and Dligach, D., & Afshar, M. (2025). Leveraging medical knowledge graphs into large language models for diagnosis prediction: Design and application study. *JMIR AI*, *4*, e58670. PMID: 39993309

Garcia, J., & Fernandez, F. (2015). A Comprehensive Survey on Safe Reinforcement Learning. *Journal of Machine Learning Research*, *16*(1), 1437–1480.

Gautam, A., & Sharma, S. (2024). Artificial Narrow Intelligence Inspired Neuromorphic Computing for Logic Operations in Healthcare Appliances. In 2024 7th International Conference on Circuit Power and Computing Technologies (ICCPCT), 714–719. https://doi.org/DOI: 10.1109/iccpct61902.2024.10672744

Gayki, Miss. Y., Chatke, Mr. P., Nandane, Miss. R., Shinde, Mr. U., Ghugare, Mr. M., Rathod, P., & Pardey, Prof. M. (2023). A Survey on "Sentiment Analysis of E-commerce Website's Reviews.". *International Journal for Research in Applied Science and Engineering Technology*, *11*(10). Advance online publication. DOI: 10.22214/ijraset.2023.56255

Genay, A., Lécuyer, A., & Hachet, M. (2021). Being an avatar "for real": A survey on virtual embodiment in augmented reality. *IEEE Transactions on Visualization and Computer Graphics*, *28*(12), 5071–5090. PMID: 34310309

Gencer, G., & Gencer, K. (2025). Large language models in healthcare: A bibliometric analysis and examination of research trends. *Journal of Multidisciplinary Healthcare*, *18*, 223–238. PMID: 39844924

Goodall, N. J. (2014). Machine ethics and automated vehicles. *Road Vehicle Automation*, 93-102.

Goodfellow, I., Shlens, J., & Szegedy, C. (2015). Explaining and harnessing adversarial examples. *International Conference on Learning Representations (ICLR)*.

Gottesman, O., Johansson, F., Komorowski, M., & Faisal, A. (2019). Guidelines for reinforcement learning in healthcare. *Nature Medicine*, *25*(1), 16–18. PMID: 30617332

Guan, Y., Wang, D., Chu, Z., Wang, S., Ni, F., Song, R., & Zhuang, C. (2024). Intelligent agents with LLM-based Process Automation. *Proceedings of the 30th ACM SIGKDD Conference on Knowledge Discovery and Data Mining*, 5018–5027. https://doi.org/DOI: 10.1145/3637528.3671646

Gupta, C., Jindal, P., & Malhotra, R. K. (2022). A Study of Increasing Adoption Trends of Digital Technologies - An Evidence from Indian Banking. In D. N. & C. A. (Eds.), *AIP Conference Proceedings* (Vol. 2481). American Institute of Physics Inc. https://doi.org/DOI: 10.1063/5.0104572

Gupta, M., Kushwaha, A. S., Sinha, A., Singh, P., & Kumar, R. (2023). Multi-Class Sentiment Analysis of Hindi Textual Data. *2023 IEEE 20th India Council International Conference, INDICON 2023*. https://doi.org/DOI: 10.1109/INDICON59947.2023.10440890

Gupta, A., & Sharma, S. (2024). Deep Learning Inspired Biomarker Diagnostic Enabled Heart Health Monitoring System for Cardiac Arrest Detection. In *2024 International Conference on Emerging Technologies and Innovation for Sustainability (EmergIN)*, 13–17. https://doi.org/DOI: 10.1109/emergin63207.2024.10960916

Gupta, J. K., Egorov, M., & Kochenderfer, M. (2017). Cooperative multi-agent control using deep reinforcement learning. *Autonomous Agents and Multi-Agent Systems*, *30*(1), 66–83.

Gupta, P., Mehlawat, M. K., Khaitan, A., & Pedrycz, W. (2021). Sentiment Analysis for Driver Selection in Fuzzy Capacitated Vehicle Routing Problem with Simultaneous Pick-Up and Drop in Shared Transportation. *IEEE Transactions on Fuzzy Systems*, *29*(5). Advance online publication. DOI: 10.1109/TFUZZ.2020.2970834

Hadi, M. U., Qureshi, R., Shah, A., Irfan, M., Zafar, A., Shaikh, M. B., & Mirjalili, S. (2023). A survey on large language models: Applications, challenges, limitations, and practical usage. *Authorea Preprints*, 3.

Han, S., Kang, H., Jin, B., Liu, X.-Y., & Yang, S. Y. (2024). XBRL Agent: Leveraging Large Language Models for Financial Report Analysis. *ICAIF 2024 - 5th ACM International Conference on AI in Finance*, 856 – 864. https://doi.org/DOI: 10.1145/3677052.3698614

Hassannejad, N. (2024). Pedagogical relations: Towards a synthesis of Dewey's child-centered education and Arendt's traditional education.

Henderson, P., Islam, R., Bachman, P., & Pineau, J.. (2018). Deep reinforcement learning that matters. *Proceedings of the AAAI Conference on Artificial Intelligence*, *32*(1).

Hernandez-Leal, P., Kartal, B., & Taylor, M. E. (2019). A survey and critique of multi-agent deep reinforcement learning. *Autonomous Agents and Multi-Agent Systems*, *33*(6), 750–797.

Herries, J. (2024). Emerging clinical applications of large language models in emergency medicine. *Emergency Medicine Australasia, 36*(4), 635–636. PMID: 39013798

Hessel, M., Silver, D., Plappert, M., Horgan, D., Modayil, J., & Doron, Y. (2018). *Learning to play in a day: Faster deep reinforcement learning by optimality tightening*. In *Proceedings of the 31st International Conference on Neural Information Processing Systems (NeurIPS 2018).*

Hidayatullah, A. F., Kalinaki, K., Aslam, M. M., Zakari, R. Y., & Shafik, W. (2023). Fine-Tuning BERT-Based Models for Negative Content Identification on Indonesian Tweets. *ICITDA 2023 - Proceedings of the 2023 8th International Conference on Information Technology and Digital Applications*. https://doi.org/DOI: 10.1109/ICITDA60835.2023.10427046

Hirano, M., & Imajo, K. (2024). Construction of Domain-Specified Japanese Large Language Model for Finance Through Continual Pre-Training. *Proceedings - 2024 16th IIAI International Congress on Advanced Applied Informatics, IIAI-AAI 2024*, 273 – 279. https://doi.org/DOI: 10.1109/IIAI-AAI63651.2024.00059

Huang, F., & Vasarhelyi, M. A. (2019). Applying robotic process automation (RPA) in Auditing: A Framework. *International Journal of Accounting Information Systems, 35*, 100433. DOI: 10.1016/j.accinf.2019.100433

Huang, S. Y., Huang, C. H., & Chang, T. W. (2022). A new concept of work engagement theory in cognitive engagement, emotional engagement, and physical engagement. *Frontiers in Psychology, 12*, 663440. PMID: 35242067

Huang, Y., Li, Y. J., & Cai, Z. (2023). Security and privacy in metaverse: A comprehensive survey. *Big Data Mining and Analytics, 6*(2), 234–247.

Hu, J., P. B. (2021). A Decentralized Cluster Formation Containment Framework for Multirobot Systems. *IEEE Transactions on Robotics*.

Hung, B. T. (2023). Joining Aspect Detection and Opinion Target Expression Based on Multi-Deep Learning Models. In *Springer Series in Reliability Engineering*. https://doi.org/DOI: 10.1007/978-3-031-21232-1_4

Ibrahim, M. A., & Salim, N. (2016). Aspect Oriented Sentiment Analysis Model of Arabic Tweets. [IJCS T]. *International Journal of Computer Science Trends and Technology, 4*(4).

Jadhav, S. G., & Sarnikar, S. (2024). Deriving Strategic Insights from Earnings Calls: Leveraging Human Experts, AI-Based Search, and Generative AI for Synthesis and Summarization. *Proceedings - 2024 Conference on AI, Science, Engineering, and Technology, AIxSET 2024*, 290 – 293. https://doi.org/DOI: 10.1109/AIxSET62544.2024.00031

Jagatheesaperumal, S. K., Ahmad, K., Al-Fuqaha, A., & Qadir, J. (2024). Advancing education through extended reality and internet of everything enabled metaverses: Applications, challenges, and open issues. *IEEE Transactions on Learning Technologies*, *17*, 1120–1139.

Jain, A. (2024). Ethical AI: A Policy Framework to Regulate Bias in Large Language Models (Doctoral dissertation).

Jain, V., & Mitra, A. (2023). Development and application of machine learning algorithms for sentiment analysis in digital manufacturing: A pathway for enhanced customer feedback. In *Emerging Technologies in Digital Manufacturing and Smart Factories*. https://doi.org/DOI: 10.4018/979-8-3693-0920-9.ch002

Jain, A. K., & Nandakumar, K. (2021). Multimodal biometrics: An overview. In *Handbook of Biometrics* (pp. 1–15). Springer.

Jain, A. K., Ross, A., & Nandakumar, K. (2020). *Introduction to biometrics*. Springer.

Jiang, Z., Xu, D., & Liang, J. (2017). A deep reinforcement learning framework for the financial portfolio management problem. *arXiv preprint arXiv:1706.10059*.

Jin, Y., Sun, Z., & Park, H. (2024). Developing an immersive game-based learning platform with generative AI and VR technologies: LearningverseVR. *Computers and Education: X Reality*, *5*(1), 100019. https://doi.org/DOI: 10.1016/j.cexr.2024.100019

Judijanto, L., Nurkhalika, R., Anurogo, D., Andari, S., & Muntasir, M. (2024). The Role of artificial intelligence in the Development of Innovative Drugs and Therapies for the Future of Health. J. of World Future Medicine. *Health and Nursing*, *2*(1), 20–36. PMID: 38183055

Junda He, C. T. (2024). LLM-Based Multi-Agent Systems for Software Engineering: Literature Review, Vision and the Road Ahead.

K, G. (2020). Supervised Machine Learning algorithm using Sentiment Analysis based on customer feedback for smart phone product. *International Journal of Emerging Trends in Engineering Research*, *8*(8). https://doi.org/DOI: 10.30534/ijeter/2020/67882020

Kadu, Mr. L., Deshpande, Dr. M., & Pawar, Dr. V. (2022). Survey of Deep Learning Approaches for Twitter Text Classification. *International Journal of Advanced Engineering Research and Science*, *9*(12). Advance online publication. DOI: 10.22161/ijaers.912.12

Kaelbling, L. P., Littman, M. L., & Moore, A. W. (1996). Reinforcement learning: A survey. *Journal of Artificial Intelligence Research*, *4*, 237–285.

Kamal, M., & Himel, A. S. (2023). Redefining Modern Marketing: An Analysis of AI and NLP's Influence on Consumer Engagement, Strategy, and Beyond. *Eigenpub Review of Science and Technology, 7*(1).

Kang, Y. M. (2021). Metaverse framework and building block. *Journal of the Korea Institute of Information and Communication Engineering*, *25*(9), 1263–1266.

Karamouzas, D., Mademlis, I., & Pitas, I. (2022). Neural Knowledge Transfer for Sentiment Analysis in Texts with Figurative Language. *IEEE International Workshop on Machine Learning for Signal Processing, MLSP, 2022-August.* https://doi.org/DOI: 10.1109/MLSP55214.2022.9943314

Kayyali, M. (2021). Positive impact of high technology on higher education.

Kayyali, M. (2024 B). Global Perspectives on Personalized Learning: Case Studies and Best Practices. In Transforming Education for Personalized Learning (pp. 66-84). IGI Global.

Kayyali, M. (2025 B). AI in Higher Education: Revolutionizing Curriculum and Administration. In AI Adoption and Diffusion in Education (pp. 31-62). IGI Global Scientific Publishing.

Kayyali, M. (Ed.). (2024 C). Building Resiliency in Higher Education: Globalization, Digital Skills, and Student Wellness: Globalization, Digital Skills, and Student Wellness. IGI Global.

Kayyali, M. (2022). Addressing Academic Freedom Challenges in Higher Education. *International Journal of Innovation and Entrepreneurship*, *1*(1), 1–3.

Kayyali, M. (2022). Equity, Equality, Diversity, and Inclusion as Key Performance Indicators in Higher Education. *Online Submission*, *3*(5), 1–3.

Kayyali, M. (2024). A). Future possibilities and challenges of AI in education. In *Transforming education with generative AI: Prompt engineering and synthetic content creation* (pp. 118–137). IGI Global Scientific Publishing.

Kayyali, M. (2024). D). Design thinking and creativity in entrepreneurial innovation. In *Applying Business Intelligence and Innovation to Entrepreneurship* (pp. 155–170). IGI Global.

Kayyali, M. (2025). A). The Impact of Personalized Learning on Student Engagement and Achievement in STEAM. In *Integrating Personalized Learning Methods Into STEAM Education* (pp. 51–78). IGI Global Scientific Publishing.

Keivandarian, N., & Carvalho, M. (2023). A Survey on Sentiment Classification Methods and Challenges. *Proceedings of the International Florida Artificial Intelligence Research Society Conference, FLAIRS, 36*. https://doi.org/DOI: 10.32473/flairs.36.133314

Kem, D. (2022). Personalised and adaptive learning: Emerging learning platforms in the era of digital and smart learning. *International Journal of Social Science and Human Research, 5*(2), 385–391.

Kendall, A., Hawke, J., & Cipolla, R. (2019). Learning to drive in a day. *2019 International Conference on Robotics and Automation (ICRA)*, 8248-8254.

Khan, H. F., & Fatima, N. (2023). Analyzing Customer Sentiment in Drug Reviews Using Natural Language Processing. *2023 7th International Conference on Electronics, Materials Engineering and Nano-Technology, IEMENTech 2023*. https://doi.org/DOI: 10.1109/IEMENTech60402.2023.10423529

Khatri, M. R. (2023). Integration of Natural Language Processing, Self-Service Platforms, Predictive Maintenance, and Prescriptive Analytics for Cost Reduction, Personalization, and Real-Time Insights Customer Service and Operational Efficiency. *International Journal of Information and Cybersecurity, 7*(9).

Khosravi, H., Sadiq, S., & Gasevic, D. (2020, February). Development and adoption of an adaptive learning system: Reflections and lessons learned. In *Proceedings of the 51st ACM technical symposium on computer science education* (pp. 58-64).

Kinsner, W. (2021, September). Digital twins for personalized education and lifelong learning. In *2021 IEEE Canadian conference on electrical and computer engineering (CCECE)* (pp. 1-6). IEEE.

Kober, J., Bagnell, J. A., & Peters, J. (2013). Reinforcement learning in robotics: A survey. *The International Journal of Robotics Research, 32*(11), 1238–1274.

Komasawa, N., & Yokohira, M. (2023). Learner-centered experience-based medical education in an AI-driven society: A literature review. *Cureus, 15*(10), e46883. PMID: 37954813

Komorowski, M., Celi, L. A., Badawi, O., Gordon, A. C., & Faisal, A. A. (2018). The artificial intelligence clinician learns optimal treatment strategies for sepsis in intensive care. *Nature Medicine*, *24*(11), 1716–1720. PMID: 30349085

Konda, V. R., & Tsitsiklis, J. N. (2000). Actor-Critic Algorithms. *Advances in Neural Information Processing Systems*, *12*, 1008–1014.

Kormushev, P., Nenchev, D. N., Calinon, S., & Sauser, E. (2013). *Bimanual robot learning of natural interaction tasks*. In *Proceedings of the IEEE/RSJ International Conference on Intelligent Robots and Systems (IROS-13).*

Krishna Pasupuleti, M. (2024). AI in Healthcare: Transforming the Future. In The New Era of Medical Intelligence: AI-Powered Diagnostics and Tailored Treatments (pp. 55–69). National Education Services.

Kukreti, M., Sehajpal, S., Tiwari, R., & Sood, K. (2025). *Driving Global Health and Sustainable Development Goals With Smart Technology* (Mohit, K., Sabina, S., Rajesh, T., & Kiran, S., Eds.; 1st ed.). IGI Global Scientific Publishing., DOI: 10.4018/979-8-3373-0240-9

Kuleto, V., Ilić, M. P., Ranković, M., Radaković, M., & Simović, A. (2024). Augmented and virtual reality in the metaverse context: the impact on the future of work, education, and social interaction. In *Augmented and virtual reality in the metaverse* (pp. 3–24). Springer Nature Switzerland.

Kumar, M. S., Vellela, S. S., Rao, G. R., Srinivas, B. R., & Javvadi, S. SyamsundaraRao, T., & Kumar, K. K. (2024). An Interactive Healthcare Recommendation System Using Big Data Analytics. In 2024 3rd International Conference for Advancement in Technology (ICONAT), 1–6. https://doi.org/DOI: 10.1109/iconat61936.2024.10774650

Kumar, R., Singh, T., Mohanty, S. N., Goel, R., Gupta, D., Alharbi, M., & Khanna, R. (2023). Study on online payments and e-commerce with SOR model. *International Journal of Retail & Distribution Management*. Advance online publication. DOI: 10.1108/IJRDM-03-2023-0137

Kwon, D., Weiss, E., Kulshrestha, T., Chawla, K., Lucas, G. M., & Gratch, J. (2024). Are llms effective negotiators? systematic evaluation of the multifaceted capabilities of llms in negotiation dialogues. arXiv preprint arXiv:2402.13550.

Langflow. (2025a). *Create custom python components: Langflow documentation*. Langflow. https://docs.langflow.org/components-custom-components

Langflow. (2025b). *Vector Stores: Langflow documentation*. Langflow. https://docs.langflow.org/components-vector-stores

Lens.org

Leventer, A. (2025, March 7). *Choosing a vector store for Langchain*. DataStax. https://www.datastax.com/blog/vector-store-langchain

Levine, S., Kumar, A., Tucker, G., & Fu, J. (2020). Offline reinforcement learning: Tutorial, review, and perspectives on open problems. *arXiv preprint arXiv:2005.01643*.

Levine, S., Finn, C., Darrell, T., & Abbeel, P. (2016). End-to-end training of deep visuomotor policies. *Journal of Machine Learning Research*, *17*(1), 1334–1373.

Li, L., Ismail, S. M., Patra, I., & Lami, D. (2024). Not a passive learner but an active one: A focus on the efficacy of philosophy-based language instruction and its consequences on EFL learners' critical thinking, engagement, and academic achievement. *BMC Psychology*, *12*(1), 148. PMID: 38486343

Lipton, Z. C. (2018). The mythos of model interpretability. *arXiv preprint arXiv:1606.03490*.

Liu, F., Zhou, H., Gu, B., Zou, Xinyu, Huang, J., Wu, J., Li, Y., Chen, S. S., Hua, Y., Zhou, P., Liu, J., Mao, Chengfeng, You, C., Wu, X., & Zheng, Y., Clifton Lei and Li, Z., Luo, J., & Clifton, D. A. (2025). Application of large language models in medicine. *Nature Reviews Bioengineering*, *3*(6), 445–464.

Li, X. W. (2024). *A survey on LLM-based multi-agent systems: workflow, infrastructure, and challenges*. Vicinagearth.

Lockhart, E. N. (2024). Creativity in the age of AI: The human condition and the limits of machine generation. *Journal of Cultural Cognitive Science*, •••, 1–6.

Lohmann, M. J., Hovey, K. A., & Gauvreau, A. N. (2018). Using a Universal Design for Learning Framework to Enhance Engagement in the Early Childhood Classroom. *The Journal of Special Education Apprenticeship*, *7*(2), n2.

Londhe, A., & Rao, P. V. R. D. P. (2022). Dynamic Classification of Sentiments from Restaurant Reviews Using Novel Fuzzy-Encoded LSTM. In *International Journal on Recent and Innovation Trends in Computing and Communication* (Vol. 10, Issue 9). https://doi.org/DOI: 10.17762/ijritcc.v10i9.5714

López Condori, J. J., & Gonzales Saji, F. O. (2021). Análisis de sentimiento de comentarios en español en Google Play Store usando BERT. *Ingeniare. Revista Chilena de Ingeniería*, *29*(3). Advance online publication. DOI: 10.4067/s0718-33052021000300557

Lo, S. C., & Tsai, H. H. (2022). Design of 3D virtual reality in the metaverse for environmental conservation education based on cognitive theory. *Sensors (Basel), 22*(21), 8329. PMID: 36366028

Lowe, R., Wu, Y., Tamar, A., & Harb, J.. (2017). Multi-agent actor-critic for mixed cooperative-competitive environments. *Advances in Neural Information Processing Systems, 30*, 6379–6390.

Luckin, R. (2025). Nurturing human intelligence in the age of AI: Rethinking education for the future. *Development and Learning in Organizations, 39*(1), 1–4.

Ludovico, A. (2024). *Tactical publishing: Using senses, software, and archives in the twenty-first century*. MIT Press.

Maibom, H. L. (2022). *The space between: How Empathy really works*. Oxford University Press.

Maltoni, D., Maio, D., Jain, A. K., & Prabhakar, S. (2022). *Handbook of fingerprint recognition* (3rd ed.). Springer.

Mannstadt, I., & Mehta, B. (2024). Large language models and the future of rheumatology: Assessing impact and emerging opportunities. *Current Opinion in Rheumatology, 36*(1), 46–51. PMID: 37729050

Marwat, M. I., Khan, J. A., Dahman Alshehri, M., & Ali, M. A., Hizbullah, Ali, H., & Assam, M. (2022). Sentiment Analysis of Product Reviews to Identify Deceptive Rating Information in Social Media: A SentiDeceptive Approach. *KSII Transactions on Internet and Information Systems, 16*(3). Advance online publication. DOI: 10.3837/tiis.2022.03.005

Marx, J., Mirbabaie, M., & Rieskamp, J. (2025). Working from the Metaverse: A distraction management perspective. *Journal of Management Information Systems, 42*(1), 206–237.

Mary Joshitta, S., & Sunil, M. P. Badriasulaimanalfurhood, Bodhankar, A., Ch.Sreedevi, & Khanna, R. (2023). The Integration of Machine Learning Technique with the Existing System to Predict the Flight Prices. *2023 3rd International Conference on Advance Computing and Innovative Technologies in Engineering, ICACITE 2023*, 398–402. https://doi.org/DOI: 10.1109/ICACITE57410.2023.10182539

Mashabab, M. F., Sheniff, M. S., Al, , Alsharief, M. S., Yami, M. A. A., Al, , Matnah, H. N. M., Abbas, A. M., Al, , Shenief, H. Y. M., & Al, , Abbas Dhaffer Ali Ali Al Al and Raseen, F. M. S. A., & Kulayb, A. H. A. Al. (2024). The role of artificial Intelligence in healthcare: A critical analysis of its implications for patient care. *JoE, 3*(7), 597–604.

McKee, M., & Correia, T. (2025). The future of the health professions: Navigating shortages, imbalances, and automation. *The International Journal of Health Planning and Management, 40*(2), 289–292. PMID: 39496993

McTear, M., & Ashurkina, M. (2024). *Transforming conversational AI: Exploring the power of large language models in interactive conversational agents*. Springer Nature.

Menghao, L. M., Yi, F., Li, Y., & Shi, Y. (2023). Research on the Application of LLM in Power Finance Middle Platform. In L. J. & L. Y. (Eds.), *Proceedings - 2023 2nd Asian Conference on Frontiers of Power and Energy, ACFPE 2023* (pp. 282 – 289). Institute of Electrical and Electronics Engineers Inc. https://doi.org/DOI: 10.1109/ACFPE59335.2023.10455549

Mevold, C. A. (2023). FROM BIASES TO BRILLIANCE An Interpretative phenomenological analysis of the connection between leadership experience and decision-making style to explore the influence of cognitive biases on decision-making and leadership potential (Master's thesis, NTNU).

Mishra, S. (2022). Artificial Intelligence: A review of progress and prospects in medicine and healthcare. *J.Electron.Electromedical.Eng.Med.Inform, 4*(1), 1–23.

Mistretta, S. (Ed.). (2024). *Reimagining Education: The Role of E-Learning, Creativity, and Technology in the Post-Pandemic Era*. BoD–Books on Demand.

Mnih, V., Kavukcuoglu, K., & Silver, D.. (2015). Human-level control through deep reinforcement learning. *Nature, 518*(7540), 529–533. PMID: 25719670

Mondal, H., & Mondal, S. (2025). Adopting augmented reality and virtual reality in medical education in resource-limited settings: Constraints and the way forward. *Advances in Physiology Education, 49*(2), 503–507. PMID: 40136005

Moody, J., & Saffell, M. (2001). Learning to trade via direct reinforcement. *IEEE Transactions on Neural Networks, 12*(4), 875–889. PMID: 18249919

Movahed, M., & Bilderback, S. (2024). Evaluating the readiness of healthcare administration students to utilize AI for sustainable leadership: a survey study. J. Health Organ. Manag., ahead-of-print(ahead-of-print), 567–582.

Murdoch, B. (2021). Privacy and artificial intelligence: Challenges for protecting health information in a new era. *BMC Medical Ethics, 22*(1), 122. PMID: 34525993

Mystakidis, S. (2022). Metaverse. *Encyclopedia, 2*(1), 486–497.

Naik, D., Naik, I., & Naik, N. (2024). Leveraging the Use of ChatGPT: Exploring Its Real-World Applications Including Their Related Ethical and Regulatory Considerations. *Lecture Notes in Networks and Systems, 884 LNNS*, 649 – 667. https://doi.org/DOI: 10.1007/978-3-031-74443-3_38

Nassani, A. A., & Javed, A., Rosak-Szyrocka Joanna and Pilar, L., Yousaf, Z., & Haffar, M. (2023). Major determinants of innovation performance in the context of healthcare sector. *International Journal of Environmental Research and Public Health, 20*(6). PMID: 36981916

Ndukwe, H., & Otukpa, E. (2025). A scoping review protocol examining the application of large language models in healthcare education and public health learning spaces. In *medRxiv*.

Ng, J. X., Lim, K. M., Lee, C. P., Lim, Q. Z., Ooi, E. K. H., & Loh, N. K. N. (2023). Sentiment Analysis Using Learning-based Approaches: A Comparative Study. *2023 11th International Conference on Information and Communication Technology, ICoICT 2023, 2023-August*. https://doi.org/DOI: 10.1109/ICoICT58202.2023.10262604

Ng, A. Y., Harada, D., & Russell, S. (1999). *Policy invariance under reward transformations: Theory and application to reward shaping*. In *Proceedings of the 16th International Conference on Machine Learning (ICML-99)*, 278-287.

Nguyen, A. H. D., Le, T. T., Dang, T. Q., & Nguyen, L. T. (2024). Understanding metaverse adoption in education: The extended UTAUMT model. *Heliyon, 10*(19). PMID: 39416817

Nguyen, T. T., Nguyen, N. D., & Nahavandi, S. (2020). Deep reinforcement learning for multi-agent systems: A review of challenges, solutions, and applications. *IEEE Transactions on Cybernetics, 50*(9), 3826–3839. PMID: 32203045

Ni, H., Meng, S., Chen, X., Zhao, Z., Chen, A., Li, P., Zhang, S., Yin, Q., Wang, Y., & Chan, Y. (2024). Harnessing Earnings Reports for Stock Predictions: A QLoRA-Enhanced LLM Approach. *2024 6th International Conference on Data-Driven Optimization of Complex Systems, DOCS 2024*, 909 – 915. https://doi.org/DOI: 10.1109/DOCS63458.2024.10704454

NIST. (2019). Face recognition vendor test (FRVT) report. https://www.nist.gov

Nufus, G. K., Mustafid, M., & Gernowo, dan R. (2021). Sentiment Analysis for Video on Demand Application User Satisfaction with Long Short Term Memory Model. *E3S Web of Conferences, 317*. https://doi.org/DOI: 10.1051/e3sconf/202131705031

Onu, P., Pradhan, A., & Mbohwa, C. (2024). Potential to use metaverse for future teaching and learning. *Education and Information Technologies, 29*(7), 8893–8924.

Open, A. I., Akkaya, I., Andrychowicz, M., Chociej, M., ... (2019). Solving Rubik's cube with a robot hand. *arXiv preprint arXiv:1910.07113.*

Ospanova, A., Pandharinath Patil, H., Arun Parekh, P., Rajendra Patil, T., & Santosh Gangatire, P. (2022). Sentiment Analysis of Text Feedback. *Article in International Journal of Innovative Research in Science Engineering and Technology.*

Painuly, S., & Sharma, S. (2024). Natural Language Processing Techniques for e-Healthcare Supply Chain Management System. In *2024 International Conference on Emerging Systems and Intelligent Computing (ESIC)*, 11–16. https://doi.org/ DOI: 10.1109/esic60604.2024.10481580

Pandey, C., Sharma, S., & Bhadula, S. (2024). Artificial Intelligence Technique in Next Generation Healthcare Systems. In *2024 IEEE International Conference on Communication, Computing and Signal Processing (IICCCS)*, 1–6. https://doi.org/ DOI: 10.1109/iicccs61609.2024.10763570

Pan, S. J., & Yang, Q. (2020). A Survey on Transfer Learning. *IEEE Transactions on Knowledge and Data Engineering*, *22*(10), 1345–1359.

Park, S. M., & Kim, Y. G. (2022). A metaverse: Taxonomy, components, applications, and open challenges. *IEEE Access : Practical Innovations, Open Solutions*, *10*, 4209–4251.

Pashangpour, S., & Nejat, G. (2024). The future of intelligent healthcare: A systematic analysis and discussion on the integration and impact of robots using large language models for healthcare. *Robotics (Basel, Switzerland)*, *13*(8), 112.

Pasupuleti, M. K. (2025). Revolutionizing healthcare: AI and Big Data for predictive analytics and precision medicine. In *AI and Big Data for Predictive Healthcare Analytics* (pp. 151–160). National Education Services.

Pendharkar, P. C. (2018). Reinforcement learning in financial trading systems: A review. *Decision Support Systems*, *115*, 48–58.

Pirjan, A., & Petroşanu, D. M. (2024). EXPLORING LARGE LANGUAGE MODELS IN THE EDUCATION PROCESS WITH A VIEW TOWARDS TRANSFORMING PERSONALIZED LEARNING. *Journal of Information Systems & Operations Management*, *18*(2).

Pomerleau, D. A. (1989). *ALVINN: An autonomous land vehicle in a neural network.* In Advances in Neural Information Processing Systems (NIPS-89), 305-313.

Poncelas, A., Lohar, P., Way, A., & Hadley, J. (2020). The Impact of Indirect Machine Translation on Sentiment Classification. *AMTA 2020 - 14th Conference of the Association for Machine Translation in the Americas, Proceedings, 1.*

Porges, S. W. (2022). Polyvagal theory: A science of safety. *Frontiers in Integrative Neuroscience, 16*, 871227. PMID: 35645742

Puiutta, E., & Veith, E. M. (2020). Explainable reinforcement learning: A survey. *arXiv preprint arXiv:2005.06247.*

Purwandari, K., Wulandari, A., Maretta, N. T., Regina, S., & Vincent. (2023). Implementation of AI Model for Sentiment Analysis of Pharmaceutical Products. *ICCA 2023 - 2023 5th International Conference on Computer and Applications, Proceedings*. https://doi.org/DOI: 10.1109/ICCA59364.2023.10401475

Puterman, M. L. (1994). *Markov Decision Processes: Discrete Stochastic Dynamic Programming*. Wiley-Interscience.

Quercia, A., Zaghir, J., Lovis, C., & Gaudet-Blavignac, C. (2024). MedFrenchmark, a small set for benchmarking generative LLMs in medical French. *Studies in Health Technology and Informatics, 316*, 601–605. PMID: 39176814

Rahul, D., George, S., & Amritha, P. S. (2025). Metaverse-Powered Human–Computer Interactions and Applications. In *Applying Metaverse Technologies to Human-Computer Interaction for Healthcare* (pp. 38–55). Auerbach Publications.

Rajeswari, S., & Kumar, T. P. (2019). Sentiment analysis over high dimensional data sets using advanced data engineering techniques. *Journal of Advanced Research in Dynamical and Control Systems, 11*(4 Special Issue).

Rambli, D. R. A., Matcha, W., & Sulaiman, S. (2013). Fun learning with AR alphabet book for preschool children. *Procedia Computer Science, 25*, 211–219.

Ramos, G., Meek, C., Simard, P., Suh, J., & Ghorashi, S. (2020). Interactive machine teaching: A human-centered approach to building machine-learned models. *Human-Computer Interaction, 35*(5-6), 413–451.

Rana, M. S., Cavaliere, L. P. L., Mishra, A. B., Padhye, P., Singh, R. R., & Khanna, R. (2022). Internet of Things (IOT) Based Assessment for Effective Monitoring Data Against Malicious Attacks on Financial Collectors. *2022 2nd International Conference on Advance Computing and Innovative Technologies in Engineering, ICACITE 2022*, 177–181. https://doi.org/DOI: 10.1109/ICACITE53722.2022.9823612

Ratha, N. K., Connell, J. H., & Bolle, R. M. (2019). Enhancing security and privacy in biometric authentication systems. *IBM Journal of Research and Development*, *63*(6), 1–12.

Rathore, M. M., Shah, S. A., Shukla, D., Bentafat, E., & Bakiras, S. (2021). The role of ai, machine learning, and big data in digital twinning: A systematic literature review, challenges, and opportunities. *IEEE Access : Practical Innovations, Open Solutions*, *9*, 32030–32052.

Ravikumar, R. N., Aarthi, S., Masharipova, G., Niyazova, N., Salaeva, N., & Buriyeva, D. (2025). Enhancing clinical decision-making and operational efficiency in healthcare using edge computing. In *Building Data-Driven Edge Systems for Business Success* (pp. 191–224). IGI Global Scientific Publishing., DOI: 10.4018/979-8-3373-1147-0.ch008

Rawat, R., Goyal, H. R., & Sharma, S. (2023). Artificial narrow Intelligence techniques in Intelligent Digital Financial Inclusion System for Digital Society. 2021 5th International Conference on Information Systems and Computer Networks (ISCON), 1–5. https://doi.org/DOI: 10.1109/iscon57294.2023.10112133

Rawat, R., Goyal, H. R., & Sharma, S. (2024). Hofstede's Cultural Dimension Driven Artificial Narrow Intelligence IDFIS for Industry 5.0 Empowered Digital Society. *Recent Patents on Engineering*, *19*. Advance online publication. DOI: 10.2174/0118722121334543241001050846

Razaque, A., Khan, M., & Alghamdi, M. (2024). Personalization of the learning path within an augmented reality spatial ability training application based on fuzzy weights. *Sensors (Basel)*, *22*(18), 7059. DOI: 10.3390/s22187059 PMID: 36146410

Restrepo, D., Wu, C., Vásquez-Venegas, C., Matos, J., Gallifant, J., Celi, L. A., Bitterman, D. S., & Nakayama, L. F. (2024). Analyzing Diversity in Healthcare LLM Research: A Scientometric Perspective. In *medRxiv*.

Retrieval Augmented Generation (RAG) in Azure AI Search. (2025). Retrieved from https://learn.microsoft.com/en-us/azure/search/retrieval-augmented-generation-overview?tabs=docs

Retrieval-Augmented Generation (RAG). (2025). Retrieved from https://www.datastax.com/guides/what-is-retrieval-augmented-generation

Rezapour, M. (2021). Sentiment classification of skewed shoppers' reviews using machine learning techniques, examining the textual features. *Engineering Reports*, *3*(1). Advance online publication. DOI: 10.1002/eng2.12280

Rondon, S., Sassi, F. C., & Furquim de Andrade, C. R. (2013). Computer game-based and traditional learning method: A comparison regarding students' knowledge retention. *BMC Medical Education, 13*(1), 30. PMID: 23442203

Russell, S., Dewey, D., & Tegmark, M. (2019). Research priorities for robust and beneficial artificial intelligence. *AI & Society*, *34*(4), 687–700.

Saad, A. I. (2020). Opinion Mining on US Airline Twitter Data Using Machine Learning Techniques. *16th International Computer Engineering Conference, ICENCO 2020*. https://doi.org/DOI: 10.1109/ICENCO49778.2020.9357390

Sadanand, V. K., & Nandini, S. (2024). AI in Indian healthcare startups. In *Advances in Medical Technologies and Clinical Practice* (pp. 1–26). IGI Global.

Sadovnik, A. R., Semel, S. F., Coughlan, R. W., Kanze, B., & Tyner-Mullings, A. R. (2017). Progressive education in the 21st century: The enduring influence of John Dewey. *The Journal of the Gilded Age and Progressive Era*, *16*(4), 515–530.

Sallab, A. E., Abdou, M., Perot, E., & Yogamani, S. (2017). Deep reinforcement learning framework for autonomous driving. *Electronic Imaging*, *2017*(19), 70–76.

Sarker, I. H. (2024). LLM potentiality and awareness: A position paper from the perspective of trustworthy and responsible AI modeling. *Discover Artificial Intelligence*, *4*(1). Advance online publication. DOI: 10.1007/s44163-024-00129-0

Sarrab, M., Elbasir, M., & Alnaeli, S. (2016). Towards a quality model of technical aspects for mobile learning services: An empirical investigation. *Computers in Human Behavior*, *55*, 100–112.

Saxena, Y., Chopra, S., & Tripathi, A. M. (2024). Evaluating Consistency and Reasoning Capabilities of Large Language Models. *2nd IEEE International Conference on Data Science and Information System, ICDSIS 2024*. https://doi.org/DOI: 10.1109/ICDSIS61070.2024.10594233

Scaravetti, D., & Doroszewski, D. (2019). Augmented Reality experiment in higher education, for complex system appropriation in mechanical design. *Procedia CIRP*, *84*, 197–202.

Schulman, J., Wolski, F., & Dhariwal, P.. (2017). *Proximal Policy Optimization Algorithms*. In *Proceedings of the 34th International Conference on Machine Learning (ICML-17)*, 12, 507-518.

Sehajpal, S., & Kaur, N. (2025). Neuroscience, Nursing, and Financial Innovation : A Synergistic Approach to Optimized Patient Care and Economic Well-Being. In Sanjay, T., Bhupinderpal Pal, S. C., Amar, J., Ercan, O., & Pawan, K. (Eds.), *Neuromarketing's Role in Sustainable Finance* (pp. 133–146). IGI Global Scientific Publishing., DOI: 10.4018/979-8-3693-9117-4.ch008

Senbekov, M., Saliev, T., Bukeyeva, Z., Almabayeva, A., & Zhanaliyeva, M. (2020). Aitenova Nazym and Toishibekov, Y., & Fakhradiyev, I. (2020). The recent progress and applications of digital technologies in healthcare: A review. *International Journal of Telemedicine and Applications*, •••, 8830200. PMID: 33343657

Shaeffer, S. (2019). Inclusive education: A prerequisite for equity and social justice. *Asia Pacific Education Review*, *20*(2), 181–192.

Shafik, W. (2023a). *A Comprehensive Cybersecurity Framework for Present and Future Global Information Technology Organizations*. https://doi.org/DOI: 10.4018/978-1-6684-9018-1.ch002

Shafik, W. (2023b). Introduction to ChatGPT. In *Advanced Applications of Generative AI and Natural Language Processing Models*. https://doi.org/DOI: 10.4018/9798369305027.ch001

Shafik, W. (2025). *Technology as a Catalyst for Achieving the Sustainable Development Goals (SDGs)* (pp. 3–39). https://doi.org/DOI: 10.1007/978-981-96-7299-8_1

Shafik, W. (2024a). Data Privacy and Security Safeguarding Customer Information in ChatGPT Systems. In *Revolutionizing the Service Industry Wth OpenAI Models* (pp. 52–86). IGI Global., DOI: 10.4018/979-8-3693-1239-1.ch003

Shafik, W. (2024b). Deep Learning Impacts in the Field of Artificial Intelligence. In *Deep Learning Concepts in Operations Research* (pp. 9–26). Auerbach Publications., DOI: 10.1201/9781003433309-2

Shafik, W., Kalinaki, K., Fahim, K. E., & Adam, M. (2024). Safeguarding Data Privacy and Security in Federated Learning Systems. In *Federated Deep Learning for Healthcare* (pp. 170–190). CRC Press., DOI: 10.1201/9781032694870-13

Shahrukh Irfan Prasanta Kumar Parida, A. B. S. D. M. N. J. D. (2023). Advancing healthcare through Artificial Intelligence: Innovations at the intersection of AI and medicine. Tuijin Jishu, 44(2).

Sharma, S. (2024). Enhancing Inclusive Learning Environments: Strategies for Curriculum Adaptation and Modification. Future of Special Education in India, 109.

Sharma, S., Jain, A., Ramola, B., Ravindar, B., Al-Taee, M., & Alazzam, M. B. (2023). Implementation of Natural Language Processing for sentiment Analysis. *2023 3rd International Conference on Advance Computing and Innovative Technologies in Engineering, ICACITE 2023*. https://doi.org/DOI: 10.1109/ICACITE57410.2023.10182452

Sharma, S., Tyagi, R., & Mohan, S. (2024). Edge Intelligence Decentralized Blockchain-Based Internet of Things (B-IoT) for sustainable healthcare. In Chapman and Hall/CRC eBooks (pp. 109–124). https://doi.org/DOI: 10.1201/9781003407096-7

Sharma, S., Tyagi, R., & Mohan, S. (2025). Blockchain-Based Security and Privacy in Digital Healthcare Recommender Systems. In In Healthcare Recommender Systems (pp. 221–237). https://doi.org/DOI: 10.1007/978-3-031-80056-6_10

Shi, W., Cao, J., Zhang, Q., & Li, Y. (2020). Edge AI for biometric authentication. *IEEE Transactions on Cloud Computing*, *8*(4), 1098–1110.

Shukla, N. K., Katikeri, R., Raja, M., Sivam, G., Yadav, S., Vaid, A., & Prabhakararao, S. (2023). Generative AI Approach to Distributed Summarization of Financial Narratives. In H. J., P. T., H. X., C. A., D. D., S. D., W. W., G. A., L. J.C.-W., & A. R. (Eds.), *Proceedings - 2023 IEEE International Conference on Big Data, BigData 2023* (pp. 2872 – 2876). Institute of Electrical and Electronics Engineers Inc. https://doi.org/DOI: 10.1109/BigData59044.2023.10386313

Shu, X., & Gu, X. (2023). An empirical study of A smart education model enabled by the edu-metaverse to enhance better learning outcomes for students. *Systems*, *11*(2), 75.

Siderska, J., Aunimo, L., Süße, T., von Stamm, J., Kedziora, D., & Aini, S. N. (2023). Towards intelligent automation (IA): Literature review on the evolution of Robotic Process Automation (RPA), its challenges, and future trends. *Engineering Management in Production and Services*, *15*(4), 90–103. DOI: 10.2478/emj-2023-0030

Silver, D., Huang, A., Maddison, C. J., & Guez, A.. (2016). Mastering the game of Go with deep neural networks and tree search. *Nature*, *529*(7587), 484–489. PMID: 26819042

Singh, B., Kushwaha, N., & Vyas, O. P. (2017). An interpretation of sentiment analysis for enrichment of Business Intelligence. *IEEE Region 10 Annual International Conference, Proceedings/TENCON*. https://doi.org/DOI: 10.1109/TENCON.2016.7847950

Solloway, A. J. (2017). *English-medium instruction in higher education in the United Arab Emirates: The perspectives of students*. University of Exeter.

Song, Y., Ezzini, S., Tang, X., Lothritz, C., Klein, J., Bissyande, T., Boytsov, A., Ble, U., & Goujon, A. (2024). Enhancing Text-to-SQL Translation for Financial System Design. *ACM International Conference Proceeding Series*, 252 – 262. https://doi.org/DOI: 10.1145/3639477.3639732

Sorin, V., Brin, D., Barash, Y., Konen, E., Charney, A., Nadkarni, G., & Klang, E. (2024). Large Language Models and Empathy: Systematic Review. *Journal of Medical Internet Research*, *26*, e52597. PMID: 39661968

Squire, K. (2010). From information to experience: Place-based augmented reality games as a model for learning in a globally networked society. *Teachers College Record*, *112*(10), 2565–2602.

Srinivas, P. V. V. S., Gayathri, K., & Bhavitha, K., Jahnavi, & Sarath, K. D. (2023). BLIP-NLP Model for Sentiment Analysis. *Proceedings of the 2nd International Conference on Edge Computing and Applications, ICECAA 2023*. https://doi.org/DOI: 10.1109/ICECAA58104.2023.10212253

Sripan, T., & Jeerapattanatorn, P. (2025). Metaverse-based learning: A comprehensive review of current trends, challenges, and future implications. *Contemporary Educational Technology*, *17*(3), ep584.

Stanoevska-Slabeva, K. (2022). Opportunities and challenges of metaverse for education: a literature review. *Edulearn22 Proceedings*, 10401-10410.

Sundararajan, K., Raj, A. N. J., & Sugumaran, M. (2021). Deep learning in biometric authentication: Trends and challenges. *IEEE Access : Practical Innovations, Open Solutions*, *9*, 102764–102779.

Sutton, R. S., & Barto, A. G. (2018). *Reinforcement learning: An introduction* (2nd ed.). MIT Press.

Sutton, R. S., McAllester, D. A., Singh, S., & Mansour, Y. (2000). *Policy Gradient Methods for Reinforcement Learning with Function Approximation*. In *Proceedings of the 12th International Conference on Neural Information Processing Systems (NIPS-00)*, 1057-1063.

Sylvester, A., Mines, R., David, R., & Campbell-Meier, J. (2023, January). Conceptualization of digital twins in an education services environment: A straw man proposal. In *Proceedings of the 56th Hawaii international conference on system sciences*.

Taicheng Guo, X. C. (2024). Large Language Model based Multi-Agents: A Survey of Progress and Challenges.

Tarnowska, K. A., & Ras, Z. W. (2019). Sentiment analysis of customer data. *Web Intelligence*, *17*(4). Advance online publication. DOI: 10.3233/WEB-190423

Taylor, S., & Soneji, S. (2022). Bioinformatics and the metaverse: Are we ready? *Frontiers in Bioinformatics*, *2*, 863676. PMID: 36304263

Teng, M., Singla, R., Yau, O., Lamoureux, D., Gupta, A., Hu, Z., Hu, R., Aissiou, A., Eaton, S., & Hamm, C., Hu Sophie and Kelly, D., MacMillan, K. M., Malik Shamir and Mazzoli, V., Teng, Y.-W., Laricheva, M., Jarus, T., & Field, T. S. (2022). Health care students' perspectives on artificial intelligence: Countrywide survey in Canada. *JMIR Medical Education*, *8*(1), e33390. PMID: 35099397

Thangavel, S. (2025). Revolutionizing Education Through Augmented Reality (AR) and Virtual Reality (VR): Innovations, Challenges and Future Prospects. *Challenges and Future Prospects (March 03, 2025)*.

Thrun, S., & Schwartz, A. (1993). *Issues in Using Function Approximation for Reinforcement Learning*. In *Proceedings of the 1993 Connectionist Models Summer School*, 255-263.

Tjoa, E., & Guan, C. (2021). A survey on explainable artificial intelligence (XAI): Toward medical AI transparency. *IEEE Transactions on Neural Networks and Learning Systems*, *32*(11), 4793–4813. PMID: 33079674

Tobin, J., Fong, R., & Ray, A.. (2017). *Domain Randomization for Transferring Deep Learning Models to New Environments*. In *Proceedings of the 2017 IEEE/RSJ International Conference on Intelligent Robots and Systems (IROS-17)*, 23-30.

Tschantz, A., Seth, A. K., & Pezzulo, G. (2020). Reinforcement learning for adaptive psychotherapy. *Trends in Cognitive Sciences*, *24*(10), 857–859.

Tuama, M. H., Mashloosh, W. M., Albehadili, H. M., Alazzawi, M., & Al-shareeda, M. A. (2023). Beyond Polarity: The Potential Applications and Impacts of Sentiment Analysis and Emotion Detection. *AlKadhum Journal of Science*, *1*(2). Advance online publication. DOI: 10.61710/akjs.v1i2.51

Twigg, C. A. (2005). Improving learning and reducing costs for online learning. In *Encyclopedia of distance learning* (pp. 1054–1060). IGI Global Scientific Publishing.

Ueland, J. S., Hinds, T. L., & Floyd, N. D. (2021). Equity at the edge of chaos: Applying complex adaptive systems theory to higher education. *New Directions for Institutional Research*, *2021*(189-192), 121–138.

Vairamani, A. D., & Nayyar, A. (2023). Decoding product sentiments: Unraveling reviews with explainable analysis using Hugging-Face transformer. In *XAI Based Intelligent Systems for Society 5.0*. https://doi.org/DOI: 10.1016/B978-0-323-95315-3.00003-6

Van Dam, A., Laidlaw, D. H., & Simpson, R. M. (2002). Experiments in immersive virtual reality for scientific visualization. *Computers & Graphics*, *26*(4), 535–555.

Van Le, N. B., & Huh, J. H. (2021). Applying sentiment product reviews and visualization for bi systems in vietnamese e-commerce website: Focusing on vietnamese context. *Electronics (Switzerland)*, *10*(20). Advance online publication. DOI: 10.3390/electronics10202481

Vemulapalli, A., & Peddi, A. (2023). A Comparative Study of Twitfeel and Transformer-Based Techniques for the Analysis of Text Data for Sentiment Classification. *Proceedings of International Conference on Contemporary Computing and Informatics, IC3I 2023*. https://doi.org/DOI: 10.1109/IC3I59117.2023.10397647

VOSviewer. https://www.vosviewer.com/

Wang, M., Bi, X., & Liu, F. (2023). Research on digital twin technology and application in campus. *The frontiers of society, science and technology, 5*(5), 118-123.

Wang, H. (2024). An Overview of the Application of Convolutional Neural Networks inSentiment Analysis. *Science and Technology of Engineering. Chemistry and Environmental Protection*, *1*(5). Advance online publication. DOI: 10.61173/t4sg2v25

Wang, Y., Zhao, H., & Liu, X. (2022). Quantum-safe encryption for biometric authentication systems. *IEEE Transactions on Quantum Engineering*, *3*, 1125–1140.

Watkins, C. J. C. H., & Dayan, P. (1992). Q-learning. *Machine Learning*, *8*(3-4), 279–292.

Williams, R. J. (1992). Simple statistical gradient-following algorithms for connectionist reinforcement learning. *Machine Learning*, *8*(3-4), 229–256.

Workum, J. D., & van de Sande, D., & Gommers Diederik and van Genderen, M. E. (2025). Bridging the gap: A practical step-by-step approach to warrant safe implementation of large language models in healthcare. *Frontiers in Artificial Intelligence*, *8*, 1504805. PMID: 39931218

Wu, W. C. V., Manabe, K., Marek, M. W., & Shu, Y. (2023). Enhancing 21st-century competencies via virtual reality digital content creation. *Journal of Research on Technology in Education*, *55*(3), 388–410. DOI: 10.1080/15391523.2021.2024049

Yadav, S. (2024). Designing Effective E-Portfolios for Authentic Assessment: Encouraging Reflection and Promoting Student Ownership. In Cases on Authentic Assessment in Higher Education (pp. 235-258). IGI Global.

Yalamanchili, A., & Sengupta, B., Song Joshua and Lim, S., Thomas, T. O., Mittal, B. B., Abazeed, M. E., & Teo, P. T. (2024). Quality of large language model responses to radiation oncology patient care questions. *JAMA Network Open*, *7*(4), e244630. PMID: 38564215

Yang, C., Liu, F., & Huang, Z. (2024). Application of artificial intelligence and virtual reality in soft skills training with modeled personality. *Applied Sciences (Basel, Switzerland)*, *15*(16), 9067. DOI: 10.3390/app15169067

Yang, L., Ni, S. T., Wang, Y., Yu, A., Lee, J. A., & Hui, P. (2025). Interoperability of the metaverse: A digital ecosystem perspective review. *IEEE Engineering Management Review*.

Yilmaz, M., O'farrell, E., & Clarke, P. (2023). Examining the training and education potential of the metaverse: Results from an empirical study of next generation SAFe training. *Journal of Software (Malden, MA)*, *35*(9), e2531.

Yu, C., Liu, J., Ma, Y., & Zhang, W. (2021). Reinforcement learning in healthcare: A survey. *ACM Computing Surveys*, *54*(5), 1–36.

Yu, H., Zhang, X., & Zhao, D. (2020). Reinforcement learning for energy-efficient driving strategies of autonomous vehicles. *IEEE Transactions on Intelligent Transportation Systems*, *21*(8), 3397–3408.

Yuheng Cheng, C. Z. (2024). Exploring arge Language Model based Intelligent Agents: Definitions, Methods and Prospects.

Zeng, A., Song, S., Welker, S., & Lee, J.. (2020). Learning synergies between pushing and grasping with self-supervised deep reinforcement learning. *IEEE Robotics and Automation Letters*, *5*(2), 2562–2569.

Zhang, H. (2017). The digital twin: Data driven simulations innovate the manufacturing process. *White paper for DXC technology*, 14-17.

Zhang, S., Vinyals, O., Munos, R., & Bengio, Y. (2018). A study on overfitting in deep reinforcement learning. *arXiv preprint arXiv:1804.06893*.

Zhang, K., Yang, Z., & Bašić, A. (2021). Multi-agent reinforcement learning: A selective overview of theories and algorithms. *Artificial Intelligence*, *301*, 103558.

Zhao, S., Bay, M., Xu, A., & Gupta, N. (2024). 3rd Workshop on End-End Customer Journey Optimization. *Proceedings of the ACM SIGKDD International Conference on Knowledge Discovery and Data Mining*, 6753 – 6754. https://doi.org/DOI: 10.1145/3637528.3671500

Zhao, C., & Kumar, A. (2022). Deep learning-based facial recognition: Challenges and opportunities. *IEEE Transactions on Biometrics, Behavior, and Identity Science*, *4*(2), 98–112.

Zhao, L., Chen, S., & Fang, X. (2024). The implementation of the cognitive theory of multimedia learning in the design and evaluation of an AI educational video assistant utilizing LLMs. *Heliyon*, *10*(4), e19326. DOI: 10.1016/j.heliyon.2024.e19326

Zhao, Y., Jiang, J., Chen, Y., Liu, R., Yang, Y., Xue, X., & Chen, S. (2022). Metaverse: Perspectives from graphics, interactions and visualization. *Visual Informatics*, *6*(1), 56–67.

About the Contributors

Soly Mathew Biju, CEng MBCS CITP FBCS FHEA, has been in the field of academic and IT industry for a total of 25 years. She has a Ph.D. in Computer Science and also an MBA in IT management. She is currently an Associate Professor at the Faculty of Engineering and Information Sciences, University of Wollongong in Dubai. Dr Biju has achieved the CEng status awarded by Engineering Council (UK). She also has achieved the Chartered IT Professional status which is a symbol of excellence in the field of IT and is also an ISTQB-certified software testing professional. She is also a Fellow Higher Education Academy, UK. She was nominated for the Teaching Excellence and Research Excellence awards at UOWD on numerous occasions and received the prestigious Teaching Excellence Award in 2012, 2015 and 2019. She was also awarded the prestigious Amity Global Academic Excellence award in 2020. She spearheads the 'Global Health and Wellbeing ' cluster at UOWD. Her research interests include machine learning, data security, software testing, cryptography, e-learning, innovations in teaching, agile software development, online teaching, network security and programming techniques. She has papers published in reputed journals and books and presented and reviewed papers at national and international conferences and journals. She has been a scientific and organizing committee member and session chair and content chair on various reputed national and international conferences. She was nominated for the Teaching Excellence and Research Excellence awards at UOWD on numerous occasions and received the prestigious Teaching Excellence Award in 2012, 2015 and 2019. She was also awarded the prestigious Amity Global Academic Excellence award in 2020. Her research interests include machine learning, data security, software testing, cryptography, e-learning, innovations in teaching, agile software development, online teaching, network security and programming techniques. She has papers published in reputed journals and books and presented and reviewed papers at national and international conferences and journals. She has been a scientific and organizing committee member and session chair and content chair on various reputed national and international conferences.

Joji Abey acting chairperson of Department of Business Management at the College of Business Administration, Kingdom University, Bahrain. She holds the prestigious Chartered Manager designation from the Chartered Management Institute (CMI), UK, and a Fellow of the Higher Education Academy (HEA), recognized for her attainment against the UK Professional Standards Framework for teaching and learning support in higher education. A life member of the Indian Commerce Association since 2019, she has published numerous articles in Scopus-indexed journals and presented papers at various international seminars and conferences

Pradnya Bhagwat serves as an Instructor in the School of Computer Science at the University of Wollongong in Dubai. Pradnya holds a Master's degree in Telecommunications and Software Engineering. Pradnya is a passionate and results-driven Software Engineer with over 15 years of experience across diverse roles and geographies, including the United States and the Middle East. Her professional journey has taken her through some of the world's most respected organizations—Motorola, Nokia, Expedia, and Wells Fargo. Her primary competencies are project management using Agile and Scrum, Software Quality Assurance and Automation. At UOWD, Pradnya currently focuses on teaching Business Information Systems courses. In this academic role, Pradnya brings industry insights into the classroom, designing interactive lab sessions, crafting practical assignments, and mentoring students to think critically and apply theoretical knowledge to real-world challenges. Pradnya is passionate about learning and has completed multiple certifications with IBM, ISTQB, Six Sigma and recently an online certification in Big Data Engineering.

Bhupinder Chahal. Yorkville University, BC, Canada.

Kashvi Chaturvedi, is studying B.Tech, specialisation in Artificial Intelligence and Data Science at Ajeenkya DY Patil University. She started solidifying her programming skills by completing various certification courses like Data Structures in C, Tableau functions and Operating Systems along with doing few projects using languages like Python, C, C++ and creating Web Page using HTML, CSS and Java Script. She had also attended an Arduino-Based Automation course at Dolphin Labs to enhance her software knowledge. There, she learned how to work with sensors, microcontrollers, and circuit design. She has also written multiple review papers on topics such as Geographic Information Systems, Comparative Analysis of BJT Configurations, Swiss Bank vs. European Central Bank: Data Analysis. She is also researching on and learning many topics such as Small Modular Reactors, Bibliometric Analysis, UNSDGs etc. Because of her interest in latest technologies, she also participated in Global Hyperloop Competition hosted by IIT Madras representing her college as team Vac-Vectoor where she learnt more about various subtopics from the mentors.

Susanta Das is a seasoned educator with a proven record of teaching and mentoring diverse students, working at multiple institutions, and providing service to the various initiatives of organizations. He received his Ph.D. and M.A. degrees from Western Michigan University (WMU), USA, and M.Sc. degree from Banaras Hindu University (BHU), India all in Physics. He continued his research as a Marie-Curie post-doctoral fellow at Stockholm University, Stockholm, Sweden on beam diagnostics for the DESIREE (Double ElectroStatic Ion Ring ExpEriment) in the project DITANET (Diagnostic Techniques for particle Accelerators – a Marie-Curie initial training NETwork), at the Indian Institute of Science Education and Research-Kolkata, India on high-pressure physics as a Project Scientist-B, and at the University of Electro-Communications, Tokyo, Japan on ion-surface interactions as a Post-doctoral fellow. Throughout his career, Dr. Das worked and collaborated with many researchers, Ph.D., master, and visiting students from different countries. He further visited many countries to discuss research and an international conference participant (UK, Italy, Germany, Greece, Belgium, Bulgaria, Romania, Brazil etc.). He co-authored several research articles in WoS/Scopus indexed international journals, conference proceedings, and scholarly book chapters published by renowned international publishing houses. Beyond his research endeavors, Dr. Das has a storied history of service to academic and administrative committees, exhibiting his commitment to the growth and development of educational institutions. His experience includes tenure at Central University South Bihar, Sri Sri University, and P.K. University before assuming his current role at Ajeenkya DY Patil University. He received the Marie-Curie post-doctoral fellowship in Sweden, Science Academies' Summer Research Fellowship in India, Gwen Frostic Doctoral Fellowship, Department Graduate Research and Creative Scholar Award by WMU, and Leo R. Parpart Doctoral Fellowship by Dept. of Physics, WMU, among many others, throughout his academic journey. At present, Dr. Das continues to delve into cutting-edge fields, with a keen interest in nanotechnology, UN SDGs, and data science. His multifaceted contributions, spanning teaching, research, and administrative leadership, showcase a dedicated professional who is instrumental in advancing the vision and mission of the institutions he serves.

Pooja Dehankar is working as an Assistant Professor at Ajeenkya D Y Patil School of Engineering, Savitribai Phule Pune University, Pune. She has completed BE in Computer Engineering from Priyadarshini College of Engineering, Nagpur, and ME in Information Technology from Sinhgad College of Engineering, Pune.

She has done Post Graduate Diploma in Advance Computing. She has 15 years of experience in academics. Her areas of interest are Artificial Intelligence, Cyber Security, and Data Mining. She has published papers in Scopus Journals. She actively participates in workshops, faculty development programs, short-term training programs, conferences, and webinars. She is pursuing Ph.D. from Symbiosis Center for Research and Innovation, Symbiosis International (Deemed University).

Mustafa Kayyali is an ardent advocate for excellence in higher education, driven by a relentless pursuit of quality, recognition, and innovation. Their journey in academia started with a Master's in Quality Management and Evaluation in Higher Education from Universitat Oberta de Catalunya, followed by a Ph.D. in Quality Management from Azteca University. These academic pursuits have laid a strong foundation for their expertise in Accreditation, Quality Assurance, and Higher Education Rankings. As an entrepreneur, researcher, translator, and publisher, they are deeply involved in various facets of the academic world. Their diverse interests encompass Management, Translation, Interpretation, and Academic consulting, contributing to a well-rounded understanding of the industry. Throughout their career, they have made significant contributions to academic literature, with more than 40 published papers and 30 book chapters to my name. Additionally, they take pride in having translated 6 books, bridging language gaps, and promoting knowledge exchange on a global scale. They are committed to fostering positive change in higher education and contributing to its continuous improvement.

Sara Majeed is an instructor at the UOWD. Experienced in AI and Machine Learning algorithms, Computer Graphics, Computer Animation, Game Programming and Development

Sultonova Mashkhura is working as Associate Professor in the Department of Pedagogy and Psychology Urgench State University named after Abu Raykhan Beruniy, Uzbekistan.

Saodat Musayeva is working in the Department of Medicine at Termez University of Economics and Service, Termez, Uzbekistan.

Izzatbek Rejapov Olimbaevich is working in Department Romano-Germanic Philology, Mamun University, Khiva, Uzbekistan

Timilehin Olubiyi is working as Dean Faculty of Management and Social Sciences West Midlands Open University Nigeria

Sonam Puri is working as Assistant Professor, New Delhi institute of Management, India

R.Bhuvaneswari working as an Assistant Professor of English at Dr.Mahalingam College of Engineering and Technology, Pollachi. To her credit she completed 10 NPTEL / SWAYAM and published few articles in Scopus indexed journals.

R. Velmurugan presently working as an Associate Professor in Commerce, Karpagam Academy of Higher Education, Coimbatore. He started his career as a Project Fellow under UGC Sponsored Major Research Project at NGM College, Pollachi. He has 18 years of teaching experience has 15 years of research experience. To his credit he produced 22 Ph.D. Scholars and 5 M.Phil. Scholars. At present 1 scholar submitter his thesis, 6 Ph.D. Scholars are under his guidance. Moreover, to his credit he published 163 articles in various International Journals, of which 56 articles are published in Scopus Indexed Journals and 15 articles in Web of Science and 76 articles in edited volumes. He also participates and presented 27 papers in various International Seminar / Conference and 54 National Seminar / Conference. He acted as an external examiner for various M.Phil. and Ph.D. Viva voce examinations. He acted as a Vice Chancellor nominee for Doctoral Committee Expert at Bharathiar University, Coimbatore and Periyar University, Salem. He acted as a Chairperson at various National Level Conferences. He also acted as an Expert for Syllabus Scrutiny Committee, Question Paper Scrutiny Committee and Expert members for Board of Studies at various reputed Colleges. Considering his meritorious contribution, he received awards like Best Paper Presenter, Best Research Supervisor and Best Faculty Awards from various research foundations and councils. He too acted as a resource person for 27 Guest Lectures, 30 Workshops and 10 faculty development programmes.

Ravikumar is an experienced educator with 11+ years of teaching in Computer Science across India and overseas. Currently an Assistant Professor at Marwadi University, Rajkot, he specializes in Advanced Java, Machine Learning, Data Science, and AI. He holds a Mini MBA from the Swiss eLearning Institute (2015), an M.E. in Computer Science Engineering from VMRF University (2013), and a B.E. from Anna University (2010). Completed PhD at Amity University, Jaipur, he is dedicated to research, professional development, and advancing education through technology.

Aarthi S is a dedicated Assistant Professor in Computer Science with over six years of teaching experience. She is currently pursuing her Ph.D. at Marwadi University, Gujarat, and holds an M.Phil. and MCA from Bharathiar University, Tamil Nadu. Throughout her academic career, Aarthi has specialized in programming languages such as C++, Java, and C, and contributed to research in recommender systems and AI-related data privacy. She has published journal articles, contributed to book chapters, and actively participated in technical workshops. Known for her student mentorship and engagement in academic events, Aarthi remains committed to fostering innovation and excellence in computer science education.

Sunil Sankathala is pursuing B. Tech Computer Science and Engineering at Ajeenkya DY Patil University, with a diverse range of interests that bridge technology, sustainability, and innovation. His academic focus lies in computer science fundamentals like programming, data structures, algorithms, and software development. He actively supplements this with hands-on experience in web development and robotics. Beyond the core curriculum, He has a strong research inclination in emerging and impactful fields. His current research interests include Artificial Intelligence in Healthcare, bioplastics, nano bioplastics, e-waste management, and solid waste management—areas where he believes technology can make a meaningful difference in solving real-world problems. He has been publishing research articles and book chapters in reputed national and international journals and books. He is also part of an ambitious Hyperloop project, which involves interdisciplinary collaboration and cutting-edge engineering aimed at revolutionizing transportation. Working on this project has enhanced his skills in teamwork, innovation, and systems thinking. In the tech domain, he has developed proficiency in web development using technologies such as HTML, CSS, JavaScript, and React. His interests in robotics further reflect building smart, responsive systems that interact with the physical world. Throughout his course, he has helped strengthen problem-solving and collaborative skills. He is proficient in languages such as Python, C, C++, MySQL, Ubuntu, Machine Learning and familiar with frameworks and tools like React, Git. He actively participates in hackathons, coding competitions, and tech events to challenge himself and learn from peers. He is also a quick learner and highly adaptable, with an eagerness to stay updated with the latest trends in the tech world. He aspires to become a skilled software engineer and contribute to building innovative solutions that have a positive impact on society. The long-term goal is to work in a dynamic environment where knowledge, grow professionally, and make meaningful contributions to the field of technology. Driven by a spirit of exploration and sustainability, he aims to contribute to technological solutions that address both human and environmental needs. The long-term goal is to become a versatile engineer and researcher, working at the intersection of computer science, environmental innovation, and human well-being.

Atharva Saraf is currently pursuing a B. Tech degree in Computer Science Engineering at Ajeenkya D Y Patil University. Throughout his academic journey, he has developed a strong foundation in various programming languages, including C, C++, and Python. His interests and focus areas lie in algorithm-based programs, artificial intelligence (with a special emphasis on neural networks), and cybersecurity. His has successfully undertaken several projects that reflect my proficiency and passion in these domains. For instance, he developed a PC-Tuner application aimed at optimizing system performance by employing various methods such as defragmentation. Additionally, he created an automated backup utility capable of securely backing up selected files, folders, and stores them in compressed backup folder in system itself it can also store backups on external hard disk and cloud storages. Beyond project work, he has contributed to the academic community through research articles and book chapters. Notable among these is my co-authored chapter on federated learning techniques, exploring their applications and advancements in the field of machine learning. Moreover, he is currently working on writing a book chapter focusing on federated learning, delving deeper into its methodologies and practical implementations. His academic experiences have honed his skills in problem-solving, critical thinking, and collaborative teamwork. He is eager to further expand His knowledge and expertise in computer science, particularly in areas that intersect with his interests in algorithms, artificial intelligence, and their practical applications.

Wasswa Shafik (Member, IEEE) received a Bachelor of Science degree in information technology from Ndejje University, Uganda, a Master of Engineering degree in Information Technology (Computer and Communication Networks) from Yazd University, Iran, and a PhD in Computer Science with the School of Digital Science, Universiti Brunei Darussalam, Brunei Darussalam. He is also the Founder and Research Director of the Dig Connectivity Research Laboratory (DCRLab) after serving as a Research Associate at the Network Interconnectivity Research Laboratory at Yazd University. Prior to this, he worked as a Community Data Analyst at Population Services International (PSI-Uganda), a Community Data Officer at the Programme for Accessible Health Communication (PACE-Uganda), a Research Assistant at the Socio-Economic Data Centre (SEDC-Uganda), Uganda, an Assistant Data Officer at TechnoServe, Kampala, Uganda, and Asmaah Charity Organization as Cheif Executive Officer. He has hundreds of publications with renowned publishers. His research interests include Artificial Intelligence, Smart Agriculture, Digital Health, Green Computing, Security and Privacy.

Meenakshi Sharma is a Professor, NIET Business School, Plot No.19, Knowledge Park-II, Greater Noida (201306) 0009-0009-4266-5928

Sachin Sharma is currently working as a Professor, Amity School of Engineering and Technology, Amity University Punjab, Mohali, India. He also worked as Associate Dean, International Affairs and Professor, Department of Computer Science and Engineering at Graphic Era Deemed to be University, Dehradun, Uttarakhand, India. He has experience of 15+ years in industry and academia. He is also Co-founder and Chief Technology officer (CTO) of IntelliNexus LLC, Arkansas, USA based company. He also worked as a Senior Systems Engineer at Belkin International, Inc., Irvine, California, USA. He received his Philosophy of Doctorate (Ph.D.) degree in Engineering Science and Systems specialization in Systems Engineering from University of Arkansas at Little Rock, USA with 4.0 out 4.0 GPA and M.S. degree in Systems engineering from University of Arkansas at Little Rock with 4.0 out 4.0 GPA. Dr. Sharma has authored/coauthored over 300+ publications in the form of books, patents, and papers in refereed journals and conference proceedings. He holds 100+ US, Indian and international patents in the area of IoT, wireless communication and AI. He has also served as a Guest Reviewer for several Special issues of IEEE/ACM Transactions. His research interests include 6G wireless communication networks, Cloud Computing, Artificial Intelligence, Quantum Computing, IoT, Vehicular ad hoc networking and Cyber security.

Aditya Shrivastav is an aspiring technologist currently pursuing a Bachelor of Technology (B. Tech.) in Computer Science and Engineering at Ajeenkya D. Y. Patil University. He holds solid programming expertise in C, C++, and Python, alongside strong command over data and business tools such as Microsoft Excel and Tally software. Aditya is a member of Team Vac-Vectoor Hyperloop and participated with the team in the Global Hyperloop Competition organized by IIT Madras, contributing to cutting-edge transportation solutions. He actively engages in hackathons and various technical events to expand his skills and contribute to innovative problem-solving. He has authored and co-authored book chapters in the domains of solid waste management, bioplastics, nanotechnology applications, and artificial intelligence, showcasing his multidisciplinary approach and research acumen. Aditya is also working on an innovative project on predictive e-waste management. The project is targeted toward IT departments, schools, and colleges, aiming to support sustainable practices and resource optimization. In parallel with his academic journey, Aditya is serving as a faculty intern at Disha Computer Institute, where he teaches C, C++, basic Python, basic Java, Excel formulas, and Tally software. His dedication and teaching proficiency earned him a Letter of Appreciation and the opportunity to conduct a workshop on Advanced Excel at G. H. Raisoni College of Arts, Commerce and Science. With a strong foundation in technology, a passion for sustainability, and hands-on experience in both teaching and project development, Aditya Shrivastav is committed to driving impact through research, education, and innovation.

Sanjay Taneja is currently an Associate Professor in Research at Graphic Era University, Dehradun, India. His significant thrust areas are Banking Regulations, Banking and Finance (Fin Tech, Green Finance), Risks, Insurance Management, Green Economics and Management of Innovation in Insurance. He holds a double master's degree (MBA &M.Com.) in management with a specialization in Finance and Marketing. He received his PG degrees in Management (Gold Medalist) from Chaudhary Devi University, Sirsa, India in 2012. He earned his Doctor of Philosophy (Sponsored By ICSSR) in Banking and Finance entitled "An Appraisal of financial performance of Indian Banking Sector: A Comparative study of Public, Private and Foreign banks in 2016 from Chaudhary Devi University, Sirsa, India. He received his Post Doctoral Degree from faculty of Social Sciences, Department of Banking and Insurance, Usak University, Turkey entitled on "Impact of the European Green Deal on Carbon (CO2) Emission in Turkey" in 2023. He has published research papers in reputed SCOPUS/Web of Science/SCI/ABDC/UGC Care Journals. Prof. Taneja has more than fifty publications in total (Scopus/ABDC/Web of Science- 27)

Anant Wairagade is Lead Cybersecurity Engineer, building IAM solutions for Organizational Cybersecurity with strong foundations in Enterprise Integrations and Technical Leadership. Started their career in Enterprise Middleware technology as middleware engineer, groomed by Enterprise architects early in their career helped laid strong foundation in Enterprise architecture design and patterns, early adopter of API programming built software productivity tools for companies leveraging native API methods provided by underpinning framework. Built Microservices using Spring Boot, PaaS by breaking down .NET monolithic application. Early adopter of JWT token for authentication and authorization of Microservices including interaction between UI and backend. Lead software development teams in Financial CRM, Core Banking, various Finance domains. Recent experience in Cybersecurity with focus on Identity and Access Management in Information Security.

Index

I

L

M

O

P

R

S

T

V

www.ingramcontent.com/pod-product-compliance
Lightning Source LLC
LaVergne TN
LVHW081522300926
849161LV00006B/1265